Historical Studies in Education

Series Editors
William J. Reese
University of Wisconsin-Madison
Department of Educational Policy Studies
Madison, WI, USA

John L. Rury
University of Kansas
Lawrence, KS, USA

This series features new scholarship on the historical development of education, defined broadly, in the United States and elsewhere. Interdisciplinary in orientation and comprehensive in scope, it spans methodological boundaries and interpretive traditions. Imaginative and thoughtful history can contribute to the global conversation about educational change. Inspired history lends itself to continued hope for reform, and to realizing the potential for progress in all educational experiences.

More information about this series at
http://www.palgrave.com/gp/series/14870

Christine A. Ogren • Marc A. VanOverbeke
Editors

Rethinking Campus Life

New Perspectives on the History of College
Students in the United States

Editors
Christine A. Ogren
Educational Policy and
Leadership Studies
University of Iowa
Iowa City, IA, USA

Marc A. VanOverbeke
College of Education
University of Illinois at Chicago
Chicago, IL, USA

Historical Studies in Education
ISBN 978-3-030-09278-8   ISBN 978-3-319-75614-1   (eBook)
https://doi.org/10.1007/978-3-319-75614-1

This Palgrave Macmillan imprint is published by the registered company Springer Nature
Switzerland AG
The registered company address is: Gewerbestrasse 11, 6330 Cham, Switzerland

SERIES FOREWORD

The lives and times of American college students have long fascinated historians, along with parents, other relatives, and the public at large. As this book amply demonstrates, moreover, the bookshelf of studies focusing on these students has become stacked high in recent years. But making sense of the wide variety of collegiate experiences in the United States, going back hundreds of years and involving thousands of institutions, remains a formidable challenge. This volume takes a bold and much needed step in the direction of resolving that dilemma.

For several decades now, Helen Horowitz's book, *Campus Life*, has stood as a landmark study of college student experiences in the United States. Extending from the colonial era to the 1980s, it offered engaging and insightful portraits of the men and women who animated student organizations and extracurricular activities across the country. But it was also generally limited to the largest and most prestigious institutions, leaving many facets of student life unexamined. A reconsideration of these themes and related questions thus has been long in order.

Christine Ogren and Marc VanOverbeke have assembled a talented group of scholars to revisit the history of American collegiate student experience, drawing upon scholarship that has illuminated its widely varied dimensions over the past several decades. Featuring chapters dealing with such traditional topics as Greek organizations, athletics, and student organizing, along with others on the experiences of African American and Mexican American students, their book also explores student experiences at normal schools, community colleges, and conservative evangelical institutions. While hardly the final word on the diversity of student

experiences in American history, it represents an important addendum—
and something of a corrective—to the accounts offered in Horowitz and
other synthetic or textbook surveys in the field.

Some of these contributions will be broadly familiar to scholars in the
field, such as Ogren's account of student life at normal schools, Nicholas
Syrett's survey of fraternities over time and Timothy Cain's treatment of
student activism, but each adds new wrinkles to consider. Other chapters
offer new topics to consider, including a consideration of "drag" on campuses by Margaret Nash, Danielle Mireles and Amanda Scott-Williams, an
account of Mexican American student organizing by Christopher Tudico,
student life at community colleges by Nicholas Strohl, and controversies
at evangelical institutions by Adam Laats. Discussions of black students life
on southern campuses by Joy Williamson-Lott and agitation for athletics
at state colleges by VanOverbeke round things out. Chapter-length considerations of relevant historiography and future directions in the field
help to maintain a larger perspective.

While acknowledging the foundational contributions of Horowitz and
other scholars in the past, this collection of essays examines the history of
student life on American campuses from the perspective of the twenty-first
century. Given the dynamic quality of research on these topics, it is unlikely
to be the final word on them. But it offers today's readers a rare opportunity to consider the vast diversity of collegiate experiences in American
history in a single sitting. We expect that this will both inform and inspire
the next generation of scholars, who will likely add yet new dimensions to
our understanding of campus life as it continues to evolve in the years
ahead.

University of Wisconsin-Madison   William J. Reese
Madison, WI, USA
University of Kansas   John L. Rury
Lawrence, KS, USA

ACKNOWLEDGMENTS

As with any book project, we are indebted to a number of people for their invaluable encouragement, ideas, and guidance. We are profoundly grateful to William Reese and John Rury, the Series Editors of Historical Studies in Education. Bill and John suggested that we undertake this project and offered crucial guidance throughout the process. We thank them not only for making this book possible but also for their support throughout both of our careers. Bill and John have been extraordinary mentors, and we cannot thank them enough or repay them for their kindness and generosity.

Michael Hevel and Amy Wells-Dolan also were invaluable as we conceptualized and began to plan this volume. We are thankful for their generosity in sharing their thoughts and ideas for this collection. Our editors at Palgrave similarly were helpful as we worked to put this volume together. We especially want to thank Milana Vernikova and Mara Berkoff.

Chris and Marc both have benefited from wonderful colleagues who have been supportive of this project. We are indebted to the University of Iowa and the University of Illinois at Chicago, and to the members of the History of Education Society (both in the United States and in the United Kingdom) and the International Standing Conference for the History of Education (ISCHE), where we discussed this project and presented versions of the research found in this volume. We are grateful for the opportunity to work with incredible scholars in both our home institutions and our professional societies. We also have benefited throughout our careers from ongoing research support, especially from the Spencer Foundation. Spencer supported the research that shaped Chris's chapter on state normal schools and Marc's chapter on state colleges.

It has been a pleasure to work with the authors whose contributions are the heart of this volume. They have been a wonderful group of contributors, who worked patiently with us and responded good naturedly to our many queries and questions. We also would like to thank each other for the privilege of collaborating on this project. During weekend meetings at each other's home and our many phone conversations, one or the other of us would often remark, "I'm so glad that we're working together on this!"

Finally, many thanks to our husbands, Bruce Hostager and John Smagner, who not only offered much-needed support but also fed us delicious food during our weekend meetings in Iowa City and Chicago.

CONTENTS

1 Introduction: Rethinking Campus Life   1
  Christine A. Ogren and Marc A. VanOverbeke

2 Trends in the Historiography of American College
  Student Life: Populations, Organizations, and Behaviors   11
  Michael S. Hevel and Heidi A. Jaeckle

3 "We Are Not So Easily to Be Overcome": Fraternities
  on the American College Campus   37
  Nicholas L. Syrett

4 "Mattie Matix" and Prodigal Princes: A Brief History
  of Drag on College Campuses from the Nineteenth
  Century to the 1940s   61
  Margaret A. Nash, Danielle C. Mireles, and Amanda
  Scott-Williams

5 "Enthusiasm and Mutual Confidence": Campus Life at
  State Normal Schools, 1870s–1900s   91
  Christine A. Ogren

6 Instruction in Living Beautifully: Social Education
  and Heterosocializing in White College Sororities   115
  Margaret L. Freeman

7 The Mexican American Movement   141
   Christopher Tudico

8 Student Activists and Organized Labor   165
   Timothy Reese Cain

9 New Voices, New Perspectives: Studying the History
   of Student Life at Community Colleges   191
   Nicholas M. Strohl

10 Activism, Athletics, and Student Life at State Colleges
   in the 1950s and 1960s   213
   Marc A. VanOverbeke

11 Campus Life for Southern Black Students in the Mid-
   Twentieth Century   237
   Joy Ann Williamson-Lott

12 Higher (Power) Education: Student Life in Evangelical
   Institutions   261
   Adam Laats

13 Conclusion: New Perspectives on Campus Life
   and Setting the Agenda for Future Research   283
   Christine A. Ogren and Marc A. VanOverbeke

Index   297

Notes on Contributors

Timothy Reese Cain is an associate professor in the Institute of Higher Education at the University of Georgia. He is author of various articles and chapters on the history of academic freedom, tenure and campus speech rights; author of *Establishing Academic Freedom: Politics, Principles, and the Development of Core Values* (Palgrave Macmillan, 2012); and co-author of *Using Evidence of Student Learning to Improve Higher Education* (Jossey-Bass, 2015).

Margaret L. Freeman has served as a university and community-college instructor and works in the software industry and as an independent scholar in Portland, Maine. She received her doctorate in American Studies from the College of William and Mary and is completing a book manuscript on the history of white sororities in the South.

Michael S. Hevel is Associate Professor of Higher Education in the College of Education and Health Professions at the University of Arkansas. His work on the history of college students has appeared in *Higher Education: Handbook of Theory and Research*, *The Journal of Higher Education*, and *History of Education Quarterly*. He is completing a book manuscript on the history of college students and alcohol use.

Heidi A. Jaeckle is a doctoral student in Higher Education at the University of Arkansas.

Adam Laats is an associate professor in the Department of Teaching, Learning, and Educational Leadership at Binghamton University. He is author of *The Other School Reformers: Conservative Activism in American*

Education (Harvard, 2015) and *Fundamentalist U: Keeping the Faith in American Higher Education* (Oxford, 2018).

Danielle C. Mireles is a doctoral student in the Education, Society, and Culture program at the University of California, Riverside. She completed her master's thesis on drag at male colleges and universities in 2017 and has published works on deaf identity.

Margaret A. Nash is a professor in the Graduate School of Education at the University of California, Riverside. She is editor of *Women's Higher Education in the United States: New Historical Perspectives* (Palgrave Macmillan, 2018) and author of *Women's Education in the United States, 1780–1840* (Palgrave Macmillan, 2005) as well as articles in *History of Education Quarterly, Journal of the Early Republic,* and *Teachers College Record.*

Christine A. Ogren is an associate professor in the Department of Educational Policy and Leadership Studies at the University of Iowa. She is author of *The American State Normal School: "An Instrument of Great Good"* (Palgrave Macmillan, 2005) and articles in *History of Education Quarterly, Higher Education: Handbook of Theory and Research,* and other journals.

Amanda Scott-Williams is a doctoral student in the Education, Society, and Culture program at the University of California, Riverside.

Nicholas M. Strohl is an adjunct instructor in the Department of Educational Policy and Leadership at Marquette University and a PhD candidate in History and Educational Policy Studies at the University of Wisconsin-Madison. His publications include a co-authored chapter on the history of US education funding in *The Convergence of K-12 and Higher Education: Policies and Programs in a Changing Era* (Harvard, 2016).

Nicholas L. Syrett is Professor of Women, Gender, and Sexuality Studies at the University of Kansas. He is co-editor of *Age in America: The Colonial Era to the Present* (NYU, 2015) and author of *The Company He Keeps: A History of White College Fraternities* (North Carolina, 2009) and *American Child Bride: A History of Minors and Marriage in the United States* (North Carolina, 2016). He has also published articles on US queer history in *American Studies, Genders,* and other journals.

Christopher Tudico is Director of College Counseling at Saint Martin de Porres High School in Cleveland, Ohio. He earned his doctorate in

Higher Education at the University of Pennsylvania and is co-editor (with Marybeth Gasman) of *Historically Black Colleges and Universities: Triumphs, Troubles, and Taboos* (Palgrave Macmillan, 2008).

Marc A. VanOverbeke is Associate Dean for Academic Affairs and an associate professor in the College of Education at the University of Illinois at Chicago. He is author of *The Standardization of American Schooling: Linking Secondary and Higher Education, 1870–1910* (Palgrave Macmillan, 2008), and is working on a book manuscript on the history of state colleges, athletics, and educational opportunity.

Joy Ann Williamson-Lott is Associate Dean of Graduate Studies and a professor in the College of Education at the University of Washington. She is author of *Black Power on Campus* (Illinois, 2003), *Radicalizing the Ebony Tower: Black Colleges and the Black Freedom Struggle in Mississippi* (Teachers College, 2008), and articles in *Journal of Southern History*, *Review of Research in Education*, and other journals.

LIST OF IMAGES

Image 4.1   Mattie Matix, 1883, Amherst College. (Source: Dramatic
             Activities Collection, Amherst College Archives and Special
             Collections)   67
Image 4.2   A Fancy Dress Party, Vassar College, 1887. (Source:
             Archives and Special Collections, Vassar College Library)   70
Image 4.3   Bryan Rivers, Haresfoot Club, University of Wisconsin,
             1924. (Source: University of Wisconsin-Madison Archives,
             Image 2017s00380)   77
Image 4.4   Prodigal Princes, University of Illinois, 1915. (Source: Illio
             Yearbook/Illini Media Company)   79
Image 4.5   Keek sent to cheer soldiers, University of Illinois, 1920.
             (Source: Illio Yearbook/Illini Media Company)   80
Image 8.1   Members of the Student Workers Federation in the late
             1930s. (Source: Ivory Photograph Collection, Box 11,
             Bentley Historical Library, University of Michigan)   175
Image 11.1   Officers of Students United for Rights and Equality (SURE)
             at Southern State College. (Source: Southern Arkansas
             University Archives)   248

CHAPTER 1

Introduction: Rethinking Campus Life

Christine A. Ogren and Marc A. VanOverbeke

Scholars have been writing about the history of student life at colleges and universities in the United States for two centuries. As in the wider field of history of higher education, much of this scholarship before the 1960s focused narrowly on individual institutions and was overly celebratory of collegiate leaders. Frederick Rudolph's 1962 *The American College and University: A History* began the reversal of this trend. Not only did Rudolph synthesize developments at multiple colleges and universities as well as critique nineteenth-century colleges, he also included three chapters devoted entirely to the extracurriculum, which—along with his publication in 1966 of an article emphasizing students' role in shaping college cultures—planted the seeds for more serious scholarly consideration of students within the larger history of higher education.[1] In the years that followed, historians further enriched our understanding of campus life with studies of particular groups of students, including women, African

C. A. Ogren (✉)
Educational Policy and Leadership Studies, University of Iowa,
Iowa City, IA, USA
e-mail: chris-ogren@uiowa.edu

M. A. VanOverbeke
College of Education, University of Illinois at Chicago, Chicago, IL, USA
e-mail: mvanover@uic.edu

© The Author(s) 2018
C. A. Ogren, M. A. VanOverbeke (eds.),
Rethinking Campus Life, Historical Studies in Education,
https://doi.org/10.1007/978-3-319-75614-1_1

1

Americans, and the poor; specific organizations and activities, including fraternities and sororities, athletics, and political movements; and students at marginalized institutions of higher education, such as academies.[2] In short, the field became more vibrant, with a stronger emphasis on understanding student life and behavior.

Two and a half decades after Rudolph's pioneering work, Helen Lefkowitz Horowitz synthesized and extended research on the history of college students in one volume that covered multiple dimensions of campus life. Published in 1987, *Campus Life: Undergraduate Cultures from the End of the Eighteenth Century to the Present* quickly became and has remained a pivotal text.[3] Although Horowitz's approach was broad, her history did not incorporate all of the diversity of students, activities, and institutions that comprise higher education in the United States. In the 30 years since the publication of *Campus Life*, historians have continued to enrich and extend the field through in-depth considerations of groups of students and elements of their lives on campus.[4] Thus, we think it is time for a new volume that captures the breadth of campus life's history, and we offer this collection to update historical understandings of being a college student.

In the chapter that follows this Introduction, "Trends in the Historiography of American College Student Life: Populations, Organizations, and Behaviors" (Chapter 2), Michael Hevel and Heidi Jaeckle use Horowitz's *Campus Life* as the launching point for their analysis of the field. They explain that Horowitz's framework of "distinct ways of being an undergraduate"—college men and women, outsiders, and rebels—allowed her to present an overview history of student populations, organizations, and behaviors over a long span of time. In the three decades since *Campus Life*, Hevel and Jaeckle further explain, historians have provided more insights into Horowitz's student groups while also adding nuance to this categorization. Hevel and Jaeckle outline how historians have broadened their focus on student populations to include not only African American and female but also Asian American, Latino, and LGBTQ students, as well as students who attended non-prestigious types of institutions not prominent in Horowitz's work, such as female seminaries and state normal schools. Regarding college student organizations, Hevel and Jaeckle describe how works published in recent decades have delved into the history of student societies, fraternities and sororities, religious organizations, and the student affairs administrators who oversaw them. They also discuss how historians have recently investigated student behaviors, including dating and sexual expression as well as singing, to trace changes in US society.

Hevel and Jaeckle end their chapter with the observation that the ensemble of recent scholarship moves far beyond Horowitz's work to provide a more complete account of the history of student life. Nevertheless, they add, *Campus Life* has remained the only book that offers a cohesive synthesis of this topic for 30 years. Our intention in this volume is to provide a new comprehensive look at historical understanding of campus life, not through one sustained narrative, but through a collection of chapters covering a range of topics, many of which move beyond even Hevel and Jaeckle's well-informed discussion of recent historiography. Taken as a whole, this collection captures at least some of the complexity of the history of campus life that is continually emerging through new scholarship in the field.

The ten chapters that follow Hevel and Jaeckle's comprehensive overview present new interpretations of traditional topics in the field, original analyses of institutions that historians of college students have tended to overlook, deeper work on marginalized student groups, and innovative research on new areas of the history of student life. While Greek-letter organizations are well-trod territory in scholarship, Nicholas Syrett and Margaret Freeman both use sophisticated gender analysis, with some attention to race, to offer new perspectives on the roles of fraternities and sororities, respectively, on campus. Along with Christine Ogren's look at campus life at state normal schools, Marc VanOverbeke's analysis of the active student cultures at the state colleges that succeeded them and Nicholas Strohl's discussion of research on student life at community colleges expand the range of institutional types in the historiography. Joy Williamson-Lott's focus on historically black and predominantly white institutions in the South deepens understanding of African American students' experiences, while Christopher Tudico's account of an organization for Mexican American students in California casts much-needed scholarly attention on students who have not been the focus of sustained historical scholarship. And Margaret Nash, Danielle Mireles, and Amanda Scott-Williams's exploration of the role of drag performances on campuses, Timothy Cain's discussion of the history of student activism in relation to labor unions, and Adam Laats's look at student experiences and protests at evangelical colleges take historical research on college students in compelling new directions.

We considered organizing this volume by grouping the ten chapters into four sections corresponding to the categories of new work on established topics, scholarship on overlooked institutions, research on often-ignored student groups, and work in compelling new areas. However, we quickly realized that most of the chapters straddle boundaries between these categories. For example, the chapters that bring new types of institutions into the historiography also discuss underrepresented student groups as well as more traditional topics. While focusing on state colleges, which have been largely absent in the historiography, VanOverbeke addresses athletics and student protests, two traditional topics in the field. Student protests also are the focus of Williamson-Lott's chapter on black students. Cain and Laats similarly discuss protests in areas not previously covered in the historiography, in relation to the larger US labor movement and among students at evangelical colleges. In short, these ten chapters defy rigid categorization because they make important contributions along multiple dimensions. So that we do not emphasize particular dimensions over others, we have ordered the ten chapters according to the chronological period they cover. Readers may find it helpful to keep in mind the four categories we outline above, as well as Hevel and Jaeckle's categories of populations, organizations, and behaviors. Our discussion of common themes in the Conclusion may also be an appealing categorization for some readers, but Chapters 3, 4, 5, 6, 7, 8, 9, 10, 11, 12 proceed chronologically, beginning with one that covers most of the nineteenth and twentieth centuries.

Chapter 3 covers the longest time span in the book. In "'We Are Not So Easily To Be Overcome': Fraternities on the American College Campus," Syrett traces the history of traditionally white college fraternities—their ideals, commitments, and behaviors—through the antebellum era, the late nineteenth century, the 1920s, and the post–World War II era. The chapter examines nearly 200 years of these fraternities from their founding in 1825 to the early twenty-first century, when they have found themselves in the news for violations of college and state laws surrounding hazing, drinking, and sexual assault. Syrett argues that fraternities have created a brotherhood that emphasizes exclusivity and defiance of university administrators, making membership decisions based on narrow standards of masculinity that have changed over time. With some exceptions, fraternal masculinity has become increasingly destructive, athletic, anti-intellectual, and heterosexually aggressive over the course of the organizations' existence.

The next two chapters also cover periods that begin in the nineteenth century. In "'Mattie Matix' and Prodigal Princes: A Brief History of Drag on College Campuses From the Nineteenth Century to the 1940s" (Chapter 4), Nash, Mireles, and Scott-Williams explore the role of drag performances on college campuses. The practice of drag on college campuses has seldom been examined by historians, as scholarly analyses of changes in types of drag focus mainly on the worlds of theater and nightclubs. The chapter documents students' engagement in multiple uses of drag, sometimes but not always mirroring Vaudeville or theatrical drag. The formats, functions, and meanings of drag were varied and complex and occurred both on and off stage, as campuses became forums where students created their own cultural meanings of drag.

In Chapter 5, "'Enthusiasm and Mutual Confidence': Campus Life at State Normal Schools, 1870s–1900s," Ogren focuses on student organizations and the social sphere at state normal schools. The majority of normal-school students, or "normalites," were female, members of racial/ethnic minority groups, and/or from the lower end of the social-class scale. While these students generally missed out on the fraternity and sorority life and culture of many universities, they created a vibrant campus life at normal schools. After briefly outlining normalites' backgrounds, Ogren demonstrates how campus life at state normal schools enhanced students' intellectual and professional growth, welcomed all students into middle-class society, and invited women students into public life. The enthusiastic and mutually confident student life at state normal schools contradicted the rigid system at private colleges and flagship universities.

The remaining chapters focus on the twentieth century. In "Instruction in Living Beautifully: Social Education and Heterosocializing in White College Sororities" (Chapter 6), Freeman explores the history of sororities in the period from roughly 1910 to 1970. She argues that while national sororities claimed to build a supportive sisterhood, their intense focus on preparing members for conventional, white, middle-class womanhood and their emphasis on physical appeal undermined positive aspects of the women's only space, as they fostered a competitive and controlling environment. Sororities promoted conventionally "feminine" activities for members and alumnae, which orbited around an ultimate goal of marriage and homemaking. Thus, heterosocializing became a primary interest of the sororities. Rather than simply instructing women in manners, social graces, and high moral character that would supposedly prepare them as "ideal" wives and mothers, sororities also specifically instructed members on appearance and personality with designs on attracting male attention.

In Chapter 7, "The Mexican American Movement," Tudico examines how the creation of an organization of Mexican American college students in California in the 1930s and 1940s signified a fundamental departure from earlier years when few Mexican students enrolled in California colleges and universities. The chapter details how these students used this organization to establish an identity and student culture on campus grounded in activism, empowerment, and education. And while the organization initially catered to young men, the movement grew to include women as well. This organization reflected the complexity of Mexican American identity during the immediate prewar period, brought students in California into contact with other college students, and represented the beginning of more active participation in California higher education among the youth of the Mexican American community.

Cain in "Student Activists and Organized Labor" (Chapter 8) discusses the history of student activism in relation to labor unions throughout the twentieth century, focusing on traditional institutions of higher education. The chapter begins with student strikebreaking activities in the early twentieth century. It then considers the first mass student movement in the 1930s, which included significant labor-related activity, before turning to student activists in the 1960s and their conflicted relationships with organized labor. Concluding with a discussion of students' re-engagement with organized labor in the late twentieth century, the chapter considers how engagement with or against labor allowed students to wrestle with their place in the economic and social order, and emphasizes that students were most supportive of labor unions when they viewed them as part of broader efforts for equity and change.

The discussion in Chapter 9, "New Voices, New Perspectives: Studying the History of Student Life at Community Colleges," also incorporates developments throughout the twentieth century. Strohl explains that historians of higher education have long acknowledged a blind spot when it comes to the history of less selective institutions, including community colleges, which today educate nearly half of all undergraduates in the United States. Even as scholars debate the merits of these institutions—at once celebrated as levers of social mobility and criticized for diverting students' ambitions—few have examined the experiences of students on these campuses, past or present. This chapter surveys the literature on the history of community colleges to identify challenges and opportunities for scholars seeking to study their campus life. Strohl considers how a better understanding of campus life at community colleges may change understanding of what it means—and has meant—to be a college student.

In "Activism, Athletics, and Student Life at State Colleges in the 1950s and 1960s" (Chapter 10), VanOverbeke explores campus life at state colleges during pivotal decades of the mid-twentieth century. Contemporary studies usually reported that students on these campuses eschewed active involvement in college life in favor of earning a degree and securing a job. As this chapter argues, however, students on these campuses built active student cultures, in great measure by advocating for football and athletics. In doing so, these students embraced the student life they saw on other campuses and argued that their campuses were real colleges. By the 1960s, they also embraced athletics as a way to push their campuses to be more open to diverse groups of students. Far from being uninterested in campus life, these students embraced active college lives that shaped their institutions in dramatic ways.

Williamson-Lott in "Campus Life for Southern Black Students in the Mid-Twentieth Century" (Chapter 11) discusses the experiences of black students at southern historically black and predominantly white institutions in the 1950s and 1960s, acknowledging roots in earlier decades and branches in later years. The chapter focuses on a subset of student activists and the organizations they created to force change at their institutions and in society. Whether in student government associations, multiracial organizations, or black-oriented groups, black student activists and their white allies demanded that their institutions participate in ameliorating America's social, political, and economic ills. By doing so, they helped narrow the distance between ebony and ivory towers and society, and forever changed the role of higher education in societal reform.

In Chapter 12, "Higher (Power) Education: Student Life at Evangelical Institutions," Laats explores students' experiences and protests at evangelical colleges in the 1960s within the context of the twentieth-century history of neo-evangelicalism and fundamentalism, as a way to understand the campus cultures these students built. The chapter focuses on neo-evangelical student protests for revised lifestyle rules and the resulting pressure placed by the evangelical public on administrators, primarily at Gordon College near Boston and Moody Bible Institute in Chicago. In the late 1960s, Gordon moved in the direction of neo-evangelical reform, while Moody remained more fundamentalist and conservative. At evangelical institutions, student protests and public commentary on them were about religion as much as they were about issues of campus life, and Laats underscores the tight connection on these campuses between religion and student life.

Finally, in the Conclusion, "New Perspectives on Campus Life and Setting the Agenda for Future Research" (Chapter 13), we summarize the collective contributions of the book's various chapters and consider what this anthology tells us about what it meant to be a college student and how students experienced college. We explore common themes and strands in campus life across chronological periods, diverse student groups, and institutional types, and discuss how the collection refines, challenges, expands, and critiques Horowitz's *Campus Life*. We also look toward the future with questions still to be answered and avenues for research that remain unexplored. While the Conclusion and the chapters that precede it demonstrate that the history of campus life has become a dynamic and far-reaching field, the Conclusion also highlights that much more research remains to be done.

Together, the varied chapters in *Rethinking Campus Life* capture some of the breadth of current historical research on campus life. Individual readers may read and digest the book differently, depending on the nature of their interest in the history of college students and their lives on campus. Those who desire to gain a sense of many aspects of student life over time may find it most useful to read all of the chapters in the order presented, letting developments across the decades unfold chronologically. Readers who are most interested in digging deeper into the history of student organizations and behaviors that have traditionally been prominent in the scholarship may want to focus on Syrett's chapter on fraternities and Freeman's chapter on sororities, and look at other chapters that discuss new aspects of student protests. Those who are most interested in campus life at non-prestigious institutions may want to begin with Ogren's chapter on state normal schools, VanOverbeke's chapter on regional colleges, and Strohl's chapter on community colleges; they may also find Williamson-Lott's discussion of student life at historically black institutions to be helpful. Readers with a particular interest in underrepresented students will be drawn to Williamson-Lott's chapter along with Tudico's chapter on Mexican American students, and may find the chapters on nonprestigious institutions to be useful as well. Those who desire to gain a sense of cutting-edge forays into heretofore unexplored areas of the history of campus life may find Nash, Mireless, and Scott-Williams's look at drag on campus, Cain's analysis of students and labor unions, and Laats's discussion of evangelical colleges to be most appealing. And readers who are particularly interested in the development and trajectory of the field itself may find Hevel and Jaecke's chapter on historiography and the Conclusion to be especially valuable. Regardless of how readers approach the book, *Rethinking Campus Life* will widen and deepen readers' understanding of the history of US college students and their lives on campus.

NOTES

1. Christine A. Ogren, "Sites, Students, Scholarship, and Structures: The Historiography of American Higher Education in the Post-Revisionist Era," in *Rethinking the History of American Education*, eds. William J. Reese and John L. Rury (New York: Palgrave Macmillan, 2008), 187–222; Michael S. Hevel, "A Historiography of College Students 30 Years After Helen Horowitz's *Campus Life*," *Higher Education: Handbook of Theory and Research* vol. 32 (The Netherlands: Springer, 2017), 419–73; Frederick Rudolph, *The American College and University: A History* (Athens: University of Georgia Press, [1962] 1990); Frederick Rudolph, "Neglect of Students as Historical Tradition," in *The College and the Student: An Assessment of Relationships and Responsibilities in Undergraduate Education by Administrators, Faculty Members, and Public Officials*, eds. Lawrence Dennis and Joseph F. Kauffman (Washington, DC: American Council on Education, 1966), 47–58.

2. Examples of works on the history of student life published in the two and a half decades following Rudolph's book include James McLachlan, "The *Choice of Hercules*: American Student Societies in the Early 19th Century," in *The University in Society*, vol. 2, ed. Lawrence Stone (Princeton: Princeton University Press, 1974), 449–94; David F. Allmindinger, *Paupers and Scholars: Transformation of Student Life in Nineteenth-Century New England* (New York: St. Martins' Press, 1975); Raymond Wolters, *The New Negro on Campus: Black College Rebellions of the 1920s* (Princeton: Princeton University Press, 1975); Joseph R. Demartini, "Student Culture as a Change Agent in American Higher Education: An Illustration From the Nineteenth Century," *Journal of Social History* 9 (Spring 1976): 526–41; Richard Angelo, "The Students at the University of Pennsylvania and the Temple College of Philadelphia, 1873–1906: Some Notes on Schooling, Class and Social Mobility in the Late Nineteenth Century," *History of Education Quarterly* 19, no. 3 (Summer 1979): 179–205; Ralph S. Brax, *The First Student Movement: Student Activism in the United States During the 1930s* (Port Washington, NY: Kennikat, 1981); Eileen Eagan, *Class, Culture and the Classroom: The Student Peace Movement of the 1930s* (Philadelphia: Temple

University Press, 1981); David W. Robson, *Educating Republicans: The College in the Era of the American Revolution, 1750–1800* (Westport, CT: Greenwood, 1985); Barbara Miller Solomon, *In the Company of Educated Women: A History of Women and Higher Education in America* (New Haven, CT: Yale University Press, 1985).

3. Helen Lefkowitz Horowitz, *Campus Life: Undergraduate Cultures from the End of the Eighteenth Century to the Present* (Chicago: University of Chicago Press, 1987).

4. For a summary of scholarship on the history of student life published since Horowitz's book, see Hevel, "A Historiography of College Students"; and Chapter 2 in this volume.

Trends in the Historiography of American College Student Life: Populations, Organizations, and Behaviors

Michael S. Hevel and Heidi A. Jaeckle

Over the last few decades, historians have focused a great deal of attention on college students, their contributions to higher education, and their role in shaping behaviors and attitudes in the larger society. But college students have not always been such popular subjects among historians. In 1966, Frederick Rudolph criticized the historiography of American higher education for "neglecting" students. The resulting narrative "was both unfair and inaccurate," Rudolph argued, for college students had been "unquestionably the most creative and imaginative force in the shaping of the American college and university." Those Americans living in the turbulent decade that followed Rudolph's critique came to realize this all too well, as enrollments in colleges and universities swelled at the same time that many college students protested war, racism, sexism, and homophobia.

M. S. Hevel (✉) • H. A. Jaeckle
Higher Education Program, College of Education and Health Professions,
The University of Arkansas, Fayetteville, AR, USA
e-mail: hevel@uark.edu

© The Author(s) 2018
C. A. Ogren, M. A. VanOverbeke (eds.),
Rethinking Campus Life, Historical Studies in Education,
https://doi.org/10.1007/978-3-319-75614-1_2

11

Responding in part to the contemporary issues on campus, historians began to pay more attention to earlier generations of college students.[1]

This initial surge of historical scholarship culminated in 1987, when Helen Lefkowitz Horowitz published *Campus Life*, which offered a 200-year history of college students and the extracurriculum. Analyzing existing historical research, memoirs and biographies of alumni, and social science research, Horowitz argued that, over time, there had been distinct ways of being an undergraduate: college men (joined, eventually, by college women), outsiders, and rebels. These undergraduate cultures began to emerge at the end of the eighteenth century. College men, the first category, were the most advantaged collegians—male, wealthy, Protestant, and white. They embraced a virulent masculinity, which manifested itself in enduring features of the extracurriculum, including fraternities and athletics, and in behaviors, such as drinking, cheating, and having sex, that troubled educators. College men believed that dominating campus life best prepared them for success after graduation. Their earliest antagonists, and Horowitz's second category, were the outsiders. The first outsiders were white men with a devout Protestant faith who came from poorer families. After the Civil War, low-income white men were joined by the first generations of white women, African American, Catholic, and Jewish students as outsiders. In contrast to college men, outsiders—both men and women—used classroom success to improve their career prospects and facilitate their social mobility.[2]

Additional undergraduate cultures formed by the early twentieth century. Unlike college men who were engrossed in the extracurriculum and outsiders who concentrated on their studies, rebels focused on developments in the larger political, economic, and artistic worlds. Rebels wrestled with college men for control of student government and campus publications, seeking to use these outlets to engage issues percolating in society. Rebels often came from wealthy families, but possessed either identities, such as being Jewish, or attitudes, such as being progressive or socialist, that were antithetical to college men. Women joined the rebel ranks, largely on equal terms with their male counterparts. Also by the early twentieth century, college women joined college men. Whereas the first generation of women students were outsiders or occasionally rebels, as higher education became more popular among wealthy white women, their campus life came to more closely resemble—and be connected to—that of college men. College women used sororities to fill their extracurricular needs and, increasingly as Victorian attitudes became obsolete, their sexual desires. Unlike the equality rebel women shared with rebel men, college women were subservient to college men. Moreover, college women's behaviors faced heightened scrutiny from college men, campus authorities, and those in the larger society.

Thus, Horowitz incorporated specific student populations, features of the extracurriculum, and student behaviors into a sweeping and insightful history of college students. However, *Campus Life* did not include much consideration of African American students and other student populations that have become increasingly prominent on college campuses over the last 30 years, including Latino, Asian American, and lesbian, gay, bisexual, or transgender (LGBTQ) students. The book also focused on elite institutions, notably those in the Northeast, and public flagship universities, without incorporating institutions that enrolled many underrepresented students, such as historically black institutions or teachers colleges. Historians writing in the decades since the publication of *Campus Life* have significantly expanded the scholarship related to college students and the types of institutions they attended. In addition to the burgeoning scholarship on activism and athletics not considered in this chapter, historians have focused on specific populations of college students, their organizations, and their behaviors. In the process, more recent historians have avoided the broad synthesis that characterized *Campus Life*. Instead, they have provided deep insights into a variety of student experiences, and their combined scholarship offers a more nuanced understanding of higher education. Synthesizing the post–*Campus Life* historiography—and organizing the discussion around college student populations, organizations, and behaviors—not only reveals a more complex history of higher education in the United States but also highlights opportunities to create an even more complete understanding of earlier generations of college students, the extracurriculum, and their influence on American higher education and society.[3]

COLLEGE STUDENT POPULATIONS

Recent historical research has mostly focused on subgroups of college students. Unlike *Campus Life*'s coverage of nearly two entire centuries, these works have often centered on shorter periods of time and specific types of institutions. Within this literature, many historians have explored gender, race and ethnicity, and socioeconomic class, illustrating how individuals from certain backgrounds accessed higher education and their experiences once on campus. In developing this body of scholarship, historians have provided insights into the varied experiences of students that Horowitz had neatly classified as college men and women, outsiders, and rebels. While recent scholarship does not necessarily challenge Horowitz's undergraduate categories, it does illustrate the potential diversity within these categories—and how groups of students might bridge multiple ones.

In *Campus Life*, Horowitz paid a great deal of attention to young white men. Since its publication, historians have continued this focus. Bruce Leslie's *Gentlemen and Scholars* traces the development of the "collegiate ideal" at Bucknell, Franklin and Marshall, Princeton, and Swarthmore in the late nineteenth and early twentieth centuries. Previous historians, epitomized by Laurence Veysey, had focused on the rise of the research university during these decades. But Leslie demonstrates that, at the same time, these four institutions became increasingly collegiate. They shifted from serving their founding religious denominations and local communities to meeting the needs of the upper- and upper-middle-class Protestants who lived in cities. White college men took classes that prepared them for professional careers alongside classes in the traditional liberal arts. They also institutionalized many features of the extracurriculum, including athletics, fraternities, performing arts, and the Young Men's Christian Associations (YMCAs). College student culture, as Leslie shows, became increasingly similar across these campuses and, indeed, throughout the nation.[4]

Several subsequent historians similarly have focused on white college men but in earlier eras. Conrad Wright uses the life histories of Harvard alumni in the 1770s to identify specific developmental milestones in the lives of the Revolutionary generation. Wright provides a lively account of student experiences at Harvard and argues that these young men used their college years to develop their intellect, character, and independence. Moving 50 years further into American history, a trio of historians has provided rich insights into the higher education experiences of white men in the South before the Civil War. Robert Pace explores how "the southern code of honor and natural adolescent development" converged to shape a distinctive student culture across colleges in the antebellum South. For example, the homogeneity of the wealthy, white, and male student body largely made fraternities irrelevant there until higher education diversified after the Civil War. Jennifer Green argues that military schools formed an important component of southern higher education by the 1840s. Their curriculum was not as "high" as that at colleges because it lacked Greek and Latin, but southern military institutions offered professionally oriented courses that became popular with the white middle class. Few alumni pursued military careers; most became doctors, engineers, businessmen, or educators. Focusing on the University of North Carolina—one of the South's most prestigious institutions before the Civil War—Timothy Williams demonstrates that white college men used their college years to promote their "intellectual manhood." These young men valued self-awareness, mental acuity, informed actions, and persuasive speaking. Williams illustrates that this emphasis on self-improvement simultaneously reflected national upper-middle-class values and regional elite values.[5]

Historians have devoted a great deal of attention to white women students as well. In 1990, Lynn Gordon's *Gender and Higher Education* joined Helen Lefkowitz Horowitz's *Alma Mater* and Barbara Miller Solomon's *In the Company of Educated Women*, published respectively in 1984 and 1985, to form a foundation of contemporary historiography regarding white college women. All of these scholars locate the establishment of women's higher education largely in the elite northeastern women's colleges—colloquially referred to as the Seven Sisters—during the decades directly following the Civil War. Whereas Horowitz and Solomon focus primarily on the first generation of college women after the Civil War, Gordon centers her study on the second generation of white college women (1890–1910) at prestigious coeducational universities and elite women's colleges. The first generation of college women focused on classroom learning to improve their career options and foster their economic mobility, while second-generation women were more interested in men and marriage and less likely after college to work outside of the home.[6]

More recent historians have complicated the foundational work of Horowitz, Solomon, and Gordon by studying the experiences of white women students at different types of institutions both before and after the Civil War. Several historians have demonstrated that antebellum white women had access to forms of higher education that proved a close equivalent to that available at men's colleges. Christine Farnham initiated this wave of interpretation in 1994. In contrast to the prevailing historiography that had claimed that southern higher education always lagged behind northern higher education and that antebellum institutions that educated women offered at most a secondary curriculum, Farnham argues that women's higher education was more accepted in the South than the North before the Civil War. In institutions named female institutes, collegiate institutes, and eventually female colleges by the late 1830s, wealthy white women experienced a curriculum that included "ornamentals" (fine arts such as drawing and dancing), modern languages (such as English, French, and German), history, and some Greek and Latin, which Farnham equates to the education available to freshmen and sophomores at men's colleges. The wealth of the student population helped explain why higher education was less controversial, and thus more widespread, in the South. These young women did not expect to enter the professions and, indeed, reinforced rather than threatened the established social order.[7]

Writing over a decade later, other scholars have further considered the opportunities for women's higher education at academies and seminaries before the Civil War. Margaret Nash demonstrates that between 1780 and 1840 these institutions offered women students a curriculum more similar to than different from that of men's colleges and helped to create an emerging white middle-class identity throughout the nation. Mary Kelley takes a similar national perspective to illustrate how white middle- and upper-class women used their education at academies and seminaries to become teachers, writers, historians, and social reformers, all positions that facilitated their involvement in the public sphere. Returning to a regional focus, Anya Jabour provides an intimate look into campus life at southern academies and seminaries. These institutions, which insisted that students live and eat on campus, better represented the Oxford-Cambridge model than most men's colleges. Jabour argues that women students resisted prescribed gender roles by breaking rules about curfews, quiet hours, and midnight meals. To the extent that these young women enjoyed a rich campus life but not necessarily equality with men, they resembled Horowitz's college women, though many decades earlier than Horowitz dated the emergence of the category.[8]

Just as some scholars have extended the periodization of women's higher education, others have explored women's experiences at less prestigious institutions and reconsidered their roles at elite institutions. Christine Ogren demonstrates how state normal schools—institutions, usually coeducational, designed to prepare teachers—served some of the first "nontraditional" students in higher education. Women comprised an overwhelming majority of students at normal schools, and students at normal schools tended to be older and from low-income families. The robust extracurriculum at normal schools resembled that of more prestigious coeducational institutions, except that women at normal schools experienced little discrimination and frequently held prominent leadership positions. Andrea Radke-Moss centers her attention on the experiences of the first women students at four coeducational land grant universities in the West. Although women disproportionately enrolled in domestic science courses, their curriculum included scientific knowledge that expanded their career possibilities. Land grant women navigated a "culture of separation" on campus, sometimes insisting on single-sex spaces in which they could develop their own talents and sometimes insisting on mixed-gender spaces that provided the same experiences that men students had. The results of these studies potentially complicate Horowitz's categories, as white women had a more inclusive education at normal schools and land grant universities, although these were less prestigious institutions than elite women's colleges or leading coeducational universities. Andrea Turpin has recently returned attention to elite women's colleges and coeducational institutions from the 1830s to the 1910s. She argues that college women's shift to more "domestic" studies resulted from the actions of educators who increasingly encouraged students to pursue educations and careers largely based on their gender by the early twentieth century.[9]

Historians have also considered white women's experiences across the twentieth century. Amy McCandless offers a century-long history of college women in the South. There, wealthy white women learned the liberal arts—the most prestigious curriculum—in preparation for spending their lives in the unpaid roles of wives and mothers. Lower-class white women and African American women experienced a more vocational curriculum to prepare for careers, mostly as teachers. Although this curriculum was less prestigious than that studied by wealthy white students, it was an effective means of social mobility, propelling many alumni into the middle class. Both white and African American college women used their sororities to become involved in community service as students and to learn social activism as alumnae, but membership in these segregated organizations was limited to the wealthier students of both races. Focusing specifically on the mid-century, Linda Eisenmann considers the women administrators and faculty who worked to create more opportunities for women on campus and in careers after college. Their efforts helped increase the number of college women from under 600,000 in 1942 to over 2,000,000 in 1965. Studying the same era as Eisenmann but returning historical focus to the Seven Sisters, Babette Faehmel critiques the conclusions of Betty Friedan's *The Feminine Mystique*, which had found that many alumnae of these elite institutions were dissatisfied as stay-at-home mothers and upset that they had forestalled promising careers by leaving college before graduation to marry. Instead, Faehmel argues, college women made savvy, or at least rational, decisions given the confines of the era's sexism. Once on campus, college women realized that rewarding and remunerative careers were available only to the most talented young women. Marrying young provided them with opportunities for greater financial security and to experience sex without social—especially parental—ostracism.[10]

Whereas McCandless incorporates African American college women into her wider history, other historians have explicitly focused on African American college students, exploring student experiences during the founding of black higher education and in subsequent generations. James Anderson situates the development of higher education within the larger educational system in the South after the Civil War. Although public institutions are perceived as the primary conduit for promoting access to higher education over time, Anderson demonstrates that southern black private liberal arts colleges enrolled the vast majority of African Americans studying at the collegiate level well into the twentieth century. This private system of higher education provided an opportunity to educate an oppressed minority despite hostility from the region's white political elites, who channeled tax dollars almost exclusively toward white students.[11]

Other historians have considered the experiences of African American college students in the North during these same decades. Linda Perkins focuses on the approximately 500 African American women who enrolled at the Seven Sisters between 1880 and 1960. These women hailed from the wealthiest African American enclaves of northeastern cities and experienced discrimination even at the most hospitable campuses. Unlike many white Seven Sisters alumnae who never worked outside the home, most African American alumnae worked as educators, lawyers, doctors, and scientists, serving the larger black community. Cally Waite provides an account of racial regression, demonstrating how Oberlin, a site of integration before the Civil War, became increasingly segregated afterward. The religious activism of Oberlin's founding generation largely dissipated after the war. Instead of the racially integrated campus life that had previously permeated Oberlin, white students increasingly ostracized African American students in dining halls, student organizations, and campus housing.[12]

Recent historians have continued to examine important aspects of black higher education. Stephanie Evans offers a national history of African American women's higher education, demonstrating how its geographical center shifted over time. It started in Ohio, Michigan, and Pennsylvania before the Civil War, shifted to the South afterward, and returned to the North in the 1930s as urban universities, in the midst of Jim Crow and the Great Migration, provided access to graduate education. Evans highlights the careers of several successful alumnae while cautioning that most African American college women did not graduate. Marcus Cox illustrates the importance of military training, mostly through the Reserve Officers' Training Corps (ROTC), at historically black institutions in the South during the century that followed the Civil War. ROTC programs provided essential funding for these meagerly resourced institutions. Military careers, similar to teaching, also fostered the social mobility of alumni into the middle class.[13]

African American college student activists have also received attention from historians. In *Black Power on Campus*, Joy Ann Williamson provides a scholarly exemplar of this genre. She focuses on the University of Illinois at Urbana-Champaign between 1965 and 1975. During this crucial decade, most of the university's African American students hailed from Chicago. Through the Black Students Association, these students helped institutionalize reform efforts. They succeeded in recruiting more African American students to the campus, and they increasingly represented their concerns on university committees. In her subsequent book, Williamson shifts attention from the University of Illinois to the entire state of Mississippi, illustrating how African American college students could be expelled or suspended for their involvement in the Civil Rights Movement. Other scholars have considered African American activists at a variety of other influential northern institutions, including the College of Holy Cross, Columbia, Cornell, and the University of Pennsylvania.[14]

Historians have begun to uncover the formative experiences of students from backgrounds that have become increasingly prominent on college campuses since the publication of *Campus Life*. Historical research about Asian and Asian American students falls into three categories. First, historians have uncovered the early experiences of Asian students studying abroad in the United States, including Liel Leibovitz and Matthew Miller's research on Chinese students in the 1870s and Emily Lawsin's research on Filipino students in the 1930s. Second, historians have considered Japanese American college students during World War II. Gary Okihiro studies students from the West Coast who were forced to leave their homes for internment camps and eventually attended colleges in the Midwest and East. Allan Austin profiles the organization that helped facilitate these enrollments, the Japanese American Student Relocation Council. This organization expected Japanese students to become "ambassadors of goodwill" on campus, and students succeeded to such a degree that they helped establish the "model minority" stereotype of Asian American students. Finally, historians have considered the involvement of college students in the Asian Movement that began in the late 1960s. Karen Umemoto describes the longest student strike in American history, which occurred at San Francisco State College from November 1968 until March 1969, involved Asian American students, and led to the creation of the first school for ethnic studies in the nation. Steve Louie and Glenn Omatsu's edited book of historical analyses, memoirs, and primary sources simultaneously documents the importance of college students to the Movement and serves as a resource for future historians. Indeed, Thai-Huy Nguyen and Marybeth Gasman draw on this book in two articles: one considers how the Movement's first years influenced Asian college students in California and the other examines its lasting impact on Vietnamese students at the University of California, Irvine, during the 1980s.[15]

Latino students have been the focus of less historical attention. Victoria-Maria MacDonald incorporates college students in *Latino Education in the United States*, including students who attended the University of California, Berkeley, and Santa Clara University in the second half of the nineteenth century. Only dozens attended Berkeley, while hundreds attended Santa Clara. Thus, the earliest Latino students largely accessed higher education through private institutions, a situation similar to that of African Americans in the South after the Civil War, although Latinos tended to enroll in Catholic colleges rather than those supported by Protestant denominations. Both MacDonald and Carlos Muñoz Jr. highlight the importance of college students in the larger Chicano Movement by the late 1960s. More recently in the *Harvard Educational Review*, MacDonald and her colleagues offer a five-stage chronology of Latino higher education. Students were the central actors of the second stage—self-determination—in the early 1970s. Then, youth activists demanded better access to higher education, adoption of culturally relevant curricula, hiring of Latino faculty, and establishment of cultural centers on campus.[16]

Native Americans have long been underrepresented in—though not absent from—higher education, but historians have begun to explore their varied experiences over time. Bobby Wright shows how colonial leaders used the pretense of converting Native Americans to Christianity to obtain charters and raise funds for Harvard, William and Mary, and Dartmouth between 1643 and 1770. Native American enrollments remained meager, however, and colonial leaders funneled the money to largely benefit wealthy young white men. More than two centuries would pass before Yale graduated a full-blood Native American, Henry Roe Cloud. In his biography, Joel Pfister argues that Roe Cloud used the oratorical skills he developed as an undergraduate debater and the connections he made at Yale to become an influential educator and activist who worked to improve Native American communities. Other scholars have considered the experiences of Native American students outside the Ivy League. Devon Mihesuah focuses on the Cherokee Female Seminary, which opened in 1851 in present-day Oklahoma and was modeled after Mount Holyoke; Donal Lindsey explores the complex race relations that occurred when over 1000 Native American students left reservations to attend the historically black (though white-controlled) Hampton Institute beginning in the 1870s; and Lisa Neuman illustrates how Native American students at Bacone College in Oklahoma used the interest of white women "collectors" of indigenous art to provide financial security in the first half of the twentieth century. Students learned traditional artistic techniques on campus, sold their artwork, and, as a result, raised funds for the institution.[17]

Despite the increase in the numbers of students with disabilities attending college in recent decades, historical research into their earlier experiences has remained quite limited. Steven Brown details the origins of the disability services program at the University of Illinois following World War II. While institutional officials were concerned that the university would become known for these services and thus attract large numbers of students with disabilities, the first director of the program and the students in the program worked to provide opportunities for students with disabilities in athletics, physical therapy, and community service. They also garnered the university's commitment to ensure the accessibility of future campus buildings decades before this requirement became a federal law. John Christiansen and Sharon Barnartt offer a history of the Deaf President Now protests at Gallaudet University in 1988. Gallaudet's deaf and hearing-impaired students resisted the board's hiring of a hearing president. With support of alumni, faculty, and the larger deaf community, the students managed to have the hearing president replaced with a deaf president and forced the resignation of the chair of the institution's governing board.[18]

Historical understanding of LGBTQ students has expanded significantly since the turn of the twenty-first century, though most studies have centered on white gay men. William Wright, Nicholas Syrett, and Margaret Nash and Jennifer Silverman describe "purges" of gay students respectively at Harvard in 1920, Dartmouth in 1925, and several public flagship universities in the 1940s. In a *Review of Higher Education* article, Patrick Dilley places these purges in the larger context of administrators' efforts to "control" gay students across the twentieth century, which also included mandatory counseling to "cure" homosexuality and refusal to recognize LGBTQ student organizations. Dilley also details the experiences of more than 60 "non-heterosexual" men who attended college in the last half of the century in *Queer Man on Campus*. Other scholars have examined LGBTQ student organizations. Brett Beemyn explores the establishment of the first two organizations at Columbia and Cornell, where gay activists were aided by students involved in the Black Power and women's rights movements. Jessica Clawson considers the significance of these organizations at Florida State University and the University of Florida in the 1970s and 1980s. LGBTQ organizations in Florida provided camaraderie and comfort for students struggling with their sexuality while, at the same time, making them more visible and thus susceptible to violence from homophobic students and community members.[19]

Over the past 30 years, historians have both reexamined the experiences of college students included in *Campus Life* and explored the experiences of those largely excluded from its pages. In doing so, they have expanded understanding of the types of institutions offering higher education and the students those institutions served. In studying eras closer to the present, historians have also captured the formative experiences of historically underrepresented but increasingly visible student populations. This research does not necessarily challenge Horowitz's categories of undergraduates, and sorting students the way she did—those advantaged on campus (college men and women), those facing more difficulty and using higher education to foster social mobility (outsiders), and those working to challenge the status quo (rebels)—remains useful. But this new research does suggest the fluidity of these categories and the varied experiences among student populations. Women at normal schools, for example, often assumed leadership positions in major student organizations and experienced little gender discrimination on campus. But they attended institutions with fewer resources than those attended by wealthier white students, and they pursued higher education to improve their social mobility after graduation. Therefore, normal women shared similarities with Horowitz's college women—or even college men—at their own institutions, but were more like outsiders within the overarching system of American higher education. In addition, while many students from historically underrepresented backgrounds fit within the outsider category, this categorization can obscure specific groups' unique paths to and challenges at college. And many of these students often worked to improve higher education and society for their communities, straddling the categories of outsider and rebel.

College Student Organizations

In addition to studies that have focused primarily on specific populations of college students, other works have centered on aspects of the extracurriculum. Horowitz, of course, incorporated organizations into her undergraduate categories, illustrating the importance of fraternities and sororities to college men and women and discussing how college men and rebels wrestled for control of student government and campus newspapers. Since the appearance of *Campus Life*, several historians have written books specifically about student organizations. They have provided new or renewed attention to Phi Beta Kappa, the oldest student organization in continued existence, the literary societies and fraternities that followed Phi Beta Kappa, and student religious organizations. Historical research also has considered the development of a new administrative field responsible, in part, for overseeing these extracurricular features. On the whole, this research reveals many contributions that college students have made to American higher education through the extracurriculum.

Richard Current provides a history of one of the oldest features of the extracurriculum, Phi Beta Kappa. Founded in 1776 at William and Mary, Phi Beta Kappa became the most prestigious honorary organization in the United States. Current contends that this organization has remained relevant for more than two centuries because it has consistently upheld the highest academic and intellectual standards promoting liberal arts education. In its infancy, the organization supplemented the classical curriculum by allowing its student members freedom of speech and creative thought that they did not enjoy in their college classrooms. As the elective system became more widespread in the late nineteenth century, the organization lost some of its original purpose and transitioned into an organization that honored scholarship. Current further shows how Phi Beta Kappa, its membership rolls long dominated by advantaged white men, worked to include more women and racial minorities by the 1950s.[20]

In its earliest form, Phi Beta Kappa exhibited characteristics that later manifested in literary societies and fraternities, two features of the extracurriculum that have also attracted the attention of historians. Many, including Rudolph and Horowitz, have long praised literary societies, arguing that they were egalitarian in membership and offered a more relevant education than the formal curriculum. Based mostly upon sources from eastern and southern men's colleges, Rudolph, Horowitz, and other scholars dated the demise of literacy societies to before the Civil War and blamed fraternities. Yet a growing body of research about literary societies illustrates how they proved useful to a greater variety of students and for a longer period of time. This research also questions whether fraternities were at fault for their demise. As the title of her book, *Learning to Stand and Speak*, implies, Mary Kelley argues that the activities of literary societies fostered women students' abilities in "learning to read critically, write lucidly, and to speak persuasively" before the Civil War.[21]

Literary societies continued to provide important educational experiences for a half century after the Civil War, and often a majority of students on campus would become members. Kolan Morelock demonstrates the importance of literary societies among the white male students at the University of Kentucky and Transylvania University in the late nineteenth and early twentieth centuries. Literary society debates, and later intercollegiate oratorical contests, served as a popular entertainment option and promoted culture among Lexington's residents into the 1900s. Turning to specific institutional types, Radke-Moss and Ogren illustrate the importance of literary societies to women students at land grant institutions and normal schools, respectively. Michael Hevel shows that these organizations developed similarly across a state university, private college, and public normal school in Iowa. At all three institutions, literary societies established debate contests, theatrical productions, and campus newspapers. Even as students became less interested in these organizations, midwestern literary societies fostered the political agency of college women a generation before women gained national suffrage. Both Morelock and Hevel argue that educators' incorporation of literary society activities—including forensics, dramatic productions, and student publications—into the formal curriculum contributed more to their demise than did fraternities. And Thomas Howard and Owen Gallogly's recent history of the Jefferson Society at the University of Virginia provides a reminder that literary societies endure on a handful of campuses today. This recent scholarship on literary societies suggests the importance of studying developments beyond a single institutional type or region in order to fully understand developments within American higher education.[22]

Fraternities and sororities, which proved to be popular among college students far longer than most literary societies, have received attention from several recent historians. In *The Company He Keeps*, Nicholas Syrett argues that for two centuries white fraternity men perpetuated the dominant form of masculinity on college campuses. At any given time, white fraternity men's behaviors reflected the privileged form of masculinity in the larger society: oratorical skills before the Civil War, athletic prowess in the late nineteenth century, and sexual conquest in the twentieth century. Laurie Wilkie offers a focused and methodologically innovative study, using archeological excavations at an elite fraternity's two chapter houses and its outdoor trash pits at the University of California, Berkeley, to reconstruct the organization's history from the 1870s through the 1950s. Advancing an argument similar to Syrett's, she demonstrates that artifacts reveal the ways in which the fraternity members embodied masculinity, whiteness, and privilege across the decades.[23]

Other historians have explored the history of fraternal organizations created by less advantaged collegians. Diana Turk considers a half-century of white women's sororities, beginning in 1870. The earliest sorority members used their organizations mostly for intellectual ends, but the subsequent generation of sorority women focused on social pursuits, including dating, and they excluded both African American and Jewish women from membership. Scholars have also turned attention to the organizations that served those students whom white sorority members ostracized. Lawrence Ross provides detailed information about the founding and founders of the historically black fraternities and sororities that came to be known as the "Divine Nine," while Paula Giddings and Deborah Whaley each focus on the history of a different historically black sorority—Delta Sigma Theta and Alpha Kappa Alpha, respectively—and situate its activities within the larger experience of African American women. These were complex organizations. Whaley, for example, shows how Alpha Kappa Alpha vacillated between promoting feminism and femininity and between social change and social life. Marianne Sanua investigates the fraternities established by and for Jewish college men beginning in the 1890s. These organizations provided social support and career guidance for Jewish students and even shelter for German Jewish refugee students. Yet Jewish fraternities also discriminated against students from less "desirable" Jewish backgrounds. Sanua claims that the decrease in anti-Semitism after World War II actually hurt the Jewish Greek system, as Jewish students became more accepted in traditionally white fraternities.[24]

Reminiscent of Leslie's focus on how some institutions embraced the collegiate ideal during the rise of the research university, David Setran's history of the YMCA demonstrates that student religious organizations became increasingly prominent during the era when Protestant denominations lost influence over institutions of higher education. Campus chapters operated with institutional approval but outside institutional authority, and were often staffed by older adults who encouraged students to assume leadership roles. Between 1900 and 1920, YMCA membership reached 25–30 percent of all male students, and local branches often "served as the de facto student services office of the universities, providing undergraduates with assistance in housing, part-time employment, career guidance, recreation, counseling, and many other necessities." Young white men comprised the majority of members in early college YMCAs, though the organization later extended its membership pool to include African Americans, Native Americans, and white women, albeit often in segregated chapters. As institutions of higher education expanded, they hired deans of women and deans of men who often assumed duties first performed by YMCA staff.[25]

Additional scholars have provided more insight into college student religious organizations and activities in general, as well as the YMCA in particular. Sara Evans compiles the memoirs of sixteen diverse college women involved in liberal Christian campus ministries between 1955 and 1975. Through these ministries, college women engaged in the Civil Rights Movement, protested the Vietnam War, questioned heteronormativity, and generally became aware of global issues. John Turner shifts historical attention to a more conservative religious group on campus, writing a history of Campus Crusade for Christ and situating the group within the larger evangelical resurgence of the second half of the twentieth century. From its meager beginnings in 1951, by the early twenty-first century, the organization operated with a $500-million budget. Returning focus to the YMCA (and to a lesser extent the Young Women's Christian Association), Dorothy Finnegan and colleagues illustrate how these organizations started much-needed programs, such as new student orientation, as swelling enrollments made institutions larger and more difficult to navigate.[26]

Both Setran and Finnegan connect activities of the YMCA to responsibilities later assumed by student affairs administrators, who themselves have been the subject of increased historical scholarship. These administrators became responsible for the extracurriculum by the early twentieth century. Historians have focused attention on formative leaders in the field, documenting their responsibilities, successes, and setbacks. They have also shown how these new leaders worked to professionalize the field. Early student affairs administrators supervised campus housing, advised student government, monitored fraternities and sororities, and staffed financial aid, campus employment, and placement offices. [27]

As this research on the development of a new administrative field to supervise the extracurriculum suggests, college students have made lasting contributions to American higher education by establishing and supporting student organizations. These organizations often have reflected the values, aspirations, and educational experiences that students missed in the formal curriculum. Many of these organizations have proved remarkably adaptable, meeting the needs of changing generations of college students. But historians have not only focused on how college students created enduring features of American higher education, they have also traced their effect on society.

COLLEGE STUDENT BEHAVIORS

While historians studying student organizations have revealed the contributions that these organizations and students have made to American higher education, other historians have focused on student behaviors. Similar to her treatment of student organizations, Horowitz connected certain behaviors on campus to a specific category of undergraduates, such as cheating to college men and studying to outsiders. In contrast, more recent historians have studied college student behaviors to trace broad changes in American society. In addition to studies of student activism, studies of college student behaviors rely primarily on sources from white collegians but strive to incorporate some from historically underrepresented students, especially African Americans. In doing so, these studies illustrate how economic, gender, and racial privilege shaped behaviors on campus. They also reveal the overall advantaged position of college students in the United States, demonstrating the ways in which college students have influenced attitudes and behaviors in the larger society.

Historian Beth Bailey has written two books that explore changes in courtship and sexuality in American society, relying mostly on sources related to college students, and in particular college women. In *From Front Porch to Back Seat*, Bailey studies the shift from courting to dating in America—mostly among white, heterosexual, college-going, middle-class youth—between 1920 and 1965. As Bailey's title suggests, courtship enjoyed increased privacy over the course of the twentieth century. Bailey argues that young women lost power over courtship as it shifted away from front porches and living rooms—women's traditional sphere of influence—toward more public arenas of cars and restaurants—men's traditional sphere of influence. Personal relationships came to be seen as commodities, with dates representing public validation of popularity, belonging, and success, a situation especially prevalent on college campuses. Men paid for public amusements associated with dating, and Bailey argues that men bought more than the movie tickets and sodas with their money; they purchased control over women.[28]

Bailey's *Sex in the Heartland* picks up largely where *From Front Porch to Back Seat* ended. Bailey focuses on how the sexual revolution in American society during the 1960s and 1970s transpired at the University of Kansas (KU). She demonstrates that the most advantaged students—white heterosexuals—achieved the greatest sexual freedoms. In contrast, KU administrators prescribed mental health treatment for gay and lesbian students. African American students experienced discrimination and segregation, and they protested for equal civil rights while white students spent their time experiencing greater sexual freedoms. Facing much stricter rules at the nearby tribal college, Native American students largely avoided public protests, leaving them unable to participate in the era's more permissive attitudes toward sexuality. Bailey concludes that the sexual revolution was less about sexual acts and behaviors and more about greater inclusiveness and equality in society; in the end, however, it mainly enabled white heterosexual college women to more fully explore their sexuality and create their own college experiences.[29]

Subsequent scholarship has continued to explore college women's sexuality and their bodies, revealing how college students contributed to societal changes and how changing social mores affected campus life. In *Rumors of Indiscretion*, Lawrence J. Nelson reveals the impact of a questionnaire about sex sent to hundreds of college women at the University of Missouri in 1929. The firestorm that resulted from the survey highlighted the tension between Victorian-era ideals about sexuality held by many community members and the more permissive attitudes that pervaded college campuses. In the aftermath, two beloved professors were fired, one student withdrew from the university without obtaining a degree, and the president lost his position. Yet, as Nelson points out, this backlash did little to stem the tide of expanding sexual boundaries of college students that the survey aimed to measure. In *Looking Good*, Margaret

Lowe focuses on college women at Smith College, Cornell University, and Spelman College to examine changes to Americans' idealized notions of the female body from 1870 through 1930. Initially, most white women focused on gaining weight and exercising at college to illustrate their healthy adjustment to campus, demonstrating that they could handle the intellectual rigor of higher education. In contrast, administrators at Spelman, a college for African American women, refused to serve traditional African American foods and encouraged African American students to lose weight and emulate the bodies of white women. For most Spelman women, physical activity came from manual labor rather than athletic exercise. Around World War I, idealized body shape became more similar among college women at all three institutions, and college women came to value weight loss and revealing flapper fashions as the best way to secure dates and husbands.[30]

J. Lloyd Winstead expands the analysis of college student behaviors beyond sexuality by examining the important role of singing on campus from the colonial era to the present. According to Winstead, singing has long connected students emotionally to each other as well as to their institutions, and served as a symbol of the college experience. At the same time, singing could serve as a means of "intimidation, protest, and defiance." At women's colleges, singing was prominent in initiations and academic ceremonies. White college students sang mostly lighthearted tunes, while black college students embraced deeper emotional songs. African American college students' singing proved particularly popular with white audiences, and some black educators arranged tours of student groups to raise funds for their colleges and universities. Winstead also makes connections between student songs and larger social change. By the 1920s, for example, as college culture came to dominate the attention of the broader public, popular college songs such as "A Girl Who Goes to Vassar Loves a Boy Who Goes to Yale" conveyed the increased romantic interest between college men and college women.[31]

College students also pushed boundaries of sexuality and established national trends during the twentieth century through the clothes they wore. Deirdre Clemente tells a fascinating story of how college students in the first half of the twentieth century popularized fashions—including jeans, khakis, shorts, sweaters, T-shirts, and pajamas—that continue to dominate contemporary American wardrobes. College students embraced styles that shifted fashion from formal to casual. College men exchanged suits for sports jackets before eventually settling on T-shirts and jeans.

College women switched out dresses, including formal evening gowns, for skirts, blouses, and shorts. They also increasingly wore items that resembled men's clothes and revealed more of their bodies. The women who experienced the greatest freedom were those attending northeastern women's colleges, as the absence of men reduced the pressure to be stylish and sizable allowances enabled them to experiment with fashion. In contrast, campus administrators enforced strict dress codes at historically black institutions well into the 1960s.[32]

These scholars' investigations into college student behaviors have both enhanced historical understanding of higher education and revealed college students' influence on the larger culture, especially in the areas of courtship and sexuality. And these works on student behaviors are some of the only historical studies since *Campus Life* that incorporate the experiences of students from different backgrounds into an overarching narrative. Collectively, these studies not only highlight how privilege influences students' experiences on campus but also reveal the advantaged position of college students in the United States.

FUTURE POSSIBILITIES

Compared to the historiography when Horowitz published *Campus Life* 30 years ago, historical understanding of college students and their experiences has increased exponentially. Horowitz's ways of being an undergraduate endure as a useful framework for considering undergraduate experiences, and *Campus Life* endures as a useful entry point into the history of college students. Yet recent historical scholarship has provided a more complete and complex portrait of higher education in the United States. Historians have revisited many types of students included in *Campus Life* and broadened their coverage to groups of students largely absent in the book but increasingly prominent on today's campuses. Instead of grouping many into a single category, such as outsiders, historians have explored the varied experiences of students from specific underrepresented backgrounds. And their focus on specific extracurricular organizations and student behavior has highlighted the importance of college students' contributions to higher education and the larger society.

While recent historical approaches have deepened coverage of the history of campus life, they have sacrificed comprehensiveness. *Campus Life* provided a broad history that included students from a variety of backgrounds in a single book, making it useful to the larger academic community and the educated public. Recent scholarship has shown that campus life has been more complicated, nuanced, and richer than Horowitz's study alone was able to highlight. As a result, no longer can individuals pick up a single volume—or even several volumes—and gain an up-to-date historical understanding of college students and campus life. At the same time, historians writing focused studies may overlook or fail to incorporate larger patterns that might more fully explain developments in the past or provide perspective to the present.

For future scholars, there is much still to be learned about specific aspects of higher education's past, especially about how traditionally marginalized groups accessed and experienced higher education. But there may also be opportunities to synthesize existing scholarship or to consider other ways to construct studies that offer long and inclusive histories of student life within higher education. A distillation of the large body of literature related to white women in higher education from the early nineteenth to the late twentieth century, for example, might reveal important trends and issues that more focused studies overlook. Moreover, members of the academic and educated communities beyond historians are more likely to read one book than ten books about a particular subject. Both approaches—specific and synthesizing studies—are poised to continue to provide new insights into the history of higher education and the past's influence on today's campuses.

NOTES

1. Frederick Rudolph, "Neglect of Students as Historical Tradition," in *The College and the Student: An Assessment of Relationships and Responsibilities in Undergraduate Education by Administrators, Faculty Members, and Public Officials*, eds. Lawrence Dennis and Joseph F. Kauffman (Washington, DC: American Council on Education, 1966), 47.

2. Helen Lefkowitz Horowitz, *Campus Life: Undergraduate Cultures from the End of the Eighteenth Century to the Present* (New York: Alfred A. Knopf, 1987).

3. Christine A. Ogren argues that college students have been one of the four main subjects of the historiography of higher education in recent decades in "Sites, Students, Scholarship, and Structures: The Historiography of American Higher Education in the Post-Revisionist Era," in *Rethinking the History of American Education*, eds. William J. Reese and John L. Rury (New York: Palgrave Macmillan, 2008), 187–222. For the longer arc of the historiography of college students in the United States and a more exhaustive consideration of the historiography of specific populations of

college students since the publication of *Campus Life* (from which this sec-
tion is adapted), see Michael S. Hevel, "A Historiography of College
Students 30 Years after Helen Horowitz's Campus Life," in *Higher
Education: Handbook of Theory and Research*, vol. 32 (The Netherlands:
Springer, 2017), 419–73.

4. William Bruce Leslie, *Gentlemen and Scholars: College and Community in
the "Age of the University," 1865–1917* (University Park: Pennsylvania State
University Press, 1992).

5. Conrad Edick Wright, *Revolutionary Generation: Harvard Men and the
Consequences of Independence* (Amherst: University of Massachusetts Press,
2005), chapter 2; Robert F. Pace, *Halls of Honor: College Men in the Old
South* (Baton Rouge: Louisiana State University Press, 2004); Jennifer
R. Green, *Military Education and the Emerging Middle Class in the Old
South* (New York: Cambridge University Press, 2008); Timothy J. Williams,
Intellectual Manhood: University, Self, and Society in the Antebellum South
(Chapel Hill: University of North Carolina Press, 2015).

6. Helen Lefkowitz Horowitz, *Alma Mater: Design and Experience in the
Women's Colleges from Their Nineteenth-Century Beginnings to the 1930s*
(New York: Alfred A. Knopf, 1984); Barbara Miller Solomon, *In the
Company of Educated Women* (New Haven, CT: Yale University Press,
1985); Lynn D. Gordon, *Gender and Higher Education in the Progressive
Era* (New Haven, CT: Yale University Press, 1990).

7. Christie Anne Farnham, *The Education of the Southern Belle: Higher
Education and Student Socialization in the Antebellum South* (New York:
New York University Press, 1994).

8. Margaret A. Nash, *Women's Education in the United States, 1780–1840*
(New York: Palgrave Macmillan, 2005); Mary Kelley, *Learning to Stand
and Speak: Women, Education and Public Life in America's Republic*
(Chapel Hill: University of North Carolina Press, 2006); Anya Jabour,
Scarlett's Sisters: Young Women in the Old South (Chapel Hill: University of
North Carolina Press, 2007).

9. Christine A. Ogren, *The American State Normal School: "An Instrument of
Great Good"* (New York: Palgrave Macmillan, 2005); Andrea G. Radke-
Moss, *Bright Epoch: Women and Coeducation in the American West* (Lincoln:
University of Nebraska Press, 2008); Andrea L. Turpin, *A New Moral
Vision: Gender, Religion, and the Changing Purposes of American Higher
Education, 1837–1917* (Ithaca, NY: Cornell University Press, 2016).

10. Amy Thompson McCandless, *The Past in the Present: Women's Higher
Education in the Twentieth-Century American South* (Tuscaloosa:
University Alabama Press, 1999); Linda Eisenmann, *Higher Education for
Women in Postwar America, 1945–1965* (Baltimore: Johns Hopkins
University Press, 2007), 5; Babette Faehmel, *College Women in the Nuclear*

Age: Cultural Literacy and Female Identity, 1940–1960 (Newark, NJ: Rutgers University Press, 2013).

11. James D. Anderson, *The Education of Blacks in the South* (Chapel Hill: The University of North Carolina Press, 1988), chapter 7.

12. Linda Perkins, "The African American Female Elite: The Early History of African American Women in the Seven Sister Colleges," *Harvard Educational Review* 67 (1997): 718–57; Cally L. Waite, *Permission to Remain Among Us: Education for Blacks in Oberlin, Ohio, 1880–1914* (Westport, CT: Praeger, 2002).

13. Stephanie Y. Evans, *Black Women in the Ivory Tower, 1850–1954: An Intellectual History* (Gainesville: University Press of Florida, 2007); Marcus S. Cox, *Segregated Soldiers: Military Training at Historically Black Colleges in the Jim Crow South* (Baton Rouge: Louisiana State University Press, 2013).

14. Joy Ann Williamson, *Black Power on Campus: The University of Illinois, 1965–75* (Urbana: University of Illinois Press, 2003); Joy Ann Williamson, *Radicalizing the Ebony Tower: Black Colleges and the Black Freedom Struggle in Mississippi* (New York: Teachers College Press, 2008); Diane Brady, *Fraternity* (New York: Spiegel & Grau, 2012); Stefan M. Bradley, *Harlem vs. Columbia University: Black Student Power in the Late 1960s* (Urbana: University of Illinois Press, 2009); Donald Alexander Downs, *Cornell '69: Liberalism and the Crisis of the American University* (Ithaca, NY: Cornell University Press, 1999); Wayne Glasker, *Black Students in the Ivory Tower: African American Student Activism at the University of Pennsylvania, 1967–1990* (Amherst: University of Massachusetts Press, 2009).

15. Liel Leibovitz and Matthew Miller, *Fortunate Sons: The 120 Chinese Boys Who Came to America, Went to School, and Revolutionized an Ancient Civilization* (New York: W.W. Norton, 2011); Emily Porcincula Lawsin, "Pensionados, Paisanos, and Pinoys: An Analysis of the Filipino Student Bulletin, 1922–1939," *Filipino American National Historical Society Journal* 4 (1996): 33–33P; Gary Y. Okihiro, *Storied Lives: Japanese American Students and World War II* (Seattle: University of Washington Press, 1999); Allan W. Austin, *From Concentration Camp to Campus: Japanese American Students and World War II* (Urbana: University of Illinois Press, 2004); Karen Umemoto, "'On Strike!': San Francisco State College Strike, 1968–69," *Amerasia* 15 (1989): 3–41; Steve Louie and Glenn Omatsu, eds., *Asian Americans: The Movement and the Moment* (Los Angeles: UCLA Asian American Studies Center Press, 2001); Thai-Huy Nguyen and Marybeth Gasman, "Activism, Identity and Service: The Influence of the Asian American Movement on the Educational Experiences of College Students," *History of Education* 44 (2015): 339–54; Thai-Huy Nguyen and Marybeth Gasman, "Cultural Identity and Allegiance Among

Vietnamese Students and Their Organizations at the University of California, Irvine: 1980–1990," *Teachers College Record* 117, no. 5 (2015): 1–22.

16. Victoria-Maria MacDonald, *Latino Education in the United States: A Narrated History from 1513–2000* (New York: Palgrave Macmillan, 2004); Carlos Muñoz, Jr., *Youth, Identity, Power: The Chicano Movement* (New York: Verso, 1989); Victoria-Maria MacDonald, John M. Botti, and Lisa Hoffman Clark, "From Visibility to Autonomy: Lations and Higher Education in the U.S., 1965–2005," *Harvard Educational Review* 77 (2007): 474–504.

17. Bobby Wright, "'For the Children of the Infidels'?: American Indian Education in the Colonial Colleges," *American Indian Culture and Research Journal* 12, no. 3 (1988): 1–14; Joel Pfister, *The Yale Indian: The Education of Henry Roe Cloud* (Durham, NC: Duke University Press, 2009); Devon A. Mihesuah, *Cultivating the Rosebuds: The Education of Women at the Cherokee Female Seminary, 1851–1909* (Urbana: University of Illinois Press, 1993); Donal F. Lindsey, *Indians at Hampton Institute, 1877–1923* (Urbana: University of Illinois Press, 1995); Lisa K. Neuman, *Indian Play: Indigenous Identities at Bacone College* (Lincoln: University of Nebraska Press, 2013).

18. Steven E. Brown, "Breaking Barriers: The Pioneering Disability Students Services Program at the University of Illinois, 1948–1960," in *The History of Discrimination in U.S. Education: Marginality, Agency, and Power*, ed. Eileen H. Tamura (New York: Palgrave Macmillan, 2008), 165–92; John B. Christiansen and Sharon N. Barnartt, *Deaf President Now! The 1988 Revolution at Gallaudet University* (Washington, DC: Gallaudet University Press, 1995).

19. William Wright, *Harvard's Secret Court: The Savage 1920 Purge of Campus Homosexuals* (New York: St. Martin's Press, 2005); Nicholas L. Syrett, "The Boys of Beaver Meadow: A Homosexual Community at 1920s Darthmouth College," *American Studies* 48 (2007): 9–18; Margaret A. Nash and Jennifer A. Silverman, "'An Indelible Mark': Gay Purges in Higher Education in the 1940s," *History of Education Quarterly* 55, no. 4 (2015): 441–59; Patrick Dilley, "20th Century Postsecondary Practices and Policies to Control Gay Students," *The Review of Higher Education* 25, no. 4 (2002): 409–31; Patrick Dilley, *Queer Man on Campus: A History of Non-Heterosexual College Men, 1945–2000* (New York: RoutledgeFarmer, 2002); Brett Beemyn, "The Silence Is Broken: A History of the First Lesbian, Gay, and Bisexual College Student Groups," *Journal of the History of Sexuality* 12, no. 2 (2003): 205–23; Jessica Clawson, "'Existing and Existing in Your Face': Hiram Ruiz and the Pedagogy of Gay Liberation Front in Tallahassee, Florida, 1970–1971," *Journal of Curriculum Theorizing* 29, no. 2 (2013): 143–48; Jessica Clawson, "Coming Out of the Campus Closet: The Emerging Visibility of Queer Students at the

University of Florida, 1970–1982," *Educational Studies* 50 (2014): 209–30.

20. Richard N. Current, *Phi Beta Kappa in American Life: The First Two Hundred Years* (New York: Oxford University Press, 1990).

21. On the traditional interpretation of literary societies, see Frederick Rudolph, *The American College and University: A History* (New York: Vintage Books, 1962), 136–45; James McLachlan, "The Choice of Hercules: American Student Societies in the Early 19th Century," in *The University in Society*, ed. Lawrence Stone, vol. 2 (Princeton, NJ: Princeton University Press, 1974), 449–94; Horowitz, *Campus Life*, 28–29. Kelley, *Learning to Stand and Speak* chapter 4, quotation on 118.

22. Kolan Thomas Morelock, *Taking the Town: Collegiate and Community Culture in the Bluegrass, 1880–1917* (Lexington: University Press of Kentucky, 2008), 5; Radke-Moss, *Bright Epoch*, chapter 3; Ogren, *The American State Normal School*, 108–19, quotation on 114; Michael S. Hevel, "Public Displays of Student Learning: The Role of Literary Societies in Early Higher Education," *The Annals of Iowa* 70, no. 1 (2011): 1–35; Michael S. Hevel, "Preparing for the Politics of Life: An Expansion of the Political Dimensions of College Women's Literary Societies," *History of Education Quarterly* 54, no. 4 (2014): 486–515; Thomas L. Howard III and Owen W. Gallogly, *Society Ties: A History of the Jefferson Society and Student Life at the University of Virginia* (Charlottesville: University of Virginia Press, 2017).

23. Nicholas L. Syrett, *The Company He Keeps: A History of White College Fraternities* (Chapel Hill: University of North Carolina Press, 2009); Laurie A. Wilkie, *The Lost Boys of Zeta Psi: A Historical Archaeology of Masculinity at a University Fraternity* (Berkeley: University of California Press, 2010).

24. Diana B. Turk, *Bound by a Mighty Vow: Sisterhood and Women's Fraternities, 1870–1920* (New York: New York University Press, 2004); Lawrence C. Ross, Jr., *The Divine Nine: The History of African American Fraternities and Sororities* (New York: Kensington, 2000); Paula Giddings, *In Search of Sisterhood: Delta Sigma Theta and the Challenge of the Black Sorority Movement* (New York: William Morrow, 1988); Deborah Elizabeth Whaley, *Disciplining Women: Alpha Kappa Alpha, Black Counterpublics, and the Cultural Politics of Black Sororities* (Albany: State University of New York Press, 2010); Marianne R. Sanua, *Going Greek: Jewish College Fraternities in the United States, 1895–1945* (Detroit: Wayne State University Press, 2003).

25. David P. Setran, *The College "Y": Student Religion in the Era of Secularization* (New York: Palgrave Macmillan, 2007), 7.

26. Sara M. Evans, ed., *Journeys That Opened the World: Women, Student Christian Movements, and Social Justice, 1955–1975* (New Brunswick, NJ:

Rutgers University Press, 2003); John G. Turner, *Bill Bright and Campus Crusade for Christ: The Renewal of Evangelicalism in Postwar America* (Chapel Hill: University of North Carolina Press, 2008); Dorothy E. Finnegan and Brian Cullaty, "Origins of the YMCA Universities: Organizational Adaptations in Urban Education," *History of Higher Education Annual* 21 (2001): 47–77; Dorothy E. Finnegan, "Raising and Leveling the Bar: Standards, Access, and the YMCA Evening Law Schools, 1890–1940," *Journal of Legal Education* 55 (2005): 208–33; Dorothy E. Finnegan, "A Potent Influence: The YMCA and YWCA at Penn College, 1882–1920s," *The Annals of Iowa* 65 (2006): 1–34; Nathan F. Alleman and Dorothy E. Finnegan, "'Believe You Have a Mission in Life and Steadily Pursue It': Campus YMCAs Presage Student Development Theory, 1894–1930," *Higher Education in Review* 6 (2009): 1–33; Dorothy E. Finnegan and Nathan F. Alleman, "The YMCA and the Origins of American Freshmen Orientation Programs," *Historical Studies in Education* 25 (2013): 95–114.

27. For an overview of this research, see Michael S. Hevel, "Toward a History of Student Affairs: A Synthesis of Research, 1995–2015," *Journal of College Student Development* 57 (2016): 844–62. Examples of books include Carolyn Terry Bashaw, *"Stalwart Women": A Historical Analysis of Deans of Women in the South* (New York: Teachers College Press, 1999); Jana Nidiffer, *Pioneering Deans of Women: More Than Wise and Pious Matrons* (New York: Teachers College Press, 2000); Robert Schwartz, *Deans of Men and the Shaping of Modern College Culture* (New York: Palgrave Macmillan, 2010); Carroll L. L. Miller and Anne S. Pruitt-Logan, *Faithful to the Task at Hand: The Life of Lucy Diggs Slowe* (Albany: State University of New York Press, 2012); Kelly C. Sartorius, *Deans of Women and the Feminist Movement: Emily Taylor's Activism* (New York: Palgrave Macmillan, 2014).

28. Beth L. Bailey, *From Front Porch to Back Seat: Courtship in Twentieth-Century America* (Baltimore, MD: Johns Hopkins University Press, 1988).

29. Beth Bailey, *Sex in the Heartland* (Cambridge: Harvard University Press, 1999).

30. Lawrence J. Nelson, *Rumors of Indiscretion: The University of Missouri's "Sex Questionnaire" Scandal in the Jazz Age* (Columbia: University of Missouri Press, 2003); Margaret A. Lowe, *Looking Good: College Women and Body Image, 1875–1930* (Baltimore, MD: Johns Hopkins University Press, 2005), 59.

31. J. Lloyd Winstead, *When Colleges Sang: The Story of Singing in American College Life* (Tuscaloosa: University of Alabama Press, 2013), 77, 79.

32. Deirdre Clemente, *Dress Casual: How College Students Redefined American Style* (Chapel Hill: University of North Carolina Press, 2014).

CHAPTER 3

"We Are Not So Easily to Be Overcome": Fraternities on the American College Campus

Nicholas L. Syrett

Over the course of a decade from the early 1910s to the early 1920s, the University of Illinois's Thomas Arkle Clark had a problem. Clark, the first "Dean of Men" on a college campus and a longtime supporter of college fraternities, was horrified that Theta Nu Epsilon (TNE) was now a presence not just on his campus but across the nation. TNE was an unsanctioned, underground fraternity that initiated both members of other fraternities and non-fraternity men, and it was secretive in its activities and its members. A member of a fraternity himself, Clark wrote to his colleagues at other universities and in other fraternities about TNE and published articles about it in a variety of venues. He explained in 1913: "The tendency to dishonesty and graft which Theta Nu Epsilon has fostered … has encouraged loose ideals generally. Drinking, gambling, cribbing, and hazing are indirectly encouraged by the low moral and political ideals for which Theta Nu Epsilon stands."[1]

Clark did not seem to realize that in describing TNE he was in essence describing all fraternities. He most seemed to dislike its secrecy, especially

N. L. Syrett (✉)
Department of Women, Gender, and Sexuality Studies,
University of Kansas, Lawrence, KS, USA
e-mail: syrett@ku.edu

© The Author(s) 2018
C. A. Ogren, M. A. VanOverbeke (eds.),
Rethinking Campus Life, Historical Studies in Education,
https://doi.org/10.1007/978-3-319-75614-1_3

in an era when fraternities had come almost fully under the supervision of men like him who were tasked with affirming fraternities' legitimacy, ensuring their future survival, and, at least to a degree, coordinating their activities on campus. Clark clearly could not understand the appeal of an organization like TNE, an appeal rooted in secrecy that it shared with the earliest fraternities and indeed still shares with fraternities' more covert activities to this day. The secrecy was precisely the point for those who joined the clandestine organization: by joining TNE they were breaking university rules.

The TNE phenomenon of the early twentieth century encapsulates the history of college fraternities writ large, in at least three overlapping ways. First, TNE members relished the fact that, in joining the organization, they were defying the faculty, which had banned TNE from campus. Following the publication of a 1922 article in which Clark claimed to have eliminated TNE from his campus by confiscating its charter, the president of the University of Illinois chapter of TNE sent him a letter, beginning "Dear Tommy," in which he explained, "I want to inform you that our chapter of Theta Nu Epsilon still lives and will continue to live here at Illinois. ... Next time you brag of your great dareing [*sic*] in exterminating us at Illinois by writing magazine articles THINK TWICE. We are not so easily to be overcome. BEWARE." Clearly the illicitness of their activity was integral to the experience for these TNE members. But that they continued to participate in sanctioned campus politics, and indeed were often leaders on campus, is also typical; fraternity men have regularly followed the rules by day and broken them by night.[2]

The second common thread between TNE and fraternities more generally is that they have always been, by definition, exclusive. Like TNE, fraternities awarded bids, then and now, only to the most desirable prospective members. Whether these prospects accepted had everything to do with the prestige of the fraternity making the offer, and that prestige was based in part on the exclusivity of its selection process. Finally, men in fraternities judged prospective members and prided themselves on their masculinity, or in nineteenth-century terms, manliness. To that end they valued certain characteristics and activities. In the nineteenth century, as a demonstration of masculinity, fraternity members espoused independence, academic skill, and some combination of charisma, family lineage, and good looks. By the later nineteenth century, fraternities increasingly focused on athletics, eschewing an earlier emphasis on academic success. From the 1920s onward, fraternities also expected their brothers to demonstrate success with women, showing their masculinity via heterosexuality. In this way fraternities often have been a microcosm of both society and the colleges and universities in which they make their homes.

This chapter takes a long view of college fraternities' ideals, commitments, and behaviors. Dividing these organizations' history into four rough chronological periods—the antebellum era, the late nineteenth century, the 1920s, and the post–World War II era—it examines nearly 200 years of traditionally white fraternities from their founding in 1825 on all-male college campuses to the early twenty-first century, when they found themselves in the news for violations of college and state laws surrounding hazing, drinking, and sexual assault. I argue that fraternities have created a brotherhood that emphasizes exclusivity and defiance of university administrators, making its membership decisions based on narrow standards of masculinity that have changed over time. With some exceptions, fraternal masculinity has become increasingly destructive, athletic, anti-intellectual, and heterosexually aggressive over the course of the organizations' existence.[3]

THE ANTEBELLUM ERA

In their earliest days in the second quarter of the nineteenth century, fraternities were, by definition, secretive and clandestine—and rooted in defiance—because on the small all-male college campuses where they were founded, administrations banned them. Antebellum colleges were quite small and often populated by students of a wide range of ages, from men in their late twenties to adolescent boys. The few faculty members, many of whom were ministers, were responsible for the moral and religious lives of their charges, and they usually saw secret societies of any variety as irreligious in and of themselves and as antithetical to the goals of the smooth functioning of college life. Francis Wayland, Brown University President, explained in an 1846 letter to Edward Hitchcock, Amherst College President: "I would incomparably rather resign my place than allow young men the right to meet in secret when they choose without the knowledge of the Faculty." In 1847, Princeton University dismissed 36 students for participating in a clandestine meeting of the sophomore class. Almost all antebellum colleges banned secret societies of any variety, fraternities being only one type.[4]

That secrecy was precisely the point, however, for the students who started and joined fraternities. When the initial chapter of Kappa Alpha, the first social fraternity to spread to other colleges, was founded at Union College in 1825, its members insisted on secrecy and followed the well-worn path of other college students who had founded a variety of academic, honorary, and secret societies for at least a half-century. Phi Beta Kappa, founded at the College of William and Mary in 1776, too was a secret society before it morphed into an academic honor society. The faculty countenanced literary societies—usually two on campus to promote competition—but most other clubs derived much of their appeal from the fact that they existed outside of the regulatory regime of college faculty and administrators.[5]

Fraternities, from their earliest iteration, broke other rules and defied faculty in other ways as well, sometimes resulting in what they called a "spree," an occasion involving alcohol and rowdiness, outlawed by university officials. One 1855 newspaper editorial explained: "Removed, by the injunction of secresy [*sic*], from faculty supervision, these societies are frequently the scenes of conviviality. They decide their own hours. If it is in the 'small hours' of the night that they adjourn, who shall call them to account? They may smoke, drink, and chat, under the disguised name of *making speeches.*" This kind of rule-breaking was one way for college youth to claim their independence in the face of college faculty who were charged with overseeing their intellectual and moral education. By asserting this independence and challenging faculty, they also sought to demonstrate their manliness.[6]

Those who joined fraternities in antebellum colleges tended not to be the men who were attending college to become ministers—the common intention of early college students—but the sons of the growing middle and upper classes seeking to gain an education and the connections and pedigree that came with a college degree. These men had greater means to afford "sprees," and they also were less concerned with the consequences for their spiritual well-being of breaking college rules. Ministers-in-training were far more likely to be older, poorer, and on a scholarship assembled by a church back home. Of the fifty men who initially joined that first Kappa Alpha chapter at Union College, for instance, only six (12 percent) became ministers, whereas 40 percent of the college's graduates during that period joined the clergy. Similar ratios characterized the careers of graduates and fraternity members at other colleges. Thus, fraternities recruited and admitted an exclusive group of students from the upper economic classes.[7]

The spiritual division between those students who joined fraternities and those who did not, or could not, was absent, however, when it came to students' attitudes toward scholarship. Almost all antebellum students prized doing well in school; it was part of how they defined their manliness. Though fraternity men were more concerned with not appearing to try all that hard, almost all of the extant evidence suggests that their behavior in the classroom, and their desire for faculty recognition of their scholarly efforts, was largely in harmony with the academic (if not the spiritual) goals of antebellum colleges. The scriptors (or secretaries) of a variety of chapters of Delta Kappa Epsilon demonstrated this concern with academics. Writing to one another, they boasted about the academic standing of their chapters, the honors they had won (honors bestowed by the very faculty whose rules they broke by night), and their standing in academics compared to other fraternity chapters with whom they perceived themselves to be in competition. The scriptor for Brown University's chapter, for instance, recounted that in addition to having the valedictorian as a member, his chapter "still occupies the front rank at Brown both in scholarship and popularity." The scriptor at Lafayette College boasted that "out of eight junior orators 4 are [Delta Kappa Epsilon] men." And the scriptor at Middlebury College proclaimed of the incoming class, "We have five of the very first in class." Contrary to accounts of antebellum college life that suggest that students generally, and men in fraternities particularly, did not care about their studies, the evidence from archival sources demonstrates that however antagonistic college students may have been with their faculty regarding regulation of their social lives, they still believed that doing well in school was desirable for its own sake, and also served as proof of their manliness.[8]

Psi Upsilon brother and Hamilton College student Alexander Hamilton Rice recounted to his fiancée in 1844: "I find since my return that I am particularly fortunate in my position upon the merit roll so far as scholarship is concerned: many who have stood above me heretofore are now below.... I do not consider the merit roll a very impartial criterion but still since they keep such a thing I am rather gratified than otherwise to share with others in its honorable place." Here was the key distinction: among fraternity brothers particularly, men wanted to do well in school, but they didn't want to appear to *want* to do well in school, to be trying *too* hard to achieve distinction. Benjamin Hall's 1856 *Collection of College Words and Customs*, derived from colleges across the country, included a large number of words for those students who studied too ostentatiously, but it also printed many words to describe those who did well at recitation. Positive terms for success included to "curl," "have a rush," "sail," "make a good shine," or "tear." By contrast, description of a recitation as a "squirt" or a "high-ti" indicated that the student was too obviously trying to please and impress the instructor.[9]

Men in fraternities, who regularly held debates, assigned essays, and maintained reading libraries, all within their own organizations, were not opposed to the primary goals of a college education, at least the secular ones; they just wanted to have fun at the same time that they honed their reasoning skills. Yale University's chapter of Kappa Sigma Epsilon, for instance, debated regularly at its meetings; in October 1849, the brothers considered the question, "Will the acquisition of New Mexico prove beneficial to the United States?" And the Delta Upsilon fraternity debated questions of womanhood in various chapters, with debate questions, including: "Ought women to have equal political rights to men?" at Waterville College; "Ought women to be allowed to vote[?]" at Williams; "Is the intellect of women equal to that of men?" at Amherst; and "Ought females to be admitted to the learned professions?" at Hamilton. In all four of these debates, the brotherhood decided in the negative.[10]

The assertion, or perhaps assumption, of masculine dominance undergirded almost all fraternity life in the antebellum era—and in many respects continues to do so to this day. While fraternity men guarded their exclusivity by selecting only those men they found to be the most manly—defined through some combination of class status, intellectual capability, healthy and attractive appearance, and charisma—they always took it for granted that as white men they were superior to white women and people of color. I have found only one man of color admitted to an antebellum college fraternity (Yung Wing, Yale Class of 1854, DKE), so overwhelmingly white and male were these organizations and the colleges at which they made their homes during the antebellum era. But fraternity men, surrounded by other white men and without women on campus, made distinctions among their fellow students based on characteristics not tied directly to phenotype or biology. The evaluations they made for membership were those made *among* similarly situated men, not between those men and racial and gendered others. They thus chose men of means whom they perceived to be manly, men who knew how to have fun by joining a secret organization and breaking the other rules laid out by their faculty, at the same time that they valued academic achievement.[11]

The Postbellum Era

As historians have demonstrated, colleges and universities changed follow-ing the Civil War. The number of colleges grew and the existing colleges and universities expanded. In many cases, especially at the newer land grant institutions, coeducation became increasingly common. In smaller numbers than women, racial and religious minorities also joined the ranks of collegiate populations. Despite these changes, which signaled the begin-nings of the democratization of higher education, the nation's elite, itself growing, began to send its sons to colleges and universities in ever grow-ing numbers, making the institutions the stomping grounds of the privileged.[12]

The most privileged among them made their homes in college fraterni-ties, sometimes quite literally, as Greek-letter organizations, aided by wealthy and influential alumni, cemented their place on campus by con-structing large and elaborate homes that replaced the earlier ramshackle clubhouses where only meetings took place. The first fraternity home built for the purpose of housing its members appeared at the University of California, Berkeley, in 1876. By 1879, thirteen fraternity chapters owned their own houses, and by 1920, that number had increased to 774 chap-ters. Fraternity houses were expensive; while alumni contributed to their building, active members took care of upkeep, which meant that only stu-dents with means could afford to join. Houses were often staffed by cooks and other servants, increasing the expense. Fraternity houses thus allowed men of means to perpetuate exclusivity on campus by self-segregating, especially in an era when many other students lived in town or with their families. With these elaborate and highly visible homes, fraternities were no longer clandestine organizations on campus, but they certainly remained exclusive.[13]

As they consolidated power in their fraternity houses, the brothers also shifted their idea of masculinity from what it had been in the antebellum period. They styled themselves as collegiate gentlemen, emphasizing the wealth of their membership, wealth that allowed them not only to live in large houses, but also to ignore the supposed purpose of college—educa-tion and preparation for the workforce—and instead focus on athletics and extracurricular activities. They gained prestige through excluding their poorer classmates, whom they called "barbs," short for barbarians. In 1873, the men of Kappa Sigma at Trinity College (later Duke University) explained that the "policy of this chapter from the very first was to exercise the greatest care in the selection of the very best men and to solicit those who were of the highest moral and social standard." Walter Hill, a Chi Phi at the University of Georgia, told his mother that those who did not belong to fraternities were "the 'OIPOLLOI' (the many)—the rabble—the plebeians. Don't think that I am getting arrogant & aristocratic, when I speak of the rabble, &c. While I do not assume any feigned condescension, I like these ordinary boys as much as I can." And at the University of California, Berkeley, one anti-fraternity newspaper explained in 1883: "The fraternities are for the most part composed of men of means, men who can pay initiation fees and regular dues and the other expenses of fraternity life. And a fact that is patent to the most careless observer, namely, that with a single exception the fraternities make money a chief requisite for membership."[14]

If fraternities made an exception to this rule, it was for the football or other athletic star in this era when sports became all the rage on college campuses. They would offer him a bid even if he did not share the social pedigree of other members. Athletics and sports were the most determinative of male students' popularity during this period, but fraternity brothers participated in all kinds of other activities in the extracurriculum: the glee club, theater, banjo club, literary and humor magazines, the yearbook, and student government. Fraternity men, like many other college students, styled this participation as "working for" their school, but for them, it was as much about working for their own popularity and that of their fraternity as it was for the benefit of the school itself. In 1897 the Stanford chapter of Zeta Psi bragged: "During the year we have been well represented in both athletics and music. On the Glee Club we have Sewall, Schneider, Macy, and Bush. On the mandolin club we are represented by Sewall—leader, and Haden—manager." Fraternity men valued these other activities. The evidence indicates that fraternity men often combined their strength to shut non-Greek men out of positions within various organizations, which only contributed to the exclusive nature of Greek life. It is also clear, however, that sports reigned supreme. As Cornelius Howard Patton and Walter Taylor Field explained in their study of college life in the 1880s, while the glee club might bring prestige, "it was a consolation prize for the man who could not make one of the athletic teams—for then as now, the college athlete occupied the first place in the public esteem." Indeed, the same Stanford chapter of Zeta Psi boasted two years later:

On Jan. 28, [18]99, William Wilson Carson of Eureka, Calif., was initiated into the fraternity. He came from Bellmont School at the beginning of the school year with an enviable record in athletics. Brother Carson was one of the most desired freshmen in college and well worthy of the name 'Zete.' He played on the freshman football team and will probably make next year's varsity team.[15]

Superior achievement in academics had been worthy of respect and admiration during the antebellum era, but athletics and other extracurricular activities in the postbellum period almost fully supplanted academics as a way of gauging a classmate's manliness and indeed his success in school more broadly. Masculinity in late-nineteenth-century US culture was undergoing shifts from its antebellum iteration; in order to combat stereotypes of the weak and sickly man trapped in an office, middle-class men aped their working-class peers and tried to define themselves as masculine by asserting their strength and virility. In growing numbers, men and boys joined the Boy Scouts, played competitive sports, and emulated Theodore Roosevelt's "strenuous life." As they embraced athleticism, students abandoned an earlier respect for those who did well academically without seeming to try. For those attending college as a sort of finishing school and aggregator of useful connections, learning was no longer the chief pursuit. This declining emphasis on academic achievement was true for many in colleges, but no one exemplified the trend more than the fraternity man. At Princeton, President James McCosh explained that secret societies "combined to lower the standards of scholarship." And as one chronicle of life at Yale explained, only about half of all compositions were original and written by the person who submitted them. Cheating was rampant and fully accepted by students, particularly the popular. By the end of this era, in 1912, Dartmouth officials worried: "One of two unpleasant conclusions seems unavoidable: either the fraternities are exercising a damaging influence upon their younger members; or they are deliberately choosing poor intellectual material. Whichever of these conclusions is correct, it constitutes a serious indictment of our Greek societies." Both were likely correct, so little did fraternities value scholarship as a mark of manliness, now recalibrated to emphasize social class and athleticism.[16]

While fraternity men adopted shifting conceptions of manhood, they did not abandon the recklessness that characterized their antebellum brethren; this illicit behavior continued to be a way for them to defy their elders. If anything they probably increased their drinking, vandalism, and breaking of rules through new fraternity practices of pledging, rushing, and initiation, most of which had little precedent in the antebellum era. By the 1870s and 1880s, fraternities had developed elaborate and competitive rituals to attract the most desirable incoming freshmen of every class. So disruptive did these activities become that officials at some colleges mandated postponing rushing until second semester or the sophomore year. In 1903, for instance, Amherst College made its fraternities abide by the resolution "that we make no appointments or pledges with prospective members of Amherst College before they leave trains upon their arrival in Amherst, or before getting off the electric cars at the corner of Northampton Road and Pleasant Street, or the Amherst terminal." These rules aimed to create a level playing field for all the fraternities and also attempted to curb the worst excesses of the process, which culminated in pledging and initiation rituals.[17]

Worse than the disruption caused by pledging was the hazing that often accompanied the initiation process for pledges. Likely originating in Civil War battalions and also harkening back to the hazing of the freshman class by sophomores in antebellum colleges, by the 1870s and 1880s, fraternity hazing had become a marked problem on college campuses. Mortimer Leggett, a Kappa Alpha pledge at Cornell University, is the nation's first recorded fraternity hazing casualty; he fell to his death in 1873 in an Ithaca gorge while blindfolded for his initiation. Other initiation rituals involved "horseplay" designed to test the mettle of a man and see if he was "yellow." Some fraternities painted their pledges, fed them nauseating concoctions, beat them, and tortured them with electricity. At Stanford in the early twentieth century, pledges were "tubbed," or stripped and submerged in cold water. These rituals, a means to cement the loyalty of brothers to the organizations, were also designed so that pledges could prove that they were manly enough to join the fraternity, to enhance the prestige of the organization by ensuring that members were tough, and in part also to recapture or redeem the manhood of the senior members who had spent the prior months or weeks groveling before freshmen in order to compel them to join their particular fraternity in the courtship ritual called rushing and pledging.[18]

It was a courtship ritual reserved for white men alone. As women and racial and religious minorities made their way onto college campuses during this period, fraternities reacted by excluding them. For "brotherhoods" of men, the exclusion of women was perhaps logical, but fraternity men often went one step further and attempted to block women from joining the membership of various boards and clubs that men had become accustomed to controlling on campus. This practice was common enough at most newly coeducational schools that women banded together in what were first known as women's fraternities, and later called sororities. At some institutions, fraternities were also open in their disdain for their new female classmates, in part because women's presence on campuses demonstrated that there was nothing inherently male about the ability to be a college student. Women students threatened men's masculinity. As one commentator from Cornell University explained, "We have the spectacle of young men sitting on the porch of a luxurious fraternity and criticizing passing 'coeds' with an acridity almost feminine, expressing disgust because their clothes do not fit them, and their hands are not neatly manicured." Fraternities at Cornell also forbade their members from courting college women, a common strategy to underscore male dominance and the exclusivity of fraternities. For fraternity men looking to socialize with women, the two acceptable avenues were courtship with middle- and upper-class women who were their peers socially if not educationally (i.e., women from other colleges or those who did not attend college at all), or working-class women and prostitutes from whom men might obtain sexual favors but to whom they owed nothing socially.[19]

Excluding African American, Asian American, Jewish, and Catholic male classmates from fraternities was more problematic than excluding women because these classmates were men. During the late nineteenth century as men from previously underrepresented minority groups began to attend colleges, most white fraternities added constitutional provisions formally banning these students. Excluding first- and second-generation immigrants, as well as people of color, was also in keeping with fraternities' emphasis upon social prestige. Most of these newly arrived students were poor, with little time or resources to devote to extracurricular activities; they also tended to study harder than fraternity men who expected a college degree but were unwilling to work hard to obtain it. Jews, in particular, were met with much ostracism, as fraternity men viewed them as the epitome of what many called the "greasy grind" or someone who always studied and supplicated himself to the desires of the faculty. At Yale in 1890, Delta Kappa Epsilon put on an anti-Semitic production entitled: "Shylock: The Sarcastic Sheeny, or the Manoeuvering Merchant of Verdant Venice." As a result of such social exclusion, students founded the first "minority fraternities" for Jews, Catholics, African Americans, and Asian Americans in this period.[20]

Fraternity men of the late nineteenth and early twentieth centuries built upon their antebellum origins to craft a version of fraternal masculinity that relied much more on socioeconomic status and athleticism. They continued to break rules and defy authority through drinking, vandalism, and the new trend of hazing. They spent far less time on their studies, with more of their college lives consumed by extracurricular activities, rushing and pledging, and socializing. By and large they also rejected the arrival of women and people of color on campuses that had previously been all white and all male. Fraternities would remain, for some time, bastions of elite white men.

THE 1920s

In the 1920s, the power of fraternities on campus increased, as the proportion of undergraduate students who joined Greek-letter organizations skyrocketed. And with a newly shared youth culture publicized across the nation via newspapers and magazines, students' cultural cachet never had been so pronounced. To really be a college student, it seemed, one also had to join a fraternity or sorority. The numbers of college students themselves also increased, along with the number of fraternity chapters, many of which were newly founded to accommodate the surge in college enrollments.[21]

In many ways, the life of fraternities followed precedents set in the late nineteenth century. Athletics and social class determined who was offered a bid, though the greater number of students and fraternities also meant that newly established chapters initiated those of lesser means and popularity. Such a shift ensured that certain chapters and fraternities became more exclusive than others. Illicit behavior, such as drinking and rule-breaking, continued to characterize many fraternity men's nighttime activities. The files in most college archives of the 1920s are filled with reports to deans of students about hazing pranks gone awry, drinking to excess, and petty acts of vandalism, even as fraternity members sought out elected student offices by day. On some campuses, they furthered the tradition of blocking unaffiliated students from meaningful extracurricular involvement. At Dartmouth College, for instance, Lambda Chi Alpha's 1923 newsletter explained that brothers participated in all the extracurricular activities. They were runners-up in basketball and beat Psi Upsilon and Sigma Chi in baseball. They played tennis and soccer and had members in the outing club, glee club, debate club, and on various social committees. At the University of Michigan 43 percent of fraternity and sorority members, compared with only 13 percent of independents, participated in some sort of activity. At Syracuse University, independents found it difficult to participate because, on that campus, 46 percent of Greeks claimed it was only right that they should maintain dominance in activities, presumably because they believed themselves to be the most talented and popular on campus; their popularity was, after all, why they had been selected for fraternity membership in the first place. But for all that participation, varsity sports remained the most important activity. As Illinois's Thomas Arkle Clark put it in 1926: "The athlete is the undergraduate idol. He is the big man in college, the god whom the freshmen worship, and to whom the young women offer incense and to whom they write congratulatory notes."[22]

Fraternity men continued to be on the leading edge of another trend that had developed in the postbellum era: they didn't study all that much and had little concern for their grades. They remained focused on college as an experience that would bring them increased connections—including among brothers and alumni in their fraternities—and the social wherewithal to compete in the world of business, where larger numbers of students sought employment after graduation. Leon B. Richardson, a professor of chemistry at Dartmouth, explained: "The moment a man shows intellectual superiority, or even manifests unusual interest in those things which a college is for, he at once falls under suspicion. He must *show* that he is not possessed of the pride of intellect; he must *show* that he has in his makeup elements of good fellowship; he must *show* that he conforms sufficiently to the normal college type not to be a marked man." It was this conformity to anti-intellectualism—academic success no longer being a marker of masculinity—that marked the life of many college students, and fraternity men especially, during the 1920s. Max McConn, dean of Lehigh University, summed up the criteria for fraternity membership in this conformist world:

The criteri[a] are: money, family, prep school, and social presentability—in an ascending scale; that is, the possession of plenty of money counts less (they are not sordidly mercenary) than family, and family less than the prestige of the prep school attended; and all three of these count less than the social presentability of the man himself. If he is a "slick" dresser (to just the right degree of "slickness") and a "smooth" talker and either a promising athlete or an adept at parlor tricks—playing the piano or the ukulele or dancing the Black Bottom—he is grabbed at once.

Fraternal masculinity also continued to be bound up in exclusivity of membership. The clauses banning people of color, Jews, and sometimes Catholics remained, but emphasis upon class generally waned. While the oldest and most established fraternities persisted in emphasizing lineage, newer fraternities that could not afford to be so picky stepped in to take those men that the older fraternities rejected.[23]

It was not just in withholding membership, however, that fraternities placed themselves above their fellow students. Their enactment of masculinity also rested more and more on the participation of college women. On an increasingly coeducational campus, the rules for interaction between college men and women had changed significantly by the 1920s. Middle-class youth had adopted the practice of dating, whereby a young man and woman went out independently, often in a car, and where the young man paid for whatever entertainment took place on the date. In exchange the young woman had to negotiate whether she wanted to reward him with any of the newly sanctioned forms of sexual expression of which middle-class youth were now availing themselves: necking, petting, and heavy petting. Most evidence indicates that middle-class college students, women especially, did not have intercourse prior to marriage, or at least engagement. They did not want to gain for themselves a reputation as being too acquiescent, but they also did not want to be known as a "flat tire," or a girl who was just no fun at all. They had to walk a blurry line between being at least somewhat sexually accommodating and becoming known as promiscuous.[24]

Most of the evidence demonstrates that fraternity men took advantage of the situation, and sexual success with women became one of the criteria for membership in a fraternity and increasingly a way for a man to prove his masculinity. He did so at a time when the newly identified category of the homosexual became culturally threatening to groups of single men who lived, ate, and slept together. This threat increased when rumors spread that homosexuality could be found among fraternities and when at least some fraternity chapters were revealed to be homes to men who did engage in same-sex sex. Thus, popularity with women became one means of demonstrating heterosexuality, now increasingly tied to masculinity. Because homosexuality as an identity category was itself still in a nascent stage, fraternity men were only beginning to believe that a disavowal of homosexuality was necessary as a precondition for masculinity. This trend would become much more pronounced in the postwar period.[25]

These changes in sexual mores and notions of masculinity had consequences for college women. Fraternity and sorority members occupied the top of the social scale, now defined through gendered performance that also incorporated attractiveness to the other sex. They tended to date one another in what one sociologist called the "rating and dating complex," whereby the social success of an individual man or woman was generally based on the number and caliber of dates he or she could manage to accrue. The difficulty for college women was maintaining popularity of the right sort. Fraternity men were particularly well poised to take advantage of the changed state of affairs, not only because they were perceived as popular and were generally wealthy enough to go on many dates, but also because they lived in fraternity houses where they could entertain women, either at parties with many attendees or alone with just one date. One frustrated female student explained: "Fraternity men can ruin a girl's reputation. If she won't 'neck' they slander her. If she does, they tell their men friends she is 'a good party,' and those men friends will pay her a call with that idea in mind. It is hard trying to go straight." Most of the extant evidence indicates that while most fraternity men did not have sexual intercourse during their college years, those who did so either visited prostitutes or extracted sexual favors from working-class women, who were themselves not always willing. Working- and middle-class women experienced the repercussions of the rise of virile masculinity among fraternity men, though in different ways. Both groups of women were increasingly on the receiving end of a new kind of competitive sport centered on sexual exploitation. Fraternity men, however, pressed further with working-class women. Men expected less sexually from college women, perceived to be "nice girls," although that perception did not mean that young men did not try to push their college classmates to be more sexually permissive.[26]

The increase in college attendance during the 1920s had brought a rapid rise in the number of fraternity men across the country, but this increase had also meant a decline in exclusivity, at least as it related to socioeconomic class status. The newer fraternities were unable to be as discerning—which helped facilitate a hierarchy of fraternities—and those traditionally white chapters continued to exclude people of color, Jews, and often Catholics as well. Almost all fraternities continued to insist upon athletic and extracurricular involvement as a demonstration of masculinity, and increasingly men in fraternities proved their masculinity through popularity with women. They publicly dated middle-class "co-eds," and they attempted to extract sexual favors from working-class women. Some became increasingly aware of homosexuality amid rumors that same-sex acts occurred secretly in some fraternities. To counter such rumors and to assert their manliness, they began to cement linkages between heterosexuality and masculinity that persist to this day.

THE POSTWAR FRATERNITY

Following the Great Depression—when college enrollment and fraternity membership both declined—and World War II—which created its own form of campus disruption as large numbers of men left to serve in the war effort—many trends from earlier periods continued unabated. After the war, college enrollments spiked and grew through the later twentieth century, but a decreasing proportion of new students chose to join Greek-letter organizations and the overall percentage of fraternity brothers on most college campuses shrank. As extracurricular alternatives, including heightened political activism, flourished both on and off campus during the 1960s, those who joined fraternities rejected more elastic styles of masculinity made popular by the anti-war and hippy movements. Fraternity members increasingly self-segregated around narrow and conformist ideals of masculinity bound up in athletics, student government, drinking, and planned careers in business. They were, studies show, also the most likely to resist the new leftist, feminist, and anti-racist politics that came to college campuses from the 1960s onward; fraternity members were more likely to be conservative politically and to see fraternity membership as a way to preserve traditional values.[27]

During the 1950s and 1960s, fraternity men defined their masculinity by participating in many of the activities that had come to dominate campus life in the late nineteenth century. Athletics reigned supreme, but participation in student government as a way of achieving fame and prestige for one's house was also encouraged. Fraternity men's vision for proper masculinity mandated a remarkable level of conformity among pledges and brothers. As a reporter for *Look* magazine found at the University of Illinois in 1963, a fraternity pledge "must view nearly every move he makes—from taking a test to getting a date—in light of what it does 'for the house'—a term so familiar at Illinois that it is abbreviated to 'FTH.'" Those men who were attracted to life in fraternities would do almost anything to achieve what many still saw as the height of social prestige on campus, and, in the postwar years, that meant engaging in activities that revolved around illicit behavior, such as destructive actions fueled by alcohol and hazing.[28]

While it may not be possible to know with certainty whether or not vandalism, alcohol consumption, and other forms of misbehavior actually increased during the 1950s and 1960s, the archives of college administrators include more reports about such activities during this period than during earlier eras. Some of these activities were of the variety that would come to have notoriety as depicted in *Animal House*, the 1978 film based on the antics of the Dartmouth College fraternity Alpha Delta during the 1960s: vomiting, destruction of physical property, and pranks meant to humiliate other fraternities. In 1969, for instance, members of Kappa Alpha at Duke, who had been drinking heavily, "acquired and burned the benches of several other fraternities in the middle of Craven quadrangle." This quadrangle on Duke's campus was known as "Animal Quad" by the 1950s, long before *Animal House* was released, and the behavior of its residents was typical of many fraternity men in this era. To be masculine in fraternal terms meant defying authority through recklessness, rule-breaking, and the consumption of copious amounts of alcohol.[29]

Hazing was also on the rise, both in its severity and in its frequency, with the intention of testing pledges' willingness to make sacrifices on behalf of the fraternity, itself a demonstration of just how exclusive the fraternity really was. While some pranks were harmless if humiliating—involving eating nauseating concoctions or committing embarrassing acts in front of female students—others were much more dangerous and even fatal. At the Massachusetts Institute of Technology (MIT), a Delta Chi pledge drowned while participating in Hell Week activities in 1956. Three years later a pledge at the University of Southern California choked to death while trying to consume an oil-soaked hunk of liver. Fraternity pledges were often made to drink excessive amounts of alcohol, sometimes in conjunction with other activities. In the 1940s, administrators at the University of North Carolina at Chapel Hill received postcards from a group calling itself "Anxious Pledges," one of which stated: "We ask your help before it will be too late. If the practice is kept up, it will end in someone being seriously injured, or perhaps killed...." These young men did not want to participate in what they believed would be dangerous activities, but they were not so opposed that they were willing to simply drop out of the process of pledging altogether. For them, even as the hold of fraternities on campus life declined, the exclusivity of fraternity membership remained crucial to their conception of college life; they just did not want to be harmed in the process of joining.[30]

Fraternity men were increasingly harming not only other pledges but also other students. In this era, sociologists and educators increasingly came to study their own students as research subjects, and some focused on the dating and sexual interactions between fraternity men and their female classmates. Most academic studies found that fraternity men continued to abide by a double standard whereby women of one social status—women who belonged to sororities that the men perceived as comparable in standing—were appropriate for dating, whereas other women were appropriate for sex. As one study put it in academic prose, "Erotic achievement is now evaluated by taking into account the desirability of the sex object and the nature of its acquisition. A successful 'snow job' on an attractive but reluctant female who may be rendered into a relatively dependable sex outlet and socially desirable companion is considerably more enhancing than an encounter with a prostitute or a 'one night stand' with a 'loose' reputation." Of course, whether a woman was or was not "loose" was determined in part by how she reacted to a man's sexual overtures or attempts at coercion. As one fraternity man explained: "A few girls living on campus are dated for another reason—sex. These girls whose moral standards allow them to engage readily in sexual intercourse are ever popular. But they are more likely to be dated in midweek and on short notice. Some of them, although they never know it, achieve great fame among the fraternities." Fraternity men were well aware of what might help their social status on the larger campus, and they recognized that sexual aggressiveness could enhance their masculine identity among their brothers. Sex could be an outlet for competition and boasting, not unlike the sports that fraternity men worshipped. Most sociological studies showed that college women reported that fraternity men were more likely than their nonaffiliated classmates to pressure women to have sex or to be physically aggressive in pursuit of sex. Sometimes they went as far as "menacing threats or coercive infliction of physical pain."[31]

The increased emphasis on aggressive heterosexuality mattered to same-sex fraternal groups within the context of a heightened awareness of homosexuality in this period. As homosexuality gained increasing publicity over the course of the twentieth century, fraternities came under greater scrutiny because they bound together large numbers of single men in an intimate domestic friendship. Most men in college fraternities were not gay, but some certainly were, and sex among fraternity men was not uncommon. At least one prominent fraternity brother, Stewart Howe, who ran a fraternity-alumni relations company, used his connections among fraternities to seek out sex with college men, and some gay men outside of fraternities eroticized Greek life. For example, by the postwar period, fraternity houses and rituals had started to appear in gay physique magazines and pornography. Fraternity men's own actions, however, only increased the likelihood that some would think them to be gay. In efforts to make the hazing of pledges as humiliating as possible, many fraternity chapters demanded that initiates perform rituals involving nudity that were openly erotic. The rites were chosen because by the postwar period homosexuality had come to be seen as antithetical to masculinity. Making pledges engage in homoerotic acts was meant to be shameful and humiliating. But it also required a concurrent disavowal of actual homosexuality. By the later twentieth century, fraternity men stood out on many campuses for their homophobia. That homophobia was in part a product of fraternities' fear that the intimacy of their all-male friendship (including evaluating all possible brothers in part on physical appearance) would be misconstrued as homosexuality. Fraternity men asserted their masculinity and actively disavowed fears of homosexuality by performing an aggressive heterosexuality with their female classmates.[32]

In one significant way, men in postwar fraternities reversed the negative trends of the past century in regard to exclusivity, but only on select campuses and in particular chapters. Beginning in the immediate aftermath of World War II, some fraternities—primarily those at elite liberal arts colleges in the Northeast and Midwest—began to integrate, though not without enormous pushback from national organizations. In March 1948, in part prodded by a supportive administration, Amherst College's chapter of Phi Kappa Psi announced that it had pledged Thomas Gibbs of Evanston, Illinois. Gibbs, in addition to being a track star and a class officer, was black. Amherst alumni of the chapter were, by and large, supportive of the move, but, after some back-and-forth with other chapters across the nation and coverage of the story in a Boston newspaper, the national office of Phi Kappa Psi revoked Amherst's charter. Instead, Gibbs had to be initiated into what had become an unaffiliated local fraternity. Similar stories played out across the nation for the following two decades, until in 1965 the newly passed Civil Rights Act mandated that schools receiving any sort of federal funding could not segregate in any officially recognized college organization. Progress before and after that decision was halting, however, with many alumni and brothers in southern schools adamantly opposed to integration. Even in the twenty-first century, many fraternities, despite the legally mandated elimination of discrimination clauses, have remained de facto white organizations. This reality may reflect the history and climate of majority-white fraternities that has propelled students of color to join organizations more welcoming of African Americans, Latinos, or Asian Americans. Throughout the 1950s and 1960s, for example, fraternities continued to host "Old South" parties and "Sharecroppers Dances," among other racially insensitive social events, and they continued to discriminate against people of color who sought to rush or pledge.[33]

As college campuses diversified in the postwar era, fraternity men were increasingly marked by their conservatism, recklessness, and exclusivity. While a minority of brothers—primarily those at elite schools in the Northeast and Midwest—openly fought segregation and sought to integrate their brotherhoods, many others resisted what they saw as an assault on their way of life. That way of life also was characterized by drinking, hazing, and a highly publicized social life with college women. Fraternity men built on the traditions of sexual exploitation that had begun in the 1920s and sought out women for conquest as a means of proving their masculinity. Because many fraternities also incorporated homoerotic ritual into their hazing practices as a means of humiliating pledges, they compensated for the possibility that they might be perceived as gay by performing a particularly aggressive version of heterosexual masculinity.

CONCLUSION

Fraternity chapters have made the news with some frequency in the early twenty-first century. Pledges and brothers have died in alarming numbers in hazing and alcohol-related incidents, with the two often overlapping. And the evidence for fraternity men's sexual exploitations has continued to mount with no end in sight. Parties, designed to get women intoxicated so they can be coerced into sex, gang rape, and games where brothers achieve points by "scoring" with as many women—willing or not—as possible, have been among the most illicit behavior to come to light in recent years. These practices have roots in fraternities' histories as organizations designed to promote exclusivity, to challenge authority, and, crucially, to enhance men's masculinity.[34]

Not all fraternity men participate in these dangerous antics, but most evidence suggests that they are *more likely* to do so than their non-Greek affiliated classmates. This reality should not be a surprise. For about two centuries now, fraternity men have built their reputations on exclusivity, and the defiance of rules, both of which contribute to their version of masculinity. Of course, some of the specific forms these behaviors take have changed over the past centuries. For example, men who once proved their manhood by performing well academically now do so through athletic prowess and heavy drinking. The importance of heterosexuality also has risen as middle-class youth increasingly have experimented with sex prior to marriage and as homosexuality has emerged as a discrete identity over the course of the twentieth century. The reputation of fraternities has been such that a new class of freshmen arrives on campus every year hoping to assert their masculine identity by partying hard and scoring with girls among other young men who look and act like themselves. As the members of TNE boasted in the 1920s, they are "not so easily to be overcome." Despite the best efforts of college administrators, these words have proved prescient.[35]

NOTES

1. Thomas Arkle Clark, "Concerning Theta Nu Epsilon," reprint from *Alumni Quarterly of the University of Illinois*, April, 1913, 7, copy in Folder: Theta Nu Epsilon, box 8, Thomas Arkle Clark Papers, Student Life and Culture Archives, University of Illinois, Urbana-Champaign (hereafter SLCA).

2. "President" to Thomas Arkle Clark, October 10, 1922, Folder: T. A. Clark, TNE, 1921–22, box 10, Thomas Arkle Clark Papers, SLCA.

3. This essay is drawn from the research for my book, *The Company He Keeps: A History of White College Fraternities* (Chapel Hill: University of North Carolina Press, 2009).

4. Francis Wayland to Edward Hitchcock, August 3, 1846, Fraternities General Files, Amherst College Archives; Minutes of Faculty, August 7, 1845–December 11, 1854, entries for March 4 and 5, 1847, Princeton University Archives. For the antebellum era more generally in fraternities, see Syrett, *Company He Keeps*, chapters 1 and 2.

5. Syrett, *Company He Keeps*, 25–27.

6. "Secret Societies in College," *New York Commercial Advertiser*, July 14, 1855, in box 162, Greek Letter Societies Folder, Historical Subject Files: Fraternities, Princeton University Archives (emphasis in original); Syrett, *Company He Keeps*, 31–35.

7. Syrett, *Company He Keeps*, 54.

8. W. G. Sufford of Brown Chapter to John Q. A. Sessions of Michigan Chapter, September 8, 1855; A. C. Trippe of Lafayette Chapter to R. C. Davis of Michigan Chapter, June 20, 1856; H. H. Thomas of Middlebury Chapter to Davis, May 15, 1856; all in Correspondence of the DKE

Fraternity, Bentley Historical Library, University of Michigan. Timothy J. Williams comes to similar conclusions using different sources. See his *Intellectual Manhood: University, Self, and Society in the Antebellum South* (Chapel Hill: University of North Carolina Press, 2015).

9. Alexander Hamilton Rice to Augusta E. McKim, January 28, 1844, Alexander Hamilton Rice Letters, MS S-9, Massachusetts Historical Society; B. H. Hall, *A Collection of College Words and Customs* (Cambridge, Mass.: John Bartlett, 1856), 146, 397, 399, 422, 455, 254, 443.

10. October 1849 entry, Kappa Sigma Epsilon records, 1847–55, box 54, folder 259, Yale University Archives, Sterling Memorial Library; Delta Upsilon debates are November 1, 1852, in Waterville minutes; February 22, 1853, in Williams minutes; June 15, 1855, in Amherst minutes; and March 21, 1849, in Hamilton minutes, all in boxes 1–3, Delta Upsilon Papers, New York Public Library.

11. Syrett, *Company He Keeps*, 69, and for a discussion of race and gender generally in antebellum fraternities, see 67–76.

12. Colin B. Burke, *American Collegiate Populations: A Test of the Traditional View* (New York: New York University Press, 1982), chapter 2, 214–23, 239–43.

13. Syrett, *Company He Keeps*, 162–3.

14. John Cooper Winslow, *Eta Prime of Kappa Sigma: An Historical Sketch, 1873–1908* (Durham, N.C.: Eta Prime of Kappa Sigma, 1908), 6; Walter B. Hill to Mary Clay Hill, May 6, 1868, in Walter B. Hill, *College Life in the Reconstruction South: Walter B. Hill's Correspondence, University of Georgia, 1869–1871*, ed. G. Ray Mathis (Athens: University of Georgia Libraries, Miscellanea Publications No. 10, 1974), 82; *Occident* 4, no. 4 (February 4, 1883): 29.

15. Syrett, *Company He Keeps*, 133–49; Zeta Psi "Delta's Journal," entry for September 1897, Zeta Psi Fraternity, Mu Chapter Records, 1893–1911, SCM 061, Stanford University Archives; Cornelius Howard Patton and Walter Taylor Field, *Eight O' Clock Chapel: A Study of New England College Life in the Eighties* (Boston: Houghton Mifflin, 1927), 292; Zeta Psi "Delta's Journal," 53.

16. Syrett, *Company He Keeps*, 144–46; Gail Bederman, *Manliness and Civilization: A Cultural History of Gender and Race in the United States, 1880–1917* (Chicago: University of Chicago Press, 1995); James McCosh, "President's Report," December 22, 1875, series 11, box 38, Reports to the Board of Trustees of the College of New Jersey, James McCosh Records, Office of the President Records, Princeton University Archives; A Graduate of '69, *Four Years at Yale* (New Haven: Charles C. Chatfield, 1871), 647; "A Report on Interfraternity Relations of Dartmouth College, Confidential, Issued May, 1914," entry for April 22, 1912, Dartmouth College Archives.

17. Syrett, *Company He Keeps*, 151–54, quotation on 154.
18. Syrett, *Company He Keeps*, 151–52.
19. Diana B. Turk, *Bound by a Mighty Vow: Sisterhood and Women's Fraternities, 1870–1920* (New York: New York University Press, 2004), esp. chapter 1; Edwin E. Slosson, *Great American Universities* (New York: Macmillan, 1910), 332–33; Syrett, *Company He Keeps*, 176–78.
20. Syrett, *Company He Keeps*, 168–69; play is described in Dan Oren, *Joining the Club: A History of Jews at Yale* (New Haven: Yale University Press, 1985), 25.
21. Paula S. Fass, *The Damned and the Beautiful: American Youth in the 1920's* (New York: Oxford University Press, 1977); Syrett, *Company He Keeps*, chapter 5.
22. *Thetagraphs*, vol. 3., no. 2, published by Theta Zeta of Lambda Chi Alpha, 1923, 8–11, Dartmouth College Archives; Roger Cooley Angell, *The Campus: A Study of Contemporary Undergraduate Life in the American University* (New York: D. Appleton, 1928), 139; Daniel Katz and Floyd Henry Allport, *Students' Attitudes: A Report of the Syracuse University Reaction Study* (Syracuse, N.Y.: Craftsman Press, 1931), 133–5; Thomas Arkle Clark, "In Defense of College Athletics," *Dearborn Independent*, June 26, 1926, 28, in box 18, 1926 folder, Thomas Arkle Clark Papers, SLCA.
23. Syrett, *Company He Keeps*, 196–200; Leon B. Richardson, *A Study of a Liberal College: A Report to the President of Dartmouth College* (Hanover, N.H.: Dartmouth College, 1924), 26; Max McConn, *College or Kindergarten?* (New York: New Republic, 1928), 160.
24. Syrett, *Company He Keeps*, 219–21.
25. Syrett, *Company He Keeps*, 203–06.
26. Willard Waller, "The Rating and Dating Complex," *American Sociological Review* 2 (1937): 727–34; R. H. Edwards, J. M. Artman, and Galen M. Fisher, *Undergraduates: A Study of Morale in Twenty-Three American Colleges and Universities* (Garden City, N.Y.: Doubleday, 1928), 218; Syrett, *Company He Keeps*, 220–27.
27. Syrett, *Company He Keeps*, 233–38.
28. Syrett, *Company He Keeps*, 238–41; "College Fraternities: The Perils of Big Brotherhood," *Look*, March 12, 1963, 56.
29. Syrett, *Company He Keeps*, 241–47; "The Kappa Alpha Case, Michael Garner for the group," October 8, 1969, record of proceedings of judicial board, Kappa Alpha Folder, Division of Student Affairs Records, Duke University Archives.
30. Syrett, *Company He Keeps*, 244–45; postcard dated January 23, 1942, box 1, series 10, folder titled Fraternities and Sororities, 1941–1943, 1946–48, Records of the Vice Chancellor for Student Affairs, University of North Carolina Archives.

31. Syrett, *Company He Keeps*, 277–83; Eugene J. Kanin, "An Examination of Sexual Aggression as a Response to Sexual Frustration," *Journal of Marriage and the Family* 29, no. 3 (August 1970): 430; Ernest W. Burgess and Paul Wallin, *Engagement and Marriage* (New York: J. B. Lippincott, 1953), 87–88; Clifford Kirkpatrick and Eugene J. Kanin, "Male Sexual Aggression on a University Campus," *American Sociological Review* 22, no. 1 (February 1957): 53–55.

32. Syrett, *Company He Keeps*, 267–74, 293–97.

33. Syrett, *Company He Keeps*, 248–61; Matthew W. Hughey, "A Paradox of Participation: Nonwhites in White Sororities and Fraternities," *Social Problems* 57, no. 4 (November 2010): 653–79.

34. Caitlin Flanagan, "The Dark Power of Fraternities," *The Atlantic*, March 2014, 72–91; John D. Foubert, Johnathan T. Newberry, and Jerry Tatum, "Behavior Differences Seven Months Later: Effects of a Rape Prevention Program," *Journal of Student Affairs Research and Practice* 44 (2007): 728–49.

35. Foubert, Newberry, and Tatum, "Behavioral Differences."

CHAPTER 4

"Mattie Matix" and Prodigal Princes: A Brief History of Drag on College Campuses from the Nineteenth Century to the 1940s

Margaret A. Nash, Danielle C. Mireles, and Amanda Scott-Williams

Students at Amherst College, a male-only institution until the late twentieth century, received a very odd invitation one day in November 1883. "The remains of the late Mattie Matix will be cremated Friday night," it read. "As one of the chief mourners of the deceased, you are hereby notified to rendezvous" for the torchlit procession to the river, where the "cremation" would occur.[1] "Mattie Matix" was a personification of the students' hated mathematics textbook. In a ritual that was common across campuses for decades, students either buried or burned math, geometry, and other loathed books.[2] Occasionally an effigy symbolized the book or its author. In Amherst's version of the ritual in 1883, "Mattie Matix" was played by a student named Clyde Fitch, and he and other "female" mourners wore

M. A. Nash (✉) • D. C. Mireles • A. Scott-Williams
Graduate School of Education, University of California, Riverside,
Riverside, CA, USA
e-mail: margaret.nash@ucr.edu

© The Author(s) 2018
C. A. Ogren, M. A. VanOverbeke (eds.),
Rethinking Campus Life, Historical Studies in Education,
https://doi.org/10.1007/978-3-319-75614-1_4

61

white dresses, wigs, and costume jewelry. While the ritual of burning textbooks deserves its own investigation as an aspect of campus life at the turn of the century, this chapter focuses on this mock funeral as but one of many instances of college students—male and female—adopting the clothing and persona of someone of another sex.

Drag has been a topic of discussion among queer theorists and cultural anthropologists for the last several decades, but the practice of drag on college campuses has received little attention. Scholars have laid out a timeline of changes in types of drag, but these analyses mostly consider the worlds of theater and nightclubs, and not the use of drag on college campuses. Because of the emphasis on theater, this scholarship discusses drag in terms of stage performance, in which men put on women's clothing and perform the roles of female characters in theatrical productions. In this chapter, however, we discuss multiple uses of drag on various college campuses. We first outline the timeline that earlier scholars have articulated for changes in drag performance. Then we show how that timeline is both supported and disrupted by a few instances of drag on college campuses. We argue that college students engaged in many uses of drag, sometimes but not always mirroring Vaudeville or theatrical drag. Rather than having a singular meaning, the formats and functions of drag were varied and complex and occurred both on and off stage, as campuses became forums where students created their own cultural meanings of drag. Through the use of drag, students developed vibrant campus cultures that shaped their college experiences and those of their peers. This chapter and other histories of drag on campus—as those emerge—will enrich views of campus culture that students built for themselves. Those cultures sometimes included drag as entertainment and protest as students worked through an understanding of their lives and the world around them.

BACKGROUND AND HISTORIOGRAPHY

Before the uprising against police brutality at the Stonewall Inn in New York in 1969, drag had not always been associated with gay culture and with gay men as female impersonators. Instead, as historians Nan Boyd, Allan Bérubé, and Sharon Ullman argue, in the first decades of the twentieth century, female impersonation was a popular and acceptable form of entertainment throughout American society. Female impersonators worked in Vaudeville, where they "functioned like magicians," amazing audiences by the skill with which they inhabited their roles.[3] They were not impersonating women in order to get a laugh, but to work as illusionists. Skilled impersonation was undetectable; an audience member who did not know that an impersonator was on the stage would assume that the performer was a woman, and would be surprised by the revelation that the performer was a man. The most successful impersonator of this period was Julian Eltinge, who played in Vaudeville and on Broadway, and opened his own theater in New York in 1912. Eltinge—a man who portrayed a woman on stage—even published his own magazine for women with "beauty tips and lessons on femininity."[4] Eltinge's heterosexuality was not questioned, in part because he made sure it would not be: he married and had children, and he showcased his masculine prowess by boxing other men in front of reporters.[5] Parading his masculinity was part of what made his female impersonation so impressive: he was a manly man who was able to fool audiences into believing he was a woman.

In the 1920s, movie talkies pushed Vaudeville off the stage, eliminating the most obvious place for female impersonators to work. At the same time, the rising popularity of Freud and psychoanalysis and the new field of sexology led to a heightened awareness of sexuality and to the new labels of sexual deviance, inversion, and homosexuality.[6] By the late 1920s, according to Boyd, sexologists and analysts spoke of female impersonators as being "motivated by gender inversion," and by the late 1920s, in the wake of morality crusades and heightened stigma of homosexuality, increasing numbers of people associated impersonators with sexual deviance.[7] As a result, according to Bérubé, impersonation went underground, and drag became a form of bawdy adult entertainment that took place in nightclubs. Many cities passed anti-vice laws banning homosexual content from stage shows, and/or banning performers from wearing the clothing of the other gender. Meanwhile, the talkies that ended Vaudeville had themselves become filled with sex and violence, leading Hollywood to establish a morality code in 1930, which went largely unenforced until 1934. The Code banned many things, including profanity, ridicule of the clergy, miscegenation, and any reference to "sex perversion."[8] "Impure love...," stated the Code, "must not be presented as attractive and beautiful."[9] Although in the 1910s female impersonation did not necessarily imply homosexuality, by the late 1920s it did. Female impersonation was now derided rather than lauded, and drag performers were seen as sexually suspect.

Drag became reinvigorated during World War II, when the military actively promoted it as a way to boost morale and provide entertainment in a nearly all-male environment. While drag had many negative associations to overcome, the military had a past it could draw on, having encouraged drag shows during World War I. Historian George Chauncey Jr. contends that "female impersonation was an unexceptional part of navy culture during the World War I years, sufficiently legitimate" for the Providence and Newport, Rhode Island, newspapers "to run lengthy stories and photo essays about the many theatrical productions at the navy base in which men took the female roles."[10] It was this history that the military could turn to when it wanted to rehabilitate drag. During World War II, the military talked about the revival as a "father-son inheritance, military bloodlines – that evoked heterosexuality, masculinity, patriotism, and family generations rather than 'moral degeneracy,' effeminacy, or homosexuality."[11]

As the war came to an end, military entertainment began to include women performing on stage with men. Women's Auxiliary Corps (WAC) members, Red Cross workers, nurses, and civilian women took female roles in productions, thus phasing out the drag shows. Bérubé writes that consequently male soldiers "who continued to don women's clothes were more easily stereotyped as homosexual and were left to face the military's expanding anti-homosexual policies."[12] After the war, drag nightclub acts began to appear again, but, unlike during the war, reporters commented explicitly on homosexuality whenever they discussed shows involving female impersonation.[13] To be acceptable in the public eye, drag performances had to take a comic form, and to not be targeted as homosexual, drag performers had to appear not to take the impersonation seriously. Instead, male performers needed to assert both their masculinity and their heterosexuality, wearing a wig or high heels for laughs and reinforcing the audience's awareness of their maleness by showing how ridiculous they looked pretending to be women. Drag took on new meaning once again in the 1970s and 1980s when it served political purposes in the growing gay liberation movement. At that time, drag was once again firmly associated with homosexuality, but the association now was used as a political tool.[14]

Most of the historical work on drag has been about men in Vaudeville, the military, and other venues; far less work has been done on men's drag traditions and customs on college campuses. The few studies of men's college drag focus on details of theatrical productions without analyzing the social meanings of drag, and without examining the uses of drag offstage.[15] Literature on college women's drag similarly is sparse, but does include examples of on-campus and offstage uses of drag. In *Campus Traditions*, Simon J. Bronner discusses comic drag, but the brief take is limited to instances after 1930.[16] He notes infrequent instances of women taking men's roles in comic rituals, listing Dutch Treat Week at North Texas

State Teachers College, in which women paid for the date, and Sadie Hawkins events at multiple campuses, in which women asked men to a dance or other festivity. Laura Horak investigates female drag in *Girls Will Be Boys: Cross-Dressed Women, Lesbians, and American Cinema, 1908–1934,* which sheds some light on the broader culture, but does not discuss college women specifically.[17] There is evidence that cross-dressing was not uncommon at women's colleges in the first decades of the twentieth century,[18] which historians most often discuss in terms of dramatic changes in women's fashion. For instance, Kendra Van Cleave notes the shift in the early twentieth century toward more masculine clothing, as well as women chopping their hair to a short "bob." She shows that "some Americans understood the less cumbersome styles now gaining in popularity to be symbolic of women's political, economic, and social progress."[19] Much more work needs to be done to fully understand drag for both college men and women, for female students both in women's colleges and in coeducational settings, and for women more generally.

Overall, the historiography suggests a trajectory, primarily for men, that moved from female impersonation during the late nineteenth and early twentieth centuries, to comic drag after World War II. Earlier drag was not associated with homosexuality, but by the late 1920s it was; postwar drag often was comic in order to distance performers from charges of homosexuality. Our research shows that this trajectory holds for drag performances on some college campuses, but not others. One important factor that complicates this arc is the variety of ways that drag was used as performance on campus in places other than the theater. Most studies have focused on drag in theater, but drag has been more widespread on college campuses. By looking outside the theater, we offer a more nuanced history of drag on campus and in society, and we gain a greater sense of the campus life that students built in these decades. We also argue that the association of drag with homosexuality may have occurred far earlier on some campuses, particularly all-male elite colleges in the East, than the historiography posits. To address these themes, we first look at instances of campus drag in places other than staged theater performances, and then turn to the stage.

CROSS-DRESSING AND DRAG OFFSTAGE

In 1712, Harvard student George Hussey appeared in women's clothing on Election Day in Cambridge. Why he did this is unclear, but the result was his expulsion from Harvard, and a revision of college laws to expressly forbid students from wearing women's clothing.[20] Scholarly literature often associates drag performance with the stage. However, college students did not just don drag on stage, as Hussey's case shows. Campus men also wore women's clothing offstage in a variety of clandestine rituals and traditions, such as mock funerals, textbook burnings, and parades.[21] Meanwhile, cross-dressing at some women's colleges was often for the practical purpose of fulfilling male roles at parties and dances. Looking at drag on college campuses thus expands the historiography to include a variety of uses of drag far broader than only theatrical productions; doing so allows us to see additional meanings of drag on campus.

Mock funerals and textbook burning rituals were two spaces in which cross-dressing occurred on the Amherst College campus. According to historian George Rugg Cutting, these events were clandestinely planned by a select group of students who would distribute pamphlets to their peers the day of the event and assign participants parts such as mourners. At the scheduled meeting time, students would march in procession to the site where the burning would take place.[22] As historian Kim Marra has emphasized, the event traditionally featured the ritual burning of "Mathew Mattix," a personified male character.[23] At some point, however, students on various campuses gave many of the personified texts female names, such as "Miss Algie Bra,"[24] "Mattie Matix," and "Anna Lytt."[25] Although students had worn costumes to these events before, it was not until 1882 that a male student donned drag to assume the role of Anna Lytt, the title character of the mock funeral that year.[26] The invitation to the 1882 funeral procession for Anna Lytt was in the form of a fold-out coffin. A photo of the cast included one character, possibly representing Anna Lytt, wearing women's apparel, holding a fan, and looking directly into the camera.[27] During 1883, Amherst students staged two separate textbook burnings in the form of funerals: the "Cremation of Miss Algie Bra" by the class of '87, and the other for "Mattie Matix" by the class of '86.[28] The pamphlet announcing the ritual for Miss Algie Bra listed a procession including "vestal virgins."[29] These "virgins" likely wore women's clothes, given that female costumes were documented in the 1875 event,[30] and because the Mattie Matix procession of the same year did include cross-dressing.[31] In the cast photo, Clyde Fitch as "Mattie Matix" is one of four female impersonators, all of whom wore white dresses and heels, wigs, and costume jewelry (Image 4.1).[32]

Drag in the context of mock funerals and textbook burnings did not appear to serve any particular function aside from student entertainment

Image 4.1   Mattie Matix, 1883, Amherst College. (Source: Dramatic Activities Collection, Amherst College Archives and Special Collections)

on the Amherst campus. Historian Cutting also briefly mentions a "very comical" Gown Parade put on by the class of 1870, providing another example of drag being used offstage for entertainment.[33] Due to the clandestine nature of some of these events, it is unclear if the administration was aware of drag in the mock funeral processions. However, cross-dressing on other campuses, such as Princeton, did occur in sight of the administration and public.[34]

At Princeton, the Alumni Parade, now known as the P-rade, formally began in the 1890s and was held on the Saturday before Commencement. While alumni had previously engaged in processions on Commencement Day, in 1897 they began to "distinguish themselves by using class hats, balloons, parasols, large palm leave fans," with younger classes "wearing colorful costumes, carrying humorous signs, and sometimes performing comic stunts."[35] In *A Princeton Companion*, a history of Princeton College, Alexander Leitch notes that at least as early as 1910 the alumni P-rade costumes included drag. That year, the class of 1900 paraded "in long gowns as suffragettes, with the former football player, 'Big Bill' Edwards, leading on horseback, as an improbable Joan of Arc."[36] The Historical Society of Princeton contains numerous images of alumni dressed in drag for the alumni parade. These include an image of men dressed as members of the "Dam Family," including "Miss U.B. Dam," and "Helen Dam," and a male alumnus in drag pushing another alumnus in an enlarged baby carriage.[37] Unlike the rituals at Amherst, Princeton's Alumni Parades were public events and participants were Princeton alumni rather than students. Drag at these parades suggests that the college itself allowed for the suspension of accepted gender roles in certain contexts and may have sanctioned it so long as it was for comedic purposes. As literary scholar Corinne Holt Sawyer states, the perception was that "the man who dresses like a woman is either insane, or he is intended to be comic, because there is no reason… a man in his right mind would willingly accept such a demotion in status."[38] According to historian Bronner, drag can "reinforce male dominance when threatening signs of change are about, by directing attention to the absurdity of men taking women's roles."[39] Consequently, the "suffragettes" of 1910 may have used drag to enforce male dominance and privilege. In this instance, Princeton alumni donned female garb to mock women who were protesting for the right to vote.[40]

Harvard's Hasty Pudding Club, one of the most well-documented social clubs of the nineteenth and twentieth centuries, may be the most famous site of college drag performances. Before Hasty Pudding launched its theatrical debut, it incorporated drag in other ways. Founded in 1795, the club transitioned into a debating society by 1800, and began staging mock trials which prosecuted both contemporary and historical figures, including Coriolanus, Cromwell, Marcus Cato, and Mary, Queen of Scots, as well as the college administrators.[41] Murder trials, cases of adultery, and breaches of promise were popular themes for mock trials. In 1836, the group's "High Court of Equity" had its first defendant and witnesses appear in costume, which, a history of Hasty Pudding explains, "transform[ed] the mock trial into a courtroom drama."[42] In the following year, the club staged the case of *Abby Roe v. Richard Doe*, which chronicled a broken promise. Future poet James Russell Lowell arrived to the trial in women's clothing to portray "Abby." Although costumes had been used for a year, this was the first documented description of a club member cross-dressing for a role. Seven years later, the Hasty Pudding Club would stage its first play and continue its trademark of having female impersonators in the cast. Eventually, Hasty Pudding Club's mock trials vanished as the organization transitioned once again, this time into a theatrical organization. The staged case of *Abby Roe* was the first of a more than century-long tradition of drag in the organization.[43]

Drag was not limited to male students. However, there is even less research on women dressing as men, and much of it focuses on fashion. This emphasis on changes in fashion and dress reform may distract from deeper discussions of gender play within these instances of cross-dressing, as there is evidence that administrators sometimes used clothing to enforce gender norms. Dorothy Elia Howells observed that, despite the wishes of the students, members of the first two classes at Radcliffe College were not permitted to wear caps and gowns for graduation, as the college president, Elizabeth Cary Agassiz, felt this attire to be "too masculine."[44] The Smith College class book for 1899 expresses a similar dissatisfaction about being required to give up the cap and gown to wear "pretty" dresses.[45] In contrast, letters that students sent home as well as pictures and articles depict college women dressing as men for various occasions and parties. For instance, a picture of a "fancy dress party" at Vassar College in 1887 shows thirteen women, seven of whom were dressed as men, complete with moustaches (Image 4.2).[46] Ruth Adams, a student at Radcliffe, wrote to her family in September 1900 about a party she attended:

> Julia Stimpson was the most stunning man that I really have ever seen. She was very large. (I don't mean fat you know.) and she did certainly look exactly like a man and an awfully handsome one too. It made you feel so funny. I was introduced to some of them I had never met before. And I really found it hard to realize they were girls. Oh I must tell you the best thing I've just heard. The first tableau was Whitmans chocolate [and] a man stands in the middle with a girl leaning on each shoulder eating out of this box of candy! Well this misguided freshman asked if the girl in the middle (dressed as a man of course) was president Taylor's son. Did you ever hear anything as rich.[47]

Female students did not wear men's clothing only at parties. Ruth Adams continued:

> Oh I must tell you about our registration. It was more fun. All the building was divided up into different wards and poles put up in each ward. The poles were manufactured out of these very high black screens. Inside were two girls (dressed as men) sitting at a table... You can't think how well they get themselves up. So every now and then a girl dressed as a policeman would come and clear away the crowd.[48]

Image 4.2 A Fancy Dress Party, Vassar College, 1887. (Source: Archives and Special Collections, Vassar College Library)

Adams described the cross-dressing in a way that made it seem both common and absurd, and showed that the women went to great lengths, off-stage, to create believable illusions. In another example, students at Vassar College recreated "The 'Harvard-Yale foot-ball game' of 1911," which was "as near 'a regular game' as [they could] make it."[49] A student explained that the "game" occurred on more than one occasion, and the students would wear sweaters from Yale and Harvard when they could be obtained, or they would wear sweaters of the proper color,

> ...buttoned up the back and bearing exaggerated paper letters on their manly chests. A few real foot-ball trousers appear (this, oh, modest alumnae, takes place in the 'secluded' circle, and the warriors wear capes to the scene of action). Bloomers serve otherwise. Head guards of many kinds, nose guards, missing teeth—of black court plaster of course—and a liberal amount of wadded muscle, and distinguished looking dirt complete the realistic appearance of foot-ball.[50]

She continued the comedy, stating that the only "fatality" was a cold, and ended by stating, "The play is very jolly and we are not ashamed of it."[51]

The literature regarding women dressing as men frequently takes the form of a discussion about changing fashion. Yet these examples show that college women engaged in regular instances of full cross-dressing with the intent to take on the appearance of men, beyond altering their own daily attire for practical purposes. Although most of the historiography on-campus drag is about its uses in theatrical productions, students used drag at other times, too. George Hussey wore female attire in the early eighteenth century in what may have been commentary on an election. Throughout the nineteenth and early twentieth centuries, students wore drag at all-male ritual textbook burials and alumni parades, and at all-female parties and dances. While both female and male students may have demonstrated the fluidity of gender roles by donning drag, other students also used drag to reinforce gender hierarchies, as when male students made fun of women's rights activists. The history of campus drag extends far beyond its use on the stage.

ONSTAGE INSTANCES OF DRAG

Just as students created many ways to use drag off the stage and for different reasons, students also embraced drag onstage on college campuses in complex ways. The trajectory of drag on campus did not adhere to the shifts from impersonation to burlesque outlined in the historiography that focuses on drag off campus. On some campuses, the association of drag with homosexuality occurred earlier than it did on professional stages, while on other campuses that association occurred much later. In Danielle Mireles's study of drag on elite all-male college campuses during the Progressive Era, she found that northeastern campuses began regulating drag through bans and restrictions as early as the 1890s. Harvard moved in this direction as early as 1915.[52] Other campuses, such as the University of Wisconsin, moved toward comedic drag much later.

Onstage, students in single-sex institutions donned drag in theatrical performances initially out of necessity, in what historian Bronner has called "collegiate role reversal."[53] Just as on the Elizabethan stage, where only men were allowed to be actors and therefore played all of the roles, students on single-sex campuses played the roles of both genders. At Princeton, students founded the Dramatic Association in 1883 as a means of funding collegiate sports organizations, which were always short of money.[54]

Princeton students were eager to establish a dramatic association, thinking it would serve dual purposes: as an additional form of student entertainment and as a source of funding for student athletic associations. In the group's first production, *David Garrick*, on May 10, 1883, George B. French, Harry A. Alexander, and Albert K. Harsha inaugurated the tradition of female impersonation in the organization.[55] According to a review in *The Daily Princetonian*, Harsha's performance of "Mrs. Browne" "called forth peals of laughter, her faint, literally"; "Mr. French as Ada Ingot, was charming, his interpretation and production of the part was fine"; and "Mrs. Smith with her seventy children was immense, and her charms surely deserved seventy repetitions."[56] The play was a success, and the production went on tour to nearby venues, including the Opera House in New Brunswick on June 1 and the Town Hall in Freehold on June 2. For the tour, "Ada" received a new costume and was described as "look[ing] more bewitching than ever."[57]

Nevertheless, by 1890, *The Princetonian* described the Dramatic Association as a "money-losing organization" and reported that it was in considerable debt. The paper predicted, "If [the dramatic association] should fail to meet with hearty approval, it is probable that the association will not attempt to continue, and will go the way of the minstrels."[58] Furthermore, its financial instability made it no longer a useful partner to the sports organizations. Rather than folding, however, the organization merged with the Glee Club to present *Po-ca-han-tas* in 1891 which "far surpassed anything ever attempted by our Dramatic Association."[59] By 1893, the Princeton University Dramatic Association had been renamed the Triangle Club of Princeton and began producing musical comedy burlesques, capitalizing on its female impersonators to dazzle audiences. The transition from serious female impersonations to comedic performances occurred earlier at Princeton than in Vaudeville. While serious female impersonations remained in vogue in the larger American public until the 1920s, some colleges began pursuing comedic presentations as early as the 1890s. It is unclear why this change occurred earlier on college campuses but Mireles suggests that constructions of masculinity, particularly Muscular Christianity, may have played a crucial role. Princeton in particular was asserting itself as an institution that produced strong male Christian leaders, and cross-dressing may have challenged that image.[60]

The turn to farce did not go uncontested, however. Many club members wanted to continue pursuing more serious plays, even though such plays did not financially fare as well as the student-produced and student-written farces.[61] According to *Princeton Alumni Weekly*, this transition to farces occurred partially due to the "audience's insistence on slapstick" and disregard for "legitimate comedy."[62] One of the most popular features was the all-male dance line in drag (often called pony ballet[63]) first documented photographically in the 1907 production of *The Mummy's Monarch*.[64]

Unlike Princeton, Amherst College's Senior Dramatics evolved from an annual tradition of senior-only productions that began in 1881. Similar to other campuses, Amherst College embraced female impersonators as part of its performances. However, unlike Princeton, productions at Amherst did not evolve from "legitimate" comedies and dramas to student-produced musical comedies, and instead began as farces and musicals.[65] This narrative differs from the larger historiography of drag off campus, which describes how drag began with serious female impersonation before transitioning into comedic forms of drag by the 1930s. In 1881, Amherst's senior class organized two productions, a farce and an operetta, *Class Day* and *Romeo and Juliet*.[66] Senior Dramatics, the new name of the organization, was firmly established with the 1884 production of *She Stoops to Conquer*, which was presented two times by the senior class. The 1885 production of *The Rivals* was also presented twice by the senior class.[67]

The 1884 and 1885 plays, *The Rivals* and *The Country Girl*, were especially significant as they featured Clyde Fitch, who later became a famous Broadway playwright and director, and who was a female impersonator during his years at Amherst College.[68] In these productions, Fitch, as a junior and then a senior, was cast in female roles: "Lydia Languish" in *The Rivals* and "Peggy Thrift" in *The Country Girl*.[69] In cast photos, Fitch, in his role of Lydia, is seen beside classmate Tod Galloway (Mrs. Malaprop) posing in costume and in-character.[70] Historian Marra concluded that Fitch most enjoyed playing the part of the "ingénue" and "coy soubrette" during his Amherst days.[71]

Fitch's peers considered him effeminate, and he accentuated this characteristic at Amherst. According to Billy J. Harbin, Kim Marra, and Robert A. Schanke, Fitch "painted the walls of his fraternity in a floral frieze, exhibited an extensive doll collection, and scented the air with mounds of potpourri in cut crystal bowls."[72] Fitch "far exceeded the conventional parameters" of female impersonation and "long remained legend at his alma mater."[73] Fitch's female impersonation extended beyond the formal stage. He participated in textbook burning ceremonies and theatrical excursions such as burlesque operettas, while in the fraternity Chi Psi. He also "improvised feminine characterizations" at faculty teas and fraternity cocktail parties, although the record does not say what clothing he wore while doing those representations.[74] To his peers, as historians have pointed out, Fitch's "nonnormative gender behavior signaled nonnormative sexual behavior."[75] According to his biographer, contemporaries referred to him as a "confirmed bachelor, a sissy-boy, a dude, and a dandy."[76] In one interview in his post-collegiate life, Fitch stated, "I knew, of course, that everyone regarded me as a sissy; but I would rather be misunderstood than lose my independence."[77] Although he was not necessarily representative of all impersonators, he seemed to embrace theater and drag as a safe haven during his time at Amherst. Student motives for donning drag no doubt varied. While individuals like Fitch may have gravitated toward drag to explore their sexuality, other students may have used drag as a form of rebellion or simply to have fun. More work on college drag needs to be done to understand the variety of reasons drag was popular on college campuses.[78]

Unlike Amherst, Harvard did not establish a formal dramatic association, the Harvard Dramatic Club, until 1908.[79] However, drag appeared on Harvard's campus in a number of plays and tragicomedy burlesques before then. The Hasty Pudding Club, which began as a debating society, became a performance-oriented club during the mid-nineteenth century, and several imitation clubs and organizations quickly followed. These included Pi Eta Society, the Dickeys (or D.K.E.), and many others, all of which utilized drag in their performances.[80]

Drag on Harvard's campus has long been a point of fascination for historians of drag. Many studies focus on Harvard's Hasty Pudding Club, whose members began donning drag as early as the 1830s. Of most interest, however, is the widespread acceptance of drag throughout the campus and the differences in the trajectory of drag at Harvard from the larger American society. As discussed previously, drag off college campuses transitioned from serious female impersonations in the early 1900s to more comedic portrayals by the 1930s. Drag at Harvard, however, seems to have begun with comedic portrayals which remained popular through the early 1900s and beyond. Although some later organizations at Harvard incorporated serious female impersonation in their plays, the dominant form of drag continued to be of the comedic variety. As we have seen, members of Hasty Pudding began showing up in costume for mock trials as early as the 1830s. According to Lemuel Hayward, Harvard class of 1845, "the first Pudding Play came off Friday evening, December 13, 1844," as it occurred to a member "that it would be a taking novelty [sic] to get up a play, instead of the Alligator or Mock Trial, as usual."[81]

Hayward described the costumes as "primitive but effective" and wrote that the male student who portrayed Distaffina, the lead female character in the play, "was rigged in a manner that was positively charming."[82] Hayward recounted:

> [she] wore a low neck and short sleeves, and on her introducing a fancy dance, the applause almost shook old Hollis [Hall] down. Another member of the club lived in the room across the entry, and there we had pudding after the play; the actors kept on their dresses, and poor Distaffina was nearly bothered to death by her admirers.[83]

In early productions, the actors were responsible for costuming themselves; thus, the quality of the female impersonators' costumes depended on the individual. According to one student regarding the play in 1850, "Chaillé was the first to hire a costume... he would not play the girl's part else... he looked a stunningly pretty girl in it."[84] Other costumes were described by their wearers as "shabby" or having been "fished out of a rag-bag."[85] Other "ladies" claimed they sought "naturalness" in their costume selection rather than "show."[86] Two of the more popular ladies were Horace Furness, class of 1854, as Signorina Furnessi who wore "tights and a thousand gauzy skirts,"[87] and Nathan Appleton who, in 1862, "has gone down in history as one of the handsomest heroines of the Pudding stage."[88] By at least the 1890s, Pudding productions included kick lines in drag.[89]

The D.K.E. Society also gave theatrical performances featuring female impersonators.[90] In 1892, George Doane Wells wrote and produced a burlesque *Antony and Cleopatra, or The Sinner, the Siren, and the Snake*. The program described the performance as a "libretto derived from suggestions from Messrs. Shakespeare, Sardou, and Co."[91] Cleopatra's description, written in verse, reads: "In dress of green and face shaved clean, in fact, at every step she walks – a queen."[92] In a production photograph, a clean-shaven John Dana Hubbell played the "beguiling" Cleopatra.[93]

Other organizations at Harvard also staged variety shows with drag, though they received less attention and many of them either abandoned theatricals or merged with other clubs by the twentieth century.[94] It wasn't until 1908, when Harvard's Dramatic Club was founded, that Radcliffe women were allowed to audition for female parts in plays at Harvard. Some clubs that had previously incorporated drag and were still in existence, including the *Deutscher Verein* and the *Cercle Français*, which gave yearly plays in German and French, respectively, opened their female roles to women shortly after.[95] The transition from men to women in female roles certainly relates to the conflation of drag with effeminacy that occurred on at least some elite all-male college campuses at the turn of the century. Faculty frequently cited effeminacy as being the chief concern for placing restrictions and limitations on students' assuming drag on stage.[96] However, this conflation did not happen everywhere at the same time.

Drag and female impersonation were prominent in Harvard's social clubs during the second half of the nineteenth century and early twentieth centuries. However, stigmatization, specifically in relation to effeminacy, surrounding male students' playing female roles may have factored into students' choice to produce comedies and farces earlier than Vaudeville performers did. In 1913, the fraternity Delta Upsilon sought a play "which contains enough humor to offset the danger arising from men's taking women's parts."[97] At Harvard and likely elsewhere, by 1913 men's taking on women's parts in theatrical productions became problematic, and by 1920, the association of drag particularly, and perhaps dramatic associations generally, with homosexuality was clear. Historian William Wright chronicles a secret court created by Harvard faculty and administrators to investigate an underground "ring" of homosexual students within the campus. By the end of the investigation, several students were expelled, a faculty member was dismissed, and one student committed suicide. Many of the students investigated had been involved with campus theater.[98] After a few years, when the purge was no longer part of current students' experiences or memories, Hasty Pudding Club's trademark again became—and continues to be—its drag kick line.[99]

All of these examples come from elite, all-male East Coast colleges. But students performed in drag at public midwestern colleges and universities as well. One example is the Haresfoot Club at the University of Wisconsin, a musical drama club that began in 1898. While students at all-male colleges could argue that their theatrical casts were single-sex out of necessity, students at coeducational institutions could not. In fact, when Haresfoot first formed at Wisconsin, a coeducational public university, it included both female and male actors. Growing out of "a common distaste for the narrow matter-of-fact rut unto which student activities of the time had fallen," the group formed a theater club with the goal of performing student-written plays.[100] In 1909 the club expanded its performances to surrounding cities and towns. The university, however, fearing the stain of moral impropriety, refused to allow women to travel with the club. The traveling show, then, featured men playing all the roles. This all-male show proved to be so popular with audiences that the members decided to no longer include women in their on-campus performances. By 1911 the club adopted its motto, "All Our Girls are Men, Yet Everyone's a Lady."[101] Cast members sat for studio photographs of themselves, clearly engaging in the illusionist form of drag rather than the comedic form. The Haresfoot Club continued throughout the 1940s (except for a few wartime years) offering all-male theatrical entertainment featuring impersonation-style drag. Long after Yale, Princeton, and Harvard had moved toward drag as comedy, Haresfoot members throughout the first half of the twentieth century staged performances and posed for glamor shots that emphasized beauty and illusion, rather than comedic burlesque (Image 4.3). By the 1950s and 1960s in the era of the now-classic film *Some Like It Hot*, Haresfoot, too, finally turned to drag as comedy.[102]

Similarly, the University of Illinois—another public midwestern coeducational university—had its own all-male theatrical troupe. In April 1913, the Illinois Union Dramatic Club presented the operetta "The Prodigal Prince," which included a pony ballet (Image 4.4).[103] Within a few years, the group reconstituted itself as the Pierrots, and in 1922 staged a production of "Perpetual Emotion."[104] Noting that its original intention of per-

Image 4.3 Bryan Rivers, Haresfoot Club, University of Wisconsin, 1924. (Source: University of Wisconsin-Madison Archives, Image 2017s00380)

forming operettas was challenging and expensive, the group moved instead to Vaudeville shows.[105] These shows were so well received that the group gave up its interest in operetta. The student yearbooks from the 1920s do not include photographs of the productions, so it is hard to tell what those shows were like. If they included drag, it may have been in the form of burlesque following the Yale and Harvard model, or in the illusionist form like Haresfoot performances.

The University of Illinois did not always support theatrical groups. A 1912 yearbook report on dramatic activities on campus detailed the work of literary societies and classes in dramatic readings, along with several student drama clubs. The author complained, however, about the lack of resources, including a hall in which to perform or any equipment. These conditions, the author said, "have taxed to the utmost the ingenuity and patience of all concerned." Pleading for support, funds, and space, the author justified theater as an activity that "is wholesome and well-directed," and has "furnished much solid amusement, apart from its genuine educational value."[106] Some of that "solid amusement" came in the form of the production "Maid of the Moon," which featured a male student in the title role and a pony ballet.[107] The article asking for more support for theater, then, characterized men in drag, including an all-male kick-line, as "wholesome" and deserving of university (and therefore of taxpayer) support. This description suggests that, to whatever extent other campuses faced a bias against drag because of a putative connection with homosexuality, such association was not prevalent everywhere, at least in the 1910s.

One of the most arresting images from this period in the Illinois yearbooks is a full-page spread in 1920 of former students as soldiers in World War I. The top half of the page is a photograph of several ships in the Atlantic fleet, with the caption naming Illinois students who had undergone training there. On the bottom left is a photo of the back of an unidentified soldier looking out of a bunker or tunnel onto a wrecked village. The final photo on this page celebrating Illinois students' participation in the war effort is of one particular thespian, Charles Keek, in drag. While the soldier in the neighboring photo is facing away, Keek, in a wig, makeup, and a woman's fur coat, is facing toward the viewer. The caption notes that Keek "was sent by the army authorities to help cheer up the soldiers of France."[108] In 1920, then, the university tacitly supported the image of a man in drag, performing both on and off the stage, and the photo spread gives as much importance to Keek as it does to the soldier in battle gear (Image 4.5).

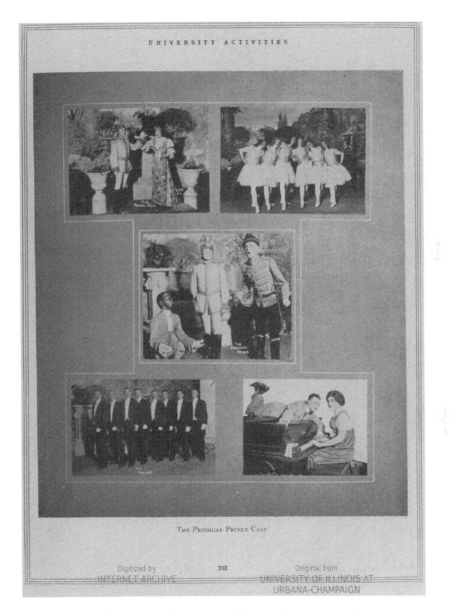

UNIVERSITY ACTIVITIES

THE PRODIGAL PRINCE CAST

Image 4.4   Prodigal Princes, University of Illinois, 1915. (Source: Illio Yearbook/ Illini Media Company)

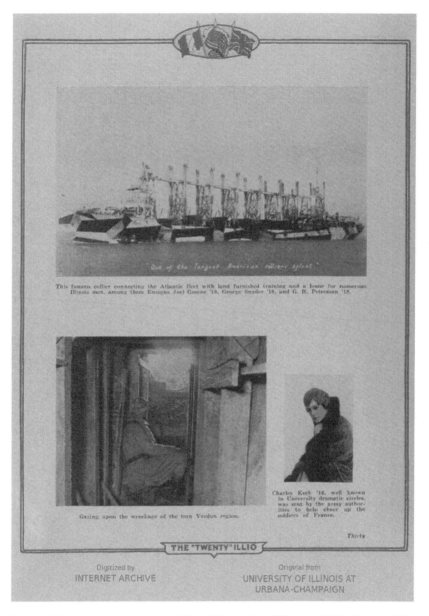

Image 4.5   Keek sent to cheer soldiers, University of Illinois, 1920. (Source: Illio Yearbook/Illini Media Company)

Women performed on stage in drag as well. As was true of men, college women had the desire to be entertained, and to engage in theater. At some women's colleges, such as Smith and Vassar, however, strict guidelines prevented students from wearing trousers even when playing men on stage.[109] Despite these restrictions, college women went to great lengths with their makeup and acting so that the audience couldn't tell that the actors were not men. Some spectators, for example, compared the acting of Radcliffe students favorably to those of the Hasty Pudding Club in 1898.[110]

During her 50th reunion speech, Elizabeth M. Richardson, Radcliffe class of 1896, spent a significant portion of her talk reminiscing about her class's "daring" costumes in theater:

> Malvolio, in 'Twelfth Night' scenes, appeared in array that shocked our elders; and when on another occasion, one character appeared in masculine attire and smoking a cubeb[111] cigarette, the fiat went forth that the limit had been reached. For some time afterward the "men" were instructed to go without smoking and to dress in coats and *skirts*. They could act behind a sofa if they wished! That edict was not very long in force, however. When Beulah Dix, '97, enacted the part of the hero in her own play, I remember clearly that no skirt hid her manly Cavalier legs.[112]

In this example, the restrictions on women wearing men's attire were far more stringent than any restrictions on men at similar institutions wearing women's attire. At Vassar, masculine costumes were forbidden, "…that is, legitimate trousers are eschewed; coats and vests are permissible, but the divided skirt marks the limit of realism!"[113] As an additional restriction, men were not permitted to attend any performances, with the exception of Smith's senior play.[114] Photographs from these performances depict "men" in bloomers; these women wore full beards and moustaches, and took on postures and facial expressions to fully embrace their parts. The discussions about actor attire continued through the early twentieth century. In 1914 *The Radcliffe Fortnightly* printed a review of "The Chinese Lantern" play:

> Miss Louise Burleigh's Mee-Mee was a delight to watch. It must have convinced any opponents of rational dress that there is no immodesty in women's wearing trousers. If anything, quite the contrary. Mee-Mee, kneeling in profile, or Mee-Mee melting to the floor, was an eloquent argument against the impedi menta which are said to encumber modern "feminine" women in America and Monte Carlo.[115]

Women and men in college, then, both engaged in theatrical productions in which some players performed in drag. At times, both women and men played up the comic effect of wearing the other's clothes, reinforcing the ridiculousness of one pretending to be the other. But at other times, both women and men played the roles seriously, working as illusionists as they showed the malleability of gender roles. Away from campus, drag in theater began as a form of magical performance: a male actor creating the illusion of being a woman. By the 1930s, drag was not welcome on stage as it had become associated with sexual deviance; any drag performance needed to be comic in order to be acceptable. On college campuses, however, this timeline is not accurate. At some elite male northeastern colleges, especially at Harvard and Princeton, the association of drag with effeminacy and/or homosexuality began several decades earlier, while at some public midwestern colleges, that association took hold much later. For women, at least at some private northeastern women's colleges, dress restrictions were strict, allowing few opportunities for women to fully adopt male roles on stage.

CONCLUSION

Drag appeared at single-sex and coeducational colleges and universities in a wide variety of settings, including mock funerals and textbook burnings at Amherst, Alumni Parades at Princeton, mock trials of the Hasty Pudding Club at Harvard, and dances at Vassar. The Alumni Parades at Princeton afforded unique opportunities for male students to engage in drag in public places without being seen as deviant or perverse.[116] Some of these "collegiate role reversals," by aiming for comedy, reinforced male dominance rather than functioning to obfuscate or complicate gender norms.[117] Students at women's colleges engaged in drag to play male roles on stage, but circumscribed roles for women were reinforced here as well, because women's colleges imposed stricter limits regarding attire. Women at Radcliffe, Smith, and Vassar also donned men's clothes at parties and dances, a use of cross-dressing that is sometimes obscured in the historiography by an emphasis on an overall change in women's fashion at the same time.

The historiography on drag posits a clear trajectory from drag as impersonation in the late nineteenth and early twentieth centuries, to drag as comic burlesque by the late 1920s as the influence of psychoanalysis and the new field of sexology rendered homosexuality deviant. There is little literature, however, on drag on college campuses. Our research, while limited and preliminary, suggests that studying drag on campuses augments the historiography on drag in theater. The association of drag with homosexuality, leading to the crackdown on drag that occurred in many cities by the late 1920s and 1930s, may have begun much earlier on some college campuses, such as Harvard and Princeton. But the association of drag with homosexuality also may have occurred much later on other campuses than the current historiography suggests, as we see in the example of the University of Wisconsin. There, drag as impersonation continued long after it had stopped elsewhere, and the strong association of drag with homosexuality was not apparent until after World War II.[118] Future research might explore regional differences, as well as differences between public and private institutions. Was Wisconsin's use of drag different from Princeton's because of cultural differences between the Midwest and the Northeast? Or is the difference better explained by Wisconsin's status as a public secular institution rather than a private denominational college? And, to what extent do class-specific ideals of masculinity explain the differences?

Because the historiography on drag has focused almost entirely on the stage, we need a new assessment that takes into account all of the many offstage uses of drag on the parts of both college women and men. Examining the multiple ways that students used drag offstage opens up new scope for understanding public and private meanings of drag. Additional research is needed to fully understand how students embraced, repudiated, or challenged rigid gender roles through the use of drag, and the ways that students used or reacted to drag's association with homosexuality as that connection changed over time. Such research will help us better understand how drag reflected, shaped, and challenged campus experiences for all students. Further research will uncover many more Mattie Mattixes and Prodigal Princes, and will enlarge our understanding of the role of drag in student life.

NOTES

1. "1883 Nov 9—Mattie Matix," digital image, Flickr, December 12, 2012, accessed October 10, 2016, https://www.flickr.com/photos/amherst_college_archives/8270579786/.
2. Andrew Fiss, "Mathematics and Mourning: Textbook Burial and Student Culture Before and After the Civil War, 1853–1880," *History of Education Quarterly* 57, no. 2 (May 2017): 221–46.

3. Nan Boyd, *Wide-Open Town: A History of Queer San Francisco to 1963* (Berkeley: University of California Press, 2003), 37; Allan Bérubé, *Coming Out Under Fire: The History of Gay Men and Women in World War Two* (New York: Free Press, 2000); Sharon R. Ullman " 'The Twentieth Century Way': Female Impersonation and Sexual Practice in Turn-of-the-Century America," *Journal of the History of Sexuality* 5, no. 4 (1995): 584–87.
4. Boyd, *Wide-Open Town*, 32.
5. Ullman, "The Twentieth Century Way."
6. Ivan Dalley Crozier, "Taking Prisoners: Havelock Ellis, Sigmund Freud, and the Construction of Homosexuality, 1897–1951," *Social History of Medicine* 13, no. 3 (2000): 447–66.
7. Boyd, *Wide-Open Town*, 36, 38.
8. Bérubé, *Coming Out Under Fire*, 73–74.
9. Thomas Doherty, *Pre-Code Hollywood: Sex, Immorality, and Insurrection in American Cinema, 1930–1934* (New York: Columbia University Press, 1999), 7.
10. George Chauncey, Jr., "Christian Brotherhood or Sexual Perversion? Homosexual Identities and the Construction of Sexual Boundaries in the World War One Era," *Journal of Social History* (2001), 189–211; 191.
11. Bérubé, *Coming Out Under Fire*, 76–77.
12. Bérubé, *Coming Out Under Fire*, 97.
13. Bérubé, *Coming Out Under Fire*, 96–97.
14. Jessica Clawson, "Queers on Campus: LGBTQ Student Visibility at Three Public Universities in Florida, 1970–1985" (Ph.D. diss., University of Florida, 2014), chapter 2.
15. Kathleen B. Casey, *The Prettiest Girl on Stage is a Man: Race and Gender Benders in Vaudeville* (Knoxville: University of Tennessee Press, 2015); Lloyd McKim Garrison, *An Illustrated History of the Hasty Pudding Club Theatricals* (Cambridge: Hasty Pudding Club, 1987); Anthony Calnek, *The Hasty Pudding Theater: A History of Harvard's Hairy-Chested Heroines* (Milan and New York: A.D.C., 1986); Donald Marsden, *The Long Kickline: A History of the Princeton Triangle Club* (Princeton, NJ: Princeton University Press, 1968); Mary Anne Long, " 'All Our Girls Are Men': The Haresfoot Club and the Original College Musical" (Ph.D. diss., The University of Wisconsin, Madison, 2004).
16. Simon J. Bronner, *Campus Traditions: Folklore from the Old-Time College to the Modern Mega-University* (Jackson: University Press of Mississippi, 2012).
17. Laura Horak, *Girls Will Be Boys: Cross-Dressed Women, Lesbians, and American Cinema, 1908–1934* (New Brunswick: Rutgers University Press, 2016).

18. Anne MacKay, ed., *Wolf Girls at Vassar: Lesbian and Gay Experiences 1930–1990* (New York: St. Martin's Press, 1993).

19. Kendra Van Cleave, "Fashioning the College Woman: Dress, Gender, and Sexuality at Smith College in the 1920s," *The Journal of American Culture* 32, no. 1 (March 2009): 6; Frances Fenton Bernard, "A Standardized Costume for Women," *Vassar Quarterly* 2, no. 2 (February 1917): 2.

20. Marjorie B. Garber, *Vested Interests: Cross-Dressing and Cultural Anxiety* (Hove, United Kingdom: Psychology Press, 1997), 61–62.

21. "1883 Nov 9—Mattie Matix"; George Rugg Cutting, *Student Life at Amherst College: Its Organizations, Their Membership, and History* (Amherst, Hatch & Williams, 1871), accessed September 2, 2016, http://archive.org/details/studentlifeatamh00cuttrich; Garber, *Vested Interests*; Alexander Leitch, *A Princeton Companion* (Princeton: Princeton University Press, 2015), 11–12; Kim Marra, "Clyde Fitch: Transvestite 'Metteur-En-Scène' of the Feminine," *New England Theatre Journal* 3 (1992): 22.

22. Cutting, *Student Life at Amherst College*.

23. Marra, "Clyde Fitch," 22.

24. This was not a reference to an article of women's underclothing, as the word "brassiere" was not in use until the 1890s.

25. "1882 Nov—Anna Lytt Funeral Pagent" digital image, Flickr, December 12, 2012, accessed October 10, 2016, https://www.flickr.com/photos/amherst_college_archives/8270583998/; "1883 Nov 9—Mattie Matix," digital image, Flickr, December 12, 2012, accessed October 10, 2016, https://www.flickr.com/photos/amherst_college_archives/8269517413/; "1883 Dec 17—Cremation of Miss Algie Bra," digital image, Flickr, December 12, 2012, accessed October 10, 2016, https://www.flickr.com/photos/amherst_college_archives/8270583728/.

26. Marra, "Clyde Fitch," 23.

27. "1882 Nov 16—Anna Lytt."

28. "1883 Nov 9—Mattie Matix"; "1883 Dec 17—Cremation of Miss Algie Bra"; Marra, "Clyde Fitch," 22–23.

29. "1883 Dec 17—Cremation of Miss Algie Bra," digital image, Flickr, December 12, 2012, accessed October 10, 2016, https://www.flickr.com/photos/amherst_college_archives/8269517499/.

30. "1875 Jul 7—Math. E. Matica! Obit.," digital image, Flickr, December 12, 2012, accessed October 10, 2016, https://www.flickr.com/photos/amherst_college_archives/8269514715/in/album-72157632236641105/.

31. "1883 Nov 9—Mattie Matix."

32. "1883 Nov 9—Mattie Matix."

33. Cutting, *Student Life*, 132.

34. Leitch, *A Princeton Companion*, 11–12.
35. Leitch, *A Princeton Companion*, 12.
36. Leitch, *A Princeton Companion*, 12.
37. "[Men in Costume]," digital image, Historical Society of Princeton, accessed September 2, 2016, http://princeton.pastperfectonline.com/photo/DF5C3B45-ABCC-42CE-9A93-708092455927; "[Alumni in Costume for P-rade, with Dog]," digital image, Historical Society of Princeton, accessed September 2, 2016, http://princeton.pastperfectonline.com/photo/F426A59F-0FC6-4E0F-B88E-923674622060. The inspiration for the costumes came from the series of postcards and lithographs depicting the infamous fictional family beginning in the late 1800s. *The Whole Dam Family and the Dam Dog* was made into a silent film by Edwin S. Porter that was released in 1905 and was a popular sketch in Vaudeville. Charles Musser, *Before the Nickelodeon: Edwin S. Porter and the Edison Manufacturing Company* (Berkeley: University of California Press, 1991), 318–19.
38. Corinne Holt Sawyer, "Men in Skirts and Women in Trousers, from Achilles to Victoria Grant: One Explanation of a Comedic Paradox," *The Journal of Popular Culture* 21, no. 2 (September 1987): 14.
39. Bronner, *Campus Traditions*, 205–7.
40. "[Class of 1900 as Suffragettes in P-rade]," digital image, Historical Society of Princeton, accessed September 2, 2016, http://princeton.pastperfectonline.com/photo/2791CBE3-6206-47E8-8E04-373440522411.
41. Anthony Calnek, *The Hasty Pudding Theater: A History of Harvard's Hairy-Chested Heroines* (New York and Milan: A.D.C., 1986), 9–10; Herman Hagedorn and John Richards, eds., *The Thirteenth Catalogue & A History of the Hasty Pudding Club* (Cambridge: Riverside Press, 1907), accessed August 19, 2016, https://archive.org/details/thirteenthcatalo00hast.
42. Calnek, *The Hasty Pudding Theatre*, 11.
43. Calnek, *The Hasty Pudding Theatre*, 11.
44. Dorothy Elia Howells, *A Century to Celebrate: Radcliffe College, 1879–1979* (Harvard University Library), 15, accessed October 17, 2016, https://iiif.lib.harvard.edu/manifests/view/drs:2573612$1i.
45. *Class of 1899 Classbook* (Smith College, 1899), accessed November 21, 2016, https://archive.org/stream/class1899smit#page/76/mode/2up/.
46. "A Fancy Dress Party in 1887," photograph, Vassar College Library, as reprinted in *Wolf Girls at Vassar: Lesbian and Gay Experiences, 1930–1990*, ed. Anne MacKay, (New York: St. Martin's Press, 1993), 6.
47. Ruth Adams, "To Family" (Letter, Vassar College, 1900?) accessed November 21, 2016, https://digitallibrary.vassar.edu/islandora/object/vassar%3A8700#page/4/mode/1up.

48. Ruth Adams, "To Family" (Letter, Vassar College, 1900?) accessed November 21, 2016, https://digitallibrary.vassar.edu/islandora/object/vassar%3A8700#page/4/mode/1up.

49. Howells, *A Century to Celebrate*, 36.

50. Howells, *A Century to Celebrate*, 36.

51. Howells, *A Century to Celebrate*, 37.

52. Danielle Mireles, "College Chorus 'Girls:' Drag at Male College and University Campuses During the Progressive Era" (Master's thesis, University of California, Riverside, 2017).

53. Bronner, *Campus Traditions*, 207.

54. "The College of Minstrels," *The Princetonian*, Match 21, 1888, 1, http://theprince.princeton.edu/princetonperiodicals/cgi-bin/princetonperiodicals?a=d&d=Princetonian18880321-01.2.9&srpos=2&e=------188-en-20--1--txt-txIN-base+ball+fund------#; *The Princetonian*, March 18, 1899, 2, http://theprince.princeton.edu/princetonperiodicals/cgi-bin/princetonperiodicals?a=d&d=Princetonian18890318-01.2.9&srpos=1&e=------188-en-20--1--txt-txIN-dramatic+association+track------#.

55. "David Garrick," *The Princetonian*, May 11, 1883, 32, http://theprince.princeton.edu/princetonperiodicals/cgi-bin/princetonperiodicals?a=d&d=Princetonian18830511-01.2.13&srpos=2&e=------188-en-20--1--txt-txIN-david+garrick----1883--;%20%E2%80%9CPrincetonian%208%20June%201883%20%E2%80%94%20Princeton%20Periodicals,%E2%80%9D%208#; "Dramatis Personæ," *The Princetonian*, May 11, 1883, 33, http://theprince.princeton.edu/princetonperiodicals/cgi-bin/princetonperiodicals?a=d&d=Princetonian18830511-01.2.14&srpos=1&e=------188-en-20--1--txt-txIN-David+Garrick----1883--#; *The Princetonian*, May 11, 1883, 25–26, http://theprince.princeton.edu/princetonperiodicals/cgi-bin/princetonperiodicals?a=d&d=Princetonian18830511-01.2.5&srpos=3&e=------188-en-20--1--txt-txIN-David+Garrick----1883--#.

56. "David Garrick," *The Princetonian*, May 11, 1883, 32; "Dramatis Personæ," *The Princetonian*, May 11, 1883, 33; *The Princetonian*, May 11, 1883, 25–26.

57. "Tour of the Dramatic Association," *The Princetonian*, June 8, 1883, 76, from http://theprince.princeton.edu/princetonperiodicals/cgi-bin/princetonperiodicals?a=d&d=Princetonian18830608-01.2.12&srpos=4&e=------188-en-20--1--txt-txIN-David+Garrick----1883--; *The Princetonian*, 25.

58. *The Princetonian*, February 17, 1890, 2, http://theprince.princeton.edu/princetonperiodicals/cgi-bin/princetonperiodicals?a=d&d=Princetonian18900217-01.2.13&srpos=6&e=------189-en-20--1--txt-txIN-minstrels-ARTICLE-----#.

59. "Pocahontas," *The Princetonian*, April 27, 1891, 1, http://theprince. princeton.edu/princetonperiodicals/cgi-bin/princetonperiodicals?a=d& d=Princetonian18910427-01.2.3&srpos=6&e=------189-en-20--1--txt-txIN-pocahontas-ARTICLE---1891--.

60. Mireles, "College Chorus Girls"; Andrea L. Turpin, "The Chief End of Man at Princeton: The Rise of Gendered Moral Formation in American Higher Education," *Journal of the Gilded Age & Progressive Era* 15, no. 4 (October 2016), 446–68.

61. Edward W. Borgers, "The Princeton Triangle Club," *Princeton Alumni Weekly*, September 29, 1950, 10–13.

62. Borgers, "The Princeton Triangle Club," 11.

63. A pony ballet is any group of dancers performing synchronized movements, usually while wearing elaborate costumes. It often but not necessarily involves high kicks. A kick line always includes synchronized high kicks. The terms often are used interchangeably.

64. "Princeton University, Triangle Club," accessed October 17, 2016, http://findingaids.princeton.edu/names/143083897.

65. Borgers, "The Princeton Triangle Club," 10–13; "Senior Dramatics," *The Amherst Student*, March 25, 1899, 177, https://www.myheritage. com/research/record-90100-39545008/the-amherst-student-newspaper-amherst-college-vol-32#fullscreen.

66. "Senior Dramatics," 177.

67. "Senior Dramatics," 177.

68. Marra, "Clyde Fitch," 15.

69. "Alumni in the Theater: Clyde Fitch, Class of 1886," Amherst College, accessed August 21, 2016, https://www.amherst.edu/library/archives/exhibitions/play/alumni/fitch.

70. "Alumni in the Theater."

71. Marra, "Clyde Fitch," 22.

72. Billy J. Harbin, Kim Marra, and Robert A. Schanke, *The Gay and Lesbian Theatrical Legacy: A Biographical Dictionary of Major Figures in American Stage History in the Pre-Stonewall Era* (Ann Arbor: University of Michigan Press, 2007), 160.

73. Harbin, et al., *The Gay & Lesbian Theatrical Legacy*, 160; Marra, "Clyde Fitch," 22.

74. Marra, "Clyde Fitch," 22.

75. Harbin, et al., *The Gay & Lesbian Theatrical Legacy*, 160.

76. Kevin Lane Dearinger, *Clyde Fitch and the American Theatre: An Olive in the Cocktail* (Lanham: Rowman & Littlefield, 2016), xiii.

77. Dearinger, *Clyde Fitch*, 10.

78. Dearinger, *Clyde Fitch*.

79. John T. Bethell, *Harvard Observed: An Illustrated History of the University in the Twentieth Century* (Cambridge, MA: Harvard University Press, 1998), 56.

80. William Dana Orcutt and William Burns Wolffe, *The Harvard Club Book: 1894–95* (Cambridge, MA: University Press, 1895), accessed October 22, 2016, https://books.google.com/books?id=gpnOAAAAMAAJ&printsec =frontcover&source=gbs_ge_summary_r&cad=0#v=onepage&q&f=false.

81. Lemuel Hayward, "The First Pudding Play," in Lloyd McKim Garrison, *An Illustrated Guide of the Hasty Pudding Club* (Cambridge, MA: Harvard University Press, 1998), 33.

82. Hayward, "The First Pudding Play," 34.

83. Hayward, "The First Pudding Play," 34.

84. Student quoted in Garrison, *An Illustrated History of the Hasty Pudding Club Theatricals*, 21.

85. Garrison, *An Illustrated History*, 21.

86. Garrison, *An Illustrated History*, 22.

87. Garrison, *An Illustrated History*, 21.

88. Hagedorn and Richards, *The Thirteenth Catalogue*, 16.

89. John T. Bethell, Richard M. Hunt and Robert Shenton, *Harvard A to Z* (Cambridge, MA: Harvard University Press, 2004), accessed July 18, 2017, https://books.google.com/books?id=WGrBJFRw1GsC&printse c=frontcover&source=gbs_ge_summary_r&cad=0#v=onepage&q&f=fa lse. For an example from 1914, see H., Jackson, Jr., B.P. Clark, Jr., and R.L. Putnam, eds., "The Fattest Calf," *Harvard Advocate*, October 9, 1914, 2.

90. Students quoted in Lucien G. Price, "American Undergraduate Dramatics," *The Bookman: A Magazine of Literature and Life*, September–February 1904, 373–88.

91. Noah Sheola, "You Seem as Dull as... A Yale Man," Houghton Library Blog, modified January 25, 2016, https://blogs.harvard.edu/hough-ton/2016/01/25/yale-man/.

92. Sheola, "You Seem as Dull."

93. Sheola, "You Seem as Dull."

94. Henry E. Cottle, "Dramatics at Harvard," *Harvard Alumni Bulletin*, September 24, 1913, 294–97; Garber, *Vested Interests*; Price, "American Undergraduate Dramatics."

95. Cottle, "Dramatics at Harvard," 294.

96. "College Athletes Act Best in Skirts: Columbia and N.Y.U. Doubt Yale Idea That Impersonations Cause Effeminacy," *New York Times*, December 12, 1915, 16; Mireles, "College Chorus Girls."

97. Cottle, "Dramatics at Harvard," 294–96.

98. William Wright, *Harvard's Secret Court: The Savage 1920 Purge of Campus Homosexuals* (New York: St. Martin's Griffin, 2006).

99. "The Pudding Story," Hasty Pudding Institute of 1770, accessed September 5, 2016, http://hastypudding.org/hasty-pudding-theatricals-history.

100. "It Was Spring and We Were Twenty," *Big As Life* Program (Madison, WI: Haresfoot Club, 1948,) 6, University of Wisconsin Archives, Madison, WI.

101. "It Was Spring and We Were Twenty," 6. For one example of the use of the motto, see "Haresfoot 'Kitty Corner' Program" (Madison, WI: Haresfoot Club, 1922), University of Wisconsin Archives.

102. For an array of images, cast photos, and theatrical programs, see "Haresfoot" at digicoll.library.wisc.edu.

103. "The Prodigal Prince," *The Illio* (Urbana: University of Illinois, 1915), 252–54.

104. "Perpetual Emotion," *The Illio* (Urbana: University of Illinois, 1922), 218.

105. "Pierrots," *The Illio* (Urbana: University of Illinois, 1921), 248.

106. "The Athenean and Ionian literary societies…," *The Illio* (Urbana: University of Illinois, 1912), 205.

107. "Maid of the Moon," *The Illio* (Urbana: University of Illinois, 1912), 206–7.

108. [no title], *The Illio* (Urbana: University of Illinois, 1920), 30.

109. Lida Rose McCabe, *The American Girl at College* (New York: Dodd, Mead & Company, 1893).

110. Karen Lepri, "Clothes Make the Man: Cross-dressing on the Radcliffe Stage," in Laurel Ulrich, ed., *Yards and Gates: Gender in Harvard and Radcliff History* (New York: Palgrave Macmillan, 2004), 235.

111. A form of cigarette that used spice and oil, primarily from a pepper plant, rather than tobacco.

112. Elizabeth Richardson, "Fifty Years On: A Speech Given at the Alumnae Dinner, 1896," *The Radcliffe Quarterly* (August 1946), 5–6, accessed Nov. 21, 2016, http://nrs.harvard.edu/urn-3:RAD. ARCH:4731683?n=6872.

113. McCabe, *The American Girl at College*, 29, 30.

114. McCabe, *The American Girl at College*, 34.

115. *The Radcliffe Fortnightly* 1, no. 4 (March 11, 1914).

116. Leitch, *A Princeton Companion*.

117. Bronner, *Campus Traditions*, 207.

118. Margaret A. Nash and Jennifer A. Silverman, "'An Indelible Mark:' Gay Purges in Higher Education in the 1940s," *History of Education Quarterly* 55, no. 4 (November 2015): 1–19.

CHAPTER 5

"Enthusiasm and Mutual Confidence": Campus Life at State Normal Schools, 1870s–1900s

Christine A. Ogren

Martha Knapp, an 1880 graduate of San Jose State Normal School in California, had fond memories of social life on campus, including one instance when women students used the "small sum of money" remaining after a specimen-gathering excursion for botany class to share a "spread" of coffee, cake, and strawberries with men students. "Everything passed off pleasantly," she recounted. "Dancing was indulged in, and thoroughly enjoyed by every one."[1] Like this spread of coffee and sweets, an observer's 1897 description of the "spirit" of Knapp's alma mater as "that of enthusiasm and mutual confidence"[2] captured student culture at state normal schools throughout the United States. First established in Massachusetts in 1839, these institutions spread to all regions of the country and numbered 180 by 1910. While their official purpose was preparing teachers for the public schools, state normal schools also offered general

C. A. Ogren (✉)
Educational Policy and Leadership Studies, University of Iowa,
Iowa City, IA, USA
e-mail: chris-ogren@uiowa.edu

© The Author(s) 2018
C. A. Ogren, M. A. VanOverbeke (eds.),
Rethinking Campus Life, Historical Studies in Education,
https://doi.org/10.1007/978-3-319-75614-1_5

academic courses and served for many students as an accessible form of higher education long before transforming in the 1910s–1930s into state teachers colleges and granting bachelor's degrees. Indeed, during their heyday between the 1870s and the 1900s, state normal schools provided a specific educational environment for a distinct student body.[3] The normal schools' enthusiastic and supportive campus life was integral to that environment and service to that student body.

In *Campus Life: Undergraduate Cultures from the End of the Eighteenth Century to the Present*, Helen Lefkowitz Horowitz argues that, while students have created and enjoyed "collective life" throughout history, the specific undergraduate culture she calls *college life* took hold in US higher education in the mid-nineteenth century and dictated student relations and experiences thereafter.[4] Focusing mainly on private and state flagship institutions, Horowitz does not discuss state normal schools or the regional colleges and universities into which they eventually grew. The history of campus life, however, is incomplete without attention to these ubiquitous institutions, which served large numbers of students to whom private colleges and flagship institutions were inaccessible.[5] This chapter focuses on student-created and -run organizations and the social sphere at state normal schools from the 1870s through the 1900s. The majority of normal-school students, or "normalites," were female, members of racial/ethnic minority groups, and/or from the lower end of the social-class scale. While these students generally did not have access to the fraternity and sorority life and football culture at the heart of the college life described by Horowitz, they created a vibrant campus life at normal schools. Whereas college life at traditional four-year institutions arose in opposition to campus rules and formal studies, normal-school student life augmented the curriculum and students' professional development as teachers. Rather than reinforcing class differences as did college life, activities at normal schools facilitated socialization into the middle class. In addition, women at normal schools were not relegated to second-class status as "coeds," but instead were active participants and leaders in campus life. After briefly outlining normalites' backgrounds, this chapter demonstrates how campus life at state normal schools enhanced students' intellectual and professional growth, welcomed all students into middle-class society, and invited women students into public life. The enthusiastic and mutually confident collective life of students at state normal schools contradicted the rigid system Horowitz describes at private colleges and flagship universities. Examining campus life at state normal schools demonstrates that *college life,* as experienced by students on more traditional campuses, was far from universal in the late nineteenth and early twentieth centuries.

NORMALITES

While Horowitz does not include normal schools in her history of campus life, she does acknowledge the presence of students who shared background characteristics with the majority of normal-school students: the group she calls *outsiders* to signify that they were uninterested or unwelcome in college life. Outsiders, she explains, tended to be from poor families. Many had grown up on farms and were older than other students. In the early nineteenth century, the first outsiders were men who were preparing for the ministry. By the late nineteenth and early twentieth centuries, pioneering women, immigrant, and ethnic and racial minority students joined the ranks of outsiders, who focused on meeting educational expectations for mobility into a range of occupations. Their professional ambitions drove them to take their academic work seriously and study hard.[6]

One of the professions for which Horowitz's outsiders prepared was teaching, and normal-school students between the 1870s and the 1900s had much in common with them. The majority of normalites were women, as most state normal schools were coeducational and enrolled more women than men, while a handful of institutions in the Northeast and South restricted their enrollment to women only. State normals in the South were segregated, and nearly two dozen of them—including those in Pine Bluff, Arkansas, Tallahassee, Florida, and Bowie, Maryland—were for African American students. Several northern normal schools enrolled students from minority racial and ethnic groups in numbers that were small yet significant for the time. Black students began appearing at state normal schools from Massachusetts to Illinois soon after the Civil War. The state normal in Albany, New York, matriculated 26 Native American students in the late nineteenth century and many South European, Polish, and Jewish immigrants in the early twentieth century. The normal schools in Pennsylvania welcomed several students from Puerto Rico and South America beginning in the 1890s, and Southwest Texas State Normal School in San Marcos enrolled some students of Mexican descent.[7]

Regardless of their race or gender, most normal-school students were the children of working people, many of whom were struggling financially.

Skilled, semiskilled, unskilled, and agricultural workers headed the homes of two-thirds of normalites in Massachusetts; the normal in Worcester reflected its location in a growing industrial city by enrolling primarily the children of skilled workers and laborers. Two-thirds of students at the normal schools in Cedar Falls, Iowa, and Emporia, Kansas, were from farming families during a period when agriculture was especially hard-hit by economic downturns and depressions. Some normal schools gained a negative reputation for serving the poor; residents of Oswego, New York, referred to students at the normal school located there as "state paupers" because state-funded teacher training was the only form of higher education that they could afford. As a result of their financial challenges, many normalites were mature in age, having entered normal school in their twenties. They often arrived with work experience, found term-time jobs to support themselves, and, in the eyes of many, lacked sophistication.[8] The principal of the state normal in Ypsilanti, Michigan, said, "Our students are working young men and women who earn their little money by the hardest toil," and a graduate of the normal school in Peru, Nebraska, remembered "girls with brown faces and plain clothing" and "boys with calloused hands."[9] The principal of the normal school in Willimantic, Connecticut, complained, "Many of our students are crude. Their manner of talking, their table manners, their actions often show a decided lack of culture."[10]

Like Horowitz's outsiders, normal-school students were also serious and studious. The visitor at San Jose in 1897 described students there as "earnest," and Oregon's State Superintendent of Public Instruction reported regarding the state's normal schools after the turn of the century that "the discipline of the student body is an easy task. Greater precaution must be exercised to prevent the ambitious from overworking than to rouse the sluggards."[11] While normalites shared the motivations and the gender, racial/ethnic, and class characteristics of Horowitz's outsiders, they were most certainly insiders on state normal-school campuses.

Enhancing Intellectual and Professional Growth

At the center of Horowitz's story is *college life*, the campus culture organized and directed by wealthier men students that held sway from the mid-nineteenth century onward. Through fraternities, athletics, and other activities, *college men* created a powerful system that opposed campus rules and formal studies. Horowitz labels poor and minority students, as well as early women students, *outsiders* because college men shunned them based on their low social status, while their concern with academic achievement and identification with the faculty made them uninterested in college life. Horowitz's outsiders were one-dimensional grinds, focused solely on achievement in the classroom.[12] Although Horowitz presents the college men-outsider schema as *the* structure of campus life between the 1870s and 1900s, it does not begin to capture student life at state normal schools. Normalites were most certainly serious about their studies, which included wide but not always deep exposure to standard academic subjects and, occasionally, classical and modern languages, as well as classroom and hands-on instruction in teaching.[13] But normalites' hunger to learn extended beyond the classroom and inspired them to create a vibrant extracurricular culture that, unlike Horowitz's college life, was inclusive and enhanced their intellectual and professional growth.

Normal-school students founded and participated in countless clubs, performing groups, publications, and literary societies. Although Horowitz and other historians suggest that Greek-letter fraternities—and, later, sororities—supplanted literary societies in the mid-nineteenth century,[14] literary societies were the most popular organizations by far at state normal schools through the opening decade of the twentieth century. Virtually all state normal schools had societies, and the majority of students belonged. As late as 1903, students established literary societies during the opening terms of new state normals in Presque Isle, Maine, and Weatherford, Oklahoma. Throughout the country, societies met weekly or biweekly, usually on Friday or Saturday afternoon or evening, to execute well-planned programs of orations, debates, moderated discussions, skits, and musical entertainment. Both single-sex and coeducational societies flourished. Meetings were occasionally open to the public, and "joint meetings" between the two societies were popular. New York State's normal schools housed branches of statewide single-sex literary societies, including Delphic, which functioned in many ways as a brother society to Clionian, as all-male Philadelphian did to all-female Agonian; the pairs held joint meetings regularly. Many societies maintained library collections and reading rooms, and students at some institutions were able to earn academic credit for society work. Most of the normals' early performing groups and publications originated within literary societies, and statewide and even interstate normal-school society debate and oratorical contests were increasingly popular.[15] J. S. Nasmith, who graduated in 1872 from Platteville, Wisconsin, remembered, "The Philadelphian literary society ... was a great help, for the training it gave in writing and speaking, and the quickening of thought that came from the debates."[16] Reinforcing and supplementing the curriculum and students' training as teachers, normal schools' literary societies and other organizations constituted the campus life of the outsider-cum-insider.

While literary societies dipped into a range of academic topics, academic clubs allowed these intellectually hungry students to focus on particular subjects. In science clubs, students enhanced their knowledge of the natural world. In the late 1870s, meetings of the Natural History Society at Brockport, New York, included reports on "Meteorites," "Ruffled Grouse," and "Motions of Plants," and a decade later, a similar club at Bridgewater, Massachusetts, organized excursions to collect plants, minerals, and animals from the surrounding area. The Astronomical Club at San Jose, California, in the early 1890s studied the moon and Jupiter.[17] Meanwhile, foreign-language clubs deepened students' cultural sensibilities while strengthening their agility in other tongues. Members of Hermania, founded at Oneonta, New York, in 1893, practiced speaking German and published a monthly paper in the language. At San Marcos, Texas, according to the 1908 yearbook, the Germanistiche Gesellschaft stood "for the cultivation of a deeper feeling of sympathy among the students of German, and a truer appreciation and broader knowledge of German life, history, literature, and music."[18]

Other clubs and, especially, literary-society meetings focused on history and the arts. Latin Club at Peru, Nebraska, in 1906 organized "a Roman Republic with a full corps of consuls, quaestors, aediles and triumvir" to enhance the study of ancient history, and an 1891 meeting of Brockport's Phothepian Society featured addresses on "England and Englishmen," "The Norman Conquest," and "Cromwell," as well as an impersonation of Sir Walter Raleigh. Many societies celebrated the February birthdays of Washington and Lincoln with programs on these American presidents, and Elizabeth Shepard won the yearly oratorical contest at the normal in Oshkosh, Wisconsin, in 1899 with her speech on Ulysses S. Grant. Great women of history did not escape the normalites' notice; for example, the Agonian Society at Geneseo, New York, debated "Resolved, that Cleopatra was a better woman than Helen of Troy." Also at Geneseo, in 1899–1900 the History of Art Club "studied German, Dutch and Flemish art," and exhibited a "large loan collection of examples of the art of those schools." A few years later, San Jose's Art Club studied "American painters, sculptors and illustrators."[19] The Pease Musical Art Club at Ypsilanti, Michigan, focused on classical music as well as art, while members of the Mendelssohn Club at San Marcos learned about "the best available works of the great composers."[20] Music was also prominent in literary societies, as most meetings featured live performances and a few also included intellectual discussions of the subject. At one meeting of Oshkosh's Phoenix, for example, several musical performances accompanied a talk entitled "Introduction of Music into the United States."[21]

While literary societies examined a range of subjects, their main focus was, of course, literature. Societies as well as other clubs regularly studied a variety of British and American authors. The Browning clubs at Florence, Alabama, and Oshkosh, Wisconsin, were named for Elizabeth Barrett Browning, just as the Shakespeare(an) societies at Cedar Falls, San Jose, and San Marcos were named for the great playwright. The programs of many other literary societies also focused on the life and work of Shakespeare and other British authors. Societies at Oneonta staged Tennyson's *The Princess* in 1892, two of Shakespeare's plays in 1901, and Dickens's *Tom Pinch* in 1905. Bertha Schuster Beach of the class of 1883 at Whitewater, Wisconsin, remembered a meeting of the Young Ladies' Literary Society devoted to Oscar Wilde, with his beloved "huge sunflowers everywhere, [and] aesthetic dresses that blinded the eyes."[22] Societies also studied the poetry and prose of American writers including Whittier, Emerson, and Twain. The program for an 1889 meeting of Brockport's Alpha Delta society included essays entitled "American Poetry," "Humor in American Poetry," and "The Poet Longfellow." San Marcos's Every Day Society declared Washington Irving its "patron saint," and imitated his writing in its 1909 yearbook entry. Literary societies also delved into American regional and vernacular literature. Together, Oneonta's societies enlivened their studies of American literature by bringing Jack London to campus, where he spoke on "Experiences of a Tramp."[23]

In addition to augmenting the curriculum in the areas of literature, the arts, history, languages, and science, normal-school student clubs, societies, and publications reached beyond academic subjects to explore contemporary developments in domestic policy and world diplomacy. Prohibition, race relations, immigration, trade unionization, regulation of business, and political reforms were common topics of society orations and debates. For example, members of Lyceum at Oshkosh debated "Shall the Negro be debarred from voting," and members of Agonian at Geneseo debated, "Resolved, That immigration is not conducive to the welfare of a country." Women's suffrage was a popular debate topic, and a special issue of Oshkosh's student publication *The Normal Advance* included editorials for and against votes for women.[24] The Normal Debating Club at Cortland, New York, in the late 1880s weighed the resolution "That England has no right to interfere in the Russo-Turkish war," while discussions of world affairs more commonly focused beyond Europe. On the eve of the Spanish-American War, Geneseo's Agonians debated, "Resolved that Cuba should be annexed to the United States," and in the wake of the war, they debated, "Resolved: That the present American war with the Phillipines [*sic*] is unjust." In 1907, students from San Marcos debated the Monroe Doctrine with representatives of North Texas State Normal School in Denton. Such topics must have been especially compelling at institutions with students from the countries under discussion, such as New Paltz, New York, where young women from Cuba studied in the "Cuban Annex" in the 1890s.[25] The normalites' world expanded as their understanding of international and domestic issues grew along with their general knowledge and intellectual acumen.

Normal-school students not only realized the intellectual benefits of involvement in academic clubs, literary societies, and publications, but also used these activities to enhance their professional preparation for teaching. Geneseo student Andrew Gilman wrote of "The Benefits of Society" membership in a 1905 yearbook, "the freedom and ease of expression and the improved compositions of the society member fully justifies the belief that this work is essential to a successful school." He explained that many normalites "come from localities where they have never had the advantages of social life"; for them, "this training is of great value, for what success can one expect as a teacher, or in any profession, if he is not able to meet others with ease."[26] Activities enhanced professional preparation more concretely by enabling students to broaden and deepen their knowledge of teaching methods and skills. Student editors published many model lesson plans. "Nature Lessons" by Stella H. Jillson in an 1894 issue of Oshkosh's *The Normal Advance* described helpful activities for fourth graders, and a regular "Practice School Department" in San Jose's *The Normal Student* during the early 1900s included lesson outlines by student teachers. The all-female Comenian Society reported in the 1911 San Marcos yearbook that its "programs" during the year had "been largely devoted to story telling and dramatization of stories that all children should know and love.... Each girl whose privilege it has been to tell a story assumed the role of teacher while the other members of the society became an enthusiastic class of young children."[27]

Beyond exploring and practicing teaching methods, normalites also engaged in these activities to extend their studies and understanding of the field of education. In Michigan, the Child Study Club at Ypsilanti deepened members' understanding of educational psychology, and the Rural Sociology Seminar at Kalamazoo explored, in the words of its founding members, "the means by which the rural school can contribute to the general progress of the community in which it is situated."[28] Student publications regularly discussed the ideas and achievements of Horace Mann, Johann Pestalozzi, and other educational reformers, and many articles and society debates focused on the relative merits of various subjects. In a Philalethean debate at Geneseo, the affirmative side convinced the judges that "the study of Latin and Greek does not repay the time spent on them." Compulsory education and other school laws were popular debate topics, as were gender issues. The members of Florence's all-male Lafayette Society revealed themselves to be progressive thinkers when the negative side won an 1880 debate on "Resolve [*sic*] that the two sexes should not be educated together" and an 1882 debate on whether "the Mental capacities of the two sexes are equal" was "decided in favor of the affirmative." Many publications had sections similar to *The Normal Advance*'s "Educational Notes," which included short quotations or facts, many of which were about schooling in other countries. This section in one 1896 issue stated, "Russia has promised to establish a public school system for Siberia," and noted, "Prussian rural schools have on average forty-two weeks of school" while "Rural schools in the United States average not quite sixteen weeks."[29]

Students' wide-ranging examination of education also facilitated their socialization as professionals. Deepening their preparation for the classroom while also broadening their understanding of larger issues in the field fostered a sense that they were becoming experts rather than simply workers. Another aspect of professional identity is involvement in professional organizations, which student journalists encouraged through coverage of the activities of teachers' associations. At San Jose, *The Normal Index* reported on meetings of the California State Teachers' Association and a county teachers' institute, and *The Normal Pennant* included "Gems From the N.E.A. [National Education Association] Speakers in Los Angeles." *The Normal Advance* remarked on the large number of Oshkosh faculty, alumni, and students who attended a meeting of the Wisconsin Teachers' Association.[30] By the latter decades of the nineteenth century, engagement in a professional occupation was a distinguishing feature of middle-class status (at least for men),[31] as was knowledge of scientific topics, European languages, world history, classical music, Western literature, and current events. In this sense, the campus life of outsiders-cum-insiders at state normal schools not only enhanced students' intellectual and professional growth, but positioned them to join the middle class.

WELCOMING ALL INTO MIDDLE-CLASS SOCIETY

According to Horowitz, the college life created by college men reified social-class differences by creating a hierarchy of social experiences that enhanced social capital for privileged white men and excluded outsiders from socializing with their higher-class peers. While acknowledging that they sought to "rise in the world," Horowitz asserts that outsiders "remained within the culture of their parents."[32] Although normalites had few if any higher-class peers with whom to interact, their social life and campus activities challenged rather than reinforced class differences by socializing them into the middle-class culture—and away from that of their parents. Early historian of Illinois State Normal University Charles A. Harper observed of normalites that "the intellectual and social poverty of their daily [home] environment" contributed to a "feeling that participation in the literary societies was the final emancipation from the crudeness, the uncouthness and the humiliating boorishness of backwards frontier life." The students, Harper explained, aimed to make their societies "as far removed as possible from the narrow, sordid, pinch-penny monotonous grind of their daily existence."[33] Together, these students from humble backgrounds used campus life to acquire the trappings of middle-class status.

As explained above, learning about literary, cultural, historical, and scientific subjects in literary societies, clubs, and publications enabled normal-school students to obtain prestigious knowledge, or the cultural capital of the middle and upper classes. As they prepared and presented orations and debates, students also refined their writing and speech, further distancing themselves from their humble class origins. By the latter part of the nineteenth century, the middle class also defined itself by taking sightseeing vacations, and knowledge of tourist attractions became another type of cultural capital.[34] In society meetings, normalites enjoyed presentations that allowed them to travel vicariously throughout the United States and the world. At a meeting of the Phoenix society at Oshkosh, Wisconsin, "Miss Dopp" described her experiences in Salt Lake City, and a program entitled "Travels in the West" figuratively took the Dixie society at Florence, Alabama, to Yellowstone National Park and other sights. Oshkosh's Ladies Literary Society explored the sights in Spain and Germany, while Comenian at San Marcos, Texas, looked at China.[35] Around the turn of the twentieth century, social issues were special concerns of many members of the middle class, who engaged in progressive reform efforts. Students at Castleton, Vermont, in 1902 debated "the Liquor Question," and the focus of both the Agonian-Philalethean joint meeting at Geneseo, New York, and the debate between the state normals in San Jose and Chico, California, in 1901 was municipal ownership of utilities. In Texas in 1908, San Marcos debated Denton on whether the state "should adopt an amendment to the constitution providing for the optional Initiative and Referendum, applicable to all laws."[36] Such considerations of progressive reforms, like their vicarious travels, furthered normalites' socialization into the middle class.

Complementing explorations of middle-class interests and cultural topics, literary society meetings' settings and structure also fostered social refinement. Beginning in the 1880s, state normal schools set aside rooms for each individual society or for pairs of societies to share, and students decorated them carefully. The Philadelphian society at Normal, Illinois, reported in 1882 on the "splendor" of its meeting hall: "The new carpet ... the richly dyed curtains swinging from the arch, the beautiful scenes of life portrayed by master hands, and the costly chandeliers, cast in a model of rare design, commend the admiration of our friends and the respect of our rivals."[37] At Brockport, New York, by the late 1890s, society rooms similarly were furnished as elegant parlors. Throughout the country, societies held their weekly or biweekly meetings in these rooms, and decorum was of the utmost importance. Between the various speeches and debates, members entertained one another with musical selections and thus enhanced their cultural capital. Many societies owned pianos and put them to good use. At Oneonta, New York, by the 1890s, all of the societies also had stringed-instrument groups. In addition to holding their regular meetings, societies also hosted dinners and receptions for other societies or faculty members in their well-adorned rooms. For example, the Literati Society at Emporia, Kansas, held a "Dickens social" and a "Shakespearean social."[38] Such gatherings called for good manners and graciousness.

Political scientist Robert Putnam observes that the years between 1870 and 1920 marked "a veritable 'boom' in association building" in the United States, one goal of which was building social capital.[39] Normalites engaged enthusiastically in association building through not only literary societies and academic clubs, but also athletic teams and religious associations. Male students took the lead in organizing sports, beginning with baseball by the early 1870s. They formed football and basketball teams beginning, respectively, in the late 1880s and the middle 1890s. Competition in these sports remained primarily intramural, with occasional inter-school match-ups, often as sideshows at inter-normal scholarly debates. Due to small numbers of male students and limited funding for athletics, men's teams often struggled to remain viable. Rather than basking in limelight, participants scrambled just to be able to field a team, which strengthened their social bonds. Women students were also active in athletics at state normals. In fact, basketball was a full-blown craze among the women, who engaged in both intramural and inter-school competition. By 1898, the women of San Jose had four basketball teams, and two years later, they formed the Normal Girls' Athletic Association with the intention of having "the best basketball team in the state, or even on the Coast." Meanwhile, the Girls' Athletic Association at Geneseo arranged for games among teams representing the different all-female literary societies. Ninety women joined the association in 1901–1902, and Geneseo played two women's basketball games against state rival Fredonia State Normal School in 1904–1905. In the early twentieth century, female and male normalites diversified their athletic endeavors and even arranged mixed tennis tournaments and bicycle clubs.[40]

In addition to sports, religious associations fostered association building among normalites. What began as informal prayer meetings of Isaac Eddy Brown and six other men students at the Presbyterian Church in Normal, Illinois, became one of the first campus chapters of the Young Men's Christian Association (YMCA) in February 1872. The following November, Brown's sister Lida invited other women students to her room for prayer and hymns, and the group soon grew into a chapter of the Young Women's Christian Association (YWCA). The Students' Christian Union founded in 1891 at Cortland Normal School in New York, aimed "to promote an earnest Christian life among students, to increase their mutual acquaintance, and make them more useful in service to God." Throughout the country, though, YM- and YWCAs were the most popular religious organizations at normal schools from the 1890s into the twentieth century. Students met for devotional services, held Bible-study classes, and undertook service projects on campus.[41] As bonds grew in worship and on the court, as well as in literary-society and club activities, normal-school students' many associations served as important vehicles for the formation of social capital, an important aspect of middle-class status.

Inclusive social events also fostered social capital and middle-class sociability among normalites. Impromptu gatherings like the "spread" that Martha Knapp and her fellow students enjoyed at San Jose and students' interactions over refreshments before and after organization meetings imitated middle-class social life. The YWCA at Normal, Illinois, held teas, and at Buffalo, New York, in the 1890s and 1900s, members of the coeducational Normal Literary Union enjoyed banquets, game parties, and even dances, before which they taught one another the correct steps.[42] Literary societies' celebrations of events such as Washington's birthday and class receptions were prominent on normal schools' social calendars. At Oshkosh, the annual fall reception that the seniors hosted for the juniors in 1898 took the form of a "Japanese party," and in 1899 it was a Halloween party. The juniors hosted a reception for the seniors each spring until 1900, when they began to take them on a boat ride instead. This annual trip across Lake Winnebago to Calumet Harbor included refreshments and dancing. Other excursions that combined socializing with a taste of tourism included regular ventures by San Jose students to Alum Rock, a nearby landform. *The Normal Index* described the day a group of juniors spent there in 1887 as "pleasantly spent in gazing at the falls and other wonders, in dancing, and in disposing of the many good things brought along for lunch." At the state normal in Richmond, Kentucky, trips to "the mountains" meant leaving on the midnight train and hiking from the Berea station in time to watch the sunrise over the peaks; after preparing and enjoying bacon and coffee together, students hiked until it was time to catch the noon train back to Richmond.[43]

Excursions to scenic areas were not the only elements of student life that took place beyond the boundaries of campus. Many normalites lived off campus because their institutions lacked the resources to provide residence halls. For students like Gordon Wilson at Bowling Green, Kentucky, boardinghouse companions—both male and female—became an important social group; he ate slowly "to lengthen out the club-like atmosphere." Other students lived with middle-class families in town. The 1898–1899 catalog for Florence, Alabama, explained that students "secure homes with cultivated, refined, discreet people, who can guide them in their amusements, advise them when necessary, and give them a pleasant social life."[44] Whether they lived in boardinghouses, with families, or on campus, normalites interacted in various ways with the middle-class society in the communities that housed their schools. They often worshipped at local churches, where they also participated in Sunday school and attended church socials, and were involved in community events ranging from "Citizens Barbeques" in San Marcos, Texas, to shows at the opera house in Greeley, Colorado. Although few state normal schools were located in urban centers, towns like Greeley, San Marcos, Oshkosh, and San Jose were generally quite a bit larger and had a more prominent middle class than normalites' home communities, and were thus new and exciting to them.[45] As students acquired cultural capital, refined their tastes, and engaged in association building in literary societies, clubs, athletic teams, and religious organizations, and as they honed their social skills at parties and on excursions, they created their own version of the middle-class society they witnessed in town. As campus life at state normal schools thus initiated students into the middle class, it also challenged one of the central tenets of the middle-class society: separate gender spheres.

INVITING WOMEN INTO PUBLIC LIFE

While Horowitz places all of the first women who attended private colleges and state flagship universities in the outsider category, she explains that some female students by the late nineteenth century became *college women*, and created sororities and a form of college life that paralleled that of college men—with lower status at coeducational institutions under the label "coed." Some college women, especially at northern women's colleges, also challenged the larger society's gender boundaries by playing sports and asserting themselves in public settings. Horowitz stresses, though, that college women were from privileged backgrounds and that their engagement in college and public life related mainly to domestic issues within the female sphere in middle-class gender ideology, which reserved public intellectual, professional, and physical pursuits for men.[46] Neither of the conditions Horowitz lists for college women held at state normal schools, where students were from non-privileged backgrounds and the culture seemed to adhere to the rural and lower-class view—necessitated by practical considerations—that gender roles were rather flexible.[47] Female normalites interacted freely with male students, and were active and visible participants as well as leaders in intellectual and social life. Instead of relegating female students to second-class status as "coeds," campus life at state normal schools socialized women into public life.

In students' intellectually and professionally oriented activities, female normalites published papers, presented orations, and debated other women and, often, men. When the female members of the Lyceum Literary Society at Oshkosh, Wisconsin, debated the male members on whether "Lincoln was a greater man than Washington," the women were victorious in their defense of the negative side. In the public joint commencement exercises of the all-female Arethusa and all-male Gamma Sigma societies at Geneseo, New York, Dorothy Covey read an oration entitled "The Influence of the Great Writers." And after Elizabeth Shepard won the coeducational oratorical contest at Oshkosh with her speech on Ulysses S. Grant, 183 supporters accompanied her to the Wisconsin state normal contest at Stevens Point, cheering, "For Grant when she spoke in electrical tones … She made the cold shivers run down our backbones."[48] In campus publications, many of the sample lesson plans and articles on education were by female students. At Florence, Alabama, the all-female Dixie society debated the usefulness of Mother Goose rhymes in teaching with members of the all-male Dialectical and Lafayette societies in the audience. And in a Lyceum-Philakean debate at Oshkosh, Ellen McDonald argued in favor of a uniform system of textbooks and Adolph Ruehl backed her with a proposal for such a system.[49] McDonald, Shepard, and Covey, like other female normalites, presented themselves as intellectuals and professionals, and thus worthy participants in the public sphere.

Normal-school social events and athletics also affirmed and encouraged women's prominence in public. Women and men interacted freely at society parties, class receptions, and excursions, and shared regular meals either on campus or in boarding clubs. Receptions often included "farces"; in one at Oshkosh, *The Normal Advance* reported, "the cowboy girls beat any on the stage."[50] Athletics also placed women in the limelight. By the late 1890s, women's basketball was not only popular among the participants, it also drew many spectators. Geneseo's *The Normalian* reported in 1902 that an inter-society game on a Saturday evening drew a "large crowd." The crowds became so large at Oshkosh in 1897 that the players barred spectators, much to the dismay of male students. Men's appeals for readmittance were eventually successful, and the 1898 yearbook stated: "Members of the foot-ball team are often found watching the [women's basketball] game from a good safe position." *The Normal Advance* reported that a later game between two class teams drew "an audience of about three hundred invited guests."[51]

Female and male normal-school students created an intellectual, social, and athletic world in which women not only played active and visible roles, but also assumed leadership positions. Of course women headed all-female literary societies, YWCA chapters, and women's basketball teams. These leaders were prominent as they represented their organizations on campus and made welcoming speeches at receptions. Women were also part of the leadership structure of coeducational clubs and societies, and of their classes and student government. Men served as organization presidents in numbers disproportionately greater than their representation on campus, but women did occasionally serve as presidents, and often occupied other offices. When Cortland, New York, instituted a new student government in 1901, the first elected chief justice of the judicial branch was Grace PerLee, who consulted a lawyer on how to proceed. At San Jose, California, when the student body in 1898 elected Harriet Quilty its first president, *The Normal Pennant* remarked, "Miss Quilty needs no further introduction to our students, her great abilities as a leader are known from Juniors to Seniors." In the 29 semesters that followed Quilty's election, 19 more student-body presidents were female and 10 were male. It was fitting, therefore, that *The Normal Pennant* in 1909 described the "highest type" of woman as "the strong, robust, Grecian type who is able to stand on both feet and look the world in the face."[52] Indeed, academically oriented activities, social life, athletics, and leadership opportunities at state normal schools encouraged women students to enter the public sphere and "look the world in the face." This emphasis would soon change.

CONCLUSION AND EPILOGUE

In the words of one observer, state normal schools during their heyday from the 1870s through the 1900s had a "spirit ... of enthusiasm and mutual confidence."[53] This spirit arose at least in part from a vibrant campus life that enhanced students' intellectual and professional growth, welcomed all students into middle-class society, and invited women students into public life. Changes in this distinctive student life accompanied the transition of state normal schools into state teachers colleges beginning in the 1910s. The 1922 yearbook at the newly minted Chico State Teachers College in California exclaimed, "How we have grown! We have cast aside the swaddling clothes of infancy and donned the vestments of manhood."[54] As students celebrated the change, they began to adopt elements of the undergraduate culture that Helen Lefkowitz Horowitz calls *college life*. An educational researcher noted the downside of this shift, reporting in 1929 that teachers colleges had merely "taken over, by imitation of the nonprofessional college and university, the good and the bad in their extracurricular practice. These activities ... have created a hodge-podge of activity which is time consuming and questionable in its ultimate effect upon the individual and institutional life."[55] Indeed, teachers-college student life did far less than normal-school student life to expand the intellectual and social worlds of economically disadvantaged and female and/or minority students.

The state normal schools' literary societies, academic clubs, and student publications enabled students to enhance their knowledge of science, languages, history, the arts, literature, and current events, as well as teaching methods and the wider field of education. With the transition into teachers colleges, however, societies began to replace literary programs and debates on educational issues with social rituals and entertainment. Most literary societies became collegiate sororities or fraternities, or were replaced by these organizations, within ten years of the teachers-college transition. As early as the mid-1910s, yearbook descriptions of societies-cum-sororities at San Jose, California, consisted of accounts of initiations, rushes, cotillions, carnivals, teas, and parties; and the Agonian Society at Geneseo, New York, reported that it focused on "sisterhood, which, after all, is our chief sorority aim."[56]

At state normal schools, literary societies and other organizations also encouraged all students to assimilate into the middle-class society they witnessed in town by acquiring cultural capital, refining their tastes, and engaging in association building. At the same time, academically oriented activities, social life, athletics, and leadership opportunities enabled female students to enter the public sphere. The new sororities and fraternities at teachers colleges, however, created new class and gender distinctions on campus. A professor at Cedar Falls, Iowa, observed that with the rise of fraternities and sororities, "Spike-tail coats, cut-a-way vests and more elaborate gowns began to be in evidence in all social functions." Several students in the early 1930s at Oneonta, New York, protested the spread of sororities on the grounds that they were exclusive. Also accompanying the teachers-college transition, the spread of residence halls on campus helped to insulate students from the middle-class town society. The majority of these new facilities were for women only, which subjected them to a higher standard of behavioral scrutiny than the men.[57]

Reinforcing the decline of intellectualism, introduction of social-class distinctions, and restriction of women students in campus life, these institutions embraced the collegiate cult of football as part of their transition into state teachers colleges. Women continued to play basketball, but spectators, including many female students, turned to men's sports. And as institutions established inter-scholastic leagues for men, they banned inter-school contests among women. A new way for individual women to seize the spotlight soon appeared, however: in 1926, freshman Hazel Cline was crowned the first homecoming queen at Southwestern State Teachers College in Weatherford, Oklahoma.[58] Along with the normal schools' transformation into teachers colleges—and later into state colleges and regional universities—student life at these institutions lost much of what had made it distinctive. Although an examination of student life at state normal schools demonstrates that Horowitz's *college life* was not as widespread in the late nineteenth and very early twentieth centuries as she claims, this brief look at student life at state teachers colleges suggests that this version of college life became more dominant by the second and third decades of the twentieth century. Horowitz, who is critical of the anti-intellectualism and elitism of college life at private and state flagship institutions,[59] would likely agree that this was not a positive development.

NOTES

1. Martha M. Knapp quoted in *Historical Sketch of the State Normal School at San Jose, California, with a Catalogue of Its Graduates and a Record of Their Work for Twenty-Seven Years* (Sacramento: J. D. Young, 1889), 69–70.

2. S. E. Rothery, "Some Educational Institutions: Pilgrimages About San Jose," *The Overland Monthly* 30 (July 1897): 75.

3. Christine A. Ogren, *The American State Normal School: "An Instrument of Great Good"* (New York: Palgrave Macmillan, 2005) (hereafter, *ASNS*). For a list of all state normal schools in the U.S., see appendix.

4. Helen Lefkowitz Horowitz, *Campus Life: Undergraduate Cultures from the End of the Eighteenth Century to the Present* (Chicago: University of Chicago Press, 1987).

5. Historians have only recently begun to analyze the role of state normal schools and former state normal schools in the US higher education system. Thelin's comprehensive history incorporates normal schools but isolates them in separate sections of chapters, while Dorn includes San Jose State Normal School as one of the 11 institutions' service to the "common

good" that he examines in depth. John R. Thelin, *A History of American Higher Education* (Baltimore: Johns Hopkins University Press, 2004); Charles Dorn, *For the Common Good: A New History of Higher Education in America* (Ithaca, NY: Cornell University Press, 2017). See also Michael S. Hevel, "Public Displays of Student Learning: The Role of Literary Societies in Early Iowa Higher Education," *The Annals of Iowa* 70, no. 1 (Winter 2011): 1–35; and Marc A. VanOverbeke, "Out of the Quietness, a Clamor: 'We Want Football!' The California State Colleges, Educational Opportunity, and Athletics," *History of Education Quarterly* 53, no. 4 (November 2013): 430–54.

6. Horowitz, *Campus Life*, 14–15, chapter 3.

7. *ASNS*, 65–8; William Marshall French and Florence Smith French, *College of the Empire State: A Centennial History of The New York State College for Teachers at Albany* ([Albany, NY?], 1944), 95, 258; Elizabeth Tyler Bugaighis, "Blackboard Diplomacy: The Role of American Normal Schools in Exporting Education to Latin America, 1891–1924" (paper presented at the annual meeting of the American Educational Research Association, New Orleans, April 2000); Tom W. Nichols, *Rugged Summit* (San Marcos, TX: The University Press, Southwest Texas State University, 1970), 94.

8. *ASNS*, 68–74; David A. Gould, "Policy and Pedagogues: School Reform and Teacher Professionalization in Massachusetts, 1840–1920" (Ph.D. diss., Brandeis University, 1977), 87; Robert T. Brown, *The Rise and Fall of the People's Colleges: The Westfield State Normal School, 1839 to 1914* (Westfield, MA: Institute for Massachusetts Studies, Westfield State College, 1988), 79; Irving H. Hart, *The First 75 Years* (Cedar Falls, IA: Iowa State Teachers College, 1951), 116; *A History of the State Normal School of Kansas for the First Twenty-Five Years* (Emporia, KS, 1889), 45; Dorothy Rogers, *Oswego: Fountainhead of Teacher Education: A Century in the Sheldon Tradition* (New York: Appleton-Century-Crofts, 1961), 58. See also Christine A. Ogren, "Rethinking the 'Nontraditional' Student from a Historical Perspective: State Normal Schools in the Late Nineteenth and Early Twentieth Centuries," *The Journal of Higher Education* 74 (November/December 2003): 640–64.

9. Egbert R. Isbell, *A History of Eastern Michigan University, 1849–1965* (Ypsilanti, MI: Eastern Michigan University Press, 1971), 138; J. M. McKenzie, *History of the Peru State Normal* (Auburn, NE: The Nemaha County Republican, 1911), 96.

10. Principal's annual report, 1910–1911, quoted in Arthur Charles Forst, Jr., "From Normal School to State College: The Growth and Development of Eastern Connecticut State College From 1899 to 1959" (Ph.D. diss., University of Connecticut, 1980), 101.

11. Rothery, "Some Educational Institutions," 74; State Superintendent quoted in Ellis A. Stebbins, *The OCE Story* (Monmouth, OR: Oregon College of Education, 1973), 46.

12. Horowitz, *Campus Life*, chapters 2–3. Horowitz's third group of college students, *rebels*, would appear in the early twentieth century. Horowitz, *Campus Life*, chapter 4.

13. *ASNS*, 85–106, 121–42.

14. Horowitz, *Campus Life*, chapter 2. Frederick Rudolph, *The American College and University: A History* (Athens, GA: University of Georgia Press, [1962] 1990), chapter 7. Hevel provides an extensive discussion of the historiography of student literary societies and argues that they remained active at three different higher-education institutions in Iowa— the (State) University of Iowa, Cornell College, and Iowa State Normal School—into the 1920s and 1930s. See Hevel, "Public Displays."

15. *ASNS*, 108–13; George Frank Sammis, "A History of the Maine Normal Schools" (Ph.D. diss., University of Connecticut, 1970), 203; Melvin Frank Fiegel, "A History of Southwestern State College, 1903–1953" (Ed.D. diss., Oklahoma State University, 1968), 26–7; Clayton C. Mau, *Brief History of the State University Teachers College, Geneseo, New York* (Geneseo, NY, 1956), 8; W. Wayne Dedman, *Cherishing This Heritage: The Centennial History of the State University College at Brockport, New York* (New York: Appleton-Century-Crofts, 1969), 124; Carey W. Brush, *In Honor and Good Faith: A History of the State University College at Oneonta, New York* (Oneonta, NY: The Faculty-Student Association of State University Teachers College at Oneonta, 1965), 49.

16. J. S. Nasmith, "An Open Letter From J. Nasmith," *Platteville Witness* 63 (April 13, 1932), 2.

17. *ASNS*, 107; Dedman, *Cherishing This Heritage*, 129; Arthur C. Boyden, *The History of Bridgewater Normal School* (Bridgewater, MA: Bridgewater Normal Alumni Association, 1933), 51; "Normal Index Department," *The Pacific Coast Teacher: A Monthly Magazine Devoted to the Educational Interests of the Pacific Coast* 1 (October 1891): 61; 1 (December 1891): 105.

18. *ASNS*, 107; Brush, *In Honor*, 50; *The Pedagogue* (San Marcos, TX, 1908), 112, Southwest Texas State University Archives, Special Collections, Alkek Library, San Marcos, TX (hereafter SWTA).

19. *ASNS*, 107, 113–14; McKenzie, *History of the Peru State Normal*, 81; Dedman, *Cherishing This Heritage*, 125–26; *The Normal Advance* 5 (March 1899): 120–23, University of Wisconsin-Oshkosh Archives, Area Research Center, Polk Library, Oshkosh, Wisconsin (hereafter UWOA); Agonian, Constitution and Alpha Chapter Secretaries' Reports, November 5, 1897, College Archives, Milne Library, State University of New York

College at Geneseo, Geneseo, NY (hereafter CASUNYG); *The Normalian* 1 (June 20, 1900): 4, CASUNYG; *The Normal Pennant* 6 (June 1903): 79, San Jose State University Archives, Special Collections, SJSU Library, San Jose, CA (hereafter SJSUA).

20. Isbell, *A History of Eastern Michigan University*, 334; *The Pegagogue* (1907), 112, SWTA.

21. *The Normal Advance* 2 (January-February 1896): 60, UWOA.

22. *ASNS*, 114–15; Susan Vaughn, "The History of State Teachers College, Florence, Alabama," *Bulletin of the State Teachers College, Florence, Alabama* 18 (Supplemental, 193?), 31, University Collection, Collier Library Archives, University of North Alabama, Florence, AL (hereafter UCUNA); *Oshkosh State Teachers College: The First Seventy-Five Years* (Oshkosh, WI: Oshkosh State Teachers College, 1946), 36; David Sands Wright, *Fifty Years at the Teachers College: Historical and Personal Reminiscences* (Cedar Falls, IA: Iowa State Teachers College, 1926), 74; *The Normal Pennant* 4 (June 1901): 18, SJSUA; *The Pedagogue* (1905), 61, SWTA.; Brush, *In Honor*, 288; Beach quoted in Albert Salisbury, *Historical Sketches of the First Quarter-Century of the State Normal School at Whitewater, Wisconsin* (Madison, WI: Tracy, Gibbs & Co., 1893), 91.

23. *ASNS*, 114; Dedman, *Cherishing This Heritage*, 125; *The Pedagogue* (1909), 98–9, SWTA; Brush, *In Honor*, 52.

24. *ASNS*, 116–18; *The Normal Advance* 5 (December 1898): 67, UWOA; Agonian, Constitution and Alpha Chapter Secretaries' Reports, December 7, 1895, CASUNYG; *The Normal Advance*, special edition (November 1, 1912), UWOA.

25. *ASNS*, 115–16; Bessie L. Park, *Cortland—Our Alma Mater: A History of Cortland Normal School and the State University of New York Teachers College at Cortland, 1869–1959* (Cortland, NY, 1960), 41; Agonian, Constitution and Alpha Chapter Secretaries' Reports, April 12, 1895 and October 31, 1899, CASUNYG; *The Pedagogue* (1907), 51, SWTA; Rogers, *Oswego: Fountainhead*, 88.

26. *Echoes from the Geneseo Normal* 1 (June 1905): no page numbers, CASUNYG.

27. *ASNS*, 143–44; *The Normal Advance* 1 (September–October 1894): 8, UWOA; *The Normal Student* 1 (November 26, 1901): 9; 2 (November 21, 1902): 7–9; 2 (May 20, 1903): 2–8, SJSUA; *The Pedagogue* (1911), 102–3, SWTA.

28. Isbell, *A History of Eastern Michigan University*, 333; Rural Sociology Seminar records quoted in James O. Knauss, *The First Fifty Years: A History of Western Michigan College of Education* (Kalamazoo, MI: Western Michigan College of Education, 1953), 18–19.

29. *ASNS*, 145–48; Philalethean Society, Constitution and 2 volumes of Meeting Minutes, vol. 1, March 18, 1892, CASUNYG; Lafayette Society: Records, April 24, 1880–May 1, 1880 and October 6, 1882–October 13, 1882, UCUNA; *The Normal Advance* 3 (November–December 1896): 31, UWOA.

30. *The Normal Index* 1 (January 1886): 41; 3 (January 1888): 55–6, SJSUA; *The Normal Pennant* 2 (September 1899): 4–6, SJSUA; *The Normal Advance* 1 (January–February 1895): 6, UWOA.

31. For further discussion of professional-status issues and normal-school teacher education, see *ASNS*, 121–122.

32. Horowitz, *Campus Life*, 14.

33. Charles A. Harper, *Development of the Teachers College in the United States, with Special Reference to the Illinois State Normal University* (Bloomington, IL: McKnight & McKnight, 1935), 112.

34. Cindy S. Aron, *Working at Play: A History of Vacations in the United States* (New York: Oxford University Press, 1999), chapter 5; Marguerite S. Shaffer, *See America First: Tourism and National Identity, 1880–1940* (Washington, DC: Smithsonian Books, 2001).

35. *ASNS*, 115; *The Normal Advance* 6 (October 1899): 33, UWOA; Dixie Club, Roll and minutes of meetings, October 25, 1912, UCUNA; Ladies Literary Society, Minutes, October 8, 1880 and February 4, 1881, UWOA; *The Normal Star* 2 (February 23, 1912): 1, SWTA.

36. *ASNS*, 115–17; *The Normal Student* 2 (November 21, 1902), 5, Castleton State College Archives, Vermont Room, Coolidge Library, Castleton, Vermont; Agonian, Constitution and Alpha Chapter Secretaries' Reports, April 12, 1901, CASUNYG; *The Normal Pennant* 4 (June 1901): 19–20, SJSUA; *The Pedagogue* (1909), 74, SWTA.

37. John W. Cook and James V. McHugh, *A History of the Illinois State Normal University* (Normal, IL: Illinois State Normal University, 1882).

38. *ASNS*, 118; Dedman, *Cherishing This Heritage*, 124–25; Brush, *In Honor*, 49; *A History of the State Normal School of Kansas*, 67.

39. Robert D. Putnam, *Bowling Alone: The Collapse and Revival of American Community* (New York: Simon & Schuster, 2000), chapter 23, quotation on 383.

40. *ASNS*, 170–73; *The Normal Pennant* 1 (November 1898): 10; 3 (October 1900): 9, SJSUA; *The Normalian* 3 (February 1902): 12, CASUNYG; *Echoes from the Geneseo Normal* 1 (June 1905), no page numbers, CASUNYG.

41. *ASNS*, 166; Helen E. Marshall, *Grandest of Enterprises: Illinois State Normal University, 1857–1957* (Normal, IL: Illinois State Normal University, 1956), 148–49; Students' Christian Union quoted in Park, *Cortland—Our Alma Mater*, 97.

42. *ASNS*, 166; Knapp quoted in *Historical Sketch of the State Normal School at San Jose*, 69–70; Marshall, *Grandest of Enterprises*, 225; *New York State Teachers College at Buffalo; A History, 1871–1946* (Buffalo, NY: New York State Teachers College at Buffalo, 1946), 143.

43. *ASNS*, 163–64; *The Normal Advance* 5 (October 1898): 32; 6 (November 1899): 55; 6 (June 1900): 205; 9 (May 1903): 164–66; 13 (June 1907): 249, UWOA; *The Normal Index* 2 (May 1887): 131, SJSUA; Mary Frances McKinney, May C. Hansen, and Gladys Tyng, "Student Life," in *Three Decades of Progress: Eastern Kentucky State Teachers College*, ed. Jonathan T. Dorris (Richmond, KY: Eastern Kentucky State Teachers College, 1936), 150.

44. Wilson quoted in Lowell H. Harrison, "Gordon Wilson's Normal Education: Western Kentucky State Normal School, 1980–1913," *Register of the Kentucky Historical Society* 86, no. 1 (Winter 1988): 29; *Annual Catalogue of the State Normal College, Florence, Alabama, 1898–99*, 41, UCUNA.

45. *ASNS*, 154–60; *The Normal Star* 1 (April 21, 1911), SWTA; William Frederick Hartman, "The History of Colorado State College of Education: The Normal School Period, 1890–1911" (Ph.D. diss., Colorado State College of Education, 1951), 164.

46. Horowitz, *Campus Life*, chapter 9. See also Lynn D. Gordon, *Gender and Higher Education in the Progressive Era* (New Haven, CT: Yale University Press, 1990); and Barbara Miller Solomon, *In the Company of Educated Women: A History of Women and Higher Education in America* (New Haven, CT: Yale University Press, 1985), chapter 7. Radke-Moss argues that female students at land-grant institutions during this period transgressed gender boundaries and negotiated a more gender-inclusive campus life. Andrea G. Radke-Moss, *Bright Epoch: Women & Coeducation in the American West* (Lincoln, NE: University of Nebraska Press, 2008).

47. Some work in women's history emphasizes that separate-spheres ideology had little impact on the less-privileged classes and races. See, for example, Gerda Lerner, *The Majority Finds Its Past: Placing Women in History* (New York: Oxford University Press, 1979), 15–30; and Sara M. Evans, *Born for Liberty: A History of Women in America* (New York: Simon & Schuster, 1997).

48. *ASNS*, 106–18; *The Normal Advance* 7 (March 1901): 122, UWOA; Arethusa Sorority, Program, "Anniversary exercises held at Normal Hall, Geneseo, by Arethusa Fraternity with Gamma Sigma Fraternity, 1900," CASUNYG; *The Normal Advance* 5 (March 1899): 120–23, UWOA.

49. *ASNS*, 142–49; Minutes of Dixie Club, April 25, 1902, in Organizations, Files, UCUNA; *The Normal Advance* 10 (June 1904): 237–38, UWOA.

50. *ASNS*, 163–67; *The Normal Advance* 13 (March 1907): 153, UWOA.

51. *ASNS*, 170–72; *The Normalian* 3 (March 1902): 10, CASUNYG; *The Normal Advance* 3 (March-April 1897): 78, UWOA; *The Quiver* (1898), 113, UWOA; *The Normal Advance* 6 (December 1899): 71, UWOA.

52. *ASNS*, 173–74; Park, *Cortland—Our Alma Mater*, 104; *The Normal Pennant* 1 (May 1898): 4, SJSUA; Estelle Greathead, *The Story of an Inspiring Past: Historical Sketches of the San Jose State Teachers College From 1862 to 1928* (San Jose, CA: San Jose State Teachers College, 1928), 69; *The Normal Pennant* 12 (June 1909): 57, SJSUA.

53. Rothery, "Some Educational Institutions," 75.

54. Chico yearbook quoted in Maxine Ollie Merlino, "A History of the California State Normal Schools—Their Origin, Growth, and Transformation into Teachers Colleges" (Ed.D. diss, University of Southern California, 1962), 337.

55. Mary Moffett Ledger, *The Social Background and Activities of Teachers College Students* (New York: Teachers College Bureau of Publications, 1929), 66.

56. *ASNS*, 206–07; *Senior Year Book: San Jose State Normal School* (1915), SJSUA; *The Normalian* (1917), 75, CASUNYG.

57. *ASNS*, 207; Wright, *Fifty Years at the Teachers College*, 213–14; Brush, *In Honor*, 187–88.

58. *ASNS*, 207–08; Jerry G. Nye, *Southwestern Oklahoma State University: The First 100 Years* (Weatherford, OK: Southwestern Oklahoma State University, 2001), 55.

59. Horowitz, *Campus Life*, chapters 1–2.

CHAPTER 6

Instruction in Living Beautifully: Social Education and Heterosocializing in White College Sororities

Margaret L. Freeman

Over the course of the twentieth century, white social sororities gained and maintained an image as preeminent and exclusive social organizations for women on college campuses in the United States. The secretive social clubs grew into powerful, national organizations by promoting themselves as alternative, or even superior, "families" for young women attending college and living away from the confines of the conventional home for the first time. Originally formed by women students in the 1870s through 1910s to provide a supportive space and social outlet comparable to white men's Greek-letter fraternities, sororities offered their members social inclusion and campus popularity. They also claimed to impart social lessons to impressionable young women who were away from the traditional home during the formative transition from girlhood to womanhood. The goal was to help women develop the habits and characteristics of white, middle-class womanhood, which required that they maintain a feminine appearance and aspire to become good housewives and nurturing mothers

M. L. Freeman (✉)
Portland, ME, USA

© The Author(s) 2018
C. A. Ogren, M. A. VanOverbeke (eds.),
Rethinking Campus Life, Historical Studies in Education,
https://doi.org/10.1007/978-3-319-75614-1_6

115

for the next generation of white Americans. Sororities guaranteed social interaction with supposedly "desirable" fraternity men from the middle- to upper classes and promised women a nationwide network of socially connected "sisters" as they became alumnae. At the same time, however, the organizations' increasing focus on what I term "heterosocializing" between sorority sisters and fraternity men undermined the supportive, women's-only space of the sorority chapter. By emphasizing the physical appeal of sorority members as a way to promote socialization and interac- tion with fraternity members, the sorority members began to connect their identity, value, and understanding of self with their physical beauty.

Few works have delved into the complicated history of men's and wom- en's Greek-letter organizations (GLOs) and their impact on college stu- dents and campus life. Diana Turk's *Bound By a Mighty Vow* examines the early decades of National Panhellenic Conference (NPC) sororities through a focus primarily on what is commonly considered the "first" sorority (or "women's fraternity"), Kappa Alpha Theta, from its founding in 1870 to 1920. Her richly detailed account ably presents the stark differ- ences in interests among the early generations of sorority women. She found that whereas late-nineteenth-century sorority women exuded a seri- ousness of purpose, driven by responsibility as the first generation of col- lege women, their counterparts in the first two decades of the twentieth century appeared to the earlier alumnae as little more than social butter- flies, planning parties and seeking dates, with little thought of the educa- tional aspect of college life.[1] Deborah Elizabeth Whaley's *Disciplining Women* critically examines black sororities, which, like the separate GLOs for Jewish and Catholic students, formed in response to the discriminatory membership practices of white, Protestant sororities. Through her study of Alpha Kappa Alpha, the first black sorority, established in 1908, Whaley argues that African American sororities in the twentieth century provided important locations of social and political organizing for black women, but that they also replicated some of the conservative, classist, and heteronor- mative aspects of the white sororities that I discuss in this chapter.[2] Nicholas Syrett's *The Company He Keeps* thoroughly explores the complexity of white sororities' male counterparts in the nineteenth and twentieth centu- ries, by focusing on fraternity membership through the lens of gender and masculinity. My work here and elsewhere highlights the troublesome nature of women's Greek-letter groups, while problematizing their will- ingness to operate ancillary to men's fraternities.[3] I see heterosocializing as fundamental to sororities' purpose in the twentieth century to provide social opportunities, but also troublesome when such socializing came to revolve primarily around attracting the admiring gazes of fraternity members.

In this chapter, which covers the period from roughly 1910 to 1970, I argue that while national sororities claimed to build a supportive sisterhood, their intense focus on preparing members for conventional, white, middle-class womanhood and their emphasis on physical appeal undermined positive aspects of the women's-only space, as it fostered a competitive and controlling environment. Sororities promoted conventionally "feminine" activities for members and alumnae, which orbited around an ultimate goal of marriage and homemaking. All of this focus meant that heterosocializing would become a primary interest of the sororities. Rather than simply instructing women in manners, social graces, and high moral character that would supposedly prepare them as "ideal" wives and mothers, by the 1920s, sororities also specifically began to instruct members on appearance and personality with designs on attracting male attention. Throughout the twentieth century, sororities relied on the acceptance of and promotion by elite fraternities to assure their popularity on campus. As such, gaining and maintaining a good reputation was tied to sorority members' physical appeal to popular men. Through training and criticism, sorority chapters monitored their members' behavior and appearance so as to fit accepted middle-class norms and to ensure that the "right" type of men (fraternity men and other "Big Men on Campus") would seek them out.

This chapter considers sororities' focus on heterosocialization through an examination of national sorority leaders' preoccupation with members' heterosocial interaction as a primary step in the development of domestic womanhood; behavioral lessons and standards for heterosocializing provided and enforced by the sorority; dangers posed by the emphasis on private, heterosocial spaces; and rush practices designed to perpetuate a membership base that would enhance future heterosocialization with popular men's fraternities. I first discuss how national sorority leaders influenced college members' interest in heterosocial interaction as early as the 1910s, when they reminded members that educated women's highest calling was to be a homemaker. College members reinforced this need for controlled heterosocialization, making sure that sisters learned socially appropriate ways to behave with men as friends or dates, so as to guard the reputation of the sorority chapter. Second, I consider the ways in which the spaces of heterosocialization could be dangerous for women. As sorority women often attended parties and other private events where alcohol was readily available and where men were often inebriated, they ran a greater risk of unwanted sexual activity, which we would now recognize as rape or sexual assault. Third, I examine how rush, the process by which sorority chapters selected new members each year, became another space where sororities attempted to further their heterosocial goals and develop strong relationships with fraternities. Chapters selected new members to meet popular standards of physical beauty and to appeal to the right fraternities. The ability of a sorority to extend "bids," or invitations, to the most physically attractive rushees was, then, a matter of chapter survival. Sorority women's attention to heterosocializing encompassed the organizations' activities, social training, membership, and ideals for sorority womanhood. This chapter is arranged chronologically and touches on all of these themes as they appear in particular time periods. Overall, it highlights how sorority chapters shaped the campus life of their members in fundamental and profound ways.

HETEROSOCIAL INTERACTION, DOMESTICITY, AND WOMANHOOD

As women's enrollment on college campuses, and their presence in the paid workplace, increased in the early decades of the twentieth century, so did public concerns over the "defeminization" of white women. In a modernizing nation with increasingly visible and unrooted populations of immigrants and African Americans, pronouncements of "race suicide," which accused Anglo-American women of endangering the supremacy of the white race by failing to fulfill their "duty" as wives and mothers, struck a chord.[4] As pseudofamilial organizations, which claimed a dignified, genteel, and often embellished Anglo-Saxon heritage, sororities believed they could provide the solution to such public fears by promoting members who would go forth to become pillars of their communities and, most importantly, mothers of the next generation of white, Protestant, middle- to upper-class American citizens. By promoting the ability to craft a homelike atmosphere for women at college, sororities were able to gain acceptance from deans of women, other university administrators, and anxious families of women leaving home to attend college from the 1870s to the 1920s. These organizations sought to reinforce a familial ideal by carving out specific domestic living spaces for their chapters and by teaching members that the ideal woman always remembered and placed first in her activities her duty to her home.[5]

Although sororities touted their organizations as models of domesticity replete with traditional sorority homes, the daily reality of sorority life did not mirror conventional, heteronormative ideals of family living. As single-sex organizations, sororities *could* be seen as a threat to heterosexuality and the status quo in gender relations. Like women's colleges in the early twentieth century that faced public scrutiny as spaces where female friend-ships might foster lesbian relationships among white, middle- to upper-class women, sororities, too, appeared as cloistered, women's-only living spaces.[6] Men were conspicuously absent from the sorority-defined familial space. Sorority women thus learned their socially prescribed roles as wives and caretakers in a space unlike what they supposedly would inhabit in adulthood. As public fears over career-minded, single women and same-sex relationships escalated during the 1920s and 1930s, these all-female spaces, once viewed as safe havens for young, impressionable women, took on a more sinister cast.[7] The fear was that sorority sisters might become so accustomed to their sorority "family" that they would be unwilling to graduate to a heteronormative model after college.

As a way to deflect attention from the possibility that sorority chapter houses could foster same-sex sexual relationships or produce "domineering," "unfeminine" women, national sororities began to publicize their greater interest in preparing members for heterosexual marriage by encouraging regular socializing with fraternity men and other men from the same social, religious, and racial backgrounds. Sorority journals, which featured chapter reports outlining successions of parties with fraternities, highlighted the importance of such parties and interactions among similar groups.[8] Pledge guidebooks from national sororities in the 1920s similarly encouraged a proper adjustment to college social life, including an emphasis on dating men of the "appropriate" background.[9] These guidebooks also focused on fashioning oneself in a manner so as to be physically attractive and socially pleasing to young men, and this emphasis only increased as the century pro-gressed. This shift in emphasis from the sorority chapter as a self-contained, women's support network to a launching pad for social improvement directed at heterosocializing and marriageability further ensured that sorori-ties and their members would not challenge male authority.

Sororities focused on more than promoting dates with the right sort of men, as they also emphasized the development of a successful domestic life as the primary goal for young women. The 1911 edition of the *Handbook of Kappa Alpha Theta* sought to describe "some distinguished members" of the sorority: "Since the home is woman's great center of activity, it follows that the distinction of a woman's fraternity cannot be gauged by her roll of members who have gained recognition in the business or professional world. Even to name the members who, as beautiful home-makers, are fulfilling the fraternity's highest ambitions for her members is out of the question. But since such ideal positions are not occupied by all members, the fraternity would also pay tribute to her many members who are courageously and cheerfully bearing a share in more public lines of endeavor."[10] Those members who did not reach what the sorority viewed as the epitome of womanhood still received encouragement, although the anonymous author's words suggested that the women in public were doing work to which sorority alumnae should not aspire. "Courageously and cheerfully," their sisters were "bearing a share" in public endeavors—a description seemingly designed to elicit sympathy more than admiration.

Particularly at universities that were majority-male, sororities sold themselves as necessary components of women's education, providing womanly guidance that the universities may not have been prepared to dispense. For those who felt that coeducation "might take the bloom off of the peach," as University of Georgia (UGA) president David C. Barrow put it in 1922, sororities could be just the antidote to contemporary fears that allowing young women to attend institutions of higher education would somehow diminish their "femininity" or "unsex" them entirely. And for those who worried that the proximity of male and female students would lead to dangerous sexual situations, sororities could also claim to teach proper modes of heterosocial engagement.[11] Sororities became a key part of the monitoring system for college women's behavior by the 1920s and would continue in that role through the 1970s, earning the respect of many campus administrators during this period.

Many college-educated women during the interwar period sought to balance career interests with the work of motherhood and homemaking. Public criticism of white women's explorations of these new "freedoms" only increased during the Great Depression, when economic strife stymied white men's employment opportunities.[12] Attuned to popular sentiment, sororities understood that the best way to continue building a positive association in the public mind was to prepare "nonthreatening" women, who saw their ideal post-college activities as wife and homemaker. While sororities' national journals in the 1910s and 1920s had focused on the primacy of members' futures as homemakers, they also had discussed employment and volunteer options for recent graduates. The journals began to shift focus in the 1930s to suggest that professional work outside of the home was not as fulfilling as heterosexual marriage and homemaking. In the 1933 issue of Zeta Tau Alpha (ZTA)'s journal *Themis,* an alumna and former dean of women lamented her initial concentration on career rather than homemaking, as well as how that might have affected the college women she advised. She realized only later, "to what extent [she] represented for those girls the glories of a 'career,' and consequently, the secondary place of home-making," when one of her former pupils wrote to congratulate her on her marriage by saying, "Well there must be something in it after all, if even you have succumbed."[13]

STANDARDS FOR HETEROSOCIALIZATION

As National Panhellenic sororities grew and spread to college campuses across the United States, leaders sought to standardize rules for rushing and to present a positive public image of the organizations. By the 1910s, national sorority leaders introduced "standards" to address issues including the "type" of women allowed to join the groups and the training given to sorority members. Sororities designed standards to safeguard traits among members, from scholarship, to appearance, to personality, to those with whom members could interact. By the 1920s and 1930s, meeting sorority standards involved greater attention to details of appearance and specific behaviors marking a "personality" type, rather than the more nebulous standards of good "character" that sororities held earlier. In nineteenth-century America, an individual's character was directly tied to moral standards and self-control, and contributed to a sense of social order. However, as cultural historian Warren Susman has noted, the United States in the first two decades of the twentieth century saw the transition from a culture valuing an individual's character and moral bearing to one invested in personality, or "the quality of being Somebody."[14] This shift in understanding clearly took root among sororities, which were, in effect, self-improvement societies for young women. "It is an established fact," stated Minnie Allen Hubbard, former grand president of Alpha Delta Pi, in 1939, "that a well-rounded education includes more than intellectual attainments. A charming personality and social graces should be the mark of a college bred woman."[15]

The sororities' focus on "personality" was also a direct result of the mental hygiene movement, which gained force in the United States during the 1920s and located "personality" as the central factor in mental health. Public attention focused on identifying personality "disorders" such as "evasiveness, seclusiveness, passivity, introversion—or the 'shut-in personality,'" all of which were designated by mental hygienists as "early symptoms of potential mental illness."[16] By seeking to identify the pledges as "types" of women who needed specific training based on their personality, sororities were unofficial participants in this mental hygiene work. By the 1920s, Kappa Alpha Theta's national prescriptions included participation in campus activities and heterosexual dating, attendance at social affairs, demonstration of hostessing skills, and an attention to "good grooming and proper clothes for proper occasions" to create an "attractive personal appearance." These behavioral standards, the sorority's national leadership held, would convey the image of "Thetas" as "good campus citizens" who displayed a successful "adjustment to social conditions" of college life and demonstrated appropriate heterosocial skills and abilities.[17]

Sororities' pledge handbooks and etiquette manuals provided women students with behavioral guidelines and were particularly important means of instructing pledges on the expectations for and limitations on their social and sexual behavior. By introducing the women to heterosocial situations, the sisters hoped to keep them from having to navigate such situations on their own without an understanding of the rules of proper social interaction. In the 1920s, Kappa Alpha Theta recommended introducing pledges to "the college social world at one or more formal parties." It would give pledges a chance to "know the chapter's friends and the most worthwhile men students." Introductions between pledges and potential suitors, the handbook's authors explained, "should be frequent." The elder sorority sisters would also monitor pledges' dating conduct when accompanying them on "double dates."[18]

Beginning in the 1930s, many sorority etiquette guides focused on how to present oneself as charming, graceful, and physically attractive for potential dates. The authors of the *Tri Delta Hostess* (1937) suggested that women maintain a charming bearing and "hold the head high (a good hairdo looks better that way), throw out the chest, and by all means pull in the abdomen."[19] Appearance and personality were the primary points of instruction in the *Hostess* because of their importance to the overall image of the sorority. "A sorority's personality," the authors explained, "is expressed through the appearance and behavior of its members. There are various reasons why a sorority 'rates' on campus, but, almost invariably, the group is a leader whose members are uniformly well groomed and posses[s] a good share of savoir faire."[20] With their comments that connected campus standing to appearance and social fluency, the *Hostess*'s authors basically admitted that a sorority chapter's popularity was based on superficial, "at-first-sight" assessments of the membership as a whole. So while sororities advocated social training to benefit the individual woman, the actual desired result of social training was to make individual members more attractive to men and, thus, to increase the standing and reputation of the sorority.

On the chapter level, sorority women learned social lessons not only through guidebooks, but also through instruction by other members who stood ready to correct any behaviors that might reflect poorly on the chapter as a whole. According to the 1931 minutes of Delta Beta Chapter of Kappa Kappa Gamma at the Woman's College of Duke University, the chapter used its Standards Committee as an authoritative body to "discipline" and "make suggestions to pledges." Instead of having individual sisters bear the responsibility for disciplining pledges, the Standards Committee would "mete out punishment."[21] The Social Standards Committee of Duke's Gamma Epsilon Chapter of Phi Mu arranged to have a female consultant visit campus in 1939 "to hold individual conferences with the girls in order to suggest improvements in their personal appearance, et cetera."[22] A sorority would monitor members' behavior in an environment where "social conduct [was] discussed freely, and criticism offered where it [was] due."[23]

During World War II, even as the lack of male students on campus limited heterosocializing, sororities continued to police women students' behavior in the unfamiliar landscape of the wartime home front, where women might date servicemen about whom they knew little or nothing. "There were so many blind dates during the war," recalled a Tri-Delta from William and Mary's class of 1944, "none of us knew them (or they us)."[24] Many perceived the demographic background of university populations to be broadening in the years after World War II as the Serviceman's Readjustment Act (1944), or G.I. Bill, enabled returning veterans to enroll at colleges. Sororities claimed to provide a protected social space where members would receive special guidance toward "appropriate" male dates and away from men who were social pariahs, possibly dangerous, or unable to meet expected middle-class standards.[25]

In the post-World War II period, as public pressure mounted for racial desegregation of social spaces in the United States, sororities' guidance toward "appropriate" dates also came to include guarding against instances of interracial heterosocialization in order to allay white fears of miscegenation.

NPC sororities' leadership sought to keep their national organizations white as a number of campus chapters sought to invite African American students into membership. On newly desegregated university campuses in the southern United States, as well as at many nonsouthern campuses where black students had enrolled in small numbers for decades but remained socially segregated, the privatized, white, heterosocial spaces of sororities and fraternities provided an insulated space where members from similar class backgrounds could interact.[26]

By the 1950s and 1960s, sorority life emphasized the idea that white college women should be pursuing an "MRS Degree." Alpha Chi Omega's 1961 etiquette guide *For She's an Alpha Chi!* emphasized that "dating is one of the concerns uppermost in every girl's mind." Whether she was "a new arrival on the college scene or an upperclassman," they explained, "the main concern for girls is where to meet the dates [they] desire."[27] The guides recommended that sorority sisters help find dates for pledges and new members. It was up to the elder sorority sisters to vet possible dates and advise new members about men on campus whom the chapter perceived to be "fast" (meaning that they expected their dates to engage in sex play, and perhaps intercourse, without establishing a firm romantic commitment beforehand). By guiding the pledges and younger members away from men who would not understand and respect the women's need to abide by middle-class standards for sexual behavior, the elder sisters were also safeguarding the sorority's reputation. If they failed to educate their members about the possible hazards of sexual activity, the entire group could suffer as a result.

At the same time, sorority chapters expected that their members would attend all parties when fraternities invited them. Regardless of the night of the week, these events took place at fraternity houses and featured alcohol, making them incompatible with schoolwork and study. The University of North Carolina's (UNC) dean of women Katherine Carmichael regularly heard concerns from sorority women and advisers over the issue of compulsory parties that were regularly held on weeknights at fraternity houses, which operated without housemothers to act as chaperones (an issue that did not seem to garner attention from national officers).[28] Despite these complaints, Carmichael still appeared to appreciate the groups' use of peer pressure to affect necessary changes in a pledge or active member's dating habits or perceived moral rectitude. In a speech to the Alpha Epsilon Chapter of Alpha Chi Omega sorority at the University of Alabama in 1956, Carmichael praised sorority life for helping young women to "develop wholesome attitudes, through group pressure, toward the opposite sex."[29]

Such "wholesome" attitudes supported the sexual double-standard, which proscribed women's sexual activity outside of marriage while also teaching that women should act as guardians against men's "uncontrollable," but socially acceptable, sexual desires and activities. Sorority women could find themselves fending off unwanted sexual advances from otherwise "suitable" fraternity men. If a potential date hailed from a top fraternity and the sorority members believed the social connections he provided were of supreme value to the chapter as a whole, the sorority might overlook his previous transgressions. In Peggy Goodin's 1950 novel, *Take Care of My Little Girl*, freshman sorority pledge Liz is pressured to date Chad, a "Big Man on Campus" from a popular fraternity. Her "sisters" see Chad as "good advertising" for their sorority. Unfortunately, he also happens to be a dull, closed-minded, drunkard, who dates around and who her sisters consider "beyond reach and dangerous."[30] When Liz is placed on probation for failing to meet scholastic requirements, she has an opportunity to view her sorority membership and her relationship with Chad with a more critical eye, and in the end decides that her true friends are those not involved in Greek life. Novels paralleled real life, since campus sororities from the 1910s onward framed heterosexual dating as an integral, even mandatory, part of college life, regardless of the consequences. In this way, sororities channeled all women, whether they chose to participate in the dating culture or not, into an environment where male students were the arbiters of their intrinsic value.

DANGERS OF HETEROSOCIALIZING

While many students, including those who both were and were not members of GLOs, heterosocialized on campus, sororities and fraternities placed a premium on the mixed-sex social event, typically preferring it to a women's-only or men's-only activity by the 1920s onward. Yet, as sorority women mixed more frequently with fraternity men, the chances of unwanted or unintended sexual encounters grew. As Syrett has argued, fraternity men of the 1920s increasingly felt the need to prove their masculinity through heterosexual performance, which increasingly played out with female classmates who were often sorority women.[31] Gatherings of fraternity men had long involved alcohol, with members often drinking to excess. With more women attending college and fraternity men beginning to view them as social companions and dates, the widening array of mixed-sex events also fostered a new drinking culture on campus that shaped the tenor of fraternity-sorority interactions at universities throughout the remainder of the twentieth century. However, as Paula Fass has noted, drinking was not typically an issue for "respectable" women students in the 1920s because they "were effectively barred from indulgence by tradition," not to mention Prohibition. Even with the end of Prohibition in 1933 and the glamorization of drinking as a sophisticated pastime by socialites and depictions in popular 1930s films, the practice was not always a regular part of heterosocializing for sorority women.[32] A Chi Omega at Louisiana State University in the mid-1930s remembered that very little drinking went on among the women: "I could name on one hand the number of girls who had ever had a drink."[33] Instead, drinking was most pronounced among fraternity men.[34]

Nevertheless, as sorority women became more frequent guests at fraternity houses and dates for fraternity men, they became accessories to the drinking culture and, eventually, they too became more frequent imbibers. The Kappa Kappa Gammas at the Woman's College of Duke University required committee reports on liquor, smoking, and "relations with men," suggesting that the leadership saw a need to monitor these behaviors. Sorority guidebooks and educational programs, however, did not appear to discuss the drinking habits of the ideal member, implying either that sorority officials believed that little drinking occurred or that they had decided to keep discussion of drinking to a minimum. Addressing the possibility that members might be found in the presence of alcohol at sorority sanctioned events could set off alarms among educators and parents, as well as critics of Greek organizations.

While university administrators of the 1920s and 1930s may have chosen to conceal instances of women students' drinking and public drunkenness to the best of their ability, in later decades, deans of women and advisory committees for campus Greek life began to note the problem of increased drinking by sorority women. Drinking among women students became a noted concern for deans of women during World War II, when heterosocializing between college women and US servicemen stationed close to some college campuses heightened administrators' efforts to control women students' behavior. After the war, when soldiers returned to campuses as students, the men's unquestioned drinking habits, along with changing American social attitudes toward drinking, influenced women students to seek a relaxation of the previously prohibitive regulations against women's drinking.[35] This increased awareness of drinking among women students suggests a concern for women's safety and perhaps an even greater concern about women's failure to maintain the sororities' moral standards while participating in the growing heterosocial drinking culture.[36] As premier guests at fraternity parties, sorority women found that saying no to alcohol could detract from their chapter's reputation for sociability. Of course, a relaxation of drinking rules on campus meant that more women could find themselves in situations where they would not always be able to control the context or consequences of drinking. Greater ease of access to alcohol at fraternity parties likely meant that more women became unintentionally inebriated in private spaces where men held the upper hand. Fraternity men's sexual assault of female guests could easily occur without repercussions for the perpetrators. When considering the androcentric nature of the shielded and often privately owned spaces where fraternity and sorority gatherings typically occurred, the addition of alcohol could create highly volatile situations. Sororities could police their own members' behavior, but not that of the fraternity men.[37]

An infamous 1961 Halloween party hosted by UNC's Upsilon Chapter of Zeta Psi fraternity and attended by the Alpha Sigma Chapter of Tri-Delta sorority illustrated this point. At the party, Zeta Psi members wore questionable costumes: one brother dressed as a prophylactic-dispensing machine, another made "suggestive use of the end of a rubber crutch," several wore diapers, and one wore nothing at all as he streaked through the house. The men also served the Tri-Delts a punch containing grain alcohol. Echoing the longstanding double-standard of sexuality, which reinforced the idea that women should serve as moral guardians and keep men from acting on their "natural" sexual desires, UNC's College Panhellenic advisers chided the sorority women for failing to live up to their "responsibility" to make sure that partygoers conducted themselves properly. The "boys will be boys" mentality that served to excuse bad behavior by men simultaneously reinforced the social expectation that women should act as good influences to quell men's misbehaviors.[38]

The College Panhellenic advisers expressed disbelief that the women consented to be guests at the party at all. They felt that the women should have "spoken to their dates" about the "tone" of the party and left the premises.[39] However, the Tri-Delta women may not have felt at liberty to leave when they were the specially invited guests of a fraternity. The sorority women may have believed that doing so would brand them as ungrateful and uptight, which most certainly would have meant an end to future social invitations from that fraternity, and, if such a reputation were to spread, an end to attention from other fraternity chapters on campus as well. While there was some dissension among the female students on the Judicial Board as to the culpability of the sorority women, the group voted to place the Tri-Delts on social probation, ending their participation in fraternity-sorority mixers for the rest of the semester.[40] Unlike many earlier drinking and behavioral cases, the men of Zeta Psi also received punishment for their antics. The administration showed an increasing unwillingness to allow fraternities the leeway they had previously enjoyed, as the school placed the chapter on "indefinite general probation" for the remainder of the 1961–1962 school year.[41] Even as fraternity and sorority parties and formal dances provided opportunities for sorority women to hone and perform heterosocial skills, they also set up interactions where sorority women could be pressured, or physically forced, to comply with fraternity men's desires for sexual activity, or to drink alcohol, which could leave them less able to fend off any physical advances by their male hosts. When sorority women, like the UNC Tri-Deltas who faced disciplinary action, failed to "regulate" the fraternity men's behavior, society usually viewed that failure as the result of women's moral weakness, not the men's.

Perpetuating Heterosocialization Through Rush

Rush had always been the most important event of the year for sorority chapters. The practice gave chapters the opportunity to gain new members who could help the chapters build their reputations on campus. Rush, in particular, helped sororities select women for membership who met or exceeded conventional, white standards of beauty. As Turk notes, by the 1890s and 1900s, sororities sought new members based on the college women's "looks, amiability, and social performance."[42] Sororities regularly publicized members' exceptional physical appearance. National journal features and chapter reports focused on those sisters chosen as homecoming queens, May Queens, and "Sweethearts of Sigma Chi," and highlighted other designations prizing physical beauty.[43] By calling attention to the attractiveness of chapter members, women sought to elevate their image and increase their status across campus as members of an elite sorority. To maintain such achievements, they needed to pledge equally "attractive" new members. A sorority's entire year (and reputation) could be made or unmade by the attributes of women they pledged during rush. Thus, the decisions about which women the chapters would pursue for membership were quite important, and, in this process, men played pivotal roles.

The case of the Gamma Epsilon Chapter of Alpha Gamma Delta at UNC offers a prime example of the difficulty in building a new chapter when campus fraternity men were not supportive. Established in 1945 as UNC's fifth national sorority, the Gamma Epsilon Chapter struggled for years, appearing to suffer a poor reputation among a majority of the student body.[44] In fall 1963, members of UNC's Advisory Committee on Special Sorority Problems, a group of women administrators and faculty that focused on campus sorority issues, discussed Alpha Gamma Delta and its small pledge class. Representatives of the sorority "expressed" to the committee "a deep concern over the number of rushees dropping out of their rush parties...for no apparent reason other than derogatory rumors and stories being spread among the student population." They also stated that they wanted to ensure that all other members of UNC's College Panhellenic were dedicated to the flourishing of every sorority chapter on campus. Without a sufficient number of new members, a sorority chapter would be unable to meet its financial obligations. A letter written by the Alpha Gamma Delta national president to the president of the UNC Panhellenic "acknowledged knowing of alleged rumors, i.e., that the Alpha Gamma Delta house would close because of its diminishing size, etc. and the need for Panhellenic to support their house as a part of the Carolina fraternity system."[45] While the grand president did not elaborate on the "etc." factors, it is likely that she referred to concerns about the financial burden of an unsuccessful chapter and the "quality," or physical attractiveness, of the sorority's members. The UNC Faculty Committee on Fraternities and Sororities, composed of men and women faculty and administrators, specifically mentioned Alpha Gamma Delta as a sorority that had trouble attracting new members because of its "reputation for pledging more 'unpopular' girls."[46] Derogatory comments about the appearance, or the heterosexual "dateability," of a sorority's members could be highly damaging to a group's reputation on campus. The Advisory Committee endorsed the letter from Alpha Gamma Delta and "urge[d] Panhellenic and all sorority women to maintain the viability of all campus chapters."[47] For the committee to issue a reminder that all sorority women on campus should support one another suggested that women in rival sorority chapters had contributed to the disparaging rumors and that competition, rather than cooperation, was the norm for sorority chapters on the campus.

Whatever the reason for its diminishing membership, Alpha Gamma Delta needed to reverse its declining fortunes. In its efforts to do so, it sought to bring in the big guns—the fraternity men. Clearly demonstrating that fraternity approval was the key to a sorority chapter's rating on campus, the Advisory Committee "suggested that the support of the IFC [Inter-Fraternity Council] be enlisted," to help bolster the reputation of the Alpha Gamma Delta house.[48] The members of the Advisory Committee were admitting that a sorority's popularity among fraternity men was imperative to its success on campus, and that fraternities had the power to rebuild the chapter's image among the student body. IFC "support" for efforts to strengthen the reputation of the Gamma Epsilon Chapter hinged on the fraternities' agreeing to have mixers with the sorority. But with the "Alpha Gams" already branded as "undesirable," fraternities would be hard pressed to invite them to mixers. Even a lower "rated" fraternity on campus would wish to avoid the stigma of associating with a sorority that had the ignominious distinction of being the butt of campus jokes. Apparently some students referred to the Alpha Gamma Deltas by the nickname "the Gamma ghouls," deriding the group's status with a dig at members' physical appearances.[49] The Advisory Committee failed to discuss the probable difficulty in getting fraternities to lend support to the Alpha Gamma Delta rehabilitation effort. While it is unclear how, or even if, this plan came to fruition, the fact that Gamma Epsilon withdrew from the UNC campus during the 1965 school year implies that the fraternity men and the other sororities had not been terribly interested in helping to save the chapter.[50]

Rush always had played a great role in the fortunes of sororities, and alumnae had long been involved in the process by sending formal recommendations for "desirable" women, as well as by providing informal gossip on "undesirable" women.[51] By the mid-to-late 1960s, rush had become a source of contention among sorority women, as many college members sought to displace alumnae's power and gain greater control over selecting the women each chapter invited into membership. In these years, larger shifts in American culture also affected student life on university campuses. Students attempted to understand their place as mature individuals within a nation altered by the civil rights movement, the rise of Black Power, the war in Vietnam, the women's rights movement, and the sexual revolution. Many students began to question authority figures such as their parents, university administrators, and their sorority's national leadership. Some student demonstrations that targeted campus administrators during this period also undermined longstanding parietals, or those university rules that governed students' behavior and that had strictly controlled women's behavior since coeducation began.[52] In this shifting environment, some college sorority women saw the need for their organizations to change. In many cases, sorority women sought an organization-wide reconsideration of educational programming and rush practices, and sought to sideline alumnae and national sorority leaders who, fearful of racial integration, attempted to maintain power over rush decisions. While this larger battle waged between alumnae and college chapter leaders, both sorority and nonsorority women students on campuses voiced displeasure with the priorities of sorority chapters at their universities. In September 1967, the president of the Panhellenic Council at Duke delivered a speech to sorority presidents, rush chairmen, and campus leaders in which she derided rush's "dehumanizing" function and announced that she was resigning her post as Panhellenic President and would be "de-sistering" from her sorority. She explained that she had begun her presidency with the hope that she could help build a greater sense of community while also overcoming the "attitude of 'parochialism'" that she saw as a part of the Greek system. A real community, she argued, need "not depend on selective membership, but can develop wherever there are people."[53] Seemingly defeated by the intransigence of the sorority system, she no longer believed that it could be changed from the inside.

The second-wave feminist movement of the 1960s and 1970s also posed challenges to the national sororities' vision for domestically inclined womanhood. As in the 1910s and 1920s, sorority leaders were conflicted by the need to keep the organizations relevant to the interests of young women, while at the same time continuing to promote the ideal of sorority women as homemakers who remained subservient to husbands and other white men. With the 1961 President's Commission on the Status of Women and the 1965 passage of Title VII of the Civil Rights Act, the US government demonstrated a new interest in and commitment to the rights of women in American society.[54] Sororities, too, acknowledged that their members participated in volunteer work outside of the private home, and that some sorority women maintained careers in addition to or instead of raising a family. However, sororities' leaders were not proponents of major changes in white, middle- to upper-class family structures and in what they believed should be women's primary goal in life. By the mid-1960s, some professional women felt that governmental commissions on the status of women had failed to hasten necessary changes, and these women splintered off to form the National Organization for Women (NOW) in 1966. As those on the forefront of possible change for the coming generation of adult women, college women were poised to help foster the movement, but the generational gap between many sorority alumnae leaders and college sorority women on the subject of women's liberation created tension within the organizations. Some of these women, enlightened by the civil rights movement and the women's movement, targeted sororities as detrimental to sisterhood because, they argued, the organizations "are based on competition and selective sisterhood," and by the late 1960s, feminist activism began to appear more robustly on college campuses. Frequently, the women students first organized around the issue of campus parietals targeted at women students, but they eventually began to question the regulations imposed by national sororities from afar.

In 1971, a group at Duke called Duke Women's Liberation not only blamed the sororities for choosing rushees that fit a certain image, but also chided *rushees* for choosing to pledge a sorority based on its ability to "satisfy [their] social needs."[55] In the group's view, both the sorority chapter and the rushees used one another to reach their goal of attracting men. Duke Women's Liberation called out the sorority women on this issue, stating that "sorority [rush] cut sessions reveal the fact that women are often judged on their ability to attract men." The group argued that sorority chapters chose rushees based on their ability to "fit in" with their specific chapter, and that "fitting in" meant that "the woman in question [wa]s higher or lower on the superficial social status scale than the sorority as a whole." The group noted that sororities' purpose in cutting women who would not "fit" their image was to eliminate the rushees whom they "considered unable to date in the same social circles or to relate to the same type of men" as the rest of the chapter. Duke Women's Liberation foresaw this "male-oriented judgment" as having "unfortunate implications for the relationships between women and 'sisterhood.'" By highlighting the point that "most men still view[ed] women in the superficial terms of appearance and physical appeal," Duke Women's Liberation claimed that in catering to male interests, sorority women gained "an excuse to view and to judge other women in these same terms."[56]

Some women students highlighted the negative implications of the heterosocial ideal on sorority rush, but the ingrained practice of heterosocializing between sororities and fraternities continued to promote a model that slotted sorority women into a conventional role of domestically centered womanhood that was subordinate to their male counterparts. Some sororities seemed happy targeting woman students who did not find these directives silly or old-fashioned. In 1971, during the period when women's rights organizations were starting at campuses across the United States, sorority women at the University of Georgia wrote proudly of being selected as "little sisters" of fraternity men. The Delta Chapter of Sigma Chi fraternity had started a "Little Sigmas" chapter for women who were pinned to Sigma Chis, but the Little Sigmas had quickly expanded to include other sorority women. In their newsletter, the university's Alpha Delta Pi chapter proudly announced that seven of the twenty women chosen by the Delta Chapter to be Little Sigmas were Alpha Delta Pis. The picture accompanying the story showed a member ironing clothes. The caption described a sister who "[found] out what it means to be a Little Sigma as she iron[ed] her boyfriend's bluejeans."[57] Apparently, she labored contentedly at what looked like pledge hazing or the daily routine of a homemaker or servant. Whether preparing oneself to physically appeal to fraternity men, or providing the men with a free labor source, many Little Sigmas—like many other college sorority women—continued to devote much of their membership time to heterosocial engagement.

CONCLUSION

While sororities' requirements that their members cultivate an attractive, "feminine" appearance and beguiling charm helped to solve the organizations' early-twentieth-century problem of appearing to separate young women from the possibility of romantic relationships with men, it also reinforced a complicated ideal for their membership. Sororities expected that their members should display their (hetero)sexuality, but without being *overtly* sexual *and* while upholding the image that they did not engage in sexual activity outside of conventional, heterosexual marriage. Within the sorority, women would occupy themselves by learning how to attract male attention, often at the expense of women's-only or educational-enrichment activities. National sorority leaders quietly applauded this ideal and college members worked with them during rush to replenish their chapters' rolls with new members who would continue to enhance the heterosocial reputation of the group. This approach meant that in many ways sororities were never strictly organizations for women, but were, instead, for the benefit of the men the sororities sought to attract.

Over the majority of the twentieth century, historically white sororities used heterosocial interactions to achieve their ideal model for white, middle- to upper-class womanhood. The goal of heterosocializing under-girded sororities' behavioral lessons for members and governed their rush practices, but also posed dangers for sorority women as the practice regularly placed them in the potentially dangerous, private spaces controlled by fraternity men. Sororities and fraternities maintained power on college campuses as their members regularly occupied prominent positions in campus activities and had greater social opportunities (through sorority- and fraternity-sponsored activities) than non-members. Deans of women and other campus administrators generally supported the organizations, and often held up sorority women as the ideal for all women students to emulate.[58] From the 1910s to the 1970s, sororities' model of domestically centered womanhood helped assuage public fears over changes in gender norms and the increasingly public activities of white, middle- to upper-class womanhood. At the same time, sororities' enforcement of members' femininity, as well as their willingness to rely on members' physical attractiveness and to operate as subservient partners to men's fraternities as a means to achieve and maintain campus popularity, set up a model of sorority sisterhood that placed relationships between women and men at a higher premium than those between sisters. This chapter sheds light on the problematic nature of these women's-only organizations during the twentieth century. It suggests that we should consider the history of GLOs as a significant social movement on college campuses that profoundly shaped members' campus experiences and even their expectations beyond campus. Historians, sociologists, and higher education professionals must continue to investigate the overlap of these organizations with other groups and individuals on campus and beyond to help us more fully understand the implications of these powerful societies that remain entrenched in campus life in the twenty-first century.

Notes

1. Diana Turk, *Bound By a Mighty Vow: Sisterhood and Women's Fraternities, 1870–1920* (New York: New York University Press, 2004), chapter 2, p. 47 in particular. For discussion on the change in terminology from "women's fraternity" to "sorority" by roughly 1890, see Turk, 165n1.
2. Deborah Elizabeth Whaley, *Disciplining Women: Alpha Kappa Alpha, Black Counterpublics, and the Cultural Politics of Black Sororities* (Albany: State University of New York Press, 2010).
3. Turk, *Bound by a Mighty Vow*; Nicholas Syrett, *The Company He Keeps: A History of White College Fraternities* (Chapel Hill: University of North Carolina Press, 2009).

4. Barbara Miller Solomon, *In the Company of Educated Women* (New Haven: Yale University Press, 1985), 56–57, 63, Table 2, 199–122.
5. Martin, *The Sorority Handbook*, 8th ed. (Boston: Ida Shaw Martin, 1923), 53–55, 58.
6. Helen Lefkowitz Horowitz, *Alma Mater: Design and Experience in the Women's Colleges from Their Nineteenth-Century Beginnings to the 1930's* (New York: Alfred A. Knopf, 1984), 308–14.
7. Christina Simmons, "Companionate Marriage and the Lesbian Threat," *Frontiers* 4, no. 3 (Autumn, 1979).
8. "Active Chapter Letters and Notes, Sigma Delta—Trinity College," *Angelos* 10, no. 2 (March, 1914): 137–38; "Chapter Letters and Notes, Sigma Delta, Trinity College," *Angelos* 20, no. 4 (June, 1924): 480.
9. *Pledge Manual or Freshman Training Guide for Kappa Alpha Theta*, 1927, 14, National Fraternity Publications (26/21/5), Howe Collection, University of Illinois at Urbana-Champaign (hereafter UI).
10. "Some Distinguished Members of Kappa Alpha Theta," *Handbook of Kappa Alpha Theta*, 1911, 16–18, National Fraternity Publications (26/21/5), Howe Collection, UI.
11. David C. Barrow, "Co-Education at the University; An Address Before the Georgia Federation of Women's Clubs, at the Twenty-Sixth Annual Convention" (Athens: University of Georgia, 1922), 9; Amy McCandless, *The Past in the Present: Women's Higher Education in the Twentieth-Century American South* (Tuscaloosa: University of Alabama Press, 1999), 55, 85.
12. Elaine Tyler May, *Homeward Bound: American Families in the Cold War Era*, rev. ed. (New York: Basic Books, 1999), 40–48.
13. Zella Brown Ragsdale, "A Former Dean of Women Looks at Homemaking," *Themis* 31, no. 3 (March, 1933): 225–27.
14. Warren I. Susman, "'Personality' and the Making of Twentieth-Century Culture" in *Culture as History: The Transformation of American Society in the Twentieth Century* (New York: Pantheon Books, 1984).
15. Minnie Allen Hubbard, "What Alpha Delta Pi Offers the College Girl," *Adelphean* 32, no. 2 (1939): 3–4.
16. Rooted in the Progressive reform movements around the turn of the twentieth century, and led by "reform-minded academicians, social workers, physicians, and psychiatrists," the National Committee for Mental Hygiene (NCMH) began in 1909. Educational historian Sol Cohen notes that mental hygienists traced all behavioral "maladjustments" back to "faulty personality development, which had its roots in childhood." The mental hygiene movement concentrated on schools as the spaces in which to "correct" individuals' "abnormal personalities" before these individual quirks developed into mental illness. See Cohen, "The Mental Hygiene Movement, the Development of Personality, and the School: The

Medicalization of Education," *History of Education Quarterly* 23, no. 2 (1983): 123–149, quotations on 125–27.

17. *Pledge Manual or Freshman Training Guide for Kappa Alpha Theta*, 12–15.

18. *Pledge Manual or Freshman Training Guide for Kappa Alpha Theta*, 14.

19. *The Tri Delta Hostess*, 1937, 6, National Fraternity Publications (26/21/5), Howe Collection, UI.

20. *Tri Delta Hostess*, 5. Sociologist Willard Waller clinicalized the term "rating" in his 1937 article "The Rating and Dating Complex," which described the system of popularity rankings he observed among undergraduates at Pennsylvania State College. In his study, Waller found that male students "rated" well as dates on criteria such as membership in a "better" fraternity, owning fashionable clothes, having ample spending money and an automobile, and displaying good manners and dancing ability. While female students also rated highly for having a fashionable wardrobe, a "smooth line," and dancing ability, the most important criterion for women was their popularity. Thus a woman's desirability as a date relied primarily on her ability to have many dates and appear sought after by men. Waller, "The Rating and Dating Complex," *American Sociological Review* 2, no. 5 (1937): 730.

21. October 13, 1931, Box 1, Series 2, KKG, Delta Beta Chapter Records, Duke University (hereafter DU).

22. April 17, 1939, Series 2, Phi Mu, Gamma Epsilon Chapter Records, DU.

23. "NPC Fraternities," 1938, 9, Box 1, Publications (41/82/800), NPC Archives, UI.

24. Class of 1944 respondent, Laura Parrish Papers, College of William and Mary (hereafter WM); *Colonial Echo*, 1944, 84, 169.

25. May, *Homeward Bound*, 68, 150.

26. Margaret L. Freeman, "Inequality for All and Mint Juleps, Too: White Social Sororities and 'Freedom of Association' in the United States," in *The Right Side of the Sixties: Reexamining Conservatism's Decade of Transformation*, eds. Laura Jane Gifford and Daniel K. Williams (New York: Palgrave Macmillan, 2012), 41–59.

27. *For She's an Alpha Chi!: A Handbooks of Collegiate Social Customs*, National Fraternity.

28. "Minutes on the Advisory Committee on Sororities," 1948, Advisory Committee on Special Sorority Problems, 1950–1955, Box 41, Series 12, Office Vice Chancellor for Student Affairs Records (#40124), University of North Carolina at Chapel Hill (hereafter UNC); Carmichael to Tri Delta member, Dec. 4, 1953, Correspondence, 1937–1957, Box 31, Series 10.2, Office of the Vice Chancellor for Student Affairs Records (#40124), UNC; Carmichael to Bill Redding, Feb. 27, 1958, Parties,

1955–1962, Box 32, Series 10.2, Office Vice Chancellor for Student Affairs Records (#40124), UNC.

29. Carmichael, "The Sorority Woman Moves Into the World of the Future," April 28, 1956, 17, Box 4, Series 2.2, Office of the Dean of Women Records (#40125), UNC.

30. Peggy Goodin, *Take Care of My Little Girl* (New York: Berkeley Medallion Books, 1950), 57–60, 109–11.

31. Syrett, *The Company He Keeps*, 183–86, 218–19.

32. Paula Fass, *The Damned and the Beautiful: American Youth in the 1920s* (New York: Oxford University Press, 1977), 310; Lori Rotskoff, *Love on the Rocks Men, Women, and Alcohol in Post-World War II America* (Chapel Hill: University of North Carolina Press, 2002), 39–40, 42–45.

33. Oct. 18, 1934, Series 2, Minutes, KKG, Delta Beta Chapter Records, DU; Jane Porter Middleton interview, 15, Louisiana State University.

34. Fass, *Damned and the Beautiful*, 318–19.

35. Mary Grace Wilson to Katherine Warren, Jan. 18, 1951, Drinking Regulations, 1942–1958, Box 29, Woman's College Records, DU.

36. *Handbook for Women Students at the University of North Carolina*, 1924–1925, UNC; *College of William and Mary Women's Student Government Handbook*, 1931–1932, Frances C. Cosby Nettles Papers, 1931–1935, WM. By 1948, UNC mentioned the prohibition of drinking in the dormitories. Women who needed to keep liquor in their rooms "for medicinal purposes," however, could do so, but had to report it to the house president. See *Handbook for Women Students at the University of North Carolina*, 1948–1949, 20, North Carolina Collection, UNC.

37. Lynn Peril, *College Girls: Bluestockings, Sex Kittens, and Coeds, Then and Now* (New York: W. W. Norton & Company 2006), 305–07; Syrett, *The Company He Keeps*, 277–78, 285–86.

38. Panhellenic Court Judicial Board Minutes, November 9, 1961, Sororities: Panhellenic Court, 1961–1965, Box 33, Series 10.2, Office of the Vice Chancellor for Student Affairs Records (#40124), UNC; Beth Bailey, *Sex in the Heartland* (Cambridge: Harvard University Press, 1999), 76–79; Peril, *College Girls*, 305–07.

39. Panhellenic Court Judicial Board Minutes, November 9, 1961, Sororities: Panhellenic Court, 1961–1965, Box 33, Series 10.2, Office of the Vice Chancellor for Student Affairs Records (#40124), UNC.

40. Panhellenic Court Judicial Board Minutes, November 9, 1961.

41. Dean Charles Henderson, Jr. to Mel Underdahl, General Secretary, Zeta Psi Fraternity, December 14, 1961, Fraternities and Sororities Correspondence, 1961, Box 32, Series 10.2, Office of the Vice Chancellor for Student Affairs Records (#40124), UNC.

42. Turk, *Bound By a Mighty Vow*, 67.

43. "Starting the Year with Beauty, Personality, Popularity, Brains..." *Themis* 35, no. 1 (1936): 1–8; "Alpha Kappa Chapter History Report—University of Tennesee-Knoxville, 1931–1934," ADPi Chapter Histories, University of Tennessee-Knoxville, Alpha Delta Pi Archives; *Key* 63, no. 2 (1946): 217; *Key* 65, no. 2 (1948): 90, 136–37.

44. Minutes of the Faculty Committee on Fraternities and Sororities, February 12, 1963, Fraternities and Sororities: Faculty Committee on Sororities, Box 41, Series 12, Office of the Vice Chancellor for Student Affairs Records (#40124), UNC.

45. Minutes of the Advisory Committee on Special Sorority Problems, October 17, 1963, Fraternities and Sororities: Advisory Committee on Special Sorority Problems, Box 41, Series 12, Office for the Vice Chancellor for Student Affairs Records (#40124), UNC.

46. Minutes of the Faculty Committee on Fraternities and Sororities, October 22, 1964, Faculty Committees: Fraternities and Sororities, 1964–1969, Box 41, Series 12, Office of the Vice Chancellor for Student Affairs Records (#40124), UNC.

47. Minutes of the Faculty Committee on Fraternities and Sororities, October 22, 1964.

48. Minutes of the Advisory Committee on Special Sorority Problems, October 17, 1963, Fraternities and Sororities: Advisory Committee on Special Sorority Problems, Box 41, Series 12, Office of the Vice Chancellor for Student Affairs Records (#40124), UNC.

49. Personal communication with UNC alumnus.

50. "Report of the Faculty Committee on Fraternities and Sororities, 1964–1965," 6–7, Fraternities and Sororities: Annual Reports, 1929; 1949; 1957–1971, Box 41, Series 12, Office of the Vice Chancellor for Student Affairs Records (#40124), UNC.

51. Turk, *Bound By a Mighty Vow*, 62–67. Correspondence between Chi Omega Chapter Advisor Guion Griffis Johnson and her North Carolinian, sorority-alumnae friends in the early 1950s demonstrates the type of unofficial, yet consequential, comments on prospective rushees that sorority alumnae would communicate through personal notes. These exchanges are found in Folders 250–275, Series 3.1: General Chi Omega Materials, Guion Griffis Johnson Papers (#04546), UNC.

52. Jeffrey Turner, *Sitting In and Speaking Out: Student Movements in the American South, 1960–1970* (Athens: University of Georgia Press, 2010), 271–74.

53. Janis Johnson, "Panhel President Quits Sororities," *Duke Chronicle*, September 20, 1967, Newspaper Clippings, 1963–1971, Box 3, Panhellenic Council Records, DU.

54. Sara Evans, *Personal Politics: The Roots of Women's Liberation in the Civil Rights Movement and the New Left* (New York: Alfred A. Knopf, 1979), 16–17.
55. Duke Women's Liberation, Program and Discussion, February 18, 1971, Newspaper Clippings, 1963–1971, Box 3, Panhellenic Council Records, DU.
56. Duke Women's Liberation, Program and Discussion, February 18, 1971.
57. "Little Sigma's," *Beta Nu's Letter* 9 (1971–1972), 4, Alpha Delta Pi—Beta Nu, University of Georgia, Chapter Histories, Alpha Delta Pi Archives.
58. Mary Alice Jones, "The Fraternity Membership: Today and Tomorrow," 24th NPC Meeting, 1935, 205–206, NPC Proceedings (41/82/10), NPC Archives, UI.

.

CHAPTER 7

The Mexican American Movement

Christopher Tudico

In the 1930s, the sons and daughters of Mexican immigrants enrolled in California colleges and universities for the first time in numbers large enough to form their own intercollegiate student organization, the Mexican American Movement (MAM), which functioned in one capacity or another from 1934 to 1950. MAM members predominantly attended higher education institutions in the greater Los Angeles area, including the University of California at Los Angeles (UCLA), the University of Southern California, Santa Barbara State College, Redlands University, Compton Junior College, and Los Angeles City College, and they emphasized the importance of a college education to their brothers and sisters living in the barrio. This chapter focuses on the history of MAM as a window into Mexican American student life and adds to a historiography that has not comprehensively detailed the history of college student life among this group of collegians.

In this chapter, I examine how the creation of an organization of Mexican American college students signified a fundamental departure from earlier years, when the few Mexican students who enrolled in

---

C. Tudico (✉)
Saint Martin de Porres High School, Cleveland, OH, USA
e-mail: ctudico@stmdphs.org

© The Author(s) 2018
C. A. Ogren, M. A. VanOverbeke (eds.),
Rethinking Campus Life, Historical Studies in Education,
https://doi.org/10.1007/978-3-319-75614-1_7

California colleges and universities were virtually invisible. I detail how these students used this organization to establish an identity and student culture on campus grounded in activism, empowerment, and education, and how they published a newspaper, *The Mexican Voice*, in order to reach a greater audience for their ideas. And while MAM initially catered to young men, I show how the movement grew to include women as well. I explore how MAM reflected the complexity of Mexican American identity during the immediate prewar period[1] and initiated contact with other college students outside California, most especially in neighboring Arizona.[2] I shed light on how MAM represented the beginning of more active participation in California higher education among the youth of the Mexican American community—and contributed to the development of a Mexican American campus student culture—a generation before Mexican American professors, students, and activists pushed for and established the first Department of Chicano Studies at California State University at Los Angeles in 1968.

MEXICAN AMERICANS AND HIGHER EDUCATION IN THE EARLY TWENTIETH CENTURY

While the greater Mexican population in California steadily grew in the first quarter of the twentieth century, the enrollment of Mexicans and Mexican Americans in California higher education remained almost non-existent. In contrast, colleges and universities grew. The University of California at Berkeley flourished and became a charter member of the prestigious Association of American Universities in 1900[3] and, as Edwin Slosson, editor of *The Independent*, put it, one of the "great American universities."[4] The State Normal School at Los Angeles morphed into the Southern Branch of the University of California and in 1927 became UCLA. Still, only a small percentage of Californians, like Americans in general, enrolled in the University of California system and in college overall; nationally, fewer than five percent of people between the ages of eighteen and twenty-two enrolled in college during this period.[5] Mexican and Mexican American participation in higher education was even lower due to limited K-12 educational opportunities for Mexican children. Overall, few Mexican Americans successfully navigated the challenges of attending predominantly under-funded, segregated, and discriminatory schools, resulting in low high-school graduation rates. As one study found, approximately fifty-four percent of Mexican girls and forty-four percent of Mexican boys dropped out of high school between the ages of fourteen and sixteen.[6]

Despite the numerous challenges facing young Mexican Americans in Los Angeles, southern California, and elsewhere throughout the state, a few individuals such as Ernesto Galarza did complete high school and go to college. Galarza and his mother fled Mexico during the revolution when he was just eight years old. He grew up in California's Sacramento Valley, where he worked as a hop picker with other members of his family. But he succeeded in earning an education while others in his community were unable to do so. Along the way, he received the assistance of teachers and a school principal, a local union leader, and the Young Men's Christian Association (YMCA). Each introduced the young man to a world outside of the fields and the barrio.[7] Galarza began his studies in 1923 at Occidental College in Los Angeles and eventually graduated from Stanford University. Looking back at his experience in college, he remembered knowing only five or so Mexican or Mexican American students attending any college in California at the same time.[8] Galarza made a concerted effort to remain attached to the community that bore and nurtured him, working there during school sessions and spending summers in the Sacramento Valley. Galarza was one of the first Mexican Americans to attend and graduate from Stanford; few if any other Mexican Americans joined him on campus. Galarza believed that students and professors thought of him as a "novelty" and a "curiosity," since few actually socialized or spent time with Mexicans or Mexican Americans prior to college.[9] Galarza did not join any Mexican American student organizations while at Stanford, since the campus had none at the time.

As Galarza and a few other Mexican American students made their way to college, students began to form Latino fraternal student organizations at the University of California in Berkeley by the 1920s, including Phi Lambda Alpha and *El Club Hispano America*.[10] These groups were not primarily for Mexican American students, however. Phi Lambda Alpha member and *El Club Hispano America* President Jesús de la Garza originally came from Mexico City.[11] Another *El Club Hispano America* member, Eduardo de Antequera Romecin, grew up in La Paz, Mexico.[12] Bartolo Guzman, of Pasadena, California, was the only Mexican American among the leadership of the student organization.[13] Similarly, a number of female students and faculty founded *Casa Hispana* for students interested in Spanish culture and language, and its membership was largely White or from abroad.[14]

Galarza and the students in the fraternal organizations were among the very first Mexican Americans to attend college in California.[15] Their stories were exceptional. The vast majority of the Mexican American population was ill equipped to even complete high school, let alone attend college. Many left school early to join their parents in working to support their families. But by the early 1930s this phenomenon changed, as the sons and daughters of Mexican immigrants reached college age and prepared to enter through the gates of California universities and earn an education.

COLLEGE ENROLLMENT AND THE DEVELOPMENT OF THE MEXICAN AMERICAN MOVEMENT

In the 1930s, as student enrollment increased, MAM emerged from the Mexican Youth Conference, a series of annual meetings sponsored by the YMCA to facilitate leadership among young men of Mexican descent and to encourage high school boys to fraternize with one another outside of the barrio. The participants in the conference took part in organized peer activities, including sports and athletics, in an effort to build character.[16] Beyond participating in sports, recreation, and socializing at the annual event, the young men took advantage of the opportunity to discuss issues pertaining to the greater Mexican community. Realizing that meeting once a year was inadequate, the most ambitious of the conference participants decided to hold their own informal monthly discussions and started a newspaper, *The Mexican Voice*, in order to share their ideas with a greater audience. Now in college, the students who published the paper described it in the following manner:

> The MEXICAN VOICE stands for encouragement, inspiration, and uplift-
> ment of our people. It tries to live up to this by giving news of outstanding
> Mexican youth, his achievements, his thoughts, his ideals, and his aspira-
> tions. The VOICE in the future will give you educational articles that per-
> tain to our people.[17]

An "inspirational/educational youth magazine," the newspaper evolved into the public mouthpiece of MAM.[18] The first student editor of *The Mexican Voice*, Felix Gutiérrez, employed the skills he learned as a part-time journalist for the *Pasadena Chronicle* in order to publish the paper. The organization's most active members, including Paul Coronel, Bert Corona, and Manuel Ceja, contributed to the newspaper on a regular basis. They produced *The Mexican Voice* with the express purpose to establish year-round communication among the Mexican Youth Conference participants, who at first were all young men. The newsletter served as a forum for the students' ideas and opinions about the issues the Mexican youth and the larger Mexican American community faced in Los Angeles and southern California. The newspaper recorded the accomplishments and successes of young Mexicans, both in the classroom and in athletics in order to inspire the young Mexican Americans in the barrio to take education seriously and to motivate students to stay out of trouble. With this focus, *The Mexican Voice* evolved into a polished publication.

Publishing the newspaper served only as the first step in the organization's attempt to broaden its work and mission. The students who created *The Mexican Voice* organized leadership institutes and regional conferences, including one for women, to supplement an annual MAM conference.[19] In 1941 the student group's leadership divorced itself from the YMCA, officially creating the MAM[20] as a full-fledged advocacy organization committed to working with Mexican American youth. As MAM membership grew to include mainly college students as well as increasing numbers of young professionals, the members supported each other in their endeavors to make a difference in their communities as teachers, counselors, and social workers.

Most importantly, throughout its duration, the publishers of and contributors to *The Mexican Voice* emphasized the importance of a college education. In its inaugural issue, José Rodriguez, then a nineteen-year-old junior-college student, wrote:

> Education is the only tool which will raise our influence, command the respect of the rich class, and enable us to mingle in their social, political and religious life.... today a college education is <u>absolutely necessary</u> for us to succeed in the professional world...If our opinion is to be had, respected, our income raised, happiness increased, we must compete! <u>EDUCATION</u> is our <u>only weapon</u>![21]

The newspaper often included profiles of the Mexican American young men and women who contributed, and, by doing so, hoped to inspire other young men and women from similar backgrounds to go to college.

Rodriquez, for instance, graduated from San Bernardino Junior College with a degree in accounting and "an eye towards the University of California at Berkeley." He originally grew up in Texas, born to parents from Mexico; Felix Gutiérrez, the editor of the paper, described Rodriquez as a "steady, conscientious fellow, fond of hard work; who is not doubtful of his success because he is dark skinned." According to Gutiérrez, Rodriguez's philosophy was that there was "always room at the top."[22] Rodriguez also argued that education can occur outside of the classroom and beyond the college campus. In the article in the inaugural issue, he wrote:

> College doors are not the only gate to education. [Abraham] Lincoln did not attend schools, but was educated. Education begins at home, education means a complete knowledge of yourself, a good knowledge of your fellowmen and a thorough knowledge of the world in which you live...We gain the equal of a college education by earnest, sincere, patient and persevering application in reading and studying at home.[23]

Manuel Ceja, a political science major and star athlete at Compton Junior College, echoed Rodriguez's point of view on the importance of earning a college education in the second issue of *The Mexican Voice*:

> But what can one individual do about this situation? He can uplift the Mexican name by constant work – hard work with others who have the same high ideals and aims. By securing education, not just high school but a college one.[24]

Ceja, a frequent contributor to *The Mexican Voice*,[25] was born in Los Angeles as the son of immigrants. Ceja attended Compton Junior College after graduating from the Spanish American Institute, where he earned varsity letters in football, basketball, and track. He also was a member of the Watts "Y" Phalanx Fraternity, a student organization composed of Mexican American high school and college students and recent college graduates.[26]

Female students also participated in MAM and pushed the organization to include more female voices and to expand the focus beyond male students. Female participants promoted improvement through education, as male students did, but they often also advocated for women more broadly within the Mexican American community. Dora Ibáñez, for example, emerged as a dynamic leader within the group. Born in Mexico, she attended public schools in Texas before taking college courses in Iowa,

Arizona, and California. She earned her teaching credentials and a B.A. from Redlands University. She worked her way through school, and earned a scholarship for voice and singing. Ibáñez had the opportunity to attend graduate school at Columbia University, but did not due to health concerns; instead, she became a teacher.[27] While a teacher, she wrote the essay, "A Challenge to the American Girl of Mexican Parentage," for the December 1938 issue of *The Mexican Voice*.[28] In the article, she applauded the efforts of MAM to champion education, but also expressed her concern that the leadership of the organization reached out primarily to a male audience. She suggested that women should be a part of this movement too, and wrote specifically to young women:

> Do you realize that you are in a country where educational opportunities for both sexes are equal? Where you too can go on ahead side by side with the boys, acquiring an education which will open up for you new horizons, a new world with a beautiful outlook, where education is gratuitous, yours only for the taking?[29]

Ibáñez encouraged Mexican American women to pursue a college education in spite of obstacles. In her opinion, the challenges Mexican women faced in California were not insurmountable:

> If you are a girl with aspirations for a college education, and your meager financial circumstances discourage you, don't let this bother you. If you have the mentality and ability to study for the profession or career on which you have set your mind, if you have enough determination, will power and spunk to meet all obstacles, you will succeed in attaining your desires.[30]

Ibáñez believed that, once successful, a Mexican American woman would be respected. "Her success," she wrote, "is an immediate result of the blend of her rich Aztec culture and the best that this country has given her."[31] Overall, MAM's members, women and men alike, hoped to fashion themselves into leaders of their people, as they viewed themselves as role models for their community. In the words of Felix Gutiérrez:

> Our job is uplifting our people, ejecting [*sic:* injecting] confidence into their veins, bolstering their depleted prides. And how can we do this? By becoming teachers, social workers, writers, lawyers, doctors, business men, trained workers, and working in every way possible for their benefit and betterment. Remember, we understand them because we are one of them and only we can bring out the best in them! We are they; they are us![32]

This focus on the value of education promoted the student culture that MAM was building on college campuses throughout the state.

The belief that earning an education could alleviate the problems the Mexican people faced in the United States was a core tenant of MAM's philosophy. But the experiences of MAM members, specifically their rare achievement of earning an education, colored their point of view. Nearly all participants in the Mexican Youth Conference were diligent and successful students, who saw their opportunities increase as they completed high school and attended college. However, the belief that it was only the lack of an education that kept Mexican Americans from advancing their position in the United State overlooked the obstacles of poverty, segregated schools, and discrimination that Mexican Americans continued to face. In that sense, students in MAM oversimplified the complex problems the Mexican people faced in California and the American Southwest. Still, the young Mexican Americans' unwavering conviction in education set them apart from their peers, and their ability to organize a college student organization was especially noteworthy.

MAM members criticized young people in the Mexican American community who they thought were not attempting to establish a better life for themselves and their families. Manuel de la Raza (Felix Gutiérrez writing under another name) specifically chastised Mexican American young men in the following passage of *The Mexican Voice*:

> Don't heed the fellows loafing at street corners, wasting their time. They'll tell you an education is worthless. Don't believe them. They don't want you to progress. They are greedy and jealous, because you have a better chance. They want you to be like them – easy-going, time-wasting Mexican fellows who drag down our name.[33]

Gutiérrez repeatedly referred to those who did not try to earn an education as "easygoing loafers."[34] Similarly, Paul Coronel admonished Mexican American young men who did not make an effort: "It's really sad to see so many young lazy fellows hanging around the corners, pool halls, gambling joints, and everywhere doing ABSOLUTELY NOTHING for themselves."[35] More often than not, however, the Mexican American students who published *The Mexican Voice* encouraged young people in their communities who did not see hope, through passages like the following:

But good or bad neighborhood, anyone with "guts" courage, determination, can arise, become educated and command respect. All you've got to do is "give yourself a chance." You're "double-crossing" yourself if you let opportunity pass. Take it or make it![36]

Coronel made a passionate plea to Mexican Americans in the barrio in an article appropriately titled "Give Yourself a Chance":

AMBITION is that strong mover that stands between desire and success... Talent and capacity are not lacking in us. What is lacking is GUTS, AMBITION, FAITH, ANIMATION, and greatest of all A DESIRE TO ELEVATE OUR MEXICAN RACE![37]

Overall, MAM leadership was overwhelmingly positive and encouraging, attempting to instill confidence in those young men and, occasionally, women in the barrio who may not have had hope in their futures.

In this vein, Mexican Youth Conference and MAM leaders printed success stories in *The Mexican Voice* of dozens of Mexican American young men and women. They did so with the expressed intent of inspiring their brethren. For example, in the September 1938 edition, contributors presented a profile of Stephen Reyes, the president of the 1937 San Pedro Conference. According to the article, Reyes picked oranges during the summers throughout high school to pay for college. He commuted seven miles to junior college, where he received an Associate of Arts degree in Letters and Science. After junior college, Reyes received student loans and worked part-time to help pay for college at UCLA. Upon graduation in 1938, he taught night school classes at a junior college and directed a local playground. Reyes hoped to return to UCLA for a master's degree.[38]

Through this and other examples, MAM not only encouraged progress through education, but also advocated for self-help through alternative means. The leadership of the organization recognized that for many in the Mexican American community, earning a college degree was nearly impossible. Consequently, MAM advocated for self-improvement through any avenue or channel available. These avenues included, among other ways, learning a trade. MAM published a story in *The Mexican Voice* about Johnny Gutiérrez—the cousin of Felix Gutiérrez—who earned a living as an aviation mechanic and supported his twelve brothers and sisters. After reciting Johnny's story, Felix Gutiérrez challenged Mexican Americans:

Why can't you do this in whatever field you choose? It takes a sacrifice to reach the goal, but once you "get there" it must be swell to have the warm feeling of accomplishment go through you. Don't let your being dark, your being of Mexican descent stop you. That is only an excuse. Johnny is dark. He works in a field few, very few, of Mexican descent do. You see, when you do a job well, expertly, people take you for what you're worth.[39]

The *Mexican Voice* also fostered discussion of topics beyond the value of education, and contributors to the newspaper expounded on any number of topics important to the Mexican American community, including Mexican American identity within the larger community and among Mexican American college students. Felix Gutiérrez penned his editorials in *The Mexican Voice* under the telling pseudonym, "Manuel De La Raza," which literally translates into the name, Manuel "Race." Manuel De La Raza created a section of the newsletter called "*Nosotros*" (meaning "we" or "us"), to demonstrate his commitment and that of MAM to a cohesive Mexican identity. In one of his last contributions to *The Mexican Voice* as Manuel De La Raza, Gutiérrez asked those in his community to be proud of their vibrant heritage. He also criticized the more affluent Mexican Americans who tried to portray themselves as "Spanish," when he wrote:

Rather discouraging has been a trend we have noticed among both our Americans of Mexican descent and others not of our national descent...The trend is towards calling any accomplished Mexican-American "Spanish," or anyone well-to-do, above average..."Spanish-American"...The whole inference...is...THAT NOTHING GOOD COMES FROM THE MEXICAN GROUP...that only the talented, the law-abiding, the part Mexican, the fair complexioned, the professionals and the tradesman are "Spanish." The drunkards, the delinquents, the very dark, the manual laborers, the pachucos, the criminals and those in the lower-socio economic scale are the Mexicans...If you don't consider this an insult, then you don't have any pride in your background! Newspapers carry this trend, prominent politicians...[and] Anglo Americans in general are guilty of this, but worst of all, our own Mexican-Americans are making this distinction! Let's have more pride in our own group. We are all the same, whether we have been here ten generations or one. We have common goals, we have community problems...Let us be proud of our heritage.[40]

As exemplified in the preceding excerpts from *The Mexican Voice*, Gutiérrez and MAM members avidly promoted pride in their Mexican American background. In *The Mexican Voice*, the student organization emphasized the commonalities, as opposed to the differences, among the increasingly diverse Mexican community in the United States and sought to build connections among Mexican Americans on campus and throughout society. MAM members also embraced a future in the United States and encouraged the readers of *The Mexican Voice* to take full advantage of what the country offered, all the while still honoring their Mexican roots. Felix Gutiérrez argued that Mexican Americans should not have to change in order to become American, stating that members of "Italian-American and German-American organizations" did not deny their national descent. He asked his readers, "Why can't we do the same?"[41] Gutiérrez urged Mexicans to "become a citizen, an American" and to "be proud of your background" as a Mexican.[42] MAM noted that Mexican Americans were American citizens, and they should be free to enjoy all the privileges of citizenship. In the initial issue of *The Mexican Voice*, Gutiérrez stated, "Remember whenever, if ever, there is a war, your being of Mexican descent won't stop you from being an American soldier. This is your country, your flag. Prepare yourself for the better positions you deserve as American citizens."[43] In response to a later proposal to rename the group to reflect a broader Latin American focus, Gutiérrez reaffirmed the group's commitment to being fundamentally Mexican American in orientation:

The name "Latin-American" applied in our case, reminds us of softened statements, honeyed words. It's like hiding behind a false front. The name "Mexican-American" is coming forth with pride, honesty, and it paints a true picture of us.[44]

In this and other ways, MAM members explicitly sought to promote their American citizenship *and* honor their Mexican heritage. In fall of 1938 Felix Gutiérrez published an anecdote regarding a Mexican American young man and self-identification. Gutiérrez wrote that the young man, when applying for a social security card, filled out "White," to the chagrin of his "paisanos," or friends, who laughed at the boy for his mistake. His "color," so they thought, should have been "Mexican."[45] Gutiérrez wrote that the young man offered the following response:

It asks for your color. Well I'm of Mexican descent, an American citizen. I was born here. It doesn't ask for your national descent, it asks for your color. Mexican is no color, nor race! Mexican is a nationality. Racially what difference is there between us South and Central Americans? Very little, if any. I have white blood in my veins as well as red. I couldn't sign this card as Indian because I'm not. The only alternative is to sign it white.[46]

According to Gutiérrez, the boy's friends "gathered the impression he had denied being of Mexican descent."[47] Significantly, Gutiérrez wrote that MAM and the leadership agreed with the young man, believing that "this young fellow spoke the truth...Saying we are Americans doesn't mean we are not of Mexican descent: Even Americans of other descents know this. So the next time anyone asks you what you are, you say, 'I'm an American.' If he questions further, say, 'I'm an American of Mexican descent.'"[48] This episode again documents how MAM members viewed themselves as Mexican American. Furthermore, the young man featured in the article was quite prescient. Even today, Mexican is not a race. On the 2010 US Census questionnaire, the terms Hispanic and Latino represent an ethnicity rather than a race. Mexican Americans today can both be "White" and "Hispanic." The anecdote speaks to the complexity of racial/ethnic identity formation in the past, as does the government's classification of race and ethnicity today. The college students who composed MAM were on the vanguard of thought on Mexican American identity and were reaffirming Mexican American identity on campus and throughout society.

MAM members' pride in their Mexican background manifested itself in other significant ways. Felix Gutiérrez and the MAM leadership thought building pride among the Mexican American community was one of the chief goals of *The Mexican Voice*, so the newspaper often publicized the athletic accomplishments of the Mexican youth in greater Los Angeles. Achievement in college sports was held in particularly high regard by the MAM leadership. Excelling in this area signified two accomplishments—athletic prowess and academic achievement, or being a successful student *and* an athlete. The newspaper included sports sections that focused on football and track, named "Sporting Around" and "On Your Marks!" respectively.[49] Each year the contributors to *The Mexican Voice* named all-star teams in the most popular sports. For instance, Gutiérrez composed a section of the March 1940 edition of *The Mexican Voice*, "Foul Shots," that documented the accomplishments of Mexican American athletes on the hardwood. Gutiérrez boasted of the difficulty in choosing high school and college all-star teams:

> "As rare as a basketball team without a paisano," may some day be a favorite expression; after what happened this past season. A year that saw almost every team with at least some Spanish name in its roster, from waterboy to coach. With a continued increase in the participation in sports our "All-Mexican Teams" are becoming harder and harder to pick.[50]

The Voice's "Los Angeles City All-Mexican Basketball Team" featured athletes from Garfield, Verdugo Hills, Jordan, Fremont, and Dorsey High Schools, while the "County High School All-Mexican Basketball Team" (including the Catholic league) included young men from Cathedral, Chino, Puente, Loyola, and Redlands High Schools. Students from Santa Barbara State, Whittier College, Chapman College, and Arizona State Teachers College were members of the "All-Mexican College Team."[51] The inclusion of scholastic and intercollegiate athletics in *The Mexican Voice* underscored the multiple ways the young Mexican American leaders hoped to inspire those in their community; the achievements of the scholar athletes demonstrated that the Mexican American people were as just as capable and talented as others in California and the United States.

Throughout its duration, MAM kept abreast of students who enrolled at colleges and universities in the Los Angeles area and often published the accomplishments of individual students. In *The Mexican Voice*, MAM leaders also heavily publicized the events and meetings of other Mexican American student organizations, both on and off the campuses of local colleges, and in the 1940 "Club Issue" of *The Mexican Voice*, MAM featured local student groups.[52] For example, the issue prominently included a piece on the female Mexican American student group at Pasadena Junior College—*El Círculo de Oro* (The Golden Circle). According to the newspaper, the Mexican American women who organized the student group did so in order to "foster social consciousness among Mexican junior college girls and to help them develop qualities for leadership among their own people."[53] Similarly, the editors of *The Mexican Voice* wrote that the Mexican American fraternity Phi Sigma Upsilon, located in southeast Los Angeles, chose "SERVICE" as its motto to underscore its commitment to promoting Mexican American pride throughout the community.[54] In addition to a vivid example of the community outreach MAM took upon itself, the "Club Issue" of *The Mexican Voice* provides evidence of the growing number of Mexican American student organizations then emerging throughout southern California, many of which were connected to local colleges and universities and which reflected the growing vibrancy of a Mexican American student culture on college campuses.

MAM also influenced college students beyond the borders of the state of California. After attending an MAM conference in Los Angeles in 1937, Rebecca Muñoz and her siblings Rosalio, Lucinda, and Josephine founded *Los Conquistadores* (the conquerors), or "*Los Conquis*," at Arizona State College, declaring:

154   C. TUDICO

> We, the Spanish-speaking students of Arizona State College at Tempe, in order to develop a better understanding between ourselves and others; to gain greater social, cultural and intellectual values through our association with others; to interest others in a college education, especially those of our own nationality, do hereby organize this club. The name of this club shall be 'Los Conquistadores.' Said club shall exist on the campus of Arizona State College at Tempe.[55]

Rebecca noted that the Mexican youth taking part in MAM were going through an "intellectual awakening" focused on promoting access to higher education and instilling a greater sense of pride among Mexican Americans.[56] Inspired, the Muñoz siblings fashioned *Los Conquis* like MAM, as an "incipient" civil rights college student organization.[57] The organization maintained ties to MAM and adopted its approach by hosting annual conferences that drew Mexican American youth from across Arizona to discuss issues pertinent to the Mexican American community.[58] In the first of her several literary contributions to *The Mexican Voice*, Rebecca Muñoz wrote:

> So we find at this time a great movement taking place among those of us who have been able to take the opportunities of education and see the immense possibilities of improvement for our people as a whole, aiming to waken our people, especially our youth to take these opportunities and thus enable themselves to become better and more productive citizens of this country.[59]

Like the leaders of MAM, Muñoz also chided the preceding generation for its loyalty primarily to Mexico:

> I have always thought that beauty of this great democracy lies in the freedom of thought and expression which grants these people the privilege of thinking as they wish, but oftentimes we see these people working a great harm for themselves by passing up great opportunities for their self-betterment because of a mistaken sense of loyalty to their cultural background.[60]

The interaction among the Mexican American youth in California and Arizona resulted in the formation of significant relationships between the leaders of the MAM and *Los Conquistadores*, including the marriage of *The Mexican Voice* founder Felix Gutiérrez and Rebecca Muñoz.[61] Many alumni of *Los Conquis* also pursued similar vocational goals to their compatriots in MAM, leading to careers in both education and advocacy (for the Mexican American communities).

The movement was growing and expanding, and in the February 1940 edition of *The Mexican Voice*, MAM President Paul Coronel reflected back on the seven-year old organization:

> It may now be said that our Mexican Youth Conference is approaching the realization of its aims and profound desires...From the very beginning most of us were conscious of an ardent feeling that did exist which showed concerned sentiment and attention in our speeches and discussion groups. Our intense interest for our Mexican youth became more vigorous and expressive year after year until we arrived to the culmination of our highest desires.[62]

With regional conferences in both California and Arizona, as well as the Mexican Girl's Conference, the organization reached its maturity. Coronel described the growing youth movement:

> Our youth movement is fundamentally non-sectarian and non-political. We are not interested in interfacing with any religious beliefs or political theories which characterize radical youth movements in our present day of political and economic struggle. Though we are extremely interested in the progress of our Mexican youth, we are not using measures which are offensive and radical. Our battle is inspirational and not material. We are using calm, determination, sincerity, and strong sense of responsibility to achieve our ends.[63]

However, the movement was progressive in that the organization's core philosophy—economic and social progress through education—was a transformative message.

By 1941, many of the original participants in MAM had graduated from college. Several were now teachers, social workers, or community organizers. As these participants matured along with the organization itself, they were more and more appreciative of the challenges their peers in the Mexican American community faced. Coronel himself reflected upon this growing realization in his 1940 column:

> Many youth would like to go to school but the family conditions do not permit many of them to do so. The average earnings of these families are astonishingly insufficient. Another situation is the class conflict in the communities and even in the schools. Many of our youth have lost much hope because they feel that there are no more opportunities available for them as

Mexicans when they observe the great numbers of people unemployed in spite of their good training. Great numbers of Mexican children are segregated in our schools thus demoralizing many of them...Another vital problem and the most serious of all is the lack of inspiration and encouragement in our homes and in the communities.[64]

To address many of these challenges and expand their organization's reach, they sought to incorporate more formally as a non-profit organization and to codify specific goals. Paul Coronel and Felix Gutiérrez were instrumental in the transition, as was Gualberto Valadez, Coronel's successor as President of MAM. In 1941, Coronel laid the foundation for formally establishing MAM, Inc. in a ten-point platform published in *The Mexican Voice*. The principles that these leaders laid out stressed themes underscored over the years at the MAM Conferences as well as in *The Mexican Voice*: "to better conditions among our Mexican race living in the United States," to be "proud to be of Mexican descent," to encourage the Mexican youth "to take greater interest in and better advantage of...educational institutions," and to promote "mutual understanding" between the Mexican American community and other racial groups.[65] As MAM transitioned to a more formal organization, it proudly recorded that in the 1941–1942 school year, "there are more students of Mexican descent now attending the University of California at Los Angeles than ever before." According to the organization, approximately thirty students were enrolled. MAM acknowledged that the number represented a modest accomplishment in comparison to the number of Mexican American young people of college age in the state. Nonetheless, the organization viewed this increase as an improvement and success story.[66]

The arrival of World War II brought opportunities and challenges for MAM, and served as a vehicle for its membership to reexamine the issues related to Mexican American youth.[67] Images of Mexican American volunteers and a Mexican American soldier, rather than the faces of students, graced the cover of *The Mexican Voice*.[68] MAM leaders, such as Manuel Ceja, enlisted and served overseas in the armed forces,[69] and newspaper columns featured titles such as "Our Heroes" and "Our Soldiers."[70] At the same time, the "activity of *pachucos* (zoot-suited street youth) provoked a severe police crackdown and an onslaught of negative media coverage that inflamed a widespread public backlash against Mexicans."[71] The ensuing Zoot Suit Riots between *pachucos* and white serviceman and sailors forced MAM to acknowledge the prejudices of the dominant white community. Paul Coronel, MAM's president and now a college graduate, attempted to make sense of the cause of the riots in the following sobering judgment published in *The Mexican Voice*:

> Much has been written on the "Pachuco" problem. Delinquency and crime waves have always victimized racial groups but it seems minority groups are always the hardest hit. The youth riots have arisen from our Mexican-American communities and now the young Mexican-Americans are faced with second generation adjustments...[72]

In the view of Coronel and MAM, the *pachucos* exhibited "antagonism and hatred towards the very society which bred them." Coronel criticized white Americans, who often did not regard the Mexican Americans "as an equal, racially or economically," as well as "American institutions," such as schools and churches, that "regarded the Mexican as a problem and not as an asset to our American society." He also challenged the policy of segregation in schools and society. At the same time, Coronel suggested that the Mexican American community shared some of the responsibility for contributing to the conditions that created the conflict: he scolded the parents of *pachucos* for not encouraging the education of their children.[73] Coronel's weighty assessment of the riots represented the complexity of MAM itself, critiquing both the Mexican American community and the dominant white hierarchy.

A year later in 1944, under less contentious circumstances, Paul Coronel again took inventory of the maturation of the MAM:

> We began as a conference, we went into a general movement and now we are in the process of organization. The local councils are made up of Mexican-Americans and Non-Mexican-Americans who are interested in the problems of the Mexican people residing in this country...As more local councils are organized it is planned to organize state organizations of the M.A.M. wherever there is a large proportion of Mexican-Americans.[74]

In the same year, MAM held a convention in Los Angeles to clarify the goals of the entity as a social services organization. Education remained the cornerstone of MAM:

> [W]e are perfectly good examples of people who are in schools, in colleges, in universities, in the professions, who have gained their place because they have earned it. We can't gain our place by simply hollering at the weaknesses or talking about the discrimination against us...[W]e accept the shortcomings that we have and we work from scratch up.[75]

Officially, MAM remained politically non-partisan and non-sectarian, and continued to foster an abiding commitment to the solution of problems through education (and in particular college), with many members citing themselves as examples of Mexican Americans who were in schools, colleges, and universities, and in various professions. But despite the need highlighted by strife and divisions during World War II and the reorganization of MAM as a non-profit, the group did not reach the zenith its leadership anticipated. World War II served as a disruptive event, not an opportunity to expand, and membership subsequently declined. Paul Coronel confessed in a 1949 letter:

> I am beginning to feel we cannot depend on the old blood in our movement. The only thing that will awaken the movement and the people in it to the responsibility we owe our people is new blood. It is wonderful to speak to people and tell them what we're trying to do and feel the enthusiasm those people radiate. We have lost so much of that feeling.[76]

MAM attempted to create a Youth Council, named the Supreme Council of the Mexican American Movement, in the hope that it would carry on in the same spirit exemplified by the previous incarnation of the organization. By then, however, MAM had lost its momentum, and it ceased to exist in 1950.

CONCLUSION

The history of MAM shows a small group of Mexican American youth on college campuses engaged and active in building an identity among themselves, in underscoring the importance of education, and encouraging more young people to enroll in college. In this way, the organization laid the foundation for later generations of Mexican American students to attend college in greater numbers. This history also highlights how Mexican American students were active and involved in building a focus and student culture on campus and off campus that valued education. While MAM members at times may have been naïve to larger challenges and segregation throughout society, they saw and valued education as a key opportunity, and they recognized the importance of building connections among Mexican American students across campuses and communities, and into neighboring states. Additionally, this study of MAM sheds light on how the complexities of race, ethnicity, class, and citizenship shaped how young Mexican Americans viewed higher education and the larger American society in general. MAM was both a Mexican *and* an American college student-led organization. In "Diferencia en la Esfera de Acción de los Padres y sus Hijos en este País," Dora Ibáñez highlighted this dual focus and the differences between MAM members and their parents' generation. She repeated the questions that the first generation of Mexican immigrants asked its children:

> What is happening with our children? Why do they reject our behavior? Why don't they respond harmoniously with our way of thinking? Don't they feel the warmth of our traditions and customs like we do?

She replied as a voice of her generation:

> Many of you don't get answers to these questions and see that your son or daughter doesn't find satisfaction in themselves, nor in the home, nor in the community nor in their own people in general.[77]

Ibáñez and her fellow MAM members believed that their parents' generation did not need to be afraid of their children's different points of view. The parents themselves brought about these different views by immigrating to the United States and California. MAM and its members simply fulfilled their parents' promise by striving for a college education and earning a part of the American dream.

MAM, in some ways, had a profound impact on the Mexican American community that resonates to this day. MAM instilled the importance of earning an education—even if at the time, this message only reached a small segment of the population. The college students who participated in MAM laid the roots of *El Movimiento* of the 1960s, when Mexican Americans advocated for equal rights, including more opportunities in higher education. MAM's Bert Corona became a leader in the Chicano Movement, as did Rosalio Muñoz, Jr., the son of Rosalio Muñoz, the cofounder of *Los Conquis*.[78] In effect, two generations of Mexican American activism were linked. Less than two decades after MAM disbanded, Mexican American students pushed for the formation of Chicano Studies programs and created college student organizations such as the *Movimiento Estudiantil Chicano de Aztlán* (MEChA). And thus, a new generation of the MAM was born.

NOTES

1. The student organization did not formally incorporate itself as the Mexican American Movement (MAM) until 1942. Until then, it was known as the Mexican Youth Conference. For continuity, I employ the term "MAM" to describe the organization.

2. Rebecca Muñoz, "Horizons," *The Mexican Voice*, August 1939, 1–3, Microform, Bancroft Library, University of California, Berkeley.

3. By 1920, the campuses that constituted the University of California enrolled around 14,000 students. See John Aubrey Douglass, *The California Idea and American Higher Education, 1850 to the 1960 Master Plan* (Stanford, CA: Stanford University Press, 2000), 130–31.

4. John Thelin, *A History of American Higher Education* (Baltimore, MD: Johns Hopkins University Press, 2004), 110–11.

5. Herman Buckner, "A Study of Pupil Elimination and Failure among Mexicans" (Master's thesis, University of Southern California, 1935), 169.

6. Buckner, "A Study of Pupil Elimination," 37–38.

7. Ernesto Galarza, *Barrio Boy* (Notre Dame: University of Notre Dame Press, [1971] 2005).

8. Carlos Muñoz, Jr., *Youth, Identity, Power: The Chicano Movement*, Revised and Expanded Edition (London: Verso Press, 2007), 34.

9. Ernesto Galarza quoted in Muñoz, *Youth, Identity, Power*, 34.

10. *Blue and Gold 1922* (Berkeley, CA: Associated Students of the University of California, 1922), 600.

11. *Blue and Gold 1928* (Berkeley, CA: Associated Students of the University of California, 1928), 78.

12. *Blue and Gold 1928*, 111.

13. *Blue and Gold 1929* (Berkeley, CA: Associated Students of the University of California, 1929), 83.

14. *Blue and Gold 1929*, 446.

15. Another example was A. A. Sandoval, a graduate of San Mateo Junior College and the University of Southern California. Sandoval became an optometrist after paying his way through school, a success story cited by MAM members. See "Dr. A.A. Sandoval—A Portrait," *The Mexican Voice*, September 1938, 8–9.

16. George J. Sánchez, *Becoming Mexican American: Ethnicity, Culture and Identity in Chicano Los Angeles, 1900–1945* (New York and Oxford: Oxford University Press, 1993), 255–56; Muñoz, *Youth, Identity, Power*, 43–44.

17. "What's The Voice All About?" *The Mexican Voice*, March 1940, 14.

18. "Leaders Meet at Pomona 'Y,'" *The Mexican Voice*, July 1938, 5; *The Mexican Voice*, Winter 1941, front cover.

19. "Leaders Meet at Glendale," *The Mexican Voice*, January–February 1939, 6–10.

20. "M.A.M. Completes Year," *The Mexican Voice*, 1943, 4.
21. José Rodriguez, "The Value of Education," *The Mexican Voice*, July 1938, 8.
22. Felix Gutiérrez, "Editor's Note," *The Mexican Voice*, July 1938, 7.
23. Rodriguez, "The Value of Education," 8.
24. Manuel Ceja, "Are We Proud of Being Mexicans?" *The Mexican Voice*, August 1938, 9.
25. "What's The Voice All About?" *The Mexican Voice*, March 1940, 14.
26. "Manuel Ceja," *The Mexican Voice*, August 1938, 8.
27. "Miss Dora Ibáñez," *The Mexican Voice*, December 1938, 2.
28. Dora Ibáñez, "A Challenge to the American Girl of Mexican Parentage," *The Mexican Voice*, December 1938, 3–5.
29. Ibáñez, "A Challenge to the American Girl of Mexican Parentage," 3.
30. Ibáñez, "A Challenge to the American Girl of Mexican Parentage," 4.
31. Ibáñez, "A Challenge to the American Girl of Mexican Parentage," 4.
32. Felix Gutiérrez, "Nosotros," *The Mexican Voice*, November–December 1939, 18–19.
33. Felix Gutiérrez, "Nosotros," *The Mexican Voice*, July 1938, 4–5.
34. Gutiérrez, "Nosotros," *The Mexican Voice*, July 1938, 4–5.
35. Paul Coronel, "Give Yourself a Chance," *The Mexican Voice*, July 1939, 6.
36. Felix Gutiérrez, "Nosotros," *The Mexican Voice*, October–November 1938, 15.
37. Paul Coronel, "Give Yourself a Chance," *The Mexican Voice*, July 1939, 5–6.
38. "Stephen Reyes Answers a Question," *The Mexican Voice*, September 1938, 10–11.
39. "Johnny Gutiérrez," *The Mexican Voice*, October–November 1938, 5–7.
40. Felix Gutiérrez, "Nosotros," *The Mexican Voice*, 1943, 8.
41. Gutiérrez, "Nosotros," *The Mexican Voice*, October–November 1938, 17.
42. Gutiérrez, "Nosotros," *The Mexican Voice*, October–November 1938, 17.
43. Gutiérrez, "Nosotros," *The Mexican Voice*, July 1938, 4–5.
44. Felix Gutiérrez, "Nosotros," *The Mexican Voice*, March 1940, 16.
45. Gutiérrez, "Nosotros," *The Mexican Voice*, September 1938, 14.
46. Gutiérrez, "Nosotros," *The Mexican Voice*, September 1938, 14.
47. Gutiérrez, "Nosotros," *The Mexican Voice*, September 1938, 14.
48. Gutiérrez, "Nosotros," *The Mexican Voice*, September 1938, 1.
49. Felix Gutiérrez, "Sporting Around," *The Mexican Voice*, November–December 1939, 15–16; Felix Gutiérrez, "On Your Marks!" *The Mexican Voice*, March 1940, 8–9.
50. "Foul Shots," *The Mexican Voice*, March 1940, 10.
51. "Foul Shots," 10.
52. "Club Issue," *The Mexican Voice*, Winter 1940.
53. "El Círculo de Oro," *The Mexican Voice*, Winter 1940, 3.
54. "Phi Sigma Upsilon," *The Mexican Voice*, Winter 1940, 10.

55. Los Conquistadores, "Preamble," 1937, Arizona State University Archives, Tempe, Arizona.
56. Rebecca Muñoz, "Horizons," *The Mexican American Voice*, August 1939, 1–3, Microform, Bancroft Library, University of California, Berkeley.
57. Laura K. Muñoz, "Desert Dreams: Mexican American Education in Arizona, 1870–1930" (Ph.D. Dissertation, Arizona State University, Tempe, Arizona, 2006), 194–95.
58. "Youth Conferences: Arizona," *The Mexican Voice*, Winter 1941, 6.
59. Rebecca Muñoz, "Horizons," *The Mexican Voice*, August 1939, 1.
60. Muñoz, "Horizons," 1.
61. Félix Gutiérrez, Professor of Journalism and Communication in the Annenberg School for Communication & Journalism and a Professor of American Studies & Ethnicity in the Dana and David Dornsife College of Letters, Arts and Sciences at the University of Southern California, is the son of Gutiérrez and Muñoz.
62. Paul Coronel, "Where Is the Mexican Youth Conference Aiming?" *The Mexican Voice*, February 1940, 1.
63. Coronel, "Where Is the Mexican Youth Conference Aiming?," 1.
64. Coronel, "Where Is the Mexican Youth Conference Aiming?," 2.
65. Gualberto Valadez, "Principles of Mexican Youth Conference," *The Mexican Voice*, Winter 1941, 1.
66. "UCLA Paisanos," *The Mexican Voice*, Winter 1941, 4.
67. For a comprehensive examination of MAM and World War II, see Félix Gutiérrez, "The Mexican Voice Goes to War: Identities, Issues, and Ideas in World War II—Era Mexican American Journalism and Youth Activism," in *Latinas/os and World War II: Mobility, Agency, and Ideology*, eds. Maggie Rivas-Rodriguez and B. V. Olguín (Austin, TX: University of Texas Press, 2014), 115–36.
68. *The Mexican Voice*, 1943, front cover; *The Mexican Voice*, Summer 1944, front cover.
69. "Dedicated to," *The Mexican Voice*, 1943, 2.
70. "Our Heroes," *The Mexican Voice*, 1943, 2; "Our Soldiers," *The Mexican Voice*, 1943, 5.
71. F. Arturo Rosales, *Chicano! The History of the Mexican American Civil Rights Movement* (Houston, TX: Arte Público Press, 1997), 102.
72. Paul Coronel, "The Pachuco Problem," *The Mexican Voice*, 1943, 3.
73. Coronel, "The Pachuco Problem," 3.
74. Paul Coronel, "As We Move," *The Mexican Voice*, Summer 1944, 2.
75. Quoted in Muñoz, *Youth, Identity, Power*, 53, from Proceedings (unpublished), First Annual Convention, Mexican-American Movement, 8 October 1944, 63.

76. Paul Coronel to Angel Cano, letter, 10 August 1949, Papers of the Supreme Council of the Mexican American Movement, Urban Archives Center, California State University, Northridge.

77. Dora Ibáñez, "Diferencia en la Esfera de Acción de los Padres y sus Hijos en este País," *The Mexican Voice*, August 1939, 4–5.

78. Muñoz, "Desert Dreams," 194–95.

CHAPTER 8

Student Activists and Organized Labor

Timothy Reese Cain

In recent years, when college and university employee unions have campaigned for improved working conditions and remuneration, they often have been supported by large groups of students. During the 2016–2017 academic year, for example, when dining hall workers at Harvard University struck for nearly three weeks before agreeing to a new contract, three thousand students signed a petition backing the workers, hundreds walked out of classes to demonstrate their support, and medical students critiqued the university's proposal for worker health care. When a union of non-tenure-line faculty at Ithaca College pursued a new agreement, the local group Students for Labor Action used phone banks, social media, petitions, and rallies to both educate students and ensure their voices were heard by the administration. And at Long Island University, large groups of students chanted "they say lock out, we say walk out" as they skipped classes in protest of the administration's unprecedented lockout of the faculty and use of replacement instructors. These and similar events across the nation point to the important role that students often play in local labor situations and highlight broader trends in student labor activity.[1]

T. R. Cain (✉)
Institute of Higher Education, University of Georgia, Athens, GA, USA
e-mail: tcain@uga.edu

© The Author(s) 2018
C. A. Ogren, M. A. VanOverbeke (eds.),
Rethinking Campus Life, Historical Studies in Education,
https://doi.org/10.1007/978-3-319-75614-1_8

165

Student engagement with organized labor may be growing but certainly is not new. For more than a century, college students have variously aligned with, joined, criticized, and countered labor unions. This chapter considers this history of student activism in relation to labor unions in the twentieth century, focusing on extracurricular activities at traditional institutions of higher education rather than on formal curricular features or institutions founded explicitly for workers' education, such as Brookwood Labor College or Commonwealth College.[2] It does so chronologically, tracing patterns of interaction beginning with the early twentieth century student strikebreaking activities and less prominent support of striking workers. It then considers the first mass student movement of the 1930s, which is best known for anti-war protests but which also included significant labor-related activity. Following a brief lull, mass student activism reemerged in the 1960s and included conflicted relationships between student militants and organized labor. The chapter concludes with a brief discussion of students' late twentieth century direct and tangential re-engagement with labor. As such, it explores the changing relationships that both brought together members of two of America's largest groups—laborers and students—and drove wedges between them. Engagement with or against labor allowed students to wrestle with their place in the economic and social order. As student populations diversified, relationships with labor often expanded, though they also became more complicated, especially when students viewed established labor organizations as part of the status quo. Students were most supportive of labor unions when they viewed them as part of broader efforts for justice, equity, and substantial societal change, rather than as organizations based narrowly on economic interests. Even during times of high student support for labor, some students aligned with capital and sought to claim or protect their class interests. Student labor activities thus were significant to the labor movement, but, more importantly to this volume, they shed light on students' political lives, the campus cultures they established, and their differing views on fundamental social issues.

Early Twentieth Century Socialists, Strikes, and Strikebreakers

Higher education expanded in the early twentieth century but at many colleges the dominant group remained the college men (and women) identified by Helen Lefkowitz Horowitz.[3] These were the upper- and upper-middle-class students who reveled in campus life as they sought to secure their places in the American economy and society. Many were not inclined to support labor and some actively opposed it. Stephen H. Norwood's "The Student as Strikebreaker" details one extreme of student-labor relations. Norwood describes most colleges as conservative institutions closely tied to leading corporations. As early as 1901, businesses recruited male students to help break strikes; into the early 1920s, these students were a crucial source of strikebreaking valued for their youth, respectability, and loyalty to management. Norwood locates these activities not only in the alliance between institutions and corporations but also in an early twentieth century societal emphasis on muscularity amid fears that societal shifts were feminizing young men. Strikebreaking—and the thrill of opposing or clashing with striking workers—provided students with an opportunity to demonstrate their masculinity in the absence of military service, as did football and other active pursuits. At the same time, strikebreaking was a class-based activity that emphasized students' allegiance to corporations, management, and the upper classes, rather than to common workers. Students also viewed strikebreaking as a fun part of college life in which they reveled in playing the role, temporarily, of wage laborers. Administrators and faculty frequently endorsed these dalliances in strikebreaking.[4]

Strikebreaking by college men is the primary image of student interaction with labor in the early twentieth century, but a minority of students were more supportive of labor. Norwood highlights that female college students and women's colleges were often more pro-labor than male students and men's colleges. Although most female college students remained politically conservative, the settlement house movement—which enlisted college and college-educated women to live in impoverished urban areas to provide educational and cultural support—provided avenues for progressive action. The movement aligned with labor, although it was highly critical of the American Federation of Labor (AFL), and provided its participants with insight into not only living conditions but also workplace issues and organizing. Some female college students also openly supported striking workers, at times even heckling their strikebreaking male peers. Founded in 1903 and headquartered in Chicago, the National Women's Trade Union League of America (WTUL) also appealed to college women and recent graduates. During the 1909–1910 strike of shirtwaist workers in New York, it raised money from female college students to support the strikers and successfully encouraged picketing by students from Barnard,

Bryn Mawr, Vassar, and Wellesley Colleges. The WTUL increasingly turned its attention to educational activities, including forming the first residential workers' education program in the country in 1914. The program provided female workers with the opportunity to take classes at Chicago colleges and universities, and became a model for later programs at Bryn Mawr College, the University of Wisconsin, and elsewhere.[5]

The Intercollegiate Socialist Society (ISS) had a larger campus footprint than the WTUL and was likewise engaged with labor issues. Founded in 1905, it had more than 1300 male and female student members and 70 campus chapters by 1915. According to Philip G. Altbach, the only national student organizations to rival its influence in the era were the Young Men's Christian Association (YMCA) and Young Women's Christian Association (YWCA). ISS was designed to engage students with socialist ideas, rather than recruit them to socialism, and among the issues that ISS considered were those involving labor. It was largely an educational organization, sponsoring tours of lecturers, producing pamphlets and the magazine *Intercollegiate Socialist*, and hosting an annual conference and summer institutes. ISS was adamantly opposed to student strikebreaking and, after considerable debate over the appropriateness of taking a partisan stand, overwhelmingly condemned the practice. Still, as a national organization, ISS was conflicted about the labor movement more broadly. As did the Socialist Party, it shared many policy positions with labor, but disagreed with the approach of Samuel Gompers and the leadership of the AFL. Moreover, it was reticent to support labor activism; for example, when members from New York City colleges marched with 60,000 workers in the 1910 May Day Parade, the national leadership told them it was ill advised.[6]

Local ISS chapters similarly sponsored lecturers and socialist study events, and in a few instances became more actively involved with labor actions. In 1911, Harvard's chapter supported cleaning women whom the institution had fired to avoid paying them the state's new minimum wage.[7] In 1913, the University of Michigan chapter highlighted the difficulties facing the many working students and called for them to organize. The chapter argued that student waiters who served in the many boarding houses in town were particularly poorly treated. In July, the student newspaper reported rumors that boarding house rates might increase due to the success of the waiters in banding together for better pay, although it would later claim that the effort had been too weak to effect change. The following fall, the waiters again attempted to organize and this time received support from the university and the YMCA, although boarding house operators claimed that the problems with low wages and poor working conditions were limited to only a few establishments. Local news coverage quickly dissipated, but, the following spring, Industrial Workers of the World co-founder and frequent ISS lecturer Frank Bohn proclaimed greater success than local evidence indicated. He wrote that Michigan's ISS chapter had "organized a union of the working students and struck in true working class style....The strike was splendidly successful as a matter of educational propaganda as well as for its material benefits." Nonetheless, the movement was short-lived and only represented one campus view on labor; on the same campus in 1912, students had served as strikebreakers when firemen and coal wheelers went on strike.[8]

Throughout the early twentieth century, then, students participated in significant but varied activities related to labor and strikes. With institutional support, male students broke strikes to demonstrate their virility and class bonds, as well as to experience the thrills associated with their riotous behaviors. At the same time, other students, especially women, studied labor, opposed strikebreaking, and even supported striking workers. Working students also pursued labor actions closer to home as they sought to better their own conditions.

The Conservative 1920s

The years just after the extreme disruption of World War I proved especially difficult for the American left and for organized labor. In the aftermath of the war and the 1917 Russian Revolution, notions of un-American activities spread and, in higher education, the wartime repression of alleged German sympathizers extended to suspected socialists. Although labor had achieved gains in working conditions and wages during the war when labor was at a premium, the conservatism of the immediate post-war period soon took a toll. In 1919, widespread labor actions intended to consolidate wartime gains were met with harsh counterattacks amid charges of communist activity.[9] Students exhibited even less affinity for labor than they had in the decade before and the student strikebreaking of the pre-war era returned, at times with violent consequences. In 1919, for example, when nearly all telephone operators in five New England states struck for better wages, students from Harvard, Massachusetts Institute of Technology (MIT), Smith and Tufts Colleges, and Brown University were among those who responded to calls for temporary workers. Many were beaten in riotous conflicts with the strikers. In the Boston Police Strike that same year, more than 200 Harvard students joined the strikebreaking efforts, making up 15 percent of the replacement force. The following year, almost all of the students from Columbia and Princeton Universities, MIT, and Stevens Institute engaged in strikebreaking activities. At Stevens, administrators canceled classes so that students could freely leave campus to do so.[10]

Some of these events reveal the complexity of the situations and the multiple perspectives of those involved. Boston police officers were staunchly anti-union, even facilitating Harvard students' strikebreaking in 1919, until they themselves unionized and struck later that year. Also, while numerous students undertook strikebreaking during the telephone operators' strike, other students condemned these activities and some administrators worried about the public reaction to students' strikebreaking. At Brown, for example, student opponents of strikebreaking resolved that the actions were not representative of the institution and the larger student body. The Smith president convinced his strikebreaking students to withdraw, and *The Harvard Crimson* editorialized against student participation. Yet, later that year, Harvard's president and football coach— who had canceled practices so his team could participate—supported, encouraged, and visited students who broke the police strike.[11]

In ensuing years, student strikebreaking largely receded, although it did periodically occur into the mid-1930s. Pro-labor activities and organizations also became rare on college campuses—any critiques of strikebreakers were generally arguments for neutrality, not in support of labor—though they did continue at least to a minimal extent. In 1921, for example, the ISS reconstituted itself as the League for Industrial Democracy (LID) and many campus chapters similarly rebranded themselves, though LID was not primarily a student organization. Despite difficulties in securing campus venues, its lecture series and events continued, including talks on labor topics by speakers such as Norman Thomas, a socialist activist and frequent candidate for state and federal office. Through its summer conferences and on-campus events, LID attempted to connect students with labor leaders and to involve them in labor activities. Moreover, LID student members at Vassar College and Yale University helped the Neckwear Makers Union publicize its members' plight with some students being jailed for their activities, while Swarthmore College LID members investigated labor conditions in the South.[12]

By the middle of the decade, LID undertook some of these activities in conjunction with the YMCA, which showed increasing interest in economic disparities. The YMCA's most relevant effort was the Summer Industrial Group program, which began in 1920. The program paid college students to work in vocational positions during the summer, bringing them into direct contact with working class laborers and the challenges that they faced. Educational components of the program presented evidence of economic struggles and included sessions with representatives of industry and labor. Many students joined unions as a result, and, in that first summer, some struck with Denver street car workers. Although historian C. Howard Hopkins saw "little evidence of direct social action in the economic arena" through the program, contemporaneous observers noted that the efforts were promising.[13] The YWCA also became increasingly committed to working class issues through its Industrial Department and, in 1920, officially supported collective bargaining. It familiarized college students with industrial issues through summer placements of female students in industrial positions, study groups of college women and workers, and interactions at the summer schools for workers that the YWCA helped coordinate. For the college women, these were largely educational activities, though they involved enough activism to draw concern from both the board of the YWCA and some college leaders.[14]

New national groups arose alongside these existing organizations, sometimes touching on labor issues without themselves being activist. One of the most prominent of these was the National Student Forum (NSF), which used annual conferences and its semi-monthly *New Student* to advocate for and report on left and radical issues, including greater connections between students and workers.[15] Still, more than in the decade before or after, college student life in the 1920s was typified by conservative self-interest and political indifference. Historian Paula S. Fass argues that "political and economic questions in the narrow sense were treated casually, almost cavalierly" by students who were "heirs apparent of American industrial capitalism."[16] Diverse institutions and populations provided for a variety of perspectives and expressions, but most college students either avoided labor issues or sided with the upper class and corporate interests.

HEIGHTENED ACTIVISM IN THE GREAT DEPRESSION

Spurred by the Great Depression and the rise of fascism in Europe, student activism in the 1930s reached a high point, with a higher percentage of students participating than in any other decade. Students protested

militarism, the Reserve Officer Training Corps (ROTC), parietal rules, violations of student and faculty free speech, and numerous other issues. They
engaged in local, national, and international politics; formed national activist associations; and rallied both on and off campus. Many, though certainly
not all, pursued more liberal political agendas than did students in most
other decades and, with the devastation of the Great Depression, they
upended class norms. That such would be the case, though, was not clear
as the decade began. Higher education was at first relatively protected from
the worst of the economic crisis and fared better than many industries. In
part due to low opportunity costs and, eventually, federal student aid,
enrollments grew in most years of the Great Depression. At the same time,
the larger national and international situation, as well as the hardships experienced by numerous students who found themselves without the part-
time work on which they relied to make ends meet, soon caused student
activism to emerge as a defining feature of higher education in the decade.[17]

The anti-war protests during the rise of fascism in Europe and the split
of the student left over communist students' allegiance to the Soviet
Union at the end of the decade are probably the best remembered aspects
of the nation's first mass student movement, but student activism around
labor issues both on and off campuses was prevalent, as well. Founded in
New York City in 1931, the communist-aligned National Student League
(NSL) was one of the most significant student organizations of the decade.
It initially drew much of its membership from the tuition-free municipal
colleges in the city, especially City College of New York. The ethnically
and religiously diverse student populations of the colleges were different
from those of many other institutions and were especially hard hit by the
Great Depression. The organization drew on the political traditions of the
immigrant communities that many of its students were part of, as well as
the leftist political scene in the city. It attracted national attention through
its March 1932 efforts to send two busloads of students to visit striking
coal miners in Harlan County, Kentucky, with the goal of providing the
miners with material support while also investigating allegations of severe
mistreatment. It was an early galvanizing event for the student left, which
Marvin Bressler and Judith Higgins later termed "the Alamo, the Maine,
and Pearl Harbor of the student movement in the thirties."[18] The students—mostly from New York institutions but also from Harvard, Smith,
and the Universities of Tennessee and Wisconsin—were followed, attacked,
and prevented from reaching Harlan, but the activity provided significant
publicity for the organization. Elsewhere, college students protested

outside of Samuel Insull's Chicago home and the Philadelphia offices of J. P. Morgan in opposition to Insull's and Morgan's mine ownership. Students from other institutions, including the University of Chicago and Commonwealth College, then undertook similar trips to aid miners. Moreover, while these students largely failed in their efforts to garner direct governmental intervention in the strike, they were instrumental in prompting a Congressional investigation into the working conditions in the coal industry.[19]

The NSL expanded nationally and served as a further alternative to the left of the student branch of the LID, soon to be known as the Student League for Industrial Democracy (SLID). The two groups vied for members but increasingly came together in efforts against militarism and the suppression of campus speech. In late December 1935, they aligned to form the American Student Union (ASU) as a new national organization that also included other liberal student groups to present a united front against fascism. Although most of its activities centered on opposing war, eliminating mandatory ROTC, and advocating for speech rights, ASU also sought to unite students and workers around common goals. The ASU's monthly *Student Advocate* reported on student labor actions and the collaborations of the ASU with the Congress of Industrial Organizations (CIO), and its national conferences included addresses by labor leaders such as CIO president John L. Lewis. The American Youth Congress (AYC), another significant leftist student group, likewise brought students and workers together, including through its efforts to lobby for greater federal economic and educational aid for young people. Indeed, the AYC intentionally looked beyond college students to those without the financial wherewithal to attend to build a broader coalition of youth to bring about substantial economic change. The student left as a whole was sympathetic to labor for personal and philosophical reasons.[20]

Widespread student support for labor clearly existed, as dozens of campus and workplace events demonstrated. In 1935, for example, the *Washington Post* reported that "with Ohio State University students in the front ranks, Columbus Packing Co. strikers and their sympathizers clashed in a 30-minute pitched battle with 200 policemen and detectives."[21] The following year, the *Student Advocate* reported on student involvement in labor difficulties at Columbia University's Teachers College resulting in the dismissal of cafeteria workers for their union activities. "Only after a strenuously-waged campaign of workers and students acting in close cooperation" did the administration agree to an impartial investigation which revealed the extreme difficulties facing the workers. The resulting union contract included the rehiring of workers and partial back pay.[22] Also in 1936, Dartmouth College students intervened in a quarry strike in Vermont, providing aid to workers while educating themselves and building cross-class understandings.[23] Yale students participated in multiple strike activities over the course of the 1930s and, at the end of the decade, helped organize university employees. In 1937, University of Michigan students who had galvanized around labor issues hitchhiked between Ann Arbor and Flint to produce and distribute the *Punch Press*, the official bulletin of autoworkers' 1936–1937 sit-down strike against General Motors. They also helped more broadly in the union's educational work and efforts to assist unemployed workers in garnering welfare.[24]

The Michigan students who supported the Flint strike were among those involved in an effort that brought labor organizing even closer to home: the founding and activities of the Student Workers Federation (SWF) (Image 8.1). Five Michigan students formed the SWF in early 1936 "with the sole aim of helping students on the campus to obtain just working conditions." The organization noted that 60 percent of male students and 25 percent of female students worked to support their schooling, mostly in unskilled positions with low wages and no job security. Students working in restaurants were often paid in leftover food rather than wages. In its lengthy tract "Why SWF?" the organization argued: "Left alone, the student worker is powerless. The coercion of necessity compels him to accept whatever job he can get."[25] The SWF noted that students had tried small shop unions but only a campus-wide organization could offer protections and benefits. Claiming 500 members the following fall, the SWF threatened boycotts to pressure local businesses to pay students the same rates that they paid non-student workers. When businesses signed on, they received placards for their windows indicating that the SWF approved of their labor practices. The SWF negotiated explicit contracts with two restaurants that had treated students especially badly and, after almost a year of effort, received an agreement from the Michigan League, a campus dining and student activities center, to raise student wages immediately. Its most visible action, though, was picketing the Ann Arbor Recreation Center in support of striking bowling pin boys, an activity that led to the arrest of several members and national attention from labor groups and the American Civil Liberties Union. Though it lasted less than two years, the SWF was influential in Ann Arbor and inspired similar groups at the Universities of Texas and California. At the latter institution, the school's

Image 8.1 Members of the Student Workers Federation in the late 1930s. (Source: Ivory Photograph Collection, Box 11, Bentley Historical Library, University of Michigan)

student government followed the lead of SWF in a campaign for better student wages under the moniker "Fair Bear" that lasted into the 1950s.[26] Of course, neither institutions nor their student populations were monolithic. Explicit opposition to unions included occasional strikebreaking, most notably in 1934, when students from the Universities of California, Southern California, and Washington broke maritime strikes. Additionally, in 1937 as many as 1500 Michigan Agricultural College students overwhelmed an attempt to extend a general strike called by the United Auto Workers from Lansing into East Lansing, where the institution was located. They dunked strikers in a campus creek and forced them back to Lansing.[27] At the end of the decade, Harvard's waiters and cooking staff unionized and sought a closed shop, and in 1940 the union successfully fought a university attempt to replace ten waitresses with student workers as a cost-cutting move. Later that year, the student council, which had been investigating the issue, called on the institution to replace the union workers with students. The request was based partly on a survey of more than 800 students in which more than half of those offering an opinion were in favor of the replacements. The reported objections related to concerns about efficiency and furthering class divisions in the student population, not the negative effect on the full-time workers.[28]

With the student left's split over communism at the end of the decade and then the changed economy and focus brought on by World War II, activism soon diminished. For much of the 1930s, though, students engaged in significant protest over on- and off-campus issues, including those involving labor and labor unions. National groups such as the ASU and AYC supported labor, local organizations formed around labor issues, and many students supported the new unions forming on their campuses. Amid the difficulties of the Great Depression, students questioned the existing economic order and sought labor action to improve both their own economic situations and those of workers with whom they were aligned more than ever before. The expansion and diversification of the student population, which drew in more students from lower socio-economic and immigrant backgrounds, partially explains this engagement. So, too, does the widespread economic hardship that affected the nation as a whole, including some college students who struggled for survival. While not all were supportive of unions and campuses such as MAC remained quite conservative, engaging with labor was both a way for many students to grapple with their roles in the world and an avenue for their efforts to achieve substantial social and economic change.

Post-war Retreat, then Radicalization

The immediate post-war period was tumultuous for organized labor with significant unrest followed by McCarthyist anti-communist crackdowns. Labor unions, including those in higher education, struggled to demonstrate that they were not dominated by communists. Although historians have paid little attention to it, the evidence suggests limited support for labor among students in the late 1940s and early 1950s. Small numbers of student activists at the University of Illinois, Harvard, and Yale, for example, participated in labor actions. At Yale, groups of students both supported and opposed a strike of janitorial and service workers for better wages and assurances that the university would not replace them with student workers. Some argued that the workers were valued members of the campus community with explicit rights, while others tried to pit the workers' needs against those of the students and university. Some performed striking workers' jobs in exchange for beer.[29] American Youth for Democracy (AYD), a successor to the Young Communist League, was the national student organization most involved with labor during this period. AYD was active on more than 60 campuses in the late 1940s, sponsoring educational programs and a California conference that brought together students and labor leaders with the understanding that labor was "the most progressive force in our country."[30] At times, local AYD chapters intervened further in labor disputes; the University of Michigan chapter, for example, attempted to raise funds to feed striking General Motors workers. A renewed SLID maintained ties to the United Auto Workers (UAW), the YMCA and YWCA brought students and labor together through their Students-in-Industry programs, and student groups such as the Labor Youth League and Students for Democratic Action considered labor issues through speakers' series and educational programs, but they usually focused their efforts elsewhere. Still, the overall picture in the immediate post-war era was one of increasingly conservative college campuses. According to historian Ellen W. Schrecker, "by the early 1950s... the student left was all but extinct on American campuses, its demise the product of external repression and personal prudence."[31]

Beginning in the early 1960s, student activism returned in profound and dramatic ways that raised questions about the nation's adherence to its founding principles. With roots in the Civil Rights Movement and the Old Left of the earlier generation, the student movements of the 1960s and early 1970s took on racism and segregation, campus speech issues, curricular relevance, women's rights, and the Vietnam War. Increasingly radicalized and influential—although still a minority activity—the various and sometimes competing efforts to upend existing power hierarchies clashed with both local and societal institutions. Throughout, student activists had complicated relationships with organized labor, in part because neither the New Left—the overarching term for the young radical activists that separated themselves from the Old Left—nor organized labor was monolithic or static. Over the tumultuous decade both experienced internal divisions and changes.

In *The New Left and Labor in the 1960s*, Peter B. Levy acknowledges the popular understanding that the two movements were in opposition.

This understanding crystalized when approximately 200 construction workers attacked, beat, and dispersed anti-war student protestors in a May 1970 clash in New York City. That event, and those in its aftermath, pointed to a significant rift between students and labor. Levy, though, complicates that view by explaining that while differing views on the war—along with the rise of Black Power and the emergence of the counter culture—drove significant wedges between students and organized labor, there were numerous ways in which unions and student activists intersected and interacted, including some in which they aligned. As Levy wrote, "the New Left's relationship to labor should be viewed dialectically. ... Indeed, if we are to arrive at a sophisticated understanding of one of the pivotal decades in American history, we must take note of both the sensational conflicts between the New Left and labor and the numerous instances of cooperation, especially on the local level."[32]

The nature of the conflicted and evolving relationship between students and labor can be demonstrated through a brief consideration of Students for a Democratic Society (SDS), the largest student activist organization of the decade. Founded in 1960 as a new start for SLID, SDS's roots were in the Old Left and it initially had strong ties to organized labor. The organization reached prominence in 1962 with the release of its manifesto, the Port Huron Statement, which had been finalized at its first convention, funded by the UAW and held at the union's retreat site. Indeed, UAW funding and in-kind support were crucial to early SDS organizing and activities. The statement was critical of organized labor, calling it "quiescent," but simultaneously recognized that labor's revitalization would be important for larger societal change. Other early SDS documents treated labor similarly. Among SDS's main activities were the Economic Research and Action Projects (ERAP), which relied on UAW funding to place community organizers mainly in urban centers, but also in rural areas, such as Hazard, Kentucky, where the organizers had a special focus on mine workers. While these activities had the potential to build coalitions between labor and students, the overall results were disappointing; indeed, in some locales, unions were skeptical and reluctant to cooperate. Later in the decade, SDS separated from the LID, radicalized, and pulled farther away from labor, but for the first few years, it actively considered the role of labor in societal change. Opinions within SDS differed but according to labor writer and one-time SDS national council member Kim Moody, much of the historiography makes SDS seem much more dismissive of organized labor than it was, even though the organization was in a difficult position: "The thing is, of course, that it's a student organization, so your ability to relate to the labor movement was severely limited. What could you do? We used to sit around and talk about these things at the first three conventions, and labor was very important to people. A lot of people became labor organizers."[33]

Broadly speaking, SDS abandoned the notion that the working class would serve as a base for a revolutionary movement but factions within the organization continued to emphasize connections. While many within SDS emphasized racial issues, the war in Vietnam, or the broader struggle between developed and developing nations, by the end of the 1960s, the increasingly influential Progressive Labor Party (PLP) instead pushed for a worker-student alliance within SDS. The PLP was formed by expelled members of the Communist Party in the early 1960s and became popular on college campuses including through sponsorship of student trips to Cuba, efforts to support miners in Kentucky, and anti-war activities. In 1965, many of its student members joined SDS, where they slowly accumulated influence and promoted activities such as a summer 1968 work-in, which placed students in industrial jobs to build bridges to and radicalize workers. The following year, a split between PLP and other internal factions caused SDS to collapse but PLP continued to pursue worker-student alliances. It emphasized student support for campus workers and sought unionization more broadly, including through significant efforts in New York's garment industry.[34]

SDS was only one of many activist organizations, and only one of many that drew upon labor support in its formative years. The Student Nonviolent Coordinating Committee (SNCC)—which inspired, informed, and cooperated with SDS—received funding from the United Packinghouse Workers of America (UPWA) and other labor unions in support of its efforts for racial justice. Unions contributed to SNCC and other civil rights organizations' 1964 Mississippi Summer Project and initially supported the Mississippi Freedom Democratic Party (MFDP), which was designed to unseat the racist southern Democrats from the presidential nominating convention. Support was reciprocal, as SNCC proved important to the early efforts of what became the United Farm Workers (UFW) and actively supported the Mississippi Freedom Labor Union (MFLU), founded by sharecroppers in 1965. It is no coincidence that these latter efforts were for independent local unions, as SNCC and other civil rights organizations were wary of the racism within the AFL-CIO and unsure whether they could count on the broader labor movement to fully support their causes. This hesitation became more pronounced after the AFL-CIO backed US President Lyndon Johnson's efforts to grant two at-large seats at the 1964 convention to the MFDP rather than allow its members to fully represent Mississippi. SNCC's turn toward Black nationalism in 1966 further moved it away from the AFL-CIO.[35]

Founded in 1964, the Southern Student Organizing Committee was a less radical activist organization for White students in the South. When its efforts to pursue White community organizing failed in 1966, it partnered with organized labor to work for improved working conditions in the region. Its most successful labor effort involved helping to organize thousands of agricultural workers into a UPWA local in Florida. It also contributed the energy of hundreds of members to efforts to organize textile workers in 1967 before folding under attacks from SDS factions.[36]

These and many other examples of student national organizations and their interactions with unions and workers, including the increasing divides between students and the AFL-CIO, tell only part of the story as numerous local efforts—some tied to national groups, others independent—also illustrate ongoing interactions between students and labor. Throughout the decade, students joined picket lines, aided striking workers, and otherwise participated in labor actions. SNCC's efforts to support César Chávez's organizing of farm workers, for example, were joined by those of numerous other organizations, including SDS, the National Student Association, and the Congress of Racial Equality, which drew many of its members from college campuses. Indeed, Chávez frequently spoke on college campuses and recruited students, while also helping to inspire the Chicano student movement.[37] According to Chávez aide Carlos LeGarratte, students "were bright-eyed and bushy-tailed and wanting to change the world. The farmworkers gave them a place where they could do so nonviolently. The college students were fantastic volunteers in the movement."[38]

At the end of the decade, notable student efforts to support labor included assistance for striking workers at General Electric in 1969–1970 and General Motors in 1970. Some students and groups supported more radical labor action against not just corporations but also the entrenched and highly bureaucratic unions that they believed were part of the problem. Included among them were students at Wayne State University who actively participated in the unauthorized wildcat strikes and racial consciousness raising of the Dodge Revolutionary Union Movement (DRUM), the forerunner of the League of Revolutionary Black Workers.

Indeed, reflecting the increasing diversity of students' backgrounds, some members of DRUM and the League were both students and autoworkers. At the end of the decade, the League helped elect an editor to Wayne State's campus paper who took the paper in a radical direction, including by hiring League activists. At the same time, many students were inactive and not all activist students supported workers' rights. Conservative campus organizations largely focused their efforts elsewhere, but some, including Young America for Freedom, spoke out against organized labor.[39]

Additional examples of student activists' support for labor in the 1960s include efforts that emphasized on-campus issues. Having been part of American Federation of Teachers (AFT) locals in the 1930s, graduate students in the 1960s formed their own locals, beginning at the University of California-Berkeley as an outgrowth of the graduate student wing of the Free Speech Movement. At the University of Wisconsin, the Teaching Assistants Association organized for greater rights and remuneration, eventually negotiating the first graduate student union contract in American higher education. Students also considered non-student workers on their campuses. At Duke University, hundreds of students responded to the killing of Martin Luther King, Jr. with an occupation of the president's house, where they demanded that he agree to support the African American workers who were organizing to overcome oppressive and racist working conditions. When the workers struck on April 8, up to 2000 students participated in a four-day silent vigil in support of them. The largest student political action in the institution's history helped build bridges between the students and community, and contributed to institutional concessions to the workers. The following year, students at the Chapel Hill and Greensboro campuses of University of North Carolina likewise participated in protests in support of the largely African American cafeteria and janitorial workers. At Greensboro, as many as 1200 people rallied in support of union workers; many were students from the nearby North Carolina A&T State University, a historically Black college at which numerous Greensboro workers were enrolled. Moreover, Black student movements on other campuses across the country included demands for better treatment for Black workers on campus.[40]

The widespread campus protests of the 1960s continued into the early 1970s but on a much smaller scale after the national student strike in protest of the killings at Kent State and Jackson State Universities; by 1972, according to sociologist Andrew Barlow, protests "were in decline everywhere."[41] Decline, of course, did not mean eradication as both on and off college campuses, activists in the 1970s and following decades still fought for equality for women, racial and ethnic minorities, and, increasingly, gay men and lesbians. Labor activity continued as well, including among the many sixties activists who moved off campus and into labor organizing. Some remained on campus and continued to organize and support labor and other movements, but by the mid-1970s the scale was decidedly smaller and the national tone was muted. At the height of protest movements in the 1960s and early 1970s, though, interactions among students and labor showed the convergence of movements to improve workers' conditions across US society. By the middle of the 1960s, disagreements among left activists spread as a number of students radicalized. Some of their efforts remained focused on workers and their rights—often in the context of racial discrimination—but students pushed for faster and more profound change than many established unions sought. Indeed, the radicalization of the student left brought it into conflict with the AFL-CIO's entrenched business unionism as many activists sought revolutionary change across a range of societal, political, and economic issues. Student activists were diverse and their efforts pushed in multiple directions, but at times they coalesced around labor issues, especially in the context of broader struggles for equality.

ACTIVISM AT THE END OF THE CENTURY

As Robert A. Rhoads captures in *Freedom's Web: Student Activism in an Age of Cultural Diversity*, the last 15 years of the twentieth century saw the return of significant activism on college campuses, much of it dealing with multicultural and identity issues. Student activism, though, received a substantial boost from the significant and successful protests against institutional and corporate ties to the apartheid regime in South Africa, protests that were supported by American labor. More explicit interaction with unions and unionizing was clearly present, as well, prodded by concerns over both local conditions and the rights and safety of workers across the globe.[42] For example, students actively participated in strike actions by clerical workers at Yale and Columbia. At Yale in the mid-1980s, according to Molly Ladd-Taylor, "Sympathetic students picketed with department and college secretaries; protested films, plays, and lectures held on campus; and organized teach-ins, discussions and departmental meetings to educate fellow students about the union.... Although the majority of students and faculty tried to remain neutral, hundreds of students attended pro-union rallies, filed a lawsuit against the university for breach of contract, staged sit-ins at the library to protest reduced hours, and withheld their second-semester tuition."[43] Others were conflicted and some opposed the workers. Students were likewise vital during strikes for recognition and contracts at Columbia in the 1980s and then again in the early 1990s, although in the latter strikes, the union struggled to build a large coalition of support due to its narrow emphasis on economics, rather than broader notions of justice.[44]

By the end of the century, scholars observed a larger revitalization of organized labor, including on college campuses. Graduate student unionization, which had slowly spread since the 1960s, took on new life, becoming one of the most vibrant areas of organizing in higher education. Lengthy battles at institutions such as Yale and New York University highlighted the contested nature of the issue, with undergraduates at times caught between their institutions and those instructing their classes.[45] In 1994, students at the University of Wisconsin-Madison formed the Staley Solidarity Action Committee, soon renamed the Student Labor Action Coalition (SLAC) in support of union workers locked out by the A. E. Staley Company in Decatur, Illinois. SLAC chapters formed on additional campuses and contributed to the AFL-CIO's 1996 launch of its Union Summer program to train students in organizing and place them in four-week union positions. Program goals included supporting organizing campaigns, attracting activist students to the labor movement, and preparing students to promote labor action on their college campuses. Perhaps the most visible early result of SLAC and Union Summers was the growth of the student anti-sweatshop movement, which took shape, in part, through the efforts of 1997 Union Summer intern Tico Alemida and resulted in significant commitments to improving conditions for workers producing university branded apparel.[46] In the closing years of the twentieth century, these student activists were joined by others focused on working conditions in collaboration with union labor, notably those in the living wage campaigns that grew at the University of Southern California, Johns Hopkins University, the University of Virginia, and elsewhere.[47]

These end-of-the-century activities were local, national, and international. They addressed both campus inequities and international human rights issues. As much or more than in any other era, they proved effective, in part due to students' abilities to apply local pressure to affect institutional behaviors in pursuit of broader justice. As part of these efforts, alliances with organized labor, which had waned over the years, were reinvigorated as students and other observers questioned the extent to which US higher education was contributing to or ameliorating economic disparities.

CONCLUSION

Over the course of the twentieth century, college student activists interacted with union workers in numerous ways, including by supporting their efforts, breaking their strikes, and learning from their tactics. At times, they pursued direct action over their own working conditions, though they more frequently considered or acted to affect the conditions of other workers, both on and off campus. Occasionally, early strikebreaking activities attracted the majority of the student population on individual campuses, while pro-union actions were generally minority efforts. Students' opinions on labor issues varied, and many students across eras were apathetic or focused on other matters. At the same time, the numerous student actions around labor were significant. During each of the high points of student protest, labor was a significant issue that generated substantial activity; in local situations, it was sometimes the primary focus of student activity. Perhaps just as significantly, union labor actions provided opportunities for students to act on wider social issues, including racial justice and gender discrimination. Indeed, while class and economic issues remained important, race and gender became much more central by the 1960s. When union efforts expanded beyond narrow economic arguments to broader concerns about justice and equity, students were more likely to engage on the side of labor.[48]

The growth and change in student populations are part of this larger story of student and labor interactions as expansion beyond the largely male, upper-middle-class clientele brought new perspectives and views on labor. The diverse student populations in 1930s New York, for example, helped turn student attention to labor issues, and those in the 1960s helped to push toward more radical labor action. At the same time, as the student uprisings in the 1960s demonstrated, it was not just the dispossessed who challenged the social and economic order. Moreover, activities were at times most effective when students worked across class lines. While many of these student actions were self-initiated, they could also be fostered and furthered by stakeholders in labor disputes. Students were valued for their views and status—early twentieth century corporations pursued students as strikebreakers for their respectability, while unions later sought their youthful enthusiasm and idealism. College was also a training ground as, throughout the century, some of the students who participated in pro-labor activities remained committed and active beyond their collegiate years. Of course, the pro-labor students were always only one part of the student population as diverse views existed throughout; in many generations, pro-labor views were in the extreme minority, but they could still affect local, national, and, at times, international situations.

The broad overview provided in this chapter sketches a long but uneven history of student activists and organized labor, pointing to historical antecedents to student-worker alliances, summer labor programs, and coalition building. It relies on some useful sources, but much more work on these and related issues is needed. This work should necessarily address issues of class, privilege, race, and gender both discretely and as they intersect. It should consider the changes in and distributions of college student populations and how those changes relate to student labor activism, including the role of students as workers. It should also include greater treatment of the opposition to labor that rarely appears in the literature on the decades after the end of widespread student strikebreaking. Perhaps most importantly, as scholars consider students' interactions with labor, they should do so in ways that do not privilege the student activists at the expense of the workers with whom they were interacting. As Erik Ludwig argues, historical treatments of a seemingly spontaneous student act can obscure the much longer and more fraught struggles of the workers themselves.[49]

NOTES

1. Fernanda Zamudio-Suaréz, "How Students Play a Supporting Role in Campus Labor Movements," *Chronicle of Higher Education*, November 21, 1916, http://www.chronicle.com/article/How-Students-Play-a-Supporting/238462; Lee Gardner, "How the Harvard Strike Fits into the Equality Conversation," *Chronicle of Higher Education*, October 19, 2016, http://www.chronicle.com/article/How-the-Harvard-Strike-Fits/238101; Kelsey O'Connor, "Strike Avoided," *Ithaca Voice*, March 27, 2017, https://ithacavoice.com/2017/03/strike-avoided-ithaca-college-contingent-faculty-reach-deal/; Fernanda Zamudio-Suaréz, "As Long Island U.'s Faculty Lockout Nears 2 Weeks, Both Sides Dig In," *Chronicle of Higher Education*, September 14, 2016, http://www.chronicle.com/article/As-Long-Island-U-s-Faculty/237773.
2. Labor colleges and workers' education programs are excluded from this chapter due to space considerations.

3. Helen Lefkowitz Horowitz, *Campus Life: Undergraduate Cultures from the End of the Eighteenth Century to the Present* (New York: Alfred A. Knopf, 1987).

4. Stephen H. Norwood, "The Student as Strikebreaker: College Youth and the Crisis of Masculinity in the Early Twentieth Century," *Journal of Social History* 28, no. 2 (1994): 331–49.

5. Norwood, "The Student as Strikebreaker," 340–41; Liz Rohan, "'The Worker Must Have Bread, but She Must Have Roses, Too': The Education Programs of the Women's Trade Union League, 1908–26," in *The Education Work of Women's Organizations, 1890–1960*, eds. Anne Meis Knupfer and Christine Woyshner (New York: Palgrave Macmillan), 121–40.

6. Max Horn, *The Intercollegiate Socialist Society, 1905–1921: Origins of the Modern American Student Movement* (Boulder, CO: Westview Press, 1979), 100–08; Philip G. Altbach, *Student Politics in America: A Historical Analysis* (New York: McGraw-Hill Book Company, 1974), 21–28.

7. Horn, *The Intercollegiate Socialist Society*, 103.

8. Altbach, *Student Politics*, 25; "Socialists Propose that Working Students Organize," *Michigan Daily*, February, 21, 1913; "Working Men in University to Form Union," *Michigan Daily*, February 25, 1913; "Rumor Spreads that the Price of Board May Soon Advance," *Michigan Daily*, July 15, 1913; "Boarding Houses Give Square Deal," *Michigan Daily*, November 5, 1913; "Working Students to Hold Meeting," *Michigan Daily*, November 6, 1913; "Waiters are to Gather Tonight," *Michigan* Daily, November 7, 1913; Frank Bohn, "A University Hunger Strike," *The Masses*, May 1914, 10; "Rah-Rah Scabs," *The Industrial Worker*, March 7, 1912.

9. Philip S. Foner, *History of the Labor Movement in the United States. Volume VIII: Postwar Struggles, 1918–1920* (New York: International Publishers, 1980), 98.

10. Norwood, "The Student as Strikebreaker," 339–43; Stephen H. Norwood, *Labor's Flaming Youth: Telephone Operators and Worker Militancy, 1878–1923* (Urbana: University of Illinois Press, 1990), 189–92.

11. Norwood, *Labor's Flaming Youth*, 189–92; Norwood, "The Student as Strikebreaker."

12. Altbach, *Student Politics*, 42–45; Robert Cohen, *When the Old Left was Young: Student Radicals and America's First Student Movement, 1929–1940* (New York: Oxford University Press, 1990), 76; *Students in Revolt: The Story of the Intercollegiate League for Industrial Democracy* (New York: League for Industrial Democracy, 1933), 7; Deborah Sue Elkin, "Labor and the Left: The Limits of Acceptable Dissent at Yale University, 1920s to 1950s" (PhD diss., Yale University, 1995), Proquest (9613972), 15–32; Kenneth Meiklejohn and Peter Nehemkis, *Southern Labor in Revolt* (New York:

Intercollegiate Student Council of the League for Industrial Democracy, 1930).

13. David P. Setran, *The College "Y": Student Religion in the Era of Secularization* (New York: Palgrave Macmillan, 2007), 229–30; C. Howard Hopkins, *History of the YMCA in North America* (New York: Association Press, 1951), 644.

14. Mary Fredrickson, "Citizens for Democracy: The Industrial Programs of the YWCA," in *Sisterhood and Solidarity: Workers Education for Women, 1914–1984*, eds. Joyce L. Kornbluh and Mary Frederickson (Philadelphia: Temple University Press, 1984), 83, 99–100; Rita Heller, "Blue Collars and Bluestockings: The Bryn Mawr Summer School for Workers," in *Sisterhood and Solidarity*, eds. Kornbluh and Frederickson, 122–27.

15. Altbach, *Student Politics*, 32–39.

16. Paula S. Fass, *The Damned and the Beautiful: American Youth in the 1920s* (New York: Oxford University Press, 1977), 328, 329.

17. Altbach, *Student Politics*; Cohen, *When the Old Left*; David O. Levine, *The American College and the Culture of Aspiration, 1915–1940* (Ithaca, NY: Cornell University Press).

18. Marvin Bressler and Judith Higgins, "The Political Left on Campus and in Society: The Active Decade. Final Report" (Washington, DC: Office of Education Bureau of Research, 1972), 56.

19. Cohen, *When the Old Left*, 17–18, 44–55.

20. Cohen, *When the Old Left*, 22–25, 188–201; *Student Advocate, Volumes 1–3* (New York: Greenwood Reprint Corporation, 1968).

21. "College Youths Lead Strikers in Ohio Rioting," *Washington Post*, June 1, 1935.

22. "University Sweatshops," *Student Advocate*, February 1936, 5–6.

23. Budd Shulberg, "Dartmouth Rejects the Academic Mind," *Student Advocate*, April 1936, 13, 30.

24. Elkin, "Labor and the Left"; Sydney Fine, *Sit-Down: The General Motors Strike of 1936–1937* (Ann Arbor: University of Michigan Press, 1969), 205, 219.

25. "Past," *Student Worker* 1, no. 1 (December 15, 1936), 1, ACLU Archives, The Roger Baldwin Years (Wilmington, DW: Scholarly Resources, 1995), microfilm, reel 141, v. 962; "Why SWF?" (Ann Arbor: Student's Workers Federation, 1937), 1, ACLU Archives, reel 141, v. 962.

26. Ed Magdol and Joseph Bernstein, "Student Workers Organize," *Student Advocate*, May 1937: 17–18; Cohen, *When the Old Left*, 203–04.

27. Norwood, "The Student as Strikebreaker," 344; Douglas W. Sprague, "Student Strikebreakers: The 1934 West Coast Waterfront Strike and the

SS Mariposa," *The Mariner's Mirror* 102, no. 2 (2016): 218–21; Madison Kuhn, *Michigan State: The First Hundred Years, 1855–1955* (East Lansing: Michigan State University Press, 1955), 395–96.

28. "Council Asks Trial of Student Waiting; But Sees Increased Dining Hall Efficiency as Main Goal," *Harvard Crimson*, September 23, 1940; "Unions Object to Putting Student Waiters in Jobs," *Harvard Crimson*, January 26, 1940; "Memories of the Harvard-Union Arguments Aroused by Yale's Struggle with CIO," *Harvard Crimson*, October 10, 1941.

29. Nella Van Dyke, "Crossing Movement Boundaries: Factors the Facilitate Coalition Protest by American College Students, 1930–1990," *Social Problems* 50, no. 2 (2003): 226–50; Elkin, "Labor and the Left," 230–56.

30. Phillip G. Altbach, "The National Student Association in the Fifties: Flawed Conscience of the Silent Generation," *Youth & Society* 5, no. 2 (1973): 184–21; "Dust off Your Dreams: The Story of the American Youth for Democracy" (New York: American Youth for Democracy, 1945), 17.

31. "MYDA Food Plan Awaits Approval," *Michigan Daily*, January 11, 1947; "Fights for Rights of Labor," *Michigan Daily*, April 18, 1947; Altbach, *Student Politics*, 132–76; Ellen W. Schrecker, *No Ivory Tower: McCarthyism and the Universities* (New York: Oxford University Press, 1986), 93.

32. Peter B. Levy, *The New Left and Labor in the 1960s* (Urbana: University of Illinois Press, 1994), 5.

33. Levy, *The New Left*; Christopher Phelps, "Port Huron at Fifty: The New Left and Labor: An Interview with Kim Moody," *Labor: Studies in the Working Class Histories of the Americas* 9, no. 2 (2012): 25–40.

34. David Barber, *A Hard Rain Fell: SDS and Why it Failed* (Jackson: University Press of Mississippi, 2008); Leigh David Benin, *The New Labor Radicalism and New York City's Garment Industry: Progressive Labor Insurgents in the 1960s* (New York: Garland Publishing, 2000); Fred Gordon, "Build The Campus Worker-Student Alliance," *New Left Notes*, September 20, 1969.

35. Michael Flug, "Organized Labor and the Civil Rights Movement of the 1960: The Case of the Maryland Freedom Union," *Labor History* 31, no. 3 (1990): 322–46; Lauren Araiza, *To March for Others: The Black Freedom Struggle and the United Farm Workers* (Philadelphia: University of Pennsylvania Press, 2014); Levy, *The New Left*, 128–36.

36. Gregg L. Michel, *Struggle for a Better South: The Southern Student Organizing Committee, 1964–1969* (New York: Palgrave Macmillan, 2004), 153–60.

37. Levy, *The New Left*; Richard Griswold del Castillo and Richard A. Garcia, *César Chávez, A Triumph of Spirit* (Norman: University of Oklahoma Press, 1995), 47–58.

38. Jennifer Pittman, "Honoring the Legacy of César E. Chávez on Campus," March 27, 2017, https://news.ucsc.edu/2017/03/chavez-campus.html.
39. Robin D. G. Kelley, "The Proletariat Goes to College," *Social Text* 49 (1996): 37–42; Manning Marable, "Dan Georgakas on the Successes and Failures of the Dodge Revolutionary Union Movement (DRUM)," *Souls* 2, no. 2, 18–26; Dan Gergakas and Marvin Surkin, *Detroit: I Do Mind Dying* (New York: St. Marten's Press, 1975); John A. Andrew, *The Other Side of the Sixties: Young Americans for Freedom and the Rise of Conservative Politics* (Rutgers University Press, 1997), 144.
40. Kelley, "The Proletariat," 39–40; Karen Sacks and Karen Brodkin, *Caring by the Hour: Women, Work, and Organizing at Duke Medical Center* (Urbana: University of Illinois Press, 1998); William A. Link, *William Friday: Power, Purpose, and American Higher Education* (Chapel Hill: University of North Carolina Press, 1995), 142–58; Joy Ann Williamson, *Black Power on Campus: The University of Illinois, 1965–1975* (Urbana: University of Illinois Press, 2000), 95.
41. Andrew Barlow, "The Student Movement of the 1960s and the Politics of Race," *Journal of Ethnic Studies* 19, no. 3 (1991): 1–22, quotation on 14.
42. Robert A. Rhoads, *Freedom's Web: Student Activism in an Age of Cultural Diversity* (Baltimore: Johns Hopkins University, 1998); Philip G. Altbach and Robert Cohen, "American Student Activism: The Post-Sixties Transformation," *Journal of Higher Education* 61, no. 1 (1990): 32–49.
43. Molly Ladd-Taylor, "Women Workers and the Yale Strike," *Feminist Studies* 11, no 3 (1985): 465–90, quotation on 481.
44. Toni Golpin, Gary Isaac, Dan Letwin, and Jack McKivigan, *On Strike for Respect: The Clerical & Technical Workers' Strike at Yale University (1984–1985)* (Chicago, IL: Charles H. Kerr Publishing Company, 1988), 56–57; Sharon Kurtz, *Workplace Justice: Organizing Multi-Identity Movements* (Minneapolis: University of Minnesota Press, 2002).
45. Kathy M. Newman, "Poor, Hungry, and Desperate? Or Privileged, Histrionic, and Demanding?" *Social Text* 49 (1996): 98–131.
46. Steven K. Ashby and C.J. Hawking, *Staley: The Fight for a New American Labor Movement* (Urbana, University of Illinois Press, 2009), 106–07; Richard Applebaum and Peter Dreier, "The Campus Anti-Sweatshop Movement," *The American Prospect* 46 (March 1999): 71–78; Liza Featherstone and the United Students Against Sweatshops, *Students Against Sweatshops* (New York: Verso, 2002); Nella Van Dyke, Marc Dixon, and Helen Carlon, "Manufactured Dissent: Labor Revitalization, Union Summer, and Student Protest," *Social Forces* 86, no. 1 (2007): 193–214.
47. Jess Walsh, "Living Wage Campaigns Storm the Ivory Tower: Low Wage Workers on Campus," *New Labor Forum* 6 (2000): 80–89; Robert D. Wilton and Cynthia Crawford, "Toward an Understanding of the

Spatiality of Social Movements: Labor Organizing at a Private University in Los Angeles," *Social Problems* 49, no. 3 (2002): 374–94.

48. Kurtz, *Workplace Justice*.

49. Erik Ludwig, "Closing in on the 'Plantation': Coalition Building and the Role of Black Women's Grievances in Duke University Labor Disputes, 1965–1968," *Feminist Studies* 25, no. 1 (1999): 79–94.

CHAPTER 9

New Voices, New Perspectives: Studying the History of Student Life at Community Colleges

Nicholas M. Strohl

Today, roughly half of all undergraduates in the United States are enrolled in community colleges: typically two-year, public open-access institutions that offer a wide range of educational services, from vocational and job training programs to college-level academic courses to adult and community education programs. Community colleges and their students have received renewed attention in recent years. In his State of the Union address in January 2015, President Barack Obama unveiled a proposal to provide federal aid to make community colleges tuition-free, so that "two years of college will become as free and universal as high school is today."[1] During his time in office, President Obama placed community colleges at the center of his administration's efforts to increase higher education attainment, and described these institutions as "well suited to promote the dual goal of academic and on-the-job preparedness for the next generation

N. M. Strohl (✉)
History and Educational Policy Studies, University of Wisconsin–Madison, Madison, WI, USA
e-mail: nstrohl@wisc.edu

© The Author(s) 2018
C. A. Ogren, M. A. VanOverbeke (eds.),
Rethinking Campus Life, Historical Studies in Education,
https://doi.org/10.1007/978-3-319-75614-1_9

191

of American workers."[2] Along the same lines, in just the last decade, states from Tennessee to New York to Oregon have proposed their own plans to make a community college education affordable, if not free, for their residents.

Despite this attention, the day-to-day experiences of students at community colleges, known more often as "junior colleges" through the 1960s, have been of marginal interest to historians of American higher education. Education historians, especially of "college life," instead have focused their attention on four-year residential colleges, where campus-based organizations and social events more often have played a central role in students' lives. In *Campus Life*, Helen Lefkowitz Horowitz acknowledges that her approach privileges the experiences of students in four-year residential colleges, even as she claims to identify patterns that may transcend particular campus environments. She wrote, "Some of the phenomena I describe depend upon the clash of different groups coexisting on campus and therefore require a residential college with a traditional college life; but other aspects are independent." As a result, she continued, "although my narrative and analysis capture most clearly the undergraduate world of the residential four-year liberal arts college nonetheless readers familiar with commuter campuses and more technically oriented schools may find something of interest."[3] Still, Horowitz's account is primarily about how adolescents and young adults, over time, created cultures for themselves on relatively elite college campuses. It offers only hints about how, or whether, such observations apply at non-elite, non-residential, and non-four-year institutions.

Historians before and after Horowitz have struggled to find an approach to studying campus life at junior and community colleges for two main reasons. First, junior and community college students do not always fit the mold of the "traditional" college student, as described in books like *Campus Life*. That is, unlike their peers in four-year residential colleges, most community college students do not live in dormitories or fraternity and sorority houses, and their lives are not organized around campus organizations and events. Rather, many live at home with parents or with families (sometimes including children) of their own. Community college students may be precocious high school students, veterans, or senior citizens; they often work part- or full-time jobs in addition to attending classes; some are homeless; and more than one-third are the first in their families to attend college. Historically, such students have been labeled "non-traditional" college students; however, in the nation's community colleges, these "non-traditional" students are the typical undergraduates.[4] Thus, historians looking for traditional forms of campus life at community colleges may be disappointed by what they find, and may need to develop new methods, and explore alternative sources, in order to identify the different ways in which student life took shape on community college campuses.

The second reason why historians of higher education may overlook the experiences of students at junior and community colleges is that, in the words of historian Philo Hutcheson, some historians "cannot even be sure that the community college is a higher education institution."[5] As discussed below, the rise of the community college in American higher education may appear to be a post–World War II phenomenon. However, the earliest two-year colleges appeared in the late nineteenth century, often as products of local efforts to articulate the pathway between high school and college.[6] And through at least the first half of the twentieth century, two-year colleges assumed many different institutional forms. The sometimes-nebulous position of two-year colleges in the ladder of American education led some historians, such as Laurence Veysey and Frederick Rudolph, to exclude these institutions entirely from their histories of American higher education.[7] As a result, only a handful of studies have examined the history of junior and community colleges, let alone the history of student life at these institutions.[8]

In this chapter, I explain why historians and other scholars should be interested in the history of student life at junior and community colleges, and how they can explore it for themselves. The chapter begins with an outline of the debate between the community college's champions and its critics, with an emphasis on scholars' remarkable lack of attention—from both champions and critics—to the voices of students, families, and local communities. The second section explains that while historians may not know much about student life at junior and community colleges, they do have access to a wealth of data about students themselves, in the form of numerous surveys and reports dating back to the 1920s. Such data about student characteristics, both historical and contemporary, may serve as a proxy for knowledge about student life when other sources, such as institutional archives, are not available. The final section considers several examples of scholarship that touch on the history of student life at junior and community colleges, and suggests new avenues for exploring campus life at these colleges, including novel source material and fresh approaches found in books, articles, and dissertations. Overall, we need a more comprehensive historical understanding of student life at these campuses to help us better understand the purposes of these institutions, how and where they fit in the larger structure of American higher education, and what students have wanted from them and how they have used them, both historically and in the present. Such knowledge is crucial not only to inform debates about the pivotal role of community colleges in the United States but also to develop a more comprehensive historical understanding of the many ways that students across higher education have experienced and developed campus life.

CHAMPIONS VERSUS CRITICS

Junior and community colleges throughout their history have been the subject of fierce debate among higher education leaders, policymakers, and scholars, including historians of higher education. Some have championed the development of community colleges as "the most important higher education innovation of the twentieth century" and as a catalyst for the expansion of access and opportunity for millions of first-generation college students.[9] At the other end, critics have charged that these institutions are "second best," "born subordinate" to four-year colleges and universities, and more often "divert," rather than further, the dreams of college students.[10] Among scholars between these two extremes, there has been a robust debate about the past and present roles of junior and community colleges in supporting democracy and opportunity in American higher education.[11] Yet, there is a glaring problem in this literature: the absence of extensive attention to the experiences of junior and community college students on campus. Without the student voice, participants in this debate lack a crucial perspective and may repeat claims about the community college student experience that the historical record does not support.

The champions emphasize the role of these institutions in expanding higher education access for millions of Americans in the three decades after World War II, often described as the "golden age" of American higher education.[12] This story usually begins with the 1947 report of the President's Commission on Higher Education, dubbed the Truman Commission—the United States' first national commission on higher education policy—and its ambitious vision of universal college access for all Americans. The commission's six-volume report, *Higher Education for American Democracy*, proposed the development of a nationwide network of tuition-free "community colleges" to serve as the initial step to higher education for millions of first-time college students in the generation after the war.[13] Community colleges, the Truman Commission wrote, should be "designed to serve chiefly local community education needs." As such, they should provide a wide range of postsecondary education programs, including "general and vocational" courses for students preparing for the workforce; courses to serve the needs of "students who will go on to a more extended general education or to specialized and professional study at some other college or university"; and a "comprehensive adult education program." The typical community college student would live at home, the commission reasoned, in part to save money, but also, the commission hoped, to benefit from continued family supervision and support in the later stages of adolescence. "Many young people want less than a full four-year college course," the commission's report stated, and two-year colleges were the institutions best suited to meet their needs.[14]

Advocates of two-year colleges, such as representatives of the American Association of Junior Colleges (AAJC), agreed. They encouraged junior and community college leaders to focus on vocational and "semiprofessional" education and to offer more terminal degrees, as opposed to general or liberal education curricula for transfer to four-year programs. In 1947, a study sponsored by the AAJC lamented that high school guidance counselors often failed to inform students about the potential benefits of terminal education programs in junior colleges. Instead, the study found that students appeared to value the institution for different purposes—namely, as a stepping-stone to further study. "Many high-school students consider the junior college as a college-preparatory institution that serves as a substitute for the two more-expensive years of a four-year institution or as an expedient for removing their subject deficiencies," wrote Phebe Ward, the coordinator of terminal education study at San Francisco Junior College. "Unfortunately, the popularity of this one-sided misperception is due, of course, to the fact that the junior college has not created an interest in terminal education among high-school students, their parents, and their teachers."[15]

By the 1970s, critics cast doubt upon assumptions, like those of the Truman Commission, about what junior and community college students wanted from a higher education. While some higher education leaders criticized community colleges as pale imitations of four-year colleges or for failing to provide meaningful opportunities for students to transfer to bachelors' degree programs, a more strident group of critics, led by historians and sociologists, charged that community colleges were inferior by design. Such "structuralist critics," as Fred Pincus has labeled them, "argue that community colleges are part of a stratified system of higher education that reproduces the race, class, and gender inequalities that are part of the larger society."[16] Whatever benefits they may provide, these critics argue, junior colleges and the community colleges into which they evolved did not prioritize extending higher education opportunity, as the Truman Commission envisioned, but rather protected the prestige and status of four-year institutions by allowing them to carefully select and maintain their student bodies.

The leading proponents of this view, historian David O. Levine and sociologists Steven Brint and Jerome Karabel, in the 1980s relied primarily on the records of elite educators and policymakers in their analysis of the historical development of junior and community colleges, thus giving readers an incomplete picture of how—and whether—high-level policy decisions affected students and institutions. In *The American College and the Culture of Aspiration, 1915–1940*, Levine makes the case that the growth of two-year junior colleges after World War I provided a way for four-year institutions to protect the status of the four-year bachelor's degree in a rapidly expanding higher education marketplace. He argues that junior college advocates, including officials like George Zook, a long-time president of the American Council on Education (1934–1950) and the chairman of the Truman Commission, were less interested in expanding higher education opportunity than they were in keeping certain students out of elite institutions. "Most public educators proclaimed that there could never be too many people in college," Levine wrote, "even as they pursued policies that would free their institutions from the need to bear all of the burden of democracy."[17] In their push for more vocational and terminal education programs in junior colleges, Levine writes, Zook and others underestimated the abilities and aspirations of many college-goers, who were "not so inadequately prepared or so unintellectual as most proponents of the terminal junior college alleged they were."[18]

In *The Diverted Dream: Community Colleges and the Promise of Educational Opportunity in America, 1900–1985*, Brint and Karabel offer a similar reading of the history of junior colleges before World War II. Between 1900 and 1925, they write, junior colleges were known for their focus on the liberal arts—not vocational and terminal education—and many provided genuine opportunity for students seeking to transfer to four-year colleges. However, between the 1920s and the 1940s, an elite vanguard of higher education leaders, national policymakers, and others associated with the newly formed AAJC campaigned to transform the form and function of junior colleges, making them clearly "subordinate" to four-year institutions in form and function. These junior college advocates, whom the authors compare to the leaders of the nineteenth-century common school movement for their "evangelical" zeal for reform, encouraged two-year colleges to emphasize vocational and "semiprofessional" education—and not transfer opportunities—in order to avoid competition with high schools and four-year colleges, while at the same time placating business interests that favored such forms of "utilitarian" education.[19] As a result, Brint and Karabel argue, post–World War II community colleges more often "diverted" the dreams of American college students than furthered them and, as institutions, served only to reinforce—and not to correct—inequality in American higher education.

Later critics of community colleges adopted this reading of history, one in which the student perspective was largely missing. Both Kevin Dougherty and J.M. Beach rely upon Brint and Karabel's analysis of the pre–World War II origins of contemporary community colleges as a basis for their own examinations of the institutions' record after the war. Building on Brint and Karabel's work, Dougherty describes community colleges as "contradictory" institutions, burdened by a sprawling, confused mission that fails to serve students effectively—a by-product of earlier efforts by elite educators and policymakers to bend the institutions to their will.[20] In *Gateway to Opportunity?*, Beach similarly adopts Brint and Karabel's premise that community colleges are fatally flawed institutions. Borrowing a phrase from the two sociologists, Beach asks his readers whether "an educational institution [the community college] 'born subordinate' as the lower-level holding pen for the university and the feeder for lower levels of the labor market can overcome its own legacy and develop into an effective, meritocratic, and democratizing institution?" Like Dougherty, Beach suggests that the contemporary institution is hampered by the efforts of pre–World War II elites to "limit access to higher education in the name of social efficiency," and often works against the wishes of students and local communities who have "other ideas" when it comes to their higher education.[21] Because of their reliance on the work of Brint and Karabel, both Dougherty and Beach further an incomplete picture of the origins of junior and community colleges that fails to account for the way in which students and local communities have also shaped the development of these institutions.

Indeed, other studies, such as John Frye's examination of the rise of public junior colleges between 1900 and 1940, suggest that critics like

Levine and Brint and Karabel grant higher education leaders and elite policymakers too much credit for their influence on junior and community college programs. In *The Vision of the Public Junior College, 1900–1940*, Frye demonstrates that elite educators and policymakers were only one of several constituencies, including students, families, and local communities, who shaped the form and function of two-year colleges at mid-century. While junior college leaders emphasized terminal education, students often preferred preparatory programs for transfer to four-year colleges. And while many higher education leaders, like the University of California's Alexis Lange, envisioned two-year colleges as the destination for students who would "go no further" in their education, the evidence suggests that many pre-World War II junior college students saw the institution differently. Ultimately, Frye argues, the "ideology" of junior college leaders had only a "weak influence over the junior college curriculum" in the decades before World War II.[22]

Absent serious inquiry into how students viewed and experienced life on junior and community college campuses, debates about the role of community colleges in American higher education, past or present, will be missing a crucial piece of the puzzle. We need to know more about how students experienced community colleges, what they wanted from these institutions, and how those expectations shaped their campus life in order to understand how administrators and policymakers, as well as students, families, and communities, defined institutional "success." Only with an enlarged perspective, and one bolstered by knowledge about student life, can we have a better sense of whether—and to what degree—junior and community colleges should be championed for expanding higher education opportunity or criticized for diverting students' dreams. Just as importantly, it is only with such an enlarged perspective and new knowledge that we can begin to understand and improve the contemporary institution in new and different ways.

INVESTIGATING WHO ATTENDED JUNIOR AND COMMUNITY COLLEGES

While we may not know much about the history of campus life at junior and community colleges, we do have access to valuable information about the characteristics of students who have attended them. Since World War I, educational researchers, often associated with state and federal governments, public research universities, or the AAJC (today the American Association of

Community Colleges, or AACC), have conducted regular surveys of two-year colleges and their students, compiling remarkable amounts of data as part of efforts to regulate and classify these institutions.[23] These studies offer a starting point for anyone interested in learning more about community college students and why these institutions appealed to students, even if they tell us little about what kind of lives students made on campus or what students hoped to accomplish while there.

Educators and policymakers were captivated by the tremendous growth of junior colleges in the decades after World War I, a moment when these institutions appeared poised to reshape the landscape of American higher education. In June 1920, at the first nationwide gathering of junior college leaders in St. Louis, U.S. Commissioner of Education Philander P. Claxton suggested that junior colleges held the potential to transform the nation's "educational machinery" and could be the key to a "better organization of higher education in the United States."[24] University of Minnesota researcher Leonard Koos agreed, writing in 1924 that the junior college "movement seems destined, like the advent of the junior high school, to affect profoundly the organization of our American system of education."[25] Broadly speaking, they were correct. In an era characterized by remarkable growth in college enrollments, junior college enrollments grew fastest. According to Levine, junior colleges enrolled about 4500 students, or 1.9 percent of undergraduates, in 1918; by 1940, they enrolled 149,854 students, or 17.6 percent of undergraduates.[26] That year, the University of Iowa's Carl Seashore declared the rapid development of junior and community colleges during the interwar period to be "the most significant mass movement in higher education that this or any other country has ever witnessed in an equal period of time .... Indeed, we have suddenly been thrown into this movement with such surprise that educational authorities and patrons find difficulty in taking its bearings."[27]

The institutional landscape of early junior colleges was highly variable. Koos's 1924 study, *The Junior College Movement*, found that junior colleges came in a variety of forms and, depending on their size and location, served many different kinds of students. Some existed as preparatory "units" in public or private universities; others were an extension of the local high school; and some stood alone as public or private junior colleges. Across different institutions, enrollment ranged "from a mere handful of students to more than a thousand."[28] Koos also examined how junior colleges promoted themselves to students, and what students appeared to gain from attending them. He identified at least 21 distinct "purposes" of junior colleges, which he then classified into seven different "groups," including preparing students for transfer to four-year programs; "rounding out of the general education"; providing occupational training; and "continuing home influences during immaturity," for students who still lived at home. Koos concluded that junior colleges—and junior college students—defied neat classification. Students enrolled for myriad reasons and with a wide variety of educational, professional, and personal goals in mind.[29]

Koos's findings provide a loose foundation for those seeking to understand the history of student life at these institutions prior to World War II. For instance, in a chapter on the "feasibility" of establishing a junior college in a community, Koos considered why some high school graduates, if given a choice, would choose to attend a four-year college instead of a junior college, and why, as statistics showed, retention rates at junior colleges lagged behind those at four-year institutions. He speculated that the allure of "college life" at four-year institutions played a role in some cases. "It takes time and effort to win acceptance of a new institution or to place it on a foundation that will justify its holding to all students who go on through two years of residence," Koos wrote. "Even if we set aside for the moment the question whether all necessary work is now going forward in these new units, it must be admitted that only after some years can the new unit become a part of the educational tradition of all the possible constituency." Koos suggested that it would be "difficult for some people to associate even a part of what they regard as the period of college training with the secondary unit below. These persons will be prone to look upon the movement disparagingly because it *is* an upward extension of the high school." In such cases, some students and parents would eschew the junior college as an inferior institution, one without the "older traditions of 'college life'" that prevailed on the campuses of four-year institutions.[30] Such statements underscore the need to gain more information on how junior college students experienced "life" on their campuses as a way to really understand these institutions and their appeal.

If Koos's study of junior colleges offers a bird's-eye view of the movement nationwide, then John Harbeson's 1932 survey of students at Pasadena Junior College (PJC) provides a detailed case study of the student population of one of the nation's largest junior colleges in the years after World War I. In a project commissioned by the Pasadena City Schools, Harbeson, the principal of PJC, examined the social and economic backgrounds, the high school and college academic records, and the standardized and psychological test scores of nearly 900 students who attended PJC between 1924 and 1927. The purpose of the study was to determine whether the practice of sorting students at the junior college level into "Certificate" or "Diploma" tracks—classifications based on the student's high school academic record and the recommendation of the high school principal and meant to identify those who were ready for college-level work and those who were not—held any indication about their performance in college. Harbeson catalogued the students' ages, place of birth (by region of the United States or country of origin), religious affiliation, favorite activities "out-of-school," parents' occupations, and "vocational aims." He found, in general, no major differences between the Certificate and the Diploma groups in terms of their reasons for attendance or their future aspirations. Students in both groups, he wrote, "hoped to continue their education in standard colleges and universities. Neither group regards the junior college as a finishing school."[31]

Harbeson's study suggests that it would be a mistake to assume anything about a junior college student's goals or aspirations based on academic or family background. That is, Certificate and Diploma students shared similar sets of personal, academic, and vocational interests. Certificate students preferred "music, reading, lectures, shows and hiking as out-of school activities," while Diploma students reportedly enjoyed "athletics and games, motoring, gardening and dancing."[32] And while Certificate and Diploma students indicated slight differences in their career goals, both groups aimed for professional occupations regardless of their parents' line of work.[33] So far as the students at Pasadena Junior College were concerned, Harbeson concluded, "It would seem from all available facts that adolescent human nature cannot be pigeon-holed into any two large, distinct and well-defined groups."[34] Indeed, as will be discussed in the next section, student life at junior and community colleges before World War II did not always square with common assumptions about the kinds of students who attended such institutions.

The characteristics of the community college population began to change significantly in the final quarter of the twentieth century, much like the American college population at large. However, in the two decades after World War II, the majority of students in two-year colleges were still "late adolescents," or about 18 to 24 years old, according to Koos's findings in *The Community College Student*, a massive volume published in 1970 in which he sought to provide a "comprehensive understanding" of the community college student population.[35] Koos devoted one-third of the volume to a general discussion of adolescent development, including data about young people's physical, mental, personal, and social development, even their sexual and dating behavior. The other parts of the study focused more directly on community college students themselves, with chapters on students' "aptitude, social status, and academic competence"; "personal characteristics, attitudes, and interests"; and "personal problems." Koos included one chapter on "adult education and the adult student," noting that adults (those over 25 years old) were a small but growing portion of the student population, especially among those who attended part-time. Yet, his portrait of community college students depicted a population not unlike that found at four-year schools: one of young adults coming of age and trying to find their way in the world.

This portrait quickly became dated. One of the best summaries of the changing demographics and characteristics of community college students since the 1970s comes from Arthur Cohen, Florence Brawer, and Carrie Kisker, in the sixth edition of *The American Community College*, published in 2014. Beginning in the 1970s, they note, the community college population grew to include greater numbers of older students (i.e., 25 and over) and many more part-time attendees. And although the mean age of community college students increased only from 27 to 29 years between 1980 and 2010, age-related patterns of enrollment shifted during that time, reflecting a growing cluster of students younger than 22 and a broader range of students 25 and older.[36] Twenty-first-century community college students also have significant, if not onerous, non-school obligations. According to a 2003–2004 survey, "one-quarter of community college students had one or more dependents; almost half of these were single parents." Nearly half worked part-time, and 33 percent full-time. And 45 percent were first-generation college students.[37] Thus, from high school students participating in dual enrollment programs to senior citizens returning to school, today's community colleges enroll a growing number of students for whom college is only one of many priorities.

Researchers should be careful not to make assumptions about student life based on statistics of student characteristics. However, these surveys of junior and community college students over the past century raise a number of compelling questions for historians studying the history of student life. Cohen, Brawer, and Kisker write that community college students have much in common with students at residential, four-year institutions; like their peers, they are motivated to pursue higher education both by a desire to "better themselves financially" and by "reasons of personal interest."[38] How do these desires play out on junior and community college campuses? And, conversely, how do junior and community college campuses structure student life? Statistics and surveys are not enough to answer these questions but they are a useful way to begin to identify pressing questions. Historians need to round out the picture of student life on junior and community college campuses. The following section provides some examples of scholars who have done just that, while offering ideas for others about to begin their exploration.

MODELS FOR HISTORIANS OF STUDENT LIFE IN JUNIOR AND COMMUNITY COLLEGES

Student life in junior and community colleges is not completely absent from the historiography. A handful of books, articles, and dissertations provide models for how historians might explore student life at these often-overlooked institutions using new methods, new sources, and new interpretative approaches—if they are creative. In contrast to elite liberal arts colleges and research universities, Hutcheson observes, the community college "does not exist as text. Its history for professional historians is not even buried; it was destroyed, since little care to [archive] records of these institutions, such as those records existed, has ever been taken."[39] Yet institutional archives, while certainly helpful, are not the only source of information about the past, and historians have discovered valuable resources in other repositories. By using archival resources available at other community institutions, such as libraries, historical societies, and even local school districts, where many junior colleges began as an extension of the high school program, scholars can paint a portrait of junior and community college life that is as full and vivid as the accounts of student life on ivy-covered quadrangles or sprawling land-grant campuses.

As noted above, the most influential works on the history of junior and community colleges, including those by Levine and by Brint and Karabel, rely primarily on the official records of institutions, higher education leaders, and state and federal policymakers. These historians do not square the broader, nationwide history with local narratives, although some have tried to do so and have relied on a broad array of sources. In his study of the development of junior colleges before World War II, Frye examines the disparity between what national leaders articulated as their vision for junior colleges and what local institutions and students hoped to gain from these institutions. For instance, in a chapter entitled "Conflict in

Vision: Local Colleges and the National Ideology," Frye uses archival material held at the Oak Park, Illinois, Public Library—such as the *Bulletin of Oak Park Junior College*, college catalogs, and documents from a local citizen's group—to examine what students, educators, and residents hoped to gain from the short-lived Oak Park Junior College (1933–1938). Frye also interviewed a former student at Oak Park Junior College nearly 60 years after his attendance at the institution.[40] Frye's research does not provide a comprehensive history of student life at Oak Park or other junior colleges prior to World War II. However, his use of local archival sources and a personal interview allows him to show that the national vision espoused by junior college leaders did not always match the expectations or perceptions of these institutions among students and in local communities. "Popular visions of the junior college were markedly different from those put forward by national writers and the university professoriate who concerned themselves with junior colleges," Frye concludes. "The popular view was that the junior college was a road to a baccalaureate degree and by extension a road to social mobility and status preferment." In contrast, he explains, "The national leadership emphasized the terminal function, necessary social control, and protection of the university."[41]

Even as the institutional records of junior and community colleges may be hard to come by, institutional histories can offer clues for how to explore the history of a school and community. Marvin Aaron's dissertation on the history of Lincoln Junior College, which was formally attached to Lincoln High School in Kansas City, Missouri, examines the role of the college in providing higher education opportunity to African Americans under segregation. Aaron's study relies on archival material from the local school district, including the high school's student newspaper, *The Lincolnite*, which covered news about the district's junior college. Aaron also uses material from the Kansas City Public Library, the Metropolitan Community College District, and the State Historical Society of Missouri.[42] These materials reveal how students at the junior college (and the high school) reacted to the Supreme Court case of Lloyd Gaines, a black man who was denied admission to the University of Missouri Law in 1936, and later, to desegregation efforts in the wake of *Brown v. Board of Education* in 1954. Ultimately, Aaron's story paints a picture of how the all-black Lincoln Junior College served as a focal point for the African-American community in Kansas City in the decades before *Brown*.

Aaron also interviewed former students, gaining insight into "their own and their family's attitudes toward the junior college, what it meant to them, and how it may have helped them with their career lives after graduation."[43] The former students' stories provide insight into how students at Lincoln Junior College, formally attached to the high school, navigated relationships with the high school students in their midst. For the most part, Aaron finds, junior college students remained separate and apart from the high school students, even having their own lounge in which to spend time between classes; however, parents of high school students expressed concern on several occasions when junior college students, including some older veterans, began to date high school girls.[44] Examining such stories is just one of several ways in which Aaron explores how junior college students sought—or did *not* seek—to distinguish themselves from their high school peers. Indeed, Lincoln Junior College was one of many public junior colleges in the first half of the twentieth century that began as an extension of a local high school. It is likely that other public school districts have records for similar postsecondary education programs, offering opportunities for historians to examine how junior college students made a life for themselves on campuses next door to the high schools from which many graduated.

Aaron's dissertation is not the only one to employ oral histories of community colleges. Nan Haugen's research on women's intercollegiate athletics in community colleges also used personal interviews to bolster information from traditional sources. In addition to exploring the archives of local newspapers and relatively robust archival collections at nine San Diego County community colleges, Haugen interviewed "teachers, coaches, physical education directors and athletics directors" in order to tell the story of the growth and development of women's sports on campus between 1955 and 1972. From the perspective of the community college, Haugen's dissertation sheds light on the relationship between the development of women's intercollegiate athletics in higher education and the rise of "women leaders" on campuses in the two decades before the 1972 passage of Title IX, a landmark federal law banning discrimination on the basis of sex in educational institutions receiving federal assistance. Haugen's dissertation reminds us that junior and community college students participated in a wide range of interscholastic activities, including sports, and often on the same level as students in four-year institutions.[45] Historians researching the experiences of community college students would be well served to investigate the archives of state and national student associations and other interscholastic networks in order to discover whether and how community college students engaged with such organizations.

Finally, Robert Pedersen's 2000 dissertation, "The Origins and Development of the Early Public Junior College: 1900–1940," is a re-examination of the history of early junior colleges that revises the narratives offered by Brint and Karabel and by Levine, and demonstrates how attention to student life can upend popular perceptions and conventional wisdom about the history of these institutions.[46] Pedersen's study explains the social and political contexts, both local and national, that supported the remarkable growth of two-year colleges between World War I and World War II. Specifically, he argues that historians of junior colleges have not looked hard enough at other primary source bases, especially "state library archives, public records maintained by local historical societies, county libraries, and newspaper morgues."[47] Based on these sources, his findings related to "student culture" at early public junior colleges question popular historical narratives that suggested early junior college students hailed from poor backgrounds or were un-interested in the "frills" of college life found on other campuses.

Indeed, late-twentieth-century advocates of community colleges, Pedersen writes, often operated on the assumption that junior colleges were created to serve the "poor and academically marginal student" and to do so at low cost.[48] He cites the Carnegie Council on Policy Studies in Higher Education's 1975 report as an example of how community college advocates characterized two-year colleges as historically low-cost institutions. The report stated, "The concept of the 'two years of free access' to higher education in the United States has a long history, dating back to some of the first public junior colleges established in the early years of the present century."[49] In fact, Pedersen explains, the cost of attending a junior college before World War II was not "substantially less" than that at a research university.[50] "Although public junior colleges operated under the sponsorship of free high schools," Pedersen writes, "most charged tuition, and many charged substantial fees in addition to tuition." In some cases, tuition and fees surpassed the cost of the state university.[51] Indeed, some early advocates for the junior college model cited high tuition and fees— and institutional reliance upon tuition revenue—as a barrier to access for students and to the broader proliferation of the institutions themselves.[52]

Pedersen's research demonstrates that student life at early junior colleges reflected a student population that engaged in sometimes-expensive social activities and was not entirely "poor" or "marginal." He writes, "There is more than ample evidence that the student culture of the typical pre-1940 junior college was no less self-absorbed and self-indulgent than the student cultures at Stanford, Ann Arbor, Berkeley, and Minneapolis." Many junior college campuses were home to interscholastic sports teams, literary and artistic societies, student newspapers, and other social organizations. "And beyond these institutionally-sponsored teams and clubs," he adds, "junior college students regularly organized elaborate social gatherings—the society pages of local newspapers most often referred to them as 'galas.' These events involved virtually all students and many faculty in activities that clearly set junior college students apart as something of a youthful social elite."[53]

Pedersen cites newspaper accounts of social events at Fort Scott Junior College, in Fort Scott, Kansas, as an example of the rich array of extracurricular activities at a typical junior college. "Within a year of the school's opening in 1919," Pedersen writes, "the theatrical productions, club meetings, and social events of the college's small student body had become a regular fixture of the *Fort Scott Tribune*'s society page." In its first decade, Fort Scott Junior College boasted a tennis team; a literary society called the "Scribbler Society," whose members held "frequent and elaborate private banquets"; and numerous theatrical productions. Student "socials" were common. The *Fort Scott Tribune* described a "Halloween gala" in 1922 for more than 70 students held at a large home. The party had all the accoutrements of an "elite" social gathering. Students "arrived in a caravan of cars," played a game called "Fox Hunt," and ate salted nuts and pumpkin pies. The *Tribune* added that the event was a wholesome affair, Pedersen observes. There was no "dancing or any other untoward behavior, and the newspaper took care to report that the entire evening's activities were chaperoned by a faculty member and his wife."[54]

Pedersen concludes that even an exploratory look at the historical record of student life at early junior colleges counters the prevailing historical narrative that these institutions served primarily poor or academically marginal students and, by extension, offered little in terms of campus life. "If junior college students were generally of socially disadvantaged backgrounds," he writes, "one might reasonably expect that they would have precious little time to expend on the diversions of an extracurriculum. After all, simply to meet their tuition expenses, let alone the cost of books and transportation, one would expect that these students devoted all of their free time employed in some marginal job or working on a local farm. Such students would have neither the means nor the leisure time to imitate the student culture of the university, with its exclusive clubs, fraternities and sororities, athletic teams, and active social life."[55] Quite the opposite, Pedersen concludes, junior college students were the toast of their (small) towns, creating a campus culture that was just as vibrant, irreverent, and, in many cases, as privileged as those found on the nation's most well-known campuses.

Following Pedersen, historians of junior and community colleges must look broadly to find their subjects—students—at work and play, on or off campus. As the above examples suggest, historians should look beyond institutional archives, if they even exist, when investigating non-elite institutions like junior and community colleges. Because they were "community" institutions, the history of many two-year colleges can likely be found in the records of local school districts and in public libraries, newspapers, and, when subjects are available, the oral histories of those who attended these institutions. While some junior and community colleges may not have possessed the traditional trappings of college life—football, fraternities, literary societies, or social clubs—many did, and those that did *not* often developed unique student cultures of their own. The question for those exploring student life at junior and community colleges is not whether such cultures existed in the ways that one might expect to find at a four-year residential college, but rather how students made a life for themselves that resembled student cultures found at residential campuses and that also reflected the unique settings of junior and community colleges.

CONCLUSION: HISTORIANS AND COMMUNITY COLLEGE STUDENTS

The history of student life at junior and community colleges, like that of the institutions themselves, remains largely unwritten. But it is possible to write this history. The studies and sources discussed in this chapter demonstrate that the task of writing the history of junior and community colleges is very different from that of writing about elite liberal arts colleges and research universities. Unlike elite institutions, community colleges typically do not possess extensive, professionally managed archives. Rather, as local institutions supported and maintained by municipal tax dollars, two-year colleges are truly the products of the communities in which they are situated. Thus, their histories are often community histories, represented not only in local archival collections, but also in the artifacts, memorabilia, private documents, and personal reflections of those who attended the schools or resided nearby.

Despite their prevalence today, community college students remain an afterthought for historians of American higher education. As a result, historians sometimes have discussed these students and their campus cultures in relation to students at four-year residential campuses—a frame of reference that is not always helpful or appropriate. Or, social scientists have taken the lead in characterizing the student experience at these institutions. Indeed, for much of the last century, social scientists have studied junior and community college students in the aggregate, as statistics, or "types," serving as a foil for students in liberal arts colleges and research universities. Studies of community college students demonstrate, even more strongly than studies of students in other institutions, that, as Cohen, Brawer, and Kisker have observed, the "classification of students into special groups is often more politically inspired than educationally pertinent."[56]

As this chapter has shown, community college students do not fit easily into boxes; to the contrary, they attend these institutions "for a variety of purposes, and the same person may have a half-dozen reasons for attending," as Cohen, Brawer, and Kisker have pointed out.[57] The question is not *whether* these students participate in "campus life," but *how* they create student cultures in ways that reflect their individual circumstances and campus environments. Historians of student life have an opportunity to re-shape our understanding of the history of junior and community colleges by telling the stories of students who have attended them. These students are not merely victims of elite educators' attempts to develop a hierarchical, differentiated system of higher education, nor are they exceptionally pragmatic or rational, eschewing the "social" side of college life in favor of a degree path that will provide a clear return on their investment. They are instead a key chapter in the history of American higher education and the American college student—and one that has not yet been fully told. Without understanding student life at junior and community colleges, we fail to understand the history of community colleges and of American higher education more generally.

NOTES

1. Barack Obama, "Remarks by the President in State of the Union Address," *The White House*, January 20, 2015, accessed April 9, 2017, https://obamawhitehouse.archives.gov/the-press-office/2015/01/20/remarks-president-state-union-address-january-20-2015.
2. The White House, "Higher Education," accessed September 17, 2013, https://obamawhitehouse.archives.gov/issues/education/higher-education.

3. Helen Lefkowitz Horowitz, *Campus Life: Undergraduate Cultures from the End of the Eighteenth Century to the Present* (New York: Alfred A. Knopf, 1987), xii.

4. "2016 Fact Sheet," *American Association of Community Colleges*, February 2016, http://www.aacc.nche.edu/AboutCC/Documents/AACCFactSheetsR2.pdf. Recent research suggests that homelessness and food insecurity among community college students is much more widespread than previously thought. See, for instance, Sara Goldrick-Rab, Jed Richardson, and Anthony Hernandez, *Hungry and Homeless in College: Results from a National Study of Basic Needs Insecurity in Higher Education* (Madison, WI: Wisconsin Hope Lab, March 2017).

5. Philo A. Hutcheson, "Reconsidering the Community College," *History of Education Quarterly* 39, no. 3 (Autumn 1999): 309.

6. See, for instance, Thomas Diener, ed., *Growth of an American Invention: A Documentary History of the Junior and Community College Movement* (New York: Greenwood Press, 1986).

7. Hutcheson, "Reconsidering the Community College," 309; Laurence R. Veysey, *The Emergence of the American University* (Chicago: University of Chicago Press, 1965); Frederick Rudolph, *The American College and University: A History* (Athens, GA: University of Georgia Press, [1962] 1990).

8. Hutcheson notes two works on the history of American higher education which devote some attention to junior and community colleges: John S. Brubacher and Willis Rudy, *Higher Education in Transition, 1636–1956* (New York: Harper and Bros., 1958) and David O. Levine, *The American College and the Culture of Aspiration, 1915–1940* (Ithaca, NY: Cornell University Press, 1986); see "Reconsidering the Community College," 309n6. Other examples of work on the history of junior and community colleges are discussed below.

9. Allen Witt, James L. Wattenberger, James F. Gollatscheck, and Joseph E. Suppiger, *America's Community Colleges: The First Century* (Washington, DC: Community College Press, 1994), 1.

10. See L. Steven Zwerling, *Second Best: The Crisis of the Junior College* (New York: McGraw-Hill, 1976) and Steven Brint and Jerome Karabel, *The Diverted Dream: Community Colleges and the Promise of Equal Educational Opportunity in America, 1900–1985* (New York: Oxford, 1989).

11. For an overview of such criticism, see Fred L. Pincus, "How Critics View the Community College's Role in the Twenty-First Century," in *A Handbook on the Community College in America: Its History, Mission, and Management*, ed. George A. Baker III (Westport, CT: Greenwood Press, 1994), 624–36.

12. See, for instance, Richard M. Freeland, *Academia's Golden Age: Universities in Massachusetts, 1945–1970* (New York: Oxford, 1992).

13. President's Commission on Higher Education, *Higher Education for American Democracy*, (New York: Harper and Bros., 1947–1948) (hereafter *HEFAD*).

14. See *HEFAD*, vol. 3, 5–14.

15. Phebe Ward, *Terminal Education in the Junior College* (New York: Harper and Bros., 1947), 103–04.

16. Pincus, "How Critics View the Community College's Role," 624–25.

17. Levine, *The American College and the Culture of Aspiration*, 164–65.

18. Levine, *The American College and the Culture of Aspiration*, 181.

19. See Brint and Karabel, *The Diverted Dream*, 23–66.

20. Kevin J. Dougherty, *The Contradictory College: The Conflicting Origins, Impacts, and Futures of the Community College* (Albany, NY: State University of New York Press, 1994).

21. J.M. Beach, *Gateway to Opportunity? A History of the Community College in the United States* (Sterling, VA: Stylus Publishing, 2011), xxxv.

22. John H. Frye, *The Vision of the Public Junior College, 1900–1940: Professional Goals and Popular Aspirations* (New York and Westport, CT: Greenwood Press, 1992), 29, 115–16.

23. See, for instance, Frederick Lamson Whitney, *The Junior College in America* (Greeley, CO: Colorado State Teachers College, 1929); James A. Starrak and Raymond M. Hughes, *The New Junior College: The Next Step in Free Public Education* (Ames, IA: The Iowa State College Press, 1948); Nelson B. Henry, ed., *The Public Junior College: The Fifty-fifth Yearbook of the National Society for the Study of Education* (Chicago, IL: University of Chicago Press, 1956); K. Patricia Cross, *the Junior College Student: A Research Description* (Berkeley, CA: Center for Research on Higher Education and American Association of Junior Colleges, 1968); James W. Thornton, Jr., *The Community Junior College*, 3rd ed. (New York: John Wiley & Sons, Inc., 1972); and other titles discussed below.

24. P. P. Claxton, "The Better Organization of Higher Education in the United States," *United States Department of Education Bulletin*, 17–26 (Washington, DC: Government Printing Office, 1922): 21–27.

25. Leonard V. Koos, *The Junior College Movement* (New York: Ginn and Co., 1925), iii.

26. Levine, *The American College and the Culture of Aspiration*, 162.

27. Carl E. Seashore, *The Junior College Movement* (New York: Henry Holt and Co., 1940), iii.

28. Koos, *The Junior College Movement*, 19.

29. Koos, *The Junior College Movement*, 17–22.

30. Koos, *The Junior College Movement*, 388–90.

31. John W. Harbeson, *Classifying Junior College Students* (Pasadena City Schools: Pasadena, CA, 1932), 20.

32. Harbeson, *Classifying Junior College Students*, 20.

33. Harbeson, *Classifying Junior College Students*, 33.
34. Harbeson, *Classifying Junior College Students*, 230.
35. Leonard V. Koos, *The Community College Student* (Gainesville, FL: University of Florida Press, 1970), xiii.
36. Arthur M. Cohen, Florence B. Brawer, and Carrie B. Kisker, *The American Community College*, 6th ed. (San Francisco: Jossey-Bass, 2014), 47–53.
37. Cohen, Brawer, and Kisker, *The American Community College*, 54.
38. Cohen, Brawer, and Kisker, *The American Community College*, 65.
39. Hutcheson, "Reconsidering the Community College," 318.
40. Frye, *The Vision of the Public Junior College*, 73–96.
41. Frye, *The Vision of the Public Junior College*, 87–88.
42. Marvin Ray Aaron, "The Higher Education of African Americans in Kansas City, Missouri: A History of Lincoln Junior College, 1936–1954" (Ph.D. diss., University of Missouri-Kansas City, 1999).
43. Aaron, "The Higher Education of African Americans," 267.
44. Aaron, "The Higher Education of African Americans," 273–78.
45. Nan Elizabeth Haugen, "A History of Women's Intercollegiate Athletics in San Diego community colleges from 1955 to 1972" (Ed.D. diss., University of San Diego, 1990).
46. Robert Patrick Pedersen, "The Origins and Development of the Early Public Junior College: 1900–1940" (Ph.D. diss., Columbia University, 2000).
47. Pedersen, "The Origins and Development of the Early Public Junior College," 32.
48. Pedersen, "The Origins and Development of the Early Public Junior College," 49.
49. The Carnegie Council on Policy Studies in Higher Education, *The Feasibility of a National Policy for the First Two Years of College* (San Francisco: Jossey-Bass, 1975), 2, quoted in Pedersen, "The Origins and Development of the Early Public Junior College," 49.
50. Pedersen, "The Origins and Development of the Early Public Junior College," 49–50.
51. Pedersen, "The Origins and Development of the Early Public Junior College," 49–50.
52. Pedersen, "The Origins and Development of the Early Public Junior College," 52–53.
53. Pedersen, "The Origins and Development of the Early Public Junior College," 54.
54. Pedersen, "The Origins and Development of the Early Public Junior College," 54–58.
55. Pedersen, "The Origins and Development of the Early Public Junior College," 53–54.
56. Cohen, Brawer, and Kisker, *The American Community College*, 63.
57. Cohen, Brawer, and Kisker, *The American Community College*, 65.

CHAPTER 10

Activism, Athletics, and Student Life at State Colleges in the 1950s and 1960s

Marc A. VanOverbeke

On a fall Saturday in 1954, 66 players from Sacramento State College ran onto the field and proceeded over the next four quarters to play football. The Sacramento team lost, but for those players and the fans cheering them on, this was a momentous game. It was the first intercollegiate football contest in the history of Sacramento State, albeit then only a few years old. While Sacramento failed to score a winning touchdown until its second season in 1955, it had succeeded in fielding a team, and was able to do so in large measure because the students pushed for it. They demanded college football, and they sought to build a campus student culture around it. Football, they reasoned, would help their new campus look and feel like other colleges. Given the public's fascination with football and the tight connection in the public's mind between the sport and college, football was a key part of their efforts to ensure that students, parents, and the public saw that Sacramento State had the trappings and customs of a real college and, thus, was a legitimate institution.[1]

M. A. VanOverbeke (✉)
College of Education, University of Illinois at Chicago, Chicago, IL, USA
e-mail: mvanover@uic.edu

© The Author(s) 2018
C. A. Ogren, M. A. VanOverbeke (eds.),
Rethinking Campus Life, Historical Studies in Education,
https://doi.org/10.1007/978-3-319-75614-1_10

213

Just over a decade later in 1967, students across the state at San José State College also turned to football, not to demand a team since the sport was already a tradition on campus, but to protest discrimination and segregation throughout the college. They expected change and pushed to develop a campus that was hospitable and welcoming to all students. Specifically, they promised to disrupt an upcoming football game if reforms did not come, and that threat created a sensation. As had been the case at Sacramento, students at San José tapped into a public fascination with football, but they focused less on building a true college, as had been the goal at Sacramento, and more on expanding access to a real college experience to greater numbers of students from diverse socioeconomic, racial, and cultural backgrounds. Football remained a focus, as it had been a decade earlier, but football also became a means of protest for students.

These two snapshots from the 1950s and 1960s span what historians and observers have sometimes called a "golden age" in higher education, when more students gained access to college and when universities became pivotal players in the social and economic growth of the country.[2] These two stories also capture campus culture, or student life, at a particular set of American colleges—state colleges and regional universities. The contemporary literature sometimes claimed that students on these campuses eschewed active involvement in college life in favor of earning a degree and securing a job, and historians, including Helen Lefkowitz Horowitz, have not comprehensively addressed these institutions or the students who attended them.[3] However, students on these campuses, as these two examples highlight, engaged actively in building campus cultures for themselves and for others. This chapter explores this active engagement at two state colleges in California, but similar levels of activism and engagement existed on state college campuses across California and the nation. The chapter first looks at and defines these state colleges, before turning specifically to student efforts at Sacramento State in the mid-1950s to bring football to campus. The chapter then focuses on the late 1960s, when students embraced the sport as a means of creating conditions to welcome diverse groups of students to campus. In the 1950s and 1960s, then, students on state college campuses in California—and elsewhere—were united by an active embrace of football and athletics to achieve their goals and aims, which included ensuring that their campuses were real colleges open to students from diverse backgrounds.

DEFINING STATE COLLEGES AND THEIR STUDENTS

San José State and Sacramento State, along with hundreds of similar institutions throughout the country, constituted a specific segment of higher education that was emerging and evolving in the years following World War II. Usually labeled state colleges and distinct from state universities, these public institutions expanded to meet the growing demand for well-educated professionals in a nation that was becoming a super power with a thriving postindustrial economy. Some of these state colleges were new institutions in the postwar years, as was the case with Sacramento State, while others, including San José State, had long histories as normal schools and then teachers colleges, or as vocational campuses and agricultural schools (often but not exclusively founded for African American students). Initially characterized as single-purpose institutions, they shed that identity in the decades following World War II and evolved as full-fledged, four-year comprehensive colleges offering bachelor's degrees and some master's degrees. In later decades, many continued to evolve and transition into regional universities. Some states eventually folded these institutions into statewide systems or built those systems anew, with the California State College (eventually University) System being among the largest such systems.[4]

Supported primarily by tax dollars and charging little, if any, tuition, these evolving institutions played an essential role in expanding educational opportunities to more young people in the postwar decades, such that by the mid-1960s, according to one study, there existed 284 state colleges, out of a total of 2400 public and private colleges and universities (both two- and four-year).[5] While a small proportion of higher education institutions overall, these colleges nonetheless educated a disproportionate share of the student body. They collectively enrolled around 1.4 million students, or about one-fifth of the nation's college population. This number was a dramatic increase over the nearly 300,000 enrolled in the mid-1950s in state colleges. More remarkably—and in line with the historic purpose of many of them—these institutions continued to graduate nearly half of the teachers working in the nation's schools.[6]

Many of the students entering and graduating from these state colleges were first-generation students. Compared to their peers in other four-year institutions, students in state colleges also came from families with lower incomes and overall socioeconomic standing. Their fathers often were skilled or semiskilled laborers, while fathers of students in other colleges generally worked in business or professional fields. Even though they came from backgrounds not then common in higher education, students who enrolled in the state colleges had strong high school records. According to one national study in the late 1960s, 85 percent of students in state colleges had graduated in the top half of their high school classes, and over 55 percent had high school averages of B or higher. These first-generation students and their parents valued the access to a college education, as well as the opportunity to gain a valuable credential and improve their socioeconomic standing and prestige, that state colleges provided. Indeed, as early as the first half of the twentieth century and as the nation developed technologically and industrially, a college degree—or even some college education—provided a valuable route to professional jobs and positions. This trend only increased in the postwar years, and college became even more important as a source of professional standing and expertise. By providing a valuable credential that led to professional careers, these state colleges ensured that more Americans had access to well-paying positions. As a result, in the postwar years, they emerged as instrumental to the growth and expansion of the middle class, to greater economic equality among Americans, and to the nation's improving economic prosperity, as Claudia Goldin and Lawrence Katz have demonstrated.[7]

BUILDING STUDENT CULTURE
THROUGH COLLEGIATE ATHLETICS

The students who enrolled at Sacramento State seeking opportunities and economic security wanted football. As new students on a new campus—Sacramento opened its campus in 1947—the students saw that older, more established colleges around them and across the nation had football teams, as well as rivalries and traditions that revolved around athletics. Football was not just a part of these more established colleges, or a core part of the culture and traditions on these campuses. It also was a popular pastime that permeated American culture for much of the late nineteenth and twentieth centuries, and, while college football was prevalent across the country, it was especially important in the southern and western regions where fewer professional teams captured public attention. After World War II, this public fascination with college football only increased, and, as the historian John Thelin has argued, "intercollegiate football flourished as public entertainment."[8] Veterans attending college on the GI

Bill further helped to fuel this spectacle and a strong connection between football and college. Many of the veterans had played prior to the war on college teams and they sought to continue their athletic feats as they returned to college, with veterans on average making up 50 percent of most college football teams between 1945 and 1950. It was difficult for these veterans to think of college without football. Similarly, it was difficult for other students, including those who did not play on college teams, to conceive of college—especially a public college—without athletics and football.[9]

Football mattered as a crucial aspect of a true college experience, and Sacramento's students were determined to have a team so that their campus would ring out with the sounds of football squads and fans cheering them on to victory. They began their campaign by delivering a petition to their president in 1953 to install a football program. They recorded over 600 signatures from their peers on campus, organized committees, and held rallies. They participated in planning meetings with faculty, produced reports, and launched campaigns to sell tickets to the public to help make the team a viable financial enterprise. Crucially, they also agreed to tax themselves and increase their fees to support a team, since the bulk of funding would have to come from the students and they would have to support a student manager to coordinate team logistics. They faced significant hurdles in convincing the president, but they succeeded when the president, seeing value in athletics, acquiesced to their demands and allowed them to build the program.[10]

As these students, their president, and others in the nation's state colleges recognized, athletics provided avenues for connection to a college and a visible indication of one's loyalties and status. Sports signaled that these students were proud members of a team and a college, even if they never stepped on the football field or basketball court. Sacramento's students understood that athletics had the potential to build their college, instill student pride and loyalty, and confer an element of prestige and standing. "For the students and alumni alike," the Sacramento students asserted in their report urging the president to embrace football, "the values [of athletics] include the development of a sense of pride in the athletic phase of the total educational program, the development of tradition and school spirit, sportsmanship, and loyalty."[11] While athletes were on the fields, other students were in the stands cheering them on, writing about them in the campus newspapers, and marching along the sidelines in their band uniforms. They too were participating in athletic traditions and in larger campus cultures, and they embraced the connection between football and college. For these students, as well as for athletes, football and athletics had become the ultimate marker of collegiate status. Athletics granted these students prestige by underscoring that they were part of a college that had the trappings and traditions found on college campuses throughout the country. Whether athletes or not, students came to understand that a college was not a real college if it lacked a football team and all of the rituals and traditions that accompanied athletic competitions. For new colleges and campuses in transition from teachers colleges to comprehensive institutions, this standing was of paramount importance and mattered deeply. Sports signaled that Sacramento State and other state colleges were on a par with colleges and universities across the country.[12]

In keeping with this sense of collegiate standing, the students built the traditions that went along with football, including rivalries and competitions with other teams, and that would help underscore the similarities between their colleges and other institutions. In 1956, for example, Sacramento's students hoped to establish a rivalry with the student body at the nearby University of California–Davis. As one student put it, "During the few short years that Sacramento State College has been in existence there has developed an intense friendly rivalry between it and the University of California at Davis." For this student, "This rivalry has grown especially in intensity since Sacramento State fielded a football team." The students wanted to encourage and promote this rivalry. To that end, they sought to create a new tradition by finding "some appropriate symbol" that would "be passed back and forth between the colleges in the manner of a perpetual trophy for the winner of the annual football game." They channeled their more established peers in hoping for a symbol that would have the same cachet "as the Stanford-California Axe, the Little Brown Jug, the U.C.L.A.-University of Southern California Bell, and other similar traditional symbols." By 1959, they had their symbol: "a surrey without a fringe on top," donated by a community member "who has taken an active interest in school activities." And with that surrey, they built a tradition to further instill student support, interest, and loyalty.[13]

Students did not want simply to build those traditions, however. They also wanted to enjoy them and participate actively in them. And, as could often be the case, the students at Sacramento, while building and enjoying their traditions, sometimes let them get out of hand. Such was the case with the Far Western Conference championship basketball game in 1957 between Sacramento and the University of Nevada. In this case, the opposing team argued that the Sacramento fans enjoyed the game a bit too much. The main offense, according to the Nevada student body president, was that Sacramento's students failed on two occasions to stand during the singing of the Nevada Alma Mater, and then attempted to drown out the Nevada spirit squad with air horns. The president hurried to state that "the students at the University of Nevada have no objections to this type of toy being used, if it is used with some discretion." In a final jab, he told Sacramento's student body president that this kind of behavior might be "your interpretation of sportsmanship."[14] As trivial as this behavior might have been, it underscored the importance of athletics and traditions to these students, and helps explain their active efforts to build an athletic culture on their campus and through that a campus student culture rooted in loyalty to their institution.

Students' interest in and focus on athletics, however, went beyond the desire to build spirit and loyalty. They were building the reputation of their institutions and the value of their degrees as crucial credentials. This focus on athletics and credentialing became even more apparent among students and alumni at San José State College in the late 1950s. There, students and former students—having been part of a football culture with a longer history than at Sacramento—rallied to force the president and university to strengthen the program and to move it closer toward big-time, championship football. They did not simply want a team; instead, they wanted a big-time, winning team. Alumni may have been at the forefront of these efforts, but they found ready allies in the student body. Together, they turned to football to strengthen their institution, as students at Sacramento had, and, they hoped, to enhance the value of their degrees.

Tracing its history back to 1857, San José State College by the 1960s had an established athletic program with a loyal following of students, alumni, and community citizens. San José State had been on the verge of becoming a major football power since the mid-1940s, but the team's fortunes started to slip in the 1950s. From 1946 to 1951, the team won 37 games, lost 10, and tied 2. However, until 1950, they were part of the California Collegiate Athletic Association, where they were able to dominate weaker teams from smaller colleges.[15] From 1952 to 1957, when the team filled its schedule with stronger opponents, the program maintained a winning record overall, although the college won only 26 games, while losing 23. The alumni and boosters cried foul. "Obviously," the alumni concluded, "San José State is not now 'on its way.'"[16]

They pointed to restrictive athletic regulations as the culprit, and advocated for a major reorganization of the athletic department with provisions for a long-range budget to adequately support a championship program. They called for more coaches and for greater financial support for athletes, including room and board. They believed that a wider network of alumni and boosters throughout the state could help secure summer jobs and on-campus jobs during the school year to help athletes afford to attend the college. As part of this plan, they suggested that alumni and boosters could volunteer as "job procurer" officers in various parts of the state.[17] They also proposed a program where alumni and interested citizens essentially would become part of the athletic department, on a voluntary basis, and serve as "field scouts" for identifying promising recruits and connecting them to the college. These alumni valued the athletic department and their college, and they were willing to tap into alumni supporters and the public to fund many of these new developments.[18]

After careful consideration, the students backed the alumni and their efforts overwhelmingly. While the students initially made no commitments and refused to take a stand on the demands for improved football, they did agree to study and discuss the issues. They debated the situation in multiple student association government meetings throughout 1957, and they also proposed a referendum so that the students could express their views on the importance of a strong football program.[19] As the students put it, we "naturally want a strong football team and we want a team we can be proud of. We put in about $42,000 of our funds into the whole athletic program, and so there is quite a bit of our money at stake."[20] In the end, the students supported a strong football program as instrumental to their lives on campus and to their futures once they graduated. They voted 2538 to 168 to endorse the program of big-time athletics.[21]

The alumni and students proposed moving toward a stronger football program, in great measure to ensure the value of the degrees that the alumni held and that current students were earning. David Heagerty, president of the alumni association, turned to the college's *Spartan Review* to make this case explicitly. He argued to current and former students that their investment in a college education and degree "can bear huge dividends or it can bring only skimpy returns." He continued, "Our investment should provide the ultimate in economic and social opportunity. No door should remain closed because of the lack of sufficient educational stature, real or imagined." The value of the degree—the return on their investment—he cautioned, was tied closely to the college's standing and reputation. Leaving little to doubt, he pushed his argument to declare that the college's standing depended on athletics. "Of the numerous influential campus endeavors," he said, "none possess the impact on public thinking and can affect an educational institution's reputation to the degree of intercollegiate athletics."[22] A substantially strengthened football program, he advocated, would "elevate athletics at [San José State] to the highest possible level and will place us on a par with the best anywhere."[23]

As a former San José student concurred in a meeting with the president, "We are the poor people. We [at San José State] have the greatest inferiority complex of any institution of higher learning" in California. But, he continued, football and athletics had given the college important traditions, as well as hope for improvement in its standing and stature. "I guarantee you," he said, "the day that every Alumni in San José State College rejoiced was the day that San José beat Stanford. Why? Because we said, for a day, for a weekend, for a week, until next year, we have lost our feeling of inferiority."[24] The future of the college rested on improving the football situation and notching more wins against prominent teams. For alumni and students, a victory against Stanford signaled that San José was no longer a sleepy teachers college but a strong and legitimate university that deserved to be seen among the nation's better colleges and universities. Athletics, he concluded, was the "heart" of the college. "If you take the heart, the spirit, the essence out of this institution, then you have killed it for all time" and demoralized the students and alumni.[25] Athletics was a serious factor in the development and identity of the college and, by extension, the students and the alumni. Their standing and their identity rested on their college and its success on the gridiron.[26]

The alumni and students reasoned that, without top-notch teams, the San José degree would not be worth as much as a degree from those colleges with national athletic reputations. San José therefore had to grasp this opportunity to showcase that it was a vibrant, comprehensive public institution. Students attended college in the hope that they would gain a credential that would unlock professional doors, allow them to move higher on the socioeconomic ladder, or, at least, retain the standing of their parents. The better the reputation of the college, the higher the value of the degree. San José could improve its image and reputation only as it played the game and furthered its athletic ambitions with an enhanced, vibrant, and winning football program.[27] Sacramento's students had earlier taken a similar position when they campaigned for football as a way to underscore the legitimacy of their institution and, thus, their degrees.

Eventually, San José did make some changes to ease restrictions on recruitment and to improve the standing of the football program.[28] As the alumni and students underscored, once a college started to play the game, it was not easy to stop playing. As they developed football at Sacramento and worked to strengthen it at San José, the students and alumni did so out of an effort to solidify the standing of their institutions and, through that, the value of their degrees as credentials. These were active students working to replicate the campus cultures they saw throughout higher education and throughout the nation. They wanted what other students had, and, in the absence of those traditions, they built them or campaigned to strengthen them, but the focus was less on the football team than on what they believed that team represented—a real college where students earned real degrees and credentials that carried weight and import. And, that standing and prestige only increased when teams won games and consistently increased their reputations. This belief among students in the importance—the necessity—of strong, successful football teams only hardened after students graduated and became alumni. For the students at Sacramento, San José, and elsewhere, the stakes of not winning were too high.

ATHLETICS AND PROTEST: EXPANDING COLLEGE LIFE TO MORE STUDENTS

Students wanted athletics, and they wanted the standing and prestige that accompanied successful feats on the football field. They were active, even as alumni, in demanding football prowess, but, throughout the 1960s and especially by the late 1960s, a new style of activism gripped colleges across the nation, as well as the state college campuses. On state college campuses, student activism in the 1960s shared similar aims—to build a true college experience—with activism in the 1950s, but some students in the 1960s deliberately campaigned to expand the benefits of that experience to more students and to make their campuses—and the student cultures on them—more open, more welcoming, and more accessible to students from different backgrounds. This activism, especially among African American and Mexican American students, was true at San José State, and again underscored the dynamic role that students played on state college campuses in building student life. As was the case earlier, athletics and football were never far from view.

While students at San José had demanded a championship football team in 1957, students there in the late 1960s, in particular African

American students, came to see athletics and football as a means of protest and as a subject of protest. They challenged their campus to be more open to African American students and, eventually, to Mexican and Mexican American students and others from diverse backgrounds. They often embraced athletics in dramatic fashion, as they did on the first day of the new semester in fall 1967. As classes were beginning, black students rallied on campus and put forth significant demands that underscored real challenges at their college. Led by their charismatic instructor, Harry Edwards, whose classes often attracted hundreds of students (black and white), this nascent union of black students demanded that the college abolish discrimination throughout the institution, develop fair and equitable housing policies, and force fraternities and sororities to integrate. They also pushed the college to enroll more students from minority backgrounds. Other students—including the college's student government association—supported these goals and called for actions and steps to rid the campus of discrimination. Groups of students across the nation similarly demanded that colleges and universities develop programs to open access to greater numbers of students. But these demands were particularly poignant on state college campuses like San José State, since black students there—and other students who supported increasing access and opportunity—were asking these colleges to live up to their mission to be more welcoming to greater numbers of students from diverse backgrounds.[29]

Football and sport were key elements of their protest, and they focused much of their frustration on athletics and challenged their institution to rid the athletic department of racism. They charged that black athletes—not just football players—were discriminated against during recruiting events and while traveling to away games. Black athletic recruits, they contended, were left on their own during recruiting and social events, while white recruits were given dates and invited to parties. Damningly, Edwards and the students pointed out that five black football players had been unable to find appropriate housing in San José, where landlords often refused to rent to black students. Instead, these players lived unhappily in a hotel. At San José and elsewhere, these charges of racism also included attacks on coaches for "stacking" football players, or assigning black players primarily to certain positions (usually on the defensive teams in football, for example), while placing white players in offensive positions, crucially as quarterbacks. The black students forcefully urged black athletic recruits hoping to play for the college in the fall to go elsewhere, "because any place is better than this," Edwards warned. The student life for black athletes and students at San José, these protestors claimed, was mired in segregation and discrimination, where the opportunities that black students had—whether that meant places to live on- and off-campus or social events to attend—were sharply limited and constrained.[30]

They declared strategically that, if their demands were not met, they would disrupt that weekend's football game through a "lie-in" or "sit-in," by sending supporters onto the field.[31] In making these threats, the students recognized the power of athletics to draw attention to a cause. The campus's athletic director understood that athletics was an easy way to emphasize a larger cause, and he admitted that the student protestors skillfully had used athletics "to strengthen their hand to bring about a solution to the whole problem" of discrimination and racism throughout the college and community.[32] Robert Clark, president of the college, also came to realize the importance of athletics to Americans and, thus, the effectiveness of using athletics to gain publicity and support. "I've learned a lot about the values of the American male," Clark said. "Athletics comes first. God, mother, and country second."[33] The black students and their allies were demanding an end to discrimination in athletics and throughout campus, but they also were using athletics—and threats to disrupt a game—to draw attention to their causes. The students gained even greater publicity when Ronald Reagan, then California's governor, declared soon after the protests started that he was prepared to call in troops to ensure that the college did not give in and cancel the game.[34]

As the protest grew, Clark took the dramatic step of canceling the game. This action only increased public interest and pressure on Clark to end the protests and get the team back on the field. Clark authorized a number of listening and working sessions over the course of the week where students, faculty, and administrators debated various aspects of the college, including fraternities and sororities, housing and equality, and athletics.[35] While he had confidence in the athletic department, he announced soon after the protests began that he was authorizing various steps and reforms to ensure that the athletic program met student needs and treated everyone equitably. All athletes, while on trips for away games, would be assigned roommates solely on a random basis, he declared. Further, all social events would be open equally to white and black athletes or would not be available to any students, and he concurred with the athletic director's proposal for a student committee (which would include black students) to help handle any grievances against the athletic department.[36]

To address segregation and discrimination more broadly throughout the college, Clark announced steps to end segregation and discrimination in fraternities and sororities, and to build programs to bring more African American students to campus and to provide them with departments and courses focused on black life and culture. Eventually these programs came to include Mexican and Mexican American students. Additionally, the college began working with other colleges and universities to develop a "College Commitment Program," which provided work-study dollars for students to tutor minority high school students and to encourage these high schoolers to enroll in college. Clark also directed the college to hire personnel specifically to recruit and work with minority students.[37] To add more weight to these recommendations and to underscore the seriousness with which Clark and the college took these charges of discrimination, Clark announced that he was creating the new position of college ombudsman—one of the first on a college campus—to continue to address and rid the college of discrimination. The ombudsman would not just react to student grievances but would actively "search out and facilitate the removal of discrimination on the basis of race, creed, or national origin, in whatever areas of the College or the College community it may occur."[38]

At the end of an eventful and tense week on campus, the black students deliberated and debated whether to accept the plans and strategies Clark outlined. If they chose to reject them, they could launch new protests and demand additional changes. After great debate, the black students welcomed these steps and voted overwhelmingly, 56 to 3, to support the changes that the president had outlined.[39] In reaching this decision, the group created various committees to work with others in the college to ensure continued success in rooting out discriminatory practices. One committee would work with Greek organizations to help them develop policies and practices to end discrimination in recruitment and housing in fraternities and sororities. Other members would work with the college to develop and fully implement tutoring programs for high school students. This outreach effort extended to the community at large, with the black students sending a committee into the community to visit "lower class homes" and determine their needs and interests. While recognizing the depth of the challenge to address discrimination in community housing, the students also committed themselves to working with community leaders to address this serious issue.[40]

The students also rescinded their pronouncement that black athletes should go elsewhere. "We are also issuing the statement that we are encouraging any athlete, in any sport, carried on San José State's campus, to come to this college, with the assurance that we have a competent, trained, professional and morally and ethically efficient staff that will do their utmost to make sure not only that this athlete comes to his fullest bloom as an athlete, but that also he develops into a well-grounded human being, which may be the more important of the two goals." Now that the group had given its assurances to potential athletes, Edwards and the students established a committee of black athletes to work with the athletic department in the recruitment and retention "of all athletes, of any athlete, black or white."[41]

The harmony reached through the open meetings and Clark's actions to address black demands was short-lived, however. Edwards and the students again commanded headlines in November 1967 when they launched a campaign encouraging black athletes to skip the 1968 Olympics. This time Edwards and the students turned their attention toward a national and international audience. They sought to raise awareness across the world of the treatment of African American athletes and students, and they embraced some of the techniques they had developed at San José to do so. While the boycott of the 1968 games did not materialize, the group succeeded in encouraging some athletes to develop their own form of protest, as was the case when two San José athletes raised their gloved fists on the winners' podium. After winning the gold and bronze medals in the 200-meter dash, Tommie Smith and John Carlos, who had participated with Edwards in protests on San José's campus, raised their fists in what has become an iconic photo. By doing so, they sparked debate and outrage across the country and world, but they also succeeded—as they had earlier at San José State—in bringing attention to discrimination and segregation.[42]

As Clark and the campus dealt with the discrimination that African Americans experienced, they also confronted charges by Mexican American students that the campus was not welcoming. Clark responded much as he had to the black students. He worked with the Mexican American students on a "Day of Concern" program to air later in the fall that would "help sensitize our faculty about the problems of discrimination encountered by the minority communities of our campus." The Mexican American students, however, protested this event when they discovered that the television show included only four Mexican American students but 11 black students. The Mexican American students argued that Mexican Americans constituted a larger proportion of California's population than African Americans (and were the largest minority group in the San José area). There were about 400 to 500 Mexican American students and a handful of Mexican American faculty at San José State College. They demanded stronger representation. Clark and his ombudsman postponed the video and worked with the students to address their concerns.[43]

These actions resolved the challenges for the moment, but in May the Mexican American students presented a list of demands to the administration. As was the case with the black students, they threatened a demonstration if the demands were not met. Rather than threatening to disrupt an athletic event, however, they promised a mass protest during college graduation exercises.[44] The group also pushed the president and college to postpone commencement until all graduating students had completed a workshop on Mexican American issues. Clark recognized the legitimacy of the student demands, and supported the need to hire more Mexican American, black, and minority instructors, to develop new courses focused on Mexican American and black subjects, and to devote more resources to recruiting and supporting minority students. And, as he admitted, the college's admission standards were problematic. "We screen them [Mexican American students] out of college with formal admission standards," he said, "that may not test the full range of their achievements." Still, he believed that bowing to the demand to postpone graduation "would be illegal."[45] Clark did hire a new ombudsman, Ralph Poblano, who had served as a counselor to the Mexican American students and chaired the advisory committee on Mexican American educational issues for the state department of education. Given these steps and ongoing discussions, the massive demonstration never materialized, although between 200 and 300 students and citizens did stage a walkout during graduation.[46]

Based on the protests of African American and Mexican American students, the San José administration, in consultation with faculty and students, moved to develop new educational opportunity programs to enroll more minority students and to provide support for them while in college. Black and Mexican American groups agreed to participate in efforts to recruit these students and to develop programs to help them adjust to college. The college also hired Al Espinoza and Tim Knowles, a recent graduate and the president of the United Black Students group who had participated with Edwards in protests, to coordinate the programs for Mexican American and African American students. Knowles understood the challenge. "Some of these kids [coming to college as part of the new program] are from the hard-core ghetto," he said. "Their high-school counselors told them they didn't have it to go to college, and many of them believed it until we came along and gave them hope."[47]

At San José, black and Mexican American students and allies actively protested this type of discrimination. They sought to build new programs and initiatives to address discrimination and segregation. They focused on expanding access to college and educational benefits to greater numbers of students, and they often turned to athletics to bring attention to their goals. At San José and elsewhere, they succeeded at least in part because they skillfully leveraged athletics to gain publicity and support.

CONCLUSION

Throughout the 1950s and 1960s, students on state college campuses—such as San José and Sacramento—built active, engaged student cultures. These efforts aimed to replicate what students saw on other, more established college campuses across the nation. They wanted football and all that it and other sports represented. They wanted to experience camaraderie, loyalty, and connection, as well as to earn a college degree and benefit from the opportunities that such a valuable credential unlocked. As they argued throughout the postwar years, and particularly in the 1950s, the value of their degrees increased as the reputation and standing of their institutions increased. For many students and the public, the way to ensure the value of a college degree was to build football programs. Sports thus became entrenched on college campuses in part as a way to build that institutional legitimacy. A decade later, as protests began to rock campuses in the late 1960s, many students remained focused on building true colleges and a true college experience, even as their efforts began to shift toward expanding the benefits of college to other students and making their campuses more welcome and accessible places. Even in these campaigns, football and athletics remained central to the activism and engagement that students participated in and to the campus cultures that they built.

NOTES

1. Josh Ellis, "A Hornet for Life: Green and Gold Courses through Snelson's Veins," *The State Hornet*, May 15, 1998 [50th Anniversary Edition], accessed June 26, 2017, http://www.csus.edu/hornet/archive/spring98/number54/50th/p3.html.
2. See, for example, Richard M. Freeland, *Academia's Golden Age: Universities in Massachusetts, 1945–1970* (Oxford: Oxford University Press, 1992); and John R. Thelin, *A History of American Higher Education* (Baltimore: The Johns Hopkins University Press, 2004), 260–62.

3. For contemporary accounts, see E. Alden Dunham, *Colleges of the Forgotten Americans: A Profile of State Colleges and Regional Universities* (New York: McGraw-Hill Book Company, 1969). Helen Lefkowitz Horowitz, *Campus Life: Undergraduate Cultures from the End of the Eighteenth Century to the Present* (Chicago: The University of Chicago Press, 1987).

4. Donald R. Gerth, *The People's University: A History of the California State University* (Berkeley: Berkeley Public Policy Press, 2010), 38, 42; Fred F. Harcleroad, H. Bradley Sagen, and C. Theodore Molen, Jr., *The Developing State Colleges and Universities: Historical Background, Current Status, and Future Plans*. (Iowa City, IA: The American College Testing Program, 1969), 8–14, 31, 76, 96; Dunham, *Colleges of the Forgotten Americans*, xii, 1, 28, 37, 51–56, 68–69; Fred F. Harcleroad and Allan W. Ostar, *Colleges and Universities for Change: America's Comprehensive Public State Colleges and Universities* (Washington, DC: American Association of State Colleges and Universities Press, 1987), 2, 4–5, 62–69, 135; Fred F. Harcleroad, C. Theodore Molen, Jr., and Jack R. Rayman, *The Regional State Colleges and Universities Enter the 1970s* (Iowa City, IA: The American College Testing Program, 1973), 6, 31–32, 93.

5. Harcleroad et al., *The Developing State Colleges and Universities*, 3.

6. Harcleroad et al., *The Developing State Colleges and Universities*, 9, 32, 39–40, 85–86, 92. Harcleroad et al., *The Regional State Colleges and Universities*, 13; Joe Smith, *Challenge to Change: The State Colleges and Universities in a Time of Expanding Responsibility* (Washington, DC: Association of State Colleges and Universities, 1965), 15; Dunham, *Colleges of the Forgotten Americans*, 39, 83, 118–19.

7. The report looking at high school records was the American Council on Education's (ACE) 1968 national norms study of incoming freshmen (Appendix C); for a discussion of this report, see Dunham, *Colleges of the Forgotten Americans*, 90–91. "Statistical Report of Regular Students, Spring Semester 1955 Compared with Fall Semester 1954–55," folder 12, box 4, Student Affairs, Sacramento State University Archives; "A First Partial Report on Student Demographic Characteristics and Financial Aid, October 1967," folder 8, box 4, Student Affairs, Sacramento State University Archives; James T. Patterson, *Grand Expectations: The United States, 1945–1974* (New York: Oxford University Press, 1996); David K. Brown, *Degrees of Control: A Sociology of Educational Expansion and Occupational Credentialism* (New York: Teachers College Press, 1995); Claudia Goldin and Lawrence F. Katz, *The Race between Education and Technology* (Cambridge: Harvard University Press, 2008); David O. Levine, *The American College and the Culture of Aspiration, 1915–1940* (Ithaca: Cornell University Press, 1986), 19–21; William G. Bowen, Matthew M. Chingos, and Michael S. McPherson, *Crossing the Finish Line:*

Completing College at America's Public Universities (Princeton: Princeton University Press, 2009).

8. John R. Thelin, *Games Colleges Play: Scandal and Reform in Intercollegiate Athletics* (Baltimore: The Johns Hopkins University Press, 1994), 5–12, 68–100, 122, 156. See also Michael Mandelbaum, *The Meaning of Sports: Why Americans Watch Baseball, Football, and Basketball and What They See When They Do* (New York: Public Affairs, 2004), 2–7, 152–53; Michael Oriard, *King Football: Sport and Spectacle in the Golden Age of Radio and Newsreels, Movies and Magazines, the Weekly & the Daily Press* (Chapel Hill: The University of North Carolina Press, 2001), 6–7, 11–13; Michael Oriard, *Reading Football: How the Popular Press Created An American Spectacle* (Chapel Hill: The University of North Carolina Press, 1993), 132–33, 144, 277; Benjamin G. Rader, *American Sports: From the Age of Folk Games to the Age of Televised Sports* (Upper Saddle River, New Jersey: Prentice Hall, 1999, 4th edition), 81, 90–91, 95–96, 173, 183, 263; Charles T. Clotfelter, *Big-Time Sports in American Universities* (Cambridge: Cambridge University Press, 2011), 14, 45, 51–52, 66, 125, 194; Ronald A. Smith, *Sports and Freedom: The Rise of Big-Time College Athletics* (New York: Oxford University Press, 1988), 218; Thelin, *A History of American Higher Education*, 208–11; John Sayle Watterson, *College Football: History, Spectacle, Controversy* (Baltimore: The Johns Hopkins University Press, 2000), 266–67.

9. Gerth, *The People's University*, 38, 42; Patterson, *Grand Expectations*, 68, 367; David D. Henry, *Challenges Past, Challenges Present: An Analysis of American Higher Education Since 1930* (San Francisco: Jossey-Bass, 1975), 62–63, 66–67, 101; Goldin and Katz, *The Race between Education and Technology*, 247; Suzanne Mettler, *Soldiers to Citizens: The G.I. Bill and the Making of the Greatest Generation* (Oxford: Oxford University Press, 2005), 7; Oriard, *King Football*, 116; Smith, *Sports and Freedom*, 218; Daniel A. Clark, "'The Two Joes Meet. Joe College, Joe Veteran:' The G.I. Bill, College Education, and Postwar American Culture," *History of Education Quarterly* 38 (Summer 1998): 167–68, 174–78.

10. "Statement Concerning the Initiation of Football Presented to the Student Assembly on December 1, 1953, by Guy A. West, President," folder 12, unprocessed collection, Office of the President (Guy West), Sacramento State University Archives; "Guy A. West to Lysle D. Leach, November 13, 1953," folder 11, unprocessed collection, Office of the President (Guy West), Sacramento State University Archives; "Present Status of the Development of the Football Issue at SSC, November 19, 1953," folder 12, unprocessed collection, Office of the President (Guy West), Sacramento State University Archives; "Minutes of the Student Council Meeting, December 2, 1953," folder 2, box 4, Student Affairs, Sacramento State

University Archives; "Report of the Football Committee, November 30, 1953," folder 12, unprocessed collection, Office of the President (Guy West), Sacramento State University Archives.

11. "Policies Governing Intercollegiate Athletics at Sacramento State College, Formulated Spring, 1953," folder 9, box 1, Coordinating Executive and Faculty Council, Sacramento State University Archives.

12. Thelin, *Games Colleges Play*, 5–9, 68–100, 122; Pamela Grundy, *Learning to Win: Sports, Education, and Social Change in Twentieth Century North Carolina* (Chapel Hill: The University of North Carolina Press, 2001), 202–03, 297–301; Brian M. Ingrassia, "Public Influence Inside the College Walls: Progressive Era Universities, Social Scientists, and Intercollegiate Football Reform," *The Journal of the Gilded Age and Progressive Era* 10 (January 2011): 61–62, 69–72; Watterson, *College Football*, xi–xii, 1–4, 241–42, 271–72, 285–87, 408; Oriard, *King Football*, 143, 365–66.

13. "James H. Morrow to Jeré Strizek, June 6, 1956," folder 3, box 4, Student Affairs, Sacramento State University Archives; "Trophy Arrives on Campus," no date, folder 5, box 4, Student Affairs, Sacramento State University Archives; "Student Council Meeting Minutes, November 16, 1959," folder 5, box 4, Student Affairs, Sacramento State University Archives. For information on college life and the development of loyalty and spirit, see Horowitz, *Campus Life*, 119.

14. "Chuck Coyle to Tom Willoughby, March 7, 1957," folder 3, box 4, Student Affairs, Sacramento State University Archives.

15. Citizens Committee for a Progressive San Jose State College, "Which Way Spartan Athletics?" *Spartan Review* 36, no. 2 (October–November 1957), 4–5, box 1, series 1, Publications Collection, San José State University Archives.

16. Citizens Committee, "Which Way Spartan Athletics?" 4–5; see also "Citizens Committee for a Progressive San Jose State College, November 7, 1957," folder 14, unprocessed collection, Office of the President (Guy West), Sacramento State University Archives; S. Glenn Hartranft, "Departments—What's going on in your dept.," *Alumni Review* 29, no. 5 (February 1951), 4, box 1, series 1, Publications Collection, San José State University Archives; Danny Hill, "Titchenal Named Football Head," *Spartan Review* 35, no. 3 (December–January 1956–57), 8, box 1, series 1, Publications Collection, San José State University Archives; Danny Hill, "Spartan Sports," *Alumni Review* 31, no. 1 (October 1952), 8, box 1, series 1, Publications Collection, San José State University Archives.

17. "An Analysis of the San Jose State College Athletic Department," n.d. [likely January 1957], 1–4, folder—athletics at SJSC, box 14, series 1,

Presidential Office Administrative Records, San José State University Archives.

18. Wes Mathis, "Frank Leahy Recognizes San Jose State Bid to Reach Football 'Big Time,'" *San Jose Evening News*, November 25, 1955, folder 4, box 20, series 3, Office of the President, John T. Wahlquist Records, San José State University Archives; Hartranft, "Departments—What's going on in your dept.," February 1951, 4; "Letter from Everett Jackson to Edwin Mosher, January 27, 1956," bound volume—Book 1, box 36, series 6, Office of the President, John T. Wahlquist Records, San José State University Archives; "An Analysis of the San Jose State College Athletic Department," 1–4.

19. "Executive Council Minutes, February 25, 1957," folder—Student Council Meetings, 1956–1957, box 32, series 3, San José State University Associated Students Records, San José State University Archives; "Student Council Agenda, November 13, 1957," folder—Student Council Meetings, 1957–1958, box 32, series 3, San José State University Associated Students Records, San José State University Archives; "Student Council Agenda, November 25, 1957, including Minutes," folder— Student Council Meetings, 1957–1958, box 32, series 3, San José State University Associated Students Records, San José State University Archives.

20. "Don Ryan, November 1957," in "Testimony from E.F. De Vilbiss, November 1957," folder—Athletic Controversy—1957, box 14, series 1, General Files, 1899–1970, San José State College Presidential Office Administrative Records, San José State University Archives.

21. Citizens Committee, "Which Way Spartan Athletics?" 4–7; student vote recorded in "Editor's Note, in "Which Way Spartan Athletics?" 7.

22. David A Heagerty, "Editorial—Your Stake in Higher Education and Athletics," *Spartan Review* 35, no. 4 (February–March 1957), 4, box 1, series 1, Publications Collection, San José State University Library Archives.

23. Heagerty, "Editorial," 4.

24. "Presentation of Mr. E. F. De Vilbiss, spokesman for the SJSC Alumni Association and member of the 'Citizens Committee for a Progressive San Jose State College,' before a community hearing on November 12, 1957," folder—Athletic Controversy, 1957, box 14, series 1, Presidential Office Administrative Records, San José State University Archives.

25. "Presentation of Mr. E. F. De Vilbiss."

26. For a discussion of athletics and identity, see Grundy, *Learning to Win*, 5–9; Watterson, *College Football*, 416; Levine, *The American College and the Culture of Aspiration*, 19, 114–20, 133–34; Oriard, *King Football*, 13–14, 19, 143, 163–64, 226–28; Clark, "'The Two Joes Meet. Joe

College, Joe Veteran,'" 174–78, 189; Daniel A. Clark, *Creating the College Man: American Mass Magazines and Middle-Class Manhood, 1890–1915* (Madison: University of Wisconsin Press, 2010), 14, 18–21, 80–89, 94–102, 109, 116–17; Smith, *Sports and Freedom*, 218.

27. Heagerty, "Editorial," 4; Levine, *The American College and the Culture of Aspiration*, 19, 114–20, 133–34; Oriard, *King Football*, 13–19, 143, 163–64, 226–28; Clark, "'The Two Joes Meet. Joe College, Joe Veteran,'" 174–78, 189; Clark, *Creating the College Man*, 14–21, 80–89, 94–102, 109, 116–17.

28. "SJS Athletic Meet Tonight," n.d. and no publication name, box 31, series V, Office of the President, John T. Wahlquist, San José State University Archives; "Dan Caputo President of SJS Foundation," *San Jose Mercury*, January 16, 1958, box 31, series V, Office of the President, John T. Wahlquist, San José State University Archives.

29. Arnold Hano, "The Black Rebel Who 'Whitelists' the Olympics," *The New York Times*, May 12, 1968, 40; Harry Edwards, "U.S.B.A. Demands, COPY, September 21, 1967," folder: Racial Discrimination, General Information, 1967–68, box 31, series 3, Office of the President, Robert D. Clark Records, San José State University Archives; "Chronology of Events in Racial Discrimination Incident, October 25, 1967," 7, 11–12, folder: Racial Discrimination, General Information, 1967–68, box 31, series 3, Office of the President, Robert D. Clark Records, San José State University Archives.

30. "Chronology of Events in Racial Discrimination Incident," 9–10; Edwards, "U.S.B.A. Demands, COPY, September 21, 1967;" Scott Moore, "Air Negro Charges, SJS President Orders," *San Jose Mercury*, September 19, 1967, no folder, box 31, series 3, Office of the President, Robert D. Clark Records, San José State University Archives. Edwards quoted in "Air Negro Charges;" "Letter from Ernest Becker to Chancellor Dumke," September 22, 1967," 1, folder: Racial Discrimination, General Information, 1967–68, box 31, series 3, Office of the President, Robert D. Clark Records, San José State University Archives.

31. "Chronology of Events in Racial Discrimination Incident," 4; "Letter from Ernest Becker to Chancellor Dumke," 1.

32. Bronzan quoted in "Rights Campaign Begun in San Jose," *The New York Times*, October 3, 1967.

33. Clark quoted in Curits J. Sitomer, "Dialogue and action prod racial reform at San Jose State," *The Christian Science Monitor*, July 2, 1968, 23a, in *San Jose State College, Student Unrest, 1967–68*, folder: Student Unrest—Student Unrest at San Jose State College, 1967–68, box 30, series 3, Office of the President, Robert D. Clark Records, San José State University Archives.

34. "Racial Discrimination Incident," in *San Jose State College, Student Unrest, 1967–68*, 2; "Chronology of Events in Racial Discrimination Incident," 13; Association of California State College Professors, "Press Release: Of 'Blackmail,' 'Appeasement,' and Prudence," September 29, 1967, folder: Racial Discrimination Problem: Letters concerning Pro G-N, 67–68, box 30, series 3, Office of the President, Robert D. Clark Records, San José State University Archives; "The Governor on 'Appeasement,'" KLIV Editorial, September 30, 31, 1967, folder: Racial Discrimination Problem: Letters concerning Pro G-N, 67–68, box 30, series 3, Office of the President, Robert D. Clark Records, San José State University Archives; "Editorial: The Real Issue at San Jose," *The Los Angeles Times*, September 28, 1967, folder: Racial Discrimination Problem: Letters concerning Pro G-N, 67–68, box 30, series 3, Office of the President, Robert D. Clark Records, San José State University Archives.
35. "Chronology of Events in Racial Discrimination Incident," 4–14; "Letter from Ernest Becker to Chancellor Dumke," 2.
36. "Statement by San Jose State College President Robert D. Clark, September 21, 1967," folder: Racial Discrimination, General Information, 1967–68, box 31, series 3, Office of the President, Robert D. Clark Records, San José State University Archives, 3–4; "Chronology of Events in Racial Discrimination Incident," 5.
37. "Statement by San Jose State College President Robert D. Clark," 5.
38. "Chronology of Events in Racial Discrimination Incident," 15; "Statement by San Jose State College President Robert D. Clark," 2.
39. "Chronology of Events in Racial Discrimination Incident," 14; "Statement by Harry Edwards, September 22, 1967," 1, folder: Edwards, Harry, 1967–68, Letters, box 29, series 3, Office of the President, Robert D. Clark Records, San José State University Archives.
40. "Statement by Harry Edwards," 1–3.
41. "Statement by Harry Edwards," 2.
42. Harry Edwards, "Why Negroes Should Boycott Whitey's Olympics," *Saturday Evening Post*, March 9, 1968, folder: Edwards, Harry, 1967–68, Letters, box 29, series 3, Office of the President, Robert D. Clark Records, San José State University Archives; Hano, "The Black Rebel Who 'Whitelists' the Olympics," 42; Al Stump, "Sports," *True: The Man's Magazine*, April 1968, 44, folder: Edwards, Harry, 1967–68, Letters, box 29, series 3, Office of the President, Robert D. Clark Records, San José State University Archives; C. Gerald Fraser, "Negroes Call Off Boycott, Reshape Olympic Protest," *The New York Times*, September 1, 1968; Joseph M. Sheehan, "2 Black Power Advocates Ousted from Olympics," *The New York Times*, October 19, 1968; Joseph M. Sheehan, "Smith Takes Olympic 200 Meters and Seagren Captures Pole Vault for U.S.," *The*

New York Times, October 17, 1968; Arthur Daley, "Sports of *The Times,* Under a Black Cloud," *The New York Times,* July 3, 1968; Arthur Daley, "Sports of *The Times,* Direct Confrontation," *The New York Times,* September 10, 1968.

43. "Clark Following Through," *San Leandro News, Fremont News-Register, Alameda Times-Star,* November 7, 1967, folder: Edwards, Harry, 1967–68, Letters, box 29, series 3, Office of the President, Robert D. Clark Records, San José State University Archives; "Mexican-American Student Protest," in *San Jose State College, Student Unrest, 1967–68,* 33–34; "Editorials: SJS chief deals ably with Chicanos," *Palo Alto Times,* June 17, 1968, in *San Jose State College, Student Unrest, 1967–68;* Robert D. Clark, "Concerning the MASC Demonstration, June 14, 1968," in *San Jose State College, Student Unrest, 1967–68,* 39. Clark quoted in "Clark Following Through."

44. "Mexican-American Student Protest," 33–34.

45. Clark, "Concerning the MASC Demonstration," 37–38.

46. "Mexican-American Student Protest," 34; "Editorials: SJS chief deals ably with Chicanos."

47. Sitomer, "Dialogue and action prod racial reform at San Jose State;" "SJSC Education Opportunity Program," *San Jose State College News,* September 13, 1968, 1–3, folder: EOP: Background Materials, 1967–68, box 29, series 3, Office of the President, Robert D. Clark Records, San José State University Archives; "Special Programs for Minority Group Students, 1968," 1–2, folder: EOP: Background Materials, 1967–68, box 29, series 3, Office of the President, Robert D. Clark Records, San José State University Archives. Knowles quoted in Sitomer, "Dialogue and action prod racial reform at San Jost State."

CHAPTER 11

Campus Life for Southern Black Students in the Mid-Twentieth Century

Joy Ann Williamson-Lott

In *Campus Life: Undergraduate Cultures from the End of the Eighteenth Century to the Present*, Helen Lefkowitz Horowitz's goal in splitting undergraduates into three categories—college men and women, outsiders, and rebels—was to provide a diversified perspective on student life and to demonstrate how battles over power, status, and control between the student groups, as well as among students, faculty, and administrators, shaped and reshaped their institutions. The book necessarily provides sweeping generalizations since it chronicles patterns and offers an overview of the contours of student life. In her own words, though, using this "wide-gauge net" has consequences: "although photographs taken at close range make all sorts of hills and valleys perceptible, from those at a distance only the broadest features of the landscape can be discerned."[1]

This chapter provides a look at some of those hills and valleys through a focus on the experiences of black students at southern historically black and predominantly white institutions in the middle of the twentieth century. The purpose is not to map Horowitz's categories onto black students or

J. A. Williamson-Lott (✉)
College of Education, University of Washington, Seattle, WA, USA
e-mail: joyann@uw.edu

© The Author(s) 2018
C. A. Ogren, M. A. VanOverbeke (Eds.),
Rethinking Campus Life, Historical Studies in Education,
https://doi.org/10.1007/978-3-319-75614-1_11

237

even to answer the question of whether her categories are appropriate for the black campus context—though both topics are worthy of study, since various student cultures certainly existed on black campuses and within black student populations at predominantly white campuses. Instead, this chapter focuses on a subset of student activists—who fit most clearly into the category of rebels, although Horowitz classifies virtually all black students as outsiders—and the organizations they created to force change at their institutions and in society. Whether in student government associations, multiracial organizations, or black-oriented groups, black student activists and their white allies demanded their institutions participate in ameliorating America's social, political, and economic ills. By doing so, they helped narrow the distance between ebony and ivory towers and society, and forever changed the role of higher education in societal reform.[2]

WHY STUDYING BLACK STUDENT ORGANIZING IS IMPORTANT

Scholars of higher education can learn a lot by studying black student activism at southern colleges and universities in the middle of the twentieth century. Though there is high-quality work in the area, particularly regarding the 1960 sit-ins and the Student Nonviolent Coordinating Committee (SNCC), holes in the literature obscure a full picture of the nature of student organizing and its targets for reform.[3] In particular, much of the existing literature extracts black students from their black campus reality and analyzes them as if their identity as activists preempted or was more important than their identity as students. It is a mistake to divorce students from their campus reality. These *activist* students also were *student* activists. Students did not terminate their interest in the black freedom struggle while on the college or university campus, nor did they terminate their student status when they participated in campaigns organized by other protest organizations. Students attended higher educational institutions to earn a degree, to expand their intellectual repertoire, and, ultimately, to get a well-paying job, not to join the movement.[4]

Characterizations of SNCC are a good example of historians' tendency to overlook activists' identity as students. The literature discusses the development of the national organization, its trajectory, mission, campaigns, and demise, but does not discuss the influence of the *student* in SNCC. Historians treat SNCC members as if their institutional affiliations were incidental beyond the fact that their status as students protected them and allowed them to participate at a higher rate than non-students—an assumption I critique elsewhere.[5] SNCC had very few full-time employees. Many members were full-time students working part-time for the organization. Campus chapters spearheaded local campaigns, raised money for SNCC projects, and used college-owned paper and machinery to publish SNCC newspapers and fliers (sometimes without the consent of the administration). The most obvious equivalent to students in SNCC would be ministers in the Southern Christian Leadership Conference who used their own churches to host meetings and rallies, took up collections to provide bail for arrested activists, and employed the church infrastructure—including phone lists, organizations, and copy machines—to advertise movement projects. Scholars have pursued this level of analysis regarding black ministers and churches, but such detailed analysis is missing from the literature on student activists and their campuses.[6] The existing literature credits students with dominating the movement after 1960 but ignores the immediate environment in which student activists functioned: the college and university campus.

The literature also focuses on black student participation in activism off campus, which obscures their activism on campus. Black students regularly co-opted black freedom struggle demands for dignity, autonomy, and self-determination in American society to accuse trustees and presidents of abridging similar on-campus rights. In fact, by the 1960s, black students had a long history of enlisting off-campus movement language and demands to fuel their own on-campus demands. The post–World War I era was particularly active for students as they tapped into the New Negro spirit in which blacks more aggressively agitated for equal rights and exalted African American culture. Black students at black institutions fought against paternalistic campus regulations as well as a curriculum focused on industrial education that trained them to be manual laborers rather than critical thinkers—both of which smacked of white supremacist notions regarding the rightful place blacks should occupy in the social, economic, and political order. Their activism opened the door for student autonomy and paved the way for future generations of black college and university students to access a curriculum that prepared them to enact racial equality for themselves and the black community in general.[7]

Student activism at Fisk University, a private institution in Nashville, Tennessee, offers a particularly vivid example of black students enacting the freedom struggle on campus. In 1924, budget problems forced trustees to seek white industrial philanthropy, which supported industrial training rather than the classical, liberal arts curriculum Fisk had offered since its founding in 1867. To solicit funds, Fisk's white president endeavored to prove that Fisk did not stray too far from the industrial model of education and that its students "were not radical egalitarians but young men and women who had learned to make peace with the reality of the caste system." He also severely restricted or removed student privileges—such as a student council and newspaper—that might have undermined his message to white funders. Students took matters into their own hands by staging a demonstration against the president and issuing a list of demands, including reinstatement of the student council and newspaper. In February 1925, the conflict came to a head when students held a demonstration and the president called in the local (white) police to arrest the students. Protesting the arrests, the student body went on strike for ten weeks. By April, the president had submitted his resignation, and later that year the new administration met many of the students' demands.[8]

Finally, the existing literature on southern black student activism neglects not only its early roots but also its later branches. Whereas scholars have focused on the 1960 sit-ins and 1964 Freedom Summer, they have almost completely ignored southern black student activism in the later 1960s and early 1970s.[9] Instead, the literature on the later 1960s focuses on the highly publicized activities of black and white students at white campuses outside the South. This focus is despite the fact that black students of the Black Power era described their actions as part of the larger and older black freedom struggle and the fact that quantitative studies found students at southern black college and universities highly active and facing more punitive forms of punishment than any other group of students.[10]

A consequence of historians' truncation of southern black college and university student participation in the black freedom struggle is that scholars credit white students, particularly those in the 1964 Free Speech Movement at the University of California at Berkeley, with providing the catalyst for widespread student activism in the second half of the 1960s.[11] This interpretation holds only if scholars strip southern black students of the early part of the decade of their student identity and ignore almost wholly those of the later 1960s and early 1970s. The lack of attention to black colleges and universities contributes to a pattern in higher educational research in which black institutions and their students are relegated to the margins of educational history and not seriously considered as a stimulus for any meaningful changes in American higher education. There is a lot remaining to be learned from studying black students as *black students.* Examining their organizations and their activism at both black and white southern institutions beyond just the early 1960s will help scholars make better sense of changes in higher education in the middle of the twentieth century and the role of students in that process.

STUDENT GOVERNMENT ASSOCIATIONS AT BLACK INSTITUTIONS

Thomas Jefferson, one of the first proponents of student self-government, believed that giving students real power to create rules and mete out disciplinary action would encourage conscientious democratic leadership. At the founding of the University of Virginia, Jefferson asked the Board of Visitors "to devise and perfect a proper system of government, which, if it be founded in reason and comity, will be more likely to nourish in the minds of our youth the combined spirit of order and self-respect, so congenial with our political institutions, and so important to be woven into the American character." According to Jefferson, investing students with a measure of responsibility encouraged a healthy respect for law and order through benign rather than punitive methods. Such proposals democratized the traditionally hierarchical structure of the university. Student governments spread from Virginia to other white campuses throughout the nation and acted as a bridge between the student body and administrators. Though black institutions lagged behind white institutions in the creation of student government associations, by the 1930s, most black campuses allowed students to form such organizations.[12]

Through the middle of the twentieth century, students at black institutions found themselves in the paradoxical situation in which they could run for campus office and vote in campus elections but could not participate in local, state, or national political life. The incongruity of being able to participate politically on campus but not in American society was not lost on them. Nor was the fact that some black institutions practiced a high level of paternalistic control over their students that was unmatched at white institutions. Student government associations attracted politically minded students who sought power as well as changes to campus regulations and climate. Though student governments most often focused on grievances against the dress code, strict supervision of male–female contact, and lack of student representation on campus committees rather than on black enfranchisement, their active involvement in campus life mirrored the burgeoning black freedom struggle's demands for participatory democracy. All black public campuses and some private institutions prohibited the formation of rights-oriented groups, particularly in the late 1950s and early 1960s as the black freedom struggle gained momentum, but administrators could not curtail political interests.

Events at Mississippi's Alcorn University and A&M College, an all-black public institution, dramatize the fact that white officials, black presidents, and students recognized the potential that student government associations offered for effecting change. Student actions were particularly brave considering the context. While whites in other southern states supported a racial caste system, subscribed to notions of black inferiority, and intimidated their black citizens into quietude, white Mississippians, according to historian V. O. Key, "put the white-supremacy case most bitterly, most uncompromisingly, most vindictively." An organized and interconnected network of white Mississippi officials and their federal-level allies used legal and extra-legal means to keep blacks undereducated, politically disenfranchised, and docile. Mississippi's all-white Board of Trustees of Institutions of Higher Learning did its part to contain activism at the states' public black institutions. So, too, did the legislature attempt to do the same at black private institutions. Their mission had become increasingly urgent as black veterans returned from World War II expecting a more just society and as the Supreme Court issued a series of decisions undermining racial segregation in educational institutions from graduate and professional school through kindergarten. Blacks and their allies additionally continued to agitate for change in the late 1950s and early 1960s.[13]

In early March 1957, Clennon King, a black minister and instructor of history at Alcorn, angered the student community with a series of articles commissioned by the *State Times*, a white Mississippi newspaper known for its racism. In his articles, King associated the National Association for the Advancement of Colored People (NAACP) with communism and declared "perhaps the NAACP is the National Association for the Agitation for Colored People after all," called African American US Congressman Adam Clayton Powell a "dupe to Northern race trickery," provided a thoroughly cleansed interpretation of American slavery, and expressed his admiration for the character of Uncle Tom in *Uncle Tom's Cabin*. The fact that pictures of Alcorn students appeared with King's articles did not endear him to them, nor did his expression of derogatory attitudes toward women in his classroom. By the time the third installment of King's series appeared, students had had enough and boycotted King's classes and demanded his resignation or his firing. The boycott spread to other classes on campus the following day, and President Jesse R. Otis recommended King's dismissal to the board of trustees. President Otis, according to rumors printed in the *State Times*, supported the students' critique of King and took action against King for drawing Alcorn into controversial issues.[14]

Days later, Ernest McEwan, the student body president, read a statement on the steps of the campus chapel endorsed by 489 of the 571 Alcorn students:

> We feel that every man is entitled to express his opinion. Every person has freedom of speech, the press. But we believe that it is unprofessional and unethical for any person to prescribe or use another's name, picture, institution in support of his convictions. The student body was not informed of this submission of the articles to the *State Times*. Therefore we were denied our freedom of speech. There is an apology owed to us by Mr. King. The only circumstance under which we will accept his apology is by the offer of his resignation.[15]

Trustees responded by closing the campus, firing the president because they believed students had "taken over, by and with the acquiescence, if not the consent and approval of the President," and renewing King's contract to assert their ultimate authority. Those students who wanted to reenroll were forced to meet with the new president, John D. Boyd, and sign a statement vowing never to participate in activism again. Governor James Coleman promised he would open the school with an entirely new student body if they did not comply. Most students signed the statement and reenrolled, but many were furious with Boyd and dubbed him a "white man's tool." Those who did not sign the statement or were identified as leaders in the walkout, including Ernest McEwan, were refused readmission.[16]

Boyd's subsequent interference with the election of Miss Alcorn (a campus pageant and tradition) and the student council in 1959 prompted a second student boycott. Boyd had appointed a committee to oversee the elections and warned the members, "you should be satisfied, as a committee, that such persons, as are nominated for positions, possess the right attitude toward law and order on the campus, as well as proper attitude toward responsibility of the administration in dealing with campus problems." In response, students submitted a list of grievances to the administration and demanded an autonomous student government, student representation on the Discipline Committee, expanded social privileges, and improved cafeteria and dormitory conditions. Boyd answered their demands by closing the campus for three days, expelling the student leaders, and calling the state police to escort students to busses waiting to transport them off campus.[17]

In March 1960, the same month as an attempted wade-in to desegregate a beach in Biloxi, Mississippi, and a month after the Greensboro, North Carolina, lunch counter sit-ins, Alcorn students again boycotted classes on campus and issued a list of grievances that closely mirrored the 1959 list. Smaller campus demonstrations continued until a two-week boycott rocked the campus in 1964. By this time, the black freedom struggle in Mississippi was full-blown with demonstrations, boycotts, sit-ins, and litigation, and SNCC and the Council of Federated Organizations (COFO) were planning to bring additional federal attention to the state through the upcoming Freedom Summer campaign. Bolstered by the escalating black freedom struggle's demands for participatory democracy off campus, hundreds of Alcorn students gathered on the football field and demanded to see the president. Their list of demands included old requests, like "a student government free of administrative domination," and new ones, like a relaxed dress code, more competent instructors, and expanded library hours.[18]

Boyd repeated his past behavior and had the Highway Patrol round up all the students and escort them off campus. This time, perhaps because he was more wary of student unrest due to intensifying civil disobedience off campus, Boyd required that parents attend a meeting with their child in order for the student to reenroll—quite a request since some students' parents lived as far away as Chicago or Detroit.[19] He used this tactic to ensure that students would submit to administrative discipline, since many parents were horrified that their child, often a first-generation college student, participated in a demonstration that put his or her academic career in jeopardy. It is not clear if the student government played a role in organizing any of the demonstrations after the 1957 crisis, particularly since the administration had a stranglehold on the organization and Boyd remained president until 1969. Demands for an autonomous student government, however, remained a centerpiece of student grievances since little had changed in terms of student autonomy.

Not all student government associations followed the same path as Alcorn's, even as the black freedom struggle escalated across the South and students became heavily involved. Many continued to focus on planning campus events, acting as a liaison between the administration and student body, and providing students with leadership opportunities. They did not press the administration for drastic changes to campus regulations or tie their work to that of activists off campus. In these cases, activist students often created their own organizations, separate from student governments, such as Grambling University's (public; Louisiana) Informers and Howard University's (private; Washington, D. C.) Nonviolent Action Group. At Southern University and A&M College, a public institution in Louisiana, the student government tried to wrestle control from activists as a way to reassert its power on campus. The Southern University campus had been rocked by a series of public and disruptive protests since the early 1960s. In 1965, student government representatives tried to end an on-campus demonstration organized by other students regarding restrictive *in loco parentis* regulations. Their reasoning was that the student government should represent the student voice in negotiating with the administration in regard to on-campus issues. According to one Southern University activist, though, it was the student government's opposition to activism and desire to control the situation that fueled the new activist organization's sudden interest in pressing for campus improvements.[20]

It was fitting that students at Alcorn (as well as at other institutions) would enlist their student government as a change agent and that their efforts would be thwarted. Organized student governments, some black campus officials and many whites worried, would do just what Thomas Jefferson had hoped: represent a shift in the hierarchical structure of the campus and give students a measure of authority and input. It was not that Mississippi's white officials and Alcorn's administrators believed that citizenship training was irrelevant. In fact, Alcorn included the notion of education for proper citizenship in its mission statement. Such learning, however, was to be confined to discussions in the history, government, or economics classroom. Students challenged this assumption when they translated republican theory into practice by demanding the right to form an advocacy organization and using it to challenge the administration. Several of the campus disturbances took place before the black freedom struggle gained a foothold in the state, but the all-white board of trustees rightly understood that black student demands to upend the hierarchical structure on campus mirrored black activist demands to upend the racial hierarchy off campus.

BLACKS AND WHITES ORGANIZING FOR RACIAL EQUALITY

Formal organizing against white supremacy by white student government associations on white campuses in the South was basically a moot issue. Student government associations, like the wider student body, at white public and private institutions held almost wholly racist ideas on the pace and value of racial equality through the middle 1960s. As one journalist visiting the University of Mississippi put it in 1962, "the range of political and social opinions is from Y to Z." Many student governments, like the one at Vanderbilt University, bolstered their conservative credentials by dropping membership in the National Student Association (NSA) after accusing it of being too liberal on race and other matters. The close ties between student government associations and Greek letter organizations at these institutions further informed their conservatism since white Greek fraternities and sororities had long histories of racist practices and policies, and, according to Horowitz, were the most conservative groups on campus. Even when there was some separation between student government officers and Greeks, rarely were the officers as formidable or influential as the Greeks who controlled campus life.[21]

There were some opportunities at segregated white institutions for students to participate in the black freedom struggle or at least to register a temperate opinion on it. Tulane University (private; Louisiana) had a Liberals Club and a Young Democrats Club, both of which condemned segregation. Many other institutions, including some public white campuses, created similarly minded organizations. Students at the University of Georgia (public), Georgia Institute of Technology (public), Emory University (private), and Oglethorpe University (private) banded together to create Georgia Students for Human Rights. University of Louisville (public) students had Students for Social Action, University of Virginia (public) students had the Virginia Council on Human Relations, and Florida State College (public) students had the Student Nonviolent Action Group. The philosophy of these organizations mirrored the tenor of the NSA's Southern Student Human Relations Project, which focused on creating positive interpersonal relationships. Though neither the NSA's project nor the campus-based organizations played a role in direct action, according to Erica Whittington, "human relations helped to provide an intellectual and moral foundation for growing student opposition to racial oppression."[22]

White students also participated in other organizations. In New Orleans, Tulane University students joined with community activists, white students from Louisiana State University, and black students from Xavier University (private) and Southern University at New Orleans (public) to swell the ranks of the New Orleans CORE. Students at white Florida State University (public) and black Florida Agricultural and Mechanical University (public) similarly joined ranks as activists. Others joined campus-based YMCAs (Young Men's Christian Associations)/YWCAs

(Young Women's Christian Associations) and participated in "free spaces" where blacks and whites interacted as equals and discussed a variety of topics. The Southern Student Organizing Committee sought to unify white students "to build together a New South which brings democracy and justice for all its people." Some of these organizations were more radical than others, but all, according to Gregg Michel, "helped to make dissent respectable on southern campuses [and] contributed to bringing progressive concerns into the mainstream of student life."[23]

As some white institutions desegregated their undergraduate student bodies in the early 1960s, the specter of on-campus interracial activism became a reality. Upper South states like Arkansas, Kentucky, and Tennessee desegregated before their Deep South counterparts, and it was in the Upper South that occasional interracial activism took root in the middle 1960s. In Arkansas, the Attorney General opened the door for desegregation by declaring in 1955 that the state's public colleges and universities were bound by the *Brown v. Board of Education* decision. During the 1957–1958 academic year, 32 black students enrolled in predominantly white institutions in the state. Black attendance at these institutions, however, was highly controversial since these campuses were located in predominantly white population centers and many local whites opposed racial equality.[24] Presidents at these campuses treaded carefully and brought as little negative attention to their institutions as possible.

By the late 1960s, 9 percent of the student body at Southern State College, a public institution in Arkansas, was black, a huge increase since the first small group of blacks had appeared on campus in 1962. Black students and their white allies formed the Students United for Rights and Equality (SURE) in fall 1968 and worked to desegregate private organizations in the local area and improve racial relations on campus. According to James Willis, an institutional biographer, the organization had 150 student members and 17 white faculty affiliates (the institution employed no black faculty members at the time) (Image 11.1). Three white faculty members most actively supported SURE's efforts and participated in the local movement. As a group, they had served as advisors for the organization, supported efforts to draw attention to segregation in the local community, and joined with students to protest the shooting of a black man by a white police officer. Arkansas newspapers covered developments on campus and reported on the nature of student and faculty activism. Nervous whites in the surrounding community took notice and expressed concern that campus constituents had a radical agenda for the local area: immediate desegregation and racial equality.[25]

Image 11.1 Officers of Students United for Rights and Equality (SURE) at Southern State College. (Source: Southern Arkansas University Archives)

President Imon E. Bruce demanded that the two faculty members serving as advisors for SURE resign from their advisory positions. They did, under protest. Bruce reminded them and SURE that they were jeopardizing Southern State's relationship with the local (white) community and undermining on-campus race-relations efforts. Soon thereafter, he recommended to the board of trustees that the three professors be fired, and the board unanimously agreed. The board chairperson, according to the American Association of University Professors (AAUP), which investigated the firings and issued a final report in 1971, told the investigating committee, "the Board would not tolerate radical, 'hippy,' or other disruptive factions on the campus" and that the professors "were simply too radical for Southern State College."[26]

The AAUP investigating committee pointed to collusion between the president and trustees in policing speech favorable of racial equality. The institution was still grappling with campus desegregation, and racial tension in the local community remained high. "It is not resistance to racial integration per se which appears to explain the position of the administration," the AAUP committee explained, "but rather a determination to retain control over the ways, means, and rate of integration." SURE and its faculty allies threatened the delicate relationship that Bruce and the board attempted to cultivate with the state legislature by using the campus to push, in their estimation, too fast and aggressively toward desegregation. The AAUP accused the institution of violating the professors' academic freedom and due process protections and censured the institution in 1971. A federal appeals court had found similarly a year earlier when it ruled that Southern State had violated the First Amendment rights of SURE members and ordered that the institution lift the organization's suspension.[27]

On-campus interracial organizing was rare in the South, especially in the later 1960s as the Black Power movement escalated and white students gravitated to protest against American involvement in the Vietnam War and toward organizations like Students for a Democratic Society (SDS). The black freedom struggle and anti-war movement were not mutually exclusive since many activists recognized links between racism at home and abroad. However, southern white campus constituents, like their counterparts outside the region, directed their efforts primarily toward opposing the war effort, the draft, and mandatory participation in the Reserve Officers' Training Corps. Black campuses experienced anti-war activism, too, but their students' attention remained focused on the black freedom struggle.

The instances of cross-racial organizing that did occur demonstrate that space existed, small though it was, for southern black and white students to work together to erode white supremacy. White student activism on behalf of black equality never matched black student activism, and black students experienced the brunt of administrative and police repression. Still, those white students who engaged in activism did so at great personal risk, as can be seen in the murders of white allies, including COFO workers Michael Schwerner and Andrew Goodman for their support of Freedom Summer in 1964 and James Reeb and Viola Liuzzo for their support of the Selma-to-Montgomery March in 1965.[28] Black and white students working together to upend the racial hierarchy, even through muted activism such as hosting conversation forums, helped bring an end to legalized white supremacy.

BLACK STUDENT ORGANIZING ON BLACK AND WHITE CAMPUSES

The philosophy of nonviolence and the goal of integration lost favor with a large segment of the black community during the middle to late 1960s. After decades of attempting to force their way into the existing social order only to meet intense white resistance and repression, many blacks, including youth, redefined both the means and the ends of the black freedom struggle. They now considered integration, rather than being the answer to black America's problems, to be a wrong-headed goal that sapped the black community of the skills and energies of its most productive members. Doubtful of the federal government's dedication to improving the conditions of blacks, suspicious regarding the extent to which white liberals were true allies, and aware of the large discrepancy between expected results and actual achievements, they shifted their ideas on the proper tactics and means to make black liberation a reality.[29]

Black students at southern black and white institutions, like their counterparts outside the region, sought to operationalize the path toward black liberation advanced by Stokely Carmichael and Charles Hamilton in their 1967 book, *Black Power: The Politics of Liberation in America*. The authors called for blacks to recognize and be proud of their heritage, build a sense of community, define their own goals, and control their own organizations. To successfully accomplish these tasks, and thereby attain Black Power, Carmichael and Hamilton declared that blacks needed to unite, stating, "before a group can enter the open society, it must first close ranks. By this we mean that group solidarity is necessary before a group can operate effectively from a bargaining position of strength in a pluralistic society." Under the banner of blackness, blacks would be able to address their grievances and demand their share of the American Dream. Biracial on-campus organizing, for the most part, came to an end.[30]

Black students at southern predominantly white institutions were few in number during the late 1960s and early 1970s, but that did not stop them from organizing to force changes at their institutions.[31] In many instances, their indictments mirrored those of Tulane University's Afro-American Congress: "Since, we, the Black Students of Tulane University are the victims of racism, we recognize all the aspects of the problem to a degree that few whites could ever hope to attain. We feel that while you may mean well in taking steps to alleviate the problem, we contend that your endeavors have been unsuccessful, too few in number, and half-heartedly undertaken." Demands across campuses often included the admission of more black students, the hiring of more black professors and staff, the creation of a black studies program or department, increased library holdings focused on the African diaspora, better treatment of black custodial staff and food workers, and an end to discrimination in white Greek organizations. Black student organizations demanded formal recognition, a share of student fees, and a direct line of communication to top-level administrators. Some also produced alternative newspapers. In 1969, the Black Student Movement at the University of North Carolina at Chapel Hill (public), began publishing *Black Ink* as an alternative to the *Daily Tar Heel*, which the group saw as a newspaper focused on the needs of white students.[32]

Infuriated by the February 1968 police murders of three black activists at South Carolina State College (public), black students less than 50 miles away at the University of South Carolina (public) accused white students, faculty, and administrators at their institution of being complicit in supporting white supremacy. Shortly after the murders at South Carolina State, the Association of African-American Students (AAAS) and the (white) Student Government Association cosponsored a memorial service to honor the victims. While the white president of the student government described the memorial as a symbol of racial cooperation and explained that it was "not intended to justify or condone any one faction," the president of AAAS declared, "sooner or later we all must die, and there is only one Heaven. We Black folks intend to make it to the promised land of Heaven, so I guess you white folks will have no alternative but to burn in Hell unless you change your ways." Black students refused to co-sponsor a memorial with white students after Dr. Martin Luther King, Jr.'s death two months later. Instead, they indicted the student government for its flaccid response after the Orangeburg murders and reminded their peers that many campus constituents celebrated after King's assassination. They also issued a list of grievances that mirrored those of black students at other predominantly white institutions and demanded that the institution move quickly to address them.[33]

White students were not silent at southern predominantly white campuses, but their attention often was focused elsewhere. For instance, the University of North Carolina at Chapel Hill had a highly active SDS chapter that focused most of its energy on forcing the legislature to repeal a speaker ban that prohibited suspected communists from speaking on public campuses in the state. A handful of students at the University of South Carolina created an organization called Aware when the institution refused to allow them to form an SDS chapter. The organization worked to broaden student access to controversial speech on campus, fought against *in loco parentis* regulations regarding women's behavior, demanded due process procedures for students accused of conduct violations, organized protests against American involvement in the Vietnam War, and advocated for more black students as well as a black studies program. The student government associations at white institutions focused their efforts on gaining more power and autonomy for students.[34] Demands regarding racial equality existed largely at the periphery of white student concerns.

Black students at black institutions issued their own lists of demands. Most resembled the grievances of their counterparts at white institutions. Though there was no need to argue for more black students, black activists demanded more decision-making power, additional library holdings focused on the black experience, creation of black studies courses and programs, and better treatment of custodial and food staff. Many even demanded more black professors. Clark College, a private black institution in Georgia, for instance, employed more white than black faculty members in the 1960s. Charlayne Hunter, one of the first black students to attend the University of Georgia, wrote, "To some, [the presence of white faculty at black colleges] may look like progress. To the black students and some of the more activist black professors this is cause for resentment."[35]

When students demanded more *black* professors they meant politically, culturally, and ideologically black rather than simply phenotypically black. They assumed that these "real" black professors would help transform the institutions into movement centers in which the black community could close ranks and plot a course for societal reform. In earlier decades, scholars like Carter G. Woodson, W. E. B. DuBois, E. Franklin Frazier, and Harold Cruse similarly had prodded black institutions and faculty, arguing that the institutions should train students for an active role in battling the racial hierarchy rather than training the black bourgeoisie to become, in Frantz Fanon's words, black skin in white masks.[36]

At some black campuses, the student governments became the vehicle for issuing demands of the administration. The student government at Mississippi Industrial College, a public institution, spearheaded protests against the administration in 1969 and 1970. Wilhelm Joseph, Jr., president of the student body in 1969, ran on a ticket that boasted, "We are going to move this place! This is a *black* college. We are going to use this opportunity to teach folks about black independence. We are going to broaden the vision." After a peaceful demonstration in February 1969 in which students protested against paternalistic campus rules, the complete absence of student representation on campus committees, and the low quality of faculty and facilities, police and campus security officers forcibly transported 196 students to Jackson (100 miles away) where family members could retrieve them, incarcerated 12 others at the Leflore County Jail,

and issued warrants for four protest leaders, including Joseph. President
James H. White then expelled all the offending students.[37] The following
year, the new student government president, Tyrone Gettis, was arrested
and expelled along with 900 other students during another student
government-sponsored protest march.[38]

Voorhees College, a private institution in South Carolina, experienced
similarly disruptive student protests the same year. The tenor and nature
of the protests were different, however, as Voorhees students injected elements of Black Power into their demands. The formation of the Black
Awareness Coordinating Committee (BACC) in 1967 was their first step.
The fact that the organization used the word "Black," instead of the word
"Negro," in its name signaled an acceptance of a new racial understanding
that included cultural and political elements. So, too, did its aggressive
tactics mirror those of Black Power–oriented groups like the Oakland,
California, Black Panther Party. In the opinion of the Voorhees administration, the BACC was a "hardcore group that was agitating and bringing
about ... confrontations" between students and administrators.[39] Whether
the administrative assessment of BACC goals was accurate, the group did
sponsor protests over the next few years.

Soon after its founding, BACC members and other students convened in
the student center to argue over the wisdom of a demonstration in the cafeteria regarding the quality of food. Most complied when security officials
asked them to leave the premises, but 25 refused. Campus security officials
tear-gassed those who remained in the building to force them out. Activism
accelerated after that, fueled in part by conditions on campus as well as the
police murders of black students at Orangeburg (only 20 miles from
Voorhees), Dr. Martin Luther King, Jr.'s assassination, and calls for Black
Power. In April 1969, an armed group of students took over the library-
administration building, christened the institution "the liberated Malcolm X
University," and demanded black studies, more black professors, and institutional involvement in the local black community. According to historian
Martha Biondi, the board of trustees, under pressure from the governor,
called in the National Guard over the objections of the Voorhees president,
and had all student activists arrested and expelled from campus.[40]

White officials often took these types of draconian measures against
black student activists. Whether at Alcorn in 1957 or Voorhees in 1967,
powerful whites attempted to block black public and private institutions
from becoming movement centers where students and their off-campus
allies could organize and mobilize against white supremacy. Black

administrators sometimes supported the faculty and student purges, whether out of a desire to keep their jobs, the need to curry favor with white legislative or private funders, political pressure and intimidation, or any number of other factors. Undoubtedly, they also were motivated by a desire to protect their students from the brutality meted out against black freedom struggle activists including those at North Carolina A&T University, Southern University and A&M College, South Carolina State, and Jackson State University who lost their lives. Maintaining calm on campus protected not only the institutions but student life as well.

CONCLUSION

This chapter's focus on black student activists and their white allies at public and private southern institutions of higher education is not meant to dismiss the activism occurring elsewhere. Southern black student activism dovetailed with black and white activism at colleges and universities across the nation, much of it aimed at enlisting the institutions in actively promoting racial equality and justice. Instead, the chapter offers a window into the experiences of a group of students and institutions almost wholly ignored in Horowitz's *Campus Life* and in most histories of higher education: black students and black campuses. It is a reminder that incorporating these students and institutions in the larger narrative about student life and student culture forces a reevaluation of that same literature.

This chapter's focus also opens areas for further research. Horowitz's characterization of black students as outsiders only applies when examining them outside the context of black colleges and universities. Scholars must be careful not to paint broad generalizations that highlight only those black experiences that occurred in the presence of whites and thus obscure the experiences of thousands of black students in black institutions. Outsiders certainly existed at black institutions, but who were they? More generally, do the categories of college men and women, outsiders, and rebels fit for black institutions, or is there another framework that can help us understand patterns in campus life and culture there? How have those patterns shifted as the institutions have diversified their own student bodies? What, exactly, is common or different about patterns in student life and culture at black versus white institutions? What might we learn by examining Hispanic-serving institutions or Tribal colleges and universities? Answering these and other questions can lead to a fuller picture of the history of how all students, not just white students, created their own environments and made their way through their undergraduate careers.

NOTES

1. Helen Lefkowitz Horowitz, *Campus Life: Undergraduate Cultures from the End of the Eighteenth Century to the Present* (New York: Alfred A. Knopf, 1987), xiii–xvi.

2. In a forthcoming book, *Jim Crow Campus: Higher Education and the Struggle for a New Southern Social Order* (Teachers College Press), I investigate southern black and white student organizing and the differences between different types of institutions (i.e. private and public, black and white) in greater depth, and provide a regional analysis of institutional change.

3. Some of the best examples include Howard Zinn, *SNCC: The New Abolitionists* (Boston: Beacon Press, 1964); William Chafe, *Civilities and Civil Rights: Greensboro, North Carolina, and the Black Struggle for Freedom* (New York: Oxford University Press, 1980); Clayborne Carson, *In Struggle: SNCC and the Black Awakening of the 1960s* (Cambridge: Harvard University Press, 1995).

4. Much of this section is taken from Joy Ann Williamson, *Radicalizing the Ebony Tower: Black Colleges and the Black Freedom Struggle in Mississippi, 1965–1975* (New York: Teachers College Press, 2008).

5. Williamson, *Radicalizing the Ebony Tower*, Introduction.

6. Aldon Morris, *Origins of the Civil Rights Movement: Black Communities Organizing for Change* (New York: Free Press, 1984).

7. James D. Anderson, *The Education of Blacks in the South, 1860–1935* (Chapel Hill: University of North Carolina Press, 1988).

8. Anderson, *The Education of Blacks in the South*.

9. Exceptions include Jeffrey Turner, *Sitting In and Speaking Out: Student Movements in the American South, 1960–1970* (Athens, GA: University of Georgia Press, 2010); Martha Biondi, *The Black Revolution on Campus* (Cambridge, MA: Harvard University Press, 2003); Ibram Kendi, *The Black Campus Movement: Black Students and the Racial Reconstitution of Higher Education, 1965–1972* (New York: Palgrave Macmillan, 2012); Williamson, *Radicalizing the Ebony Tower*.

10. Urban Research Corporation, *Student Protests 1969: Summary* (Chicago: Urban Research Corporation, 1969).

11. Alexander W. Astin, Helen S. Astin, Alan E. Bayer, and Ann S. Bisconti, "Overview of the Unrest Era," in *The History of Higher Education*, 2nd ed., eds. Lester F. Goodchild and Harold S. Wechsler (New York: Simon and Schuster, 1997); Philip Altbach, *Student Politics in America: A Historical Analysis* (New York: McGraw-Hill, 1976); Horowitz, *Campus Life*. Doug McAdam examines the catalytic importance of the Free Speech Movement but highlights how white students were influenced by the black southern freedom struggle in *Freedom Summer* (New York: Oxford University Press, 1988).

12. Thomas Jefferson, "Report of the Commissioners Appointed to Fix the Site of the University of Virginia" (Richmond: Virginia Senate, 1818), quotation on 12.

13. V. O. Key, Jr., *Southern Politics in State and Nation*, 2nd ed. (Knoxville: University of Tennessee Press, 1984), 130. See also Neil R. McMillen, *Dark Journey: Black Mississippians in the Age of Jim Crow* (Urbana: University of Illinois Press, 1989). For a lengthy discussion of how the legislature interfered at a private institution see Williamson, *Radicalizing the Ebony Tower*, chapter 5.

14. Clennon King, "NAACP Claimed Closing Doors of Opportunity to Negroes," *State Times*, March 3, 1957; "Adam Powell Called 'Dupe' to Northern Race Trickery," *State Times*, March 4, 1957, 14; and "Real Uncle Toms May Come from North, Be College Bred," *State Times*, March 6, 1957; Jerry Proctor, "King Tries to Stop Student Walk-Outs," *State Times*, March 8, 1957.

15. "Alcorn A&M College, March 1957," Newsfilm Collection, Reel D03, Mississippi Department of Archives and History, Jackson, Mississippi (hereafter MDAH). The number of students arrested varies in different sources, but all cite the overwhelming participation of students in the boycott.

16. Board of Trustees, minutes, March 9, 1957, MDAH (first quotation); "The End of Uncle Tom Teachers," [*Ebony*, 1957], and "Integration Feud Rocks Alcorn," *Chicago Defender*, March 16, 1957 (second quotation); Strikes and Protest Movements File, Alcorn State University Archives, Lorman, Mississippi (hereafter ASUA).

17. Trezzvant Anderson, "More Charges Against Boyd Hurled at Alcorn," *Pittsburgh Courier*, September 10, 1960, Student Strikes and Protest Movements File, ASUA; J. D. Boyd to J. A. Morris, et al., May 1, 1959 (quotation), enclosure in Corrine Craddock Carpenter to E. R. Jobe, June 26, 1960, American Association of University Professors Papers, Box 4, Folder Corrine Carpenter, George Washington University Archives, Washington D.C. (hereafter AAUPP); The Special Grievance Committee to Administration of Alcorn College, October 29, 1959, and Student Body of Alcorn A&M College to President's Advisory Committee, J. D. Boyd, and Alumni Association, [March or April] 1960, enclosure in Carpenter to Jobe; "More Charges Against Boyd Hurled at Alcorn."

18. Student Body of Alcorn to President's Advisory Committee; Faculty of Alcorn A&M College to J. D. Boyd, March 24, 1960, enclosure in Carpenter to Jobe; "Hundreds Sent Home," *The Free Press*, May 9, 1964 (first quotation); and "Alcorn Education Tragedy Gets Press Cover-Up," *The Free Press*, May 9, 1964 (second quotation), AAUPP, Box 4, Folder Frank Purnell.

19. Frank and Rosentene Purnell to Bertram Davis, May 11, 1964, AAUPP, Box 4, Folder A. D. Sumberg.

20. Turner, *Sitting In and Speaking Out*, 179, 191, 176–77.

21. *New York Times*, October 21 1962, cited in Charles Eagles, *The Price of Defiance: James Meredith and the Integration of Ole Miss* (Chapel Hill: University of North Carolina Press, 2009), quotation on 15; Paul K. Conkin, *Gone with the Ivy: A Biography of Vanderbilt University* (Knoxville, Vanderbilt University Press, 1985), 614. See also Erica Whittington, "'Human Relations' and the Freedom Movement: The NSA Southern Student Human Relations Project, 1958–1968," in *Rebellion in Black and White: The Southern Student Movement in Perspective*, eds. Robert Cohen and David Snyder (Baltimore: Johns Hopkins University Press, 2013), 83–105; Horowitz, *Campus Life*, 144. For another example of close ties between Greeks and Student Government Associations see Clarence L. Mohr and Joseph E. Gordon, *Tulane: the Emergence of a Modern University, 1945–1980* (Baton Rouge: Louisiana State University Press, 2001), 312–15. Also, Greek organizations were found to be the most conservative nationwide, not just in the South (Horowitz, *Campus Life*).

22. Mohr and Gordon, *Tulane*, 294–95, 240–41, 216–23; Gregg Michel, *Struggle for a Better South: The Southern Student Organizing Committee, 1964–1969* (New York: Palgrave Macmillan: 2004), 22; Whittington, "'Human Relations,'" quotation on 84.

23. Alan Gartner and Christopher Ferreira, "A State of Action," *New York Law Review* 59 (2014/2015): 95–109; *Lombard v. Louisiana*, 373 U.S. 267 (1963); Sara Evans and Harry Boyte, *Free Spaces: The Sources of Democratic Change in America* (Chicago: University of Chicago Press, 2002); Michel, *Struggle for a Better South*, 41, 5.

24. A. Stephen Stephan, "Desegregation of Higher Education in Arkansas," *Journal of Negro Education* 27, no. 3 (Summer 1958): 243–52.

25. "Southern State College (Arkansas)," *AAUP Bulletin* (Spring 1971): 40–49; James F. Willis, *Southern Arkansas University: The Mulerider School's Centennial History, 1909–2009* (Magnolia: Southern Arkansas University Foundation, 2009). The institution is now called Southern Arkansas University.

26. "Southern State College," 48; Willis, *Southern Arkansas University*, 260–65. There were no black faculty members employed on campus.

27. "Southern State College," 48; Willis, *Southern Arkansas University*, 260–65; *Pickings v. Bruce*, 430 F. 2d 595 (8th Circuit 1970).

28. Michel, *Struggle for a Better South*.

29. Stokely Carmichael and Charles V. Hamilton, *Black Power: The Politics of Liberation in America* (New York: Vintage Books, 1967).

30. Carmichael and Hamilton, *Black Power*, 44 (second quotation); Peniel Joseph, *Waiting 'Til the Midnight Hour: A Narrative History of Black Power in America* (New York: Henry Holt, 2006).

31. It should be noted that the number of black students enrolled in predominantly white institutions outside the South was also small. For instance, at the University of Illinois at Urbana-Champaign, black students constituted only 3.6 percent of the undergraduate population in 1975. D. J. Wermers, *Enrollment at the University of Illinois by Racial/Ethnic Categories: Fall Terms, 1967–1975* (Urbana: University Office of Academic Policy Analysis, December 1976), 12, obtained from the University Office of Academic Policy Analysis, University of Illinois, at Urbana-Champaign.

32. Mohr and Gordon, *Tulane*, quotation on 357; "Founding of the Black Student Movement," *The Carolina Story: A Virtual Museum of University History*, accessed January 3, 2017, https://museum.unc.edu/exhibits/show/integration/preston-dobbins--left--and-reg; "Black Student Movement and Black Ink," *The Carolina Story: A Virtual Museum of University History*, accessed January 3, 2017, https://museum.unc.edu/exhibits/show/student-organizations/black-student-movement-and-bla.

33. Elsie Watts, "The Freshman Year Experience, 1962–1990: An Experiment in Humanistic Higher Education" (Ph.D. diss., Queen's University, Kingston, Ontario Canada, 1999), 144 (both quotations), 145.

34. William Billingsley, *Communists on Campus: Race, Politics, and the Public University in Sixties North Carolina* (Athens: University of Georgia Press, 1999); Elsie Watts, "The Freshman Year Experience," 134, 156–60, 171–200.

35. Turner, *Sitting In*, 190; Charlayne Hunter, "Black Colleges and the Black Mood," *Southern Education Report* 4, no.9 (May 1969): 28–31, quotation on 30.

36. Carter G. Woodson, *The Mis-Education of the Negro* (Nashville: Winston-Derek, [1933] 1990); W. E. B. DuBois, *The Souls of Black Folk* (New York: Vintage Books, [1903] 1990); E. Franklin Frazier, *Black Bourgeoisie* (New York: Free Press, 1957); Harold Cruse, *The Crisis of the Negro Intellectual* (New York: Morrow, 1967); Frantz Fanon, *Black Skin, White Masks* (New York: Grove, 1967).

37. "Major Demands as Presented to the Administrative Council," 1960, cited in Sammy Jay Tinsley, "A History of Mississippi Valley State College" (Ph.D. diss., University of Mississippi, 1972), 222–26, 227. Many students in both 1969 and 1970 were allowed to reenroll after hearings before the Administrative Council.

38. Exhibit A in Board of Trustees, minutes, February 19, 1970, MDAH; J. H. White to Mississippi Legislature, letter reprinted in *Commercial Appeal*, March 26, 1971, 3, cited in Tinsley, "A History of Mississippi Valley," 243.

39. Orlanda H. White, "Testimony before Hearings before the Permanent Subcommittee on Investigations, Riots, Civil and Criminal Disorders," 91st Congress, 1st session, July 1969, part 22, quotation on 4796.

40. White, "Testimony before Hearings," 4785; Robert Romer, *1969/1970: Protests and State Troopers at Voorhees College*, accessed December 4, 2106, http://www.americancenturies.mass.edu/centapp/oh/story. do?shortName=romer1969; "Voorhees College (South Carolina)," *AAUP Bulletin* (Spring 1974): 82–89; Biondi, *The Black Revolution*, 153–57, quotation on 154.

CHAPTER 12

Higher (Power) Education: Student Life in Evangelical Institutions

Adam Laats

By 1968, it had become painfully clear, at least to some students. Life at evangelical institutions, they protested, was not living up to either the demands of modern higher education or authentic evangelical Christianity. The tradition of tight limits on behavior had infantilized evangelical students, they insisted, and the all-encompassing obsession with keeping students safe had robbed them of their ability to have the kind of college experience they desired. As one neo-evangelical student protester complained plaintively, "We want to be treated like real college students."[1] Some evangelical students wanted to have their political voices heard just as secular students did; they wanted to take part in protests and push for social change. Most of all, they wanted to overturn the lifestyle rules that had made them feel like they were not "real college students" at all.

This chapter explores these students' experiences and protests at evangelical colleges within a larger evangelical history, as a way to understand the campus cultures and student life they built. The names of the universities

A. Laats (✉)
Department of Teaching, Learning, and Educational Leadership,
Binghamton University (SUNY), Binghamton, NY, USA
e-mail: alaats@binghamton.edu

© The Author(s) 2018
C. A. Ogren, M. A. VanOverbeke (eds.),
Rethinking Campus Life, Historical Studies in Education,
https://doi.org/10.1007/978-3-319-75614-1_12

261

and colleges where they protested are not as well-known as institutions such as Harvard and Yale, but they have always played a leading part in evangelical culture. Even outside of evangelical circles, those who follow presidential politics may be familiar with institutions such as Liberty University in Virginia or Wheaton College near Chicago. Historians of America's culture wars are keenly aware of schools such as Bob Jones University (BJU) in South Carolina and Bryan College in Tennessee. Other colleges and institutes might not attract as much attention outside of evangelical circles, but institutions such as Gordon College near Boston, Moody Bible Institute (MBI) in Chicago, Biola University in Los Angeles, and a host of others are as well known to the evangelical public as the Ivy League is to striving secular suburbanites.[2]

In many cases, the twentieth-century trajectories of these colleges and universities were very similar to those of other institutions of higher education. By the middle of the twentieth century, for example, most had earned regional accreditation. They had tightened and standardized their admissions requirements. When enrollment at state colleges spiked after World War II, enrollment shot up at evangelical schools as well. When admissions officers at secular schools began insisting on more rigorous credentials for admission, so too did administrators at evangelical colleges. And, when students in the 1960s demanded greater freedom from strict lifestyle rules, so too did some students on evangelical campuses.[3]

In important ways, however, student life had always been different at evangelical institutions. The rulebooks were thicker and were quoted far more often. The schools promised their constituencies that they enforced student rules far more vigorously than did administrators at secular schools. Also, instead of evolving from traditional liberal-arts colleges, many evangelical institutions started as non-degree-granting missionary-training schools and had long emphasized missionary preparation instead of professional certification. In addition, faculty members always had to sign detailed statements of religious belief and students had to agree to often-draconian rules and supervision.[4]

Student life at evangelical colleges, institutes, and universities was also profoundly shaped by the history of evangelical Protestantism itself. As discussed more fully in the next section, in the early twentieth century, a conservative protest movement known as fundamentalism—a movement that embraced divine biblical interpretations, strict lifestyle rules, and deeply conservative political principles—split many evangelical denominations. By the 1940s and 1950s, however, a faction of fundamentalists known as "new-evangelicals," "neo-evangelicals," or, confusingly, simply as "evangelicals" mobilized as a counter-reform movement focused on a more liberal loosening of fundamentalist traditions. Some fundamentalists embraced the new reforms and became neo-evangelicals. Others fought against the movement and remained firmly fundamentalist. Still other evangelicals vacillated, unsure whether to support forward-looking neo-evangelical reform or faithful fundamentalist steadfastness. Often, evangelical colleges, universities, and institutes waffled as well, sympathetic to both neo-evangelical calls for change and fundamentalist insistence on tradition. College administrators, in particular, hesitated to alienate either neo-evangelicals or fundamentalists, especially when they were deep-pocketed alumni. The language of these conflicting cross-currents in evangelical higher education can become particularly confusing, since all sides tended to see themselves as the adherents of true evangelical Christianity. In this chapter, "evangelical" will refer to the entire network of evangelical higher education throughout the twentieth century, but "fundamentalist" will refer to the network between the 1920s and the 1940s. When describing the 1940s onward, this chapter will differentiate between "neo-evangelical" and "fundamentalist" factions.

In this context of tension and disruption within evangelicalism, students at evangelical institutions of higher education in the late 1960s and early 1970s staged their own versions of campus protests. Both neo-evangelical and fundamentalist protesters often adopted the tone and the ideas of secular protesters. They protested for and against the war in Vietnam, and they fought for and against civil-rights reform, but this chapter focuses on another aspect of neo-evangelical student protest: Protests in favor of revised lifestyle rules. At some institutions, tentative student protests quickly dissolved amid conservative student counter-protests. At other schools, neo-evangelical students protested lifestyle constraints and mimicked the styles of campus rebellion that had popped up in non-evangelical institutions across the country. They staged sit-in protests and dramatic marches. They sometimes copied the "hippie" fashions of secular rebels as well. Even when the student protesters adopted the dramatic style of secular leftist protesters, however, they did so in a radically different context. For one thing, students at evangelical colleges and universities usually wrapped their protests in the language of the continuing feud between fundamentalists and neo-evangelicals. In addition, administrators at evangelical schools came under intense pressure from the evangelical public, either to support or to oppose the student protests. As had student protesters, evangelical commenters always framed their arguments in terms of evangelical religion itself. In short, campus protests at evangelical schools were always at least as much about evangelicalism as about the issues of race, war, and campus life.

In order to make sense of this complicated history and to understand student life at evangelical campuses, this chapter explores the larger context and the history of student protest at two schools in this network: Gordon College near Boston and MBI in Chicago. Each of these institutions had its own idiosyncratic history. Gordon had opened as Gordon Missionary Training School in 1895. By 1921, it had become Gordon College of Theology and Missions,[5] and the college had begun offering bachelor's degrees to satisfy the demands of students.[6] MBI, founded in 1886, never changed its name, but by 1963 it had also begun offering a standard four-year college course capped with a bachelor's degree.[7] These two institutions did not represent the entirety of evangelical higher education in the twentieth century, and as this chapter demonstrates, they were very different throughout the late 1960s. As an institution, Gordon College moved more decisively in the direction of neo-evangelical reform. MBI remained more conservative, more thoroughly guided by fundamentalist tradition. Analyzing the history of student protest at these two institutions, however, does provide a sense of the ways that students at evangelical schools built their campus cultures, sometimes with bitter disputes, and how those campus cultures differed from life at mainstream colleges and universities.

FUNDAMENTALIST HIGHER EDUCATION

Though they had much longer histories, it was only in the 1920s that Gordon and Moody began to consider themselves part of a fundamentalist movement, a self-conscious movement that had emerged as part of a protest among American evangelical Protestants in that turbulent decade. Most prominently, the fundamentalist movement of the 1920s arose as a result of a denominational battle among conservative and liberal factions in leading American Protestant denominations such as the Baptists and the Presbyterians. Conservative intellectuals and activists, sometimes calling themselves "fundamentalists," fought for control of these denominations. In general, fundamentalist Baptists and Presbyterians wanted their conventions and presbyteries to insist on certain supernatural truths—the "fundamentals"—as inviolable beliefs of true Christianity. As modernist theologians took a new look at the history of the Bible, for example, and suggested that it had been cobbled together from a set of traditional myths over a long stretch of time by imperfect human editors, fundamentalists insisted on the inerrancy or divine inspiration of the Bible. And as liberal theologians questioned the facts of Biblical miracles and Christ's divinity, fundamentalists argued that such beliefs were beyond question, beyond mere reasoning and skepticism.[8]

As historian George Marsden has noted, the fundamentalist impulse in the 1920s ranged far beyond specific theological demands and denominational struggles for control.[9] In the 1920s, fundamentalist leaders often combined an array of vague conservative impulses—including ardent patriotism, defense of free-market economics, and traditional ideas about gender and family roles—into a powerful and popular vision of fundamentalism. Many of the fundamentalist schools founded in the 1920s inherited this broad notion of fundamentalism, a sort of cultural fundamentalism. Fundamentalist schools were to teach and preach fundamentalist religion, of course. But fundamentalists also expected their institutions to adhere rigidly to a long list of traditionalist and culturally conservative rules that did not result directly from the theological imperatives of the fundamentalist movement. Male students generally were expected to avoid wearing beards, for example, when even the staunchest conservatives admitted such rules did not result directly from a fundamentalist interpretation of the Bible.[10]

For fundamentalist school leaders, the notion of student safety was paramount. Fundamentalist colleges and universities promised to protect students from dangerously liberal theology. They would also shield students from every cultural menace that fundamentalists assumed plagued the world of modern America and higher education. This tendency was widespread and consistent. For example, when fundamentalist evangelist Bob Jones Sr. opened his eponymous fundamentalist college in Florida in 1926 (it would move twice, finally settling in its current location in Greenville, South Carolina, and renaming itself BJU in 1947), he promised parents that "[f]athers and mothers who place their sons and daughters in our institution can go to sleep at night with no haunting fear that some skeptical teachers will steal the faith of their precious children."[11] There was more than just liberal theology to worry about, however. Jones also fulminated against the moral dangers of "paved highways, automobiles, and modern travel."[12] Such modern amenities, Jones preached, took young people into a dizzying and dangerous world of unsupervised moral abandon. His school, Jones promised, would protect fundamentalist youth from the specific dangers of liberal theology, but it would also keep kids safe from the vague and multifaceted dangers of life in modern America.

Between the 1920s and the 1950s, colleges and universities in general—not just fundamentalist ones—imposed strict student rules to control behavior.[13] The network of fundamentalist colleges and universities took these strictures on student behavior much further and insisted on them much more stringently as a basic and non-negotiable tenet of proper fundamentalist higher education. For instance, non-fundamentalist colleges and universities in the 1920s often required students to sign in or out of their dorms. Students everywhere, especially female students, were often required to arrange chaperones for dates and off-campus trips. All those rules applied at fundamentalist schools such as Bob Jones College (BJC) as well. At BJC, though, the rules went even further, and sometimes in idiosyncratic directions. BJC students were not allowed to listen to "jazz," or even to talk about it.[14] They were not allowed to "loiter" on campus or speak to members of the opposite sex outside of approved social encounters.[15] BJC students were forbidden to drink or smoke, as was the case on many campuses, but they were also not allowed to dance, except at formal supervised school events. Attendance at those formal school social events was mandatory, and every student—male and female alike—was required to attend with a formal date. If they could not find one, BJC arranged one for them.[16] At times, the stringent rules seemed to reflect mainly President Bob Jones Sr.'s peculiar chauvinism. For example, Jones explicitly forbade women from borrowing one another's clothes. He assumed that women were uniquely susceptible to vanity and competition, and by banning clothes-sharing, he hoped to encourage a culture of feminine modesty and self-effacement.[17]

The goal of near-total control of student life remained a feature of fundamentalist schools throughout the twentieth century. In the 1950s, for instance, any college student might have been in trouble for getting caught with his girlfriend in an empty administrative office at midnight, the way one student did at BJU.[18] But few schools stationed a spy outside a downtown movie theater to make sure no students were attending movies, the way Wheaton College did in the 1920s.[19] During the 1930s, one ousted faculty member from BJC penned a ferocious denunciation of student life at the fundamentalist college. Dorothy Seay had been hired in 1936 to teach French. By May 1938 she had been fired based on accusations of being too friendly with students and of encouraging them to listen to forbidden jazz music. In frustration, Seay took to the pages of *American Mercury* to describe the unhealthy atmosphere. At BJC, Seay wrote, the frenzy for student safety had devolved into a furious culture of witch hunts and furtive spying. As she put it, the school "needs no Gestapo, since every person there is a potential informer."[20]

In all the schools of the network, concerned fundamentalists subjected their schools to a withering scrutiny. They were looking for signs of theological or intellectual slippage: Did a biology professor teach evolution? Did a theology professor teach liberal modernism? Fundamentalist schools, by definition, were to protect students from those sorts of intellectual threats. But concerned fundamentalists also sought to ensure that these institutions remained havens from some of the non-theological temptations of college life. At Biola University in California, for example, President Samuel Sutherland was forced continually to defend the true fundamentalist purity of his institution. As late as 1969, one concerned fundamentalist wrote Sutherland to complain of an advertisement in the student newspaper for "Me-n-Ed's Pizza Parlor," in which a plump and jolly-looking customer ate a slice of pizza and cheerfully swung a stein of beer. "Do you feel," the fundamentalist asked, "this is the type of advertisement a Christian publication should print?" To this fundamentalist neighbor, the notion of a Biola student drinking beer challenged the legitimacy of Biola as a truly fundamentalist institution.[21] Sutherland rushed to reassure him that the ad was a terrible mistake and it had already been fixed. The image of the beer stein had been removed; the implication that Biola students enjoyed alcohol was eliminated.[22]

Perhaps not surprisingly, at fundamentalist colleges and universities, many students in the first half of the twentieth century bucked the strict rules. The archival files of every school bulge with examples of students who tried to evade fundamentalist strictures. At MBI in Chicago, for example, the files from the 1920s, 1930s, 1940s, and 1950s show a consistent record of student misbehavior and institutional response. For instance, in 1932 one student was expelled for sneaking out of a mandatory chapel service and lying about it.[23] Also in 1932, a different student was caught smoking. When he lied about it, he was also expelled.[24] Another student the same year was kicked out for cheating on exams.[25] Yet another was forced out in 1933 for drinking alcohol and having an "untidy room."[26] Before the 1960s, students could be—and often were—expelled for a range of other offenses, sometimes as vague as "moral delinquency"[27] or for having the "wrong attitude."[28]

Not every student broke the rules, of course. The disciplinary records cannot definitively prove how many students obeyed or rebelled against the strict guidelines. It is clear, however, that many students not only followed the rules but embraced them as part of an authentic evangelical experience. As one student who attended Wheaton College in 1938 later remembered, "there was constantly the Christian atmosphere, which I appreciated, and which sort of held me together with the College."[29]

By the late 1940s, however, even the most earnest students, faculty, and administrators might have disagreed about the proper definition of a healthy "Christian atmosphere." By that time, a reform movement had swept the world of American fundamentalism. Calling themselves "new-evangelicals," "neo-evangelicals," or simply "evangelicals," these reformers wanted fundamentalism to open up to the world. As a general rule, neo-evangelical reformers hoped to scrape away some of the non-theological accretions that had come to be associated with fundamentalism.[30] They argued, for example, that at colleges there was no theological reason why students could not be allowed more personal freedom, as long as those students always freely chose healthy evangelical behaviors. As one frustrated neo-evangelical reformer put it, too often fundamentalists lost sight of the big picture in their frantic enforcement of the "big five": Students were told too often that being a good Christian meant avoiding smoking, drinking, dancing, gambling, and movies. Instead of teaching young people the positive truths of real evangelical religion, this reformer worried, schools were merely stunting their spiritual growth with rigid rules.[31]

REAL COLLEGE STUDENTS

In the 1960s, when students at Gordon College near Boston protested against their fundamentalist-era lifestyle rules, they often framed their campus protests as part of this neo-evangelical protest movement. They assumed that neo-evangelical reform was simply the evangelical variant of wider 1960s-style campus protests. For example, students brought Jonathon Kozol, a writer who often penned books about social justice and against racism, to campus to encourage their fellow students to embrace civil-rights activism.[32] Other Gordon students—to the chagrin of their college president—protested ferociously against US military involvement in Southeast Asia.[33] When they did so, students insisted that their politics and their demands represented a truer evangelical Christianity. They claimed that fundamentalist strictures and traditions had obliterated true

Christianity. To represent authentic evangelical religion, student protesters insisted repeatedly, Gordon College needed to shake off its fundamentalist past; Gordon needed to root out the profound racism and imperialism that had wormed its way into fundamentalist culture. Nowhere did neo-evangelical student protesters have more success than in their campaign against stultifying 1920s-era lifestyle rules, as this section will explore. When they protested dress codes, and against strictures on dancing, smoking, and drinking, however, students often did not understand the intense pressure under which their administrators worked. Both fundamentalists and neo-evangelicals from around the country peppered the Gordon administration with demands, just as student protesters did, placing great strain on campus leaders. In the end, student protesters at Gordon won significant concessions, especially when students connected lifestyle changes with neo-evangelical reform.

In late 1967, President James Forrester heard complaints about a recent youth leadership conference on Gordon's campus, at which some students displayed their sympathies for hippie fashions and rock and roll music. Some fundamentalist members of the community were shocked by the implied abandonment of traditional fundamentalist campus rules. One attendee worried that Gordon's students no longer adhered to the "traditional Christian" rules of evangelical colleges.[34] Another fretted that some students seemed to be playing "rock and roll" quite openly. The lyrics of this sort of music, the concerned observer warned Forrester, were always disgustingly "in line with this new moral philosophy in our country."[35] Did Gordon no longer stand as a moral rebuke to such twisted, secular philosophies? As a way to express his displeasure with these neo-evangelical changes, one concerned Gordon alumnus pledged never to donate another dollar to his alma mater. He was shocked by the "ridiculous, hippy type, God dishonoring, student behavior" he saw on display on Gordon's campus. Not only did he state that he would be holding on to his donations, but he threatened to warn young people not to apply to Gordon "until corrections are made."[36] That sort of dollars-and-cents threat scared Gordon's administrators. They hastened to reassure outraged conservatives that any "hippy type" protests did not fairly represent Gordon College. President Forrester assured one correspondent that the "unfortunate rebels" were only "about one percent of the total student body." Forrester promised he had "no intention to tolerate these things."[37] Another administrator similarly condemned Gordon's "rebels and nonconformists." Don't worry, he wrote, "steps were taken to correct the situation."[38]

All in all, Forrester insisted that Gordon would always remain a different sort of school. In 1967, he proudly announced that on his campus, students would remain true to fundamentalist principles and never engage in "mere negative and uninformed protests made noisily and dramatically." Instead, Gordon's students would work for positive change "by rational means within a framework of law and order under God." At Gordon, Forrester pledged, "youth is encouraged to have faith in the historical validity and continuity of the principles of competitive free enterprise." Most of all, at Gordon, students and faculty alike were "unembarrassed" by their "biblical faith."[39]

In less public environments, Gordon's leaders admitted that not all of their students embraced free-enterprise economics and fundamentalist traditions. When leading neo-evangelical scholar and public intellectual Harold Ockenga took over as Gordon's president in 1969, he noted that there was "considerable tendency" on campus to engage in Sixties-style protests. But Ockenga vowed that he would never allow the school to veer from true evangelical rules, even as the fundamentalist focus of his predecessor receded somewhat. In just one day, he explained to a concerned former faculty member, he had suspended six students. To Ockenga, such drastic punishments served as proof that he was willing to go to any lengths to preserve Gordon's continuing role as a different sort of school. In Ockenga's words, he would unflinchingly "maintain the school as a truly Christian College."[40]

Ockenga had his work cut out for him. Gordon's leaders faced pressure from all sides at once—from alumni and community members as well as from student activists. At least one alumnus agreed with some of the students and worried in 1968 that Gordon had timidly retreated from needed neo-evangelical reforms. So far, he charged, the school had done nothing to escape the "extra-scriptural requirements" that went along with "the fundamentalist subculture." Such requirements, he worried, led students away from real religion by pushing empty "customs, folkways, mores and taboos" instead of authentic evangelicalism.[41] Never fear, an administrator assured him. There had already been significant revision of lifestyle rules. At Gordon, students were still required to abstain from alcohol and tobacco. But the new rules no longer defined movies as "inherently wrong." And Gordon students—female ones, at any rate—were now allowed to wear makeup.[42]

Such changes had not come easily. In 1968, students engaged in a sit-in to protest the strict behavioral rules. As one student protester explained, they were not against real evangelical Christianity. They were not sitting in to protest against their college, but rather to push against the fundamentalist rut in which their college remained stuck. They hoped to point out that the thick rulebook governing student behavior itself was anti-evangelical. It only promoted a "subculture," the protester explained, devoted to "maintaining the mores" of short-sighted fundamentalist tradition. If Gordon were to remain a true evangelical college, it needed to ditch those mindless fundamentalist rules and demand more authentic evangelical ones. Moreover, the students demanded, such reforms were necessary for other reasons as well. Neo-evangelical students wanted to participate in the sorts of campus protests that had become synonymous with higher education nationwide. And they wanted a taste of the sorts of personal freedom that seemed to be on offer at non-evangelical schools, or the freedoms that students at those schools were pushing to gain. As one protest leader put it, "we want to be treated like real college students." That meant a radical reform of the strict rules. It also meant a call for a new culture of student engagement and leadership, a new culture of Sixties-style student protests. Perhaps to their surprise, the Gordon administration agreed. Instead of castigating the protesters, Dean Richard Gross publicly commended their devotion to "activism over apathy."[43]

The administration's willingness to consider some changes in the student rulebook encouraged other student protesters to make their cases as well. As they discovered, there was no simple way to discern in advance what changes administrative leaders would support and which ones they would oppose. In early 1968, for example, one anonymous Gordon student lamented his or her punishment for smoking. This student saw no religious reason for being subjected to "such extreme mental torment regarding tobacco[.]"[44] In this case, Dean Richard Gross defended the school's tobacco policy. If Gordon did not ban tobacco, Gross argued in the pages of the *Gordon Tartan*, "we would have basically a non-Christian student body." Real Christians, Gross explained, abstained. He did not limit himself to religious exhortation, however, as he cautioned that any sort of group protest such as a Sixties-style campus smoke-in would result in mass expulsions.[45] At least one Gordon student agreed. Although non-Christians did not think smoking was a moral issue, this student told *Tartan* readers, real Christians knew that it was. As this student-writer asked tendentiously, what kind of missionaries could they be with cigarettes dangling from their mouths?[46] In some cases, student activists successfully tied changes in the rulebook to healthy neo-evangelical reform. In the case of smoking, however, that approach failed.

Dancing might have been a different matter entirely. One administrator told Gordon students in early 1968 that the institution actually had no rule against dancing. Any organized dance, however, would have to be approved and regulated by the administration. Overall, one *Tartan* writer reported, a slim majority of students wanted the campus to have a dance.[47] Predictably, the pro-dance party made its case in the language of the neo-evangelical–fundamentalist divide. Too often, a student wrote, anti-dancers suffered from a mindless "new legalism." Instead of thinking about promoting an authentic evangelical message, such traditionalists stuck to rules merely for the sake of the rules themselves. What Gordon and the rest of evangelical America needed was more "Christian liberty" and less stuck-in-the-mud fundamentalism.[48]

At Gordon and other evangelical colleges, however, there was no precise way to separate the two.[49] The public debates on Gordon's campus between student protesters and cautious administrators masked the private deliberations and exhortations that filled administrators' mailboxes. In order to settle the riotous student demand for revisions to the student rulebook, administrators in 1970 offered a list of changes that they could defend to the conservative evangelical community. Trustees who approved the new rules in May 1970 insisted that changes never threatened the core evangelical beliefs of Gordon College. Nor did trustees abandon efforts to enforce relatively stringent rules. But the new rules also recognized the central demands of student protesters. For example, the new rules specified that dancing would not be permitted, either on or off campus. Smoking and drinking among students were discouraged in general and absolutely forbidden on campus. Drugs, specifically marijuana, were absolutely banned, on or off campus. Trustees hoped this list of prohibitions would satisfy the insistence of conservatives on stringent control of student behavior. Students, though, won significant concessions. The new rulebook guaranteed that the administration would never misrepresent the political activism of Gordon students. They promised, that is, never to preach to fundamentalist audiences that neo-evangelical Gordon students never protested. Vaguely but importantly, the new rules gave students "the right to live and pursue learning in a democratic social atmosphere." Students had often felt oppressed by administration decisions. The new rules promised that they would never lose their ability to voice their opinions without fear of rebuke.[50]

By the standards of a liberal college town like Madison or Berkeley, these concessions seemed mild. For neo-evangelical students, however, the new guarantee that they would "retain, while a student, the freedom of a private citizen" represented a significant change from fundamentalist tradition.[51] Since the 1920s, fundamentalist institutions had insisted on total control of student lives. At Gordon College—and at many other evangelical colleges that embraced the neo-evangelical reform—at least, those fundamentalist restrictions had successfully been challenged as a defining moment of the evangelical "Sixties."

In short, by 1970 the Gordon community had a new type of rulebook. Yes, Gordon's students were real college students. They could not be treated like children. They could not be given rules for no good reason, nor simply dictated to as if their protests were merely tantrums. On the other hand, Gordon's students were also real evangelical Christians. That meant they could be expected to embrace higher behavioral standards. The school could claim control over student lifestyles, but only if it could justify that control as part of authentic evangelical Christianity and not as part of a mindless adherence to fundamentalist tradition. At neo-evangelical colleges like Gordon—or, more precisely, evangelical colleges with large numbers of students, faculty, alumni, and administrators sympathetic to the neo-evangelical reform movement—student protesters succeeded only when they convinced cautious administrators of their evangelical merit. Students won a new list of explicit rights, but only when they made their cases in the language of neo-evangelical reform. Such protests may have looked on the surface like the sit-ins on secular campuses, but the issues involved were unique to the network of evangelical institutions of higher education.

Keeping the Faith

Gordon College was not the only school that struggled to figure out the role of student protest and student lifestyle rules at evangelical campuses in the late 1960s. Some schools rigidly refused to consider any whiff of neo-evangelical reform. BJU, for example, had always prided itself on its uncompromising fundamentalist rules and atmosphere. In 1945, fundamentalist pundit John R. Rice praised the feel of the campus. While non-fundamentalist colleges had lapsed into a permissive sloth, Rice wrote, BJC never varied from its restrictive rules for students. As a result, Rice rejoiced that students were able to engage in romantic relationships without succumbing to carnal temptation. As he put it in his widely read fundamentalist newspaper *Sword of the Lord*, "I felt like thanking God that young love could blossom in a Christian environment without the tawdry license and necking and looseness so customary among worldly young people."⁵² In campus politics, too, the BJU community never challenged its conservative, fundamentalist traditions, even under extreme pressure. In 1970, for example, as secular campuses endured violent waves of student protests and police crackdowns, and as even neo-evangelical-friendly institutions such as Gordon College revised their fundamentalist student rulebooks, the Alumni Association of BJU reaffirmed its commitment to uncompromising fundamentalism. "Whereas" the association resolved,

> we note the tragic results of tolerant, soft-core administrators who are permitting the breakdown of principles and policies ... and Whereas many graduates of these restless institutions are shocked and stand in disbelief at destruction of buildings, property, discipline, and moral integrity ... we declare our continued allegiance and loyalty to the school.

The BJU Alumni Association sided proudly with BJU's top leadership, in spite of "unwarranted attack by the Neo-Evangelical forces and liberals."⁵³ At BJU, there was no whisper of student dissent or student protest.

By the late 1960s, however, most colleges, universities, and institutes of higher education that had embraced the fundamentalist movement in the 1920s had a more conflicted institutional relationship to reform. Gordon College moved tentatively toward an institutional embrace of neo-evangelical reform. Other schools, such as MBI, remained friendlier to fundamentalist-style rules and traditions. At MBI, students shied away from dramatic protests such as sit-ins. Yet some activists did mobilize for reforms to restrictive student rules. In general, the student body at Moody was more divided than that of Gordon. As at Gordon and other schools in the network, student protesters at MBI framed their appeals in the language of neo-evangelical reform. They insisted they did not want to drink or smoke, yet they criticized the old-fashioned fundamentalist rules that kept them from fully evolving as true evangelical Christians. By and large, tentative student objections met with stern resistance from the administration. As at Gordon, administrators at MBI felt intense pressure from fundamentalists outside the MBI community. Unlike at Gordon, however, internal pressure from neo-evangelical student reformers did not have enormous popular appeal among MBI students. To onlookers, it may have seemed that the administration's clampdown was the end of the story. As this section explores, however, some evidence suggests that MBI students simply moved to quieter forms of rebellion.

The political climate at MBI was, in general, more conservative than that at most colleges. When it came to the war in Vietnam, for example, in 1968 a majority of 54 percent of MBI students supported US military involvement. In comparison, only 21 percent of students nationwide did so.[54] Similarly, though some white students at MBI called for "self-examination" of racist attitudes among white evangelicals, in general those anti-racist sentiments failed to generate widespread support among the student body.[55]

When it came to the student rulebook, too, MBI students remained profoundly divided. As at Gordon College, some called for neo-evangelical reforms that would allow students to engage in more authentic evangelical religion. Many student voices, however, supported the traditional rules. Debates among students peaked in late 1970, when the administration announced its plans to re-examine the student rulebook. Student Council President Don Wipf publicly called for an overhaul. Rules were not a bad thing, Wipf wrote in the pages of the student newspaper. However, every young person needed "freedom to make decisions on his [sic] own." Without the freedom to decide, Wipf argued, "A person will not mature nor be able to face today's world."[56] Some students countered that the rules should remain strict. "I didn't come to Moody to change the rules," one student argued. "I came to study God's Word and let it change me."[57] The editor of the student paper argued that the rules needed adjusting, not replacing. Yes, the student editor wrote in late 1970, some of the rules show "definite inconsistency or no logical reasoning." And those kinds of rules should change. In general, though, the editor believed that such decisions should be left in the hands of trusted college administrators. Students, he insisted, "should work more on changing our attitudes than on changing the rules."[58]

In December 1970, student reporters at MBI conducted an informal survey of student attitudes. As at other evangelical and fundamentalist colleges, some students framed their complaints about the rules in neo-evangelical terms. One student, for example, responded that all the curfews and restrictions kept him from preaching on street corners as much as he wanted to. Why shouldn't he be able to stay out late, he wondered, if that's when the streets of Chicago needed the most Christian exhortation? Other students firmly supported the traditional rules. Becky Martin, for instance, responded that the rules were "good, sensible, and backed by solid reasoning." Overall, the student reporters concluded, many students griped about the rules, but in general the student body thought the "rules were basically OK."[59]

Perhaps because of the continued support of many conservative students, the MBI administration did not relent much when it came to its official student rules. Instead, campus leaders tended to give in to steady pressure from the wider fundamentalist community. President B. Myron Cedarholm of Maranatha Baptist Bible College in Wisconsin, for instance, pressed MBI President William Culbertson to reject any neo-evangelical-inspired reforms. If MBI were to loosen student rules, Cedarholm worried, it would send a dangerous signal to the rest of the network of Bible colleges and universities. Cedarholm had heard rumors about new trends in "music and ecumenical trends" at MBI. He hoped Culbertson would continue to keep MBI on the side of fundamentalist traditionalism.[60]

In the end, such pressure to remain true to traditional fundamentalist rules won the day at MBI. Administrators especially never retreated from the position they took in the turbulent summer of 1969, when the streets of Chicago and many other American cities seemed full of radically dressed young people. In spite of the seeming universality of such radical chic, administrators reminded students that they must continue to set a "Good Example" on Chicago's streets. In spite of widespread rumors to the contrary, administrators warned, MBI students were still prohibited from drinking alcohol, dancing, smoking, or attending the cinema or dramatic performances. Women still had to wear skirts no higher than the tops of their knees. And no students were allowed to wear blue jeans and T-shirts, the de facto uniform of Sixties protests. Men needed to wear "sport shirts with casual slacks and/or sport coats or suits." Perhaps most importantly, male students were never to adopt any of the latest fashions for men, including "long hair, long sideburns, beards and 'Fu-manchu' moustaches." To fulfill their mission as Christian voices in the gritty urban wilderness, MBI students needed to stand out. They needed to comport themselves differently; they needed to look different from the young people who were filling Chicago's streets with what were seen as starkly unChristian messages.[61]

It would be tempting to conclude that scattered voices of student protest at more conservative institutions such as MBI had made no impact at all. A more careful examination, however, shows that student rebellion at MBI was actually widely successful, but only when it took quieter forms. One survey in 1974, for example, found that students tended to pick and choose which of MBI's restrictive lifestyle rules they would embrace. When it came to rules with direct religious intent, most students in the late 1960s respected the strictures. They continued, for instance, to engage in mandatory daily prayer and chapel attendance. They respected the college's rule about daily Bible reading. Rules forbidding card playing and movie attendance, however, did not retain the same universal respect among MBI students. A journalist who interviewed professors and alumni from MBI concluded that large numbers of students—30–60 percent—simply rejected such rules. They did not stage sit-ins or protest marches, but large numbers of MBI students quietly and intentionally attended movies, played cards, drank alcohol, or smoked cigarettes.[62]

Even when an institution such as MBI seemed to reject tentative student efforts at protest, many of the traditional lifestyle rules changed in practice. MBI did not witness the same style of rebellion as did Gordon, but students did voice their dissatisfaction with rules that kept them from practicing what they saw as authentic evangelical religion. When the administration proved intractable, MBI students sometimes simply transgressed the rules on their own. Such transgressions, students believed, did not take away from their understanding of authentic evangelical Christianity.

THE EVANGELICAL CAMPUS SIXTIES

As this chapter has demonstrated, pressure from fundamentalists nationwide made it difficult for leaders at schools like MBI and Gordon to loosen their student rules in response to neo-evangelical student protests. Students, too, often supported traditional rules in significant numbers. Every institution had its own unique experience and its own mix of student, alumni, administration, and community influence. At Gordon, and other neo-evangelical-friendly institutions, Sixties-style protests achieved a measure of success. Students agitated for a reexamination of strict rules and administrators often agreed. Instead of knee-jerk assumptions about traditional fundamentalist prohibitions on movies, smoking, and alcohol, many evangelical colleges embraced a looser sort of ban. Instead of simply telling students "no," evangelical colleges in the late 1960s and thereafter encouraged students to examine their lifestyle decisions prayerfully, always keeping in mind their need to set a good example as evangelical missionaries. At MBI and other institutions friendlier to fundamentalist tradition, student challenges to fundamentalism made less headway. For one thing, student sentiment itself strongly supported traditional rules. For another, outside pressure from fundamentalist activists weighed heavily. At MBI, with its close links to the Bible-college network, fundamentalist pressure from both students and outsiders combined to push student protest into quieter forms of misbehavior.

At all evangelical and fundamentalist institutions, student protesters had the most success when they articulated their grievances in the language of neo-evangelical reform. The campus protests about fundamentalist lifestyle rules—as well as about the Vietnam War and racism—at schools such as Gordon were not merely echoes of the protests at mainstream schools. Rather, students at Gordon, and, to a lesser degree, at MBI, engaged in a uniquely evangelical form of activism. Yes, they agitated against strict *in loco parentis* rules, similar to such protests at non-evangelical schools. By and large, however, they agitated not in the name of secular freedom, but rather in the name of authentic evangelical Christianity. When evangelical students protested for greater freedom in the 1960s, they made their cases in the language of the neo-evangelical reform movement itself. Yes, students wanted more freedom to choose their clothes, their bedtimes, and their dating patterns, but when they got their way—as they sometimes did—it was because they had insisted that such notions were an inherent part of true evangelical religion. Students navigated a larger neo-evangelical–fundamentalist divide as they struggled to figure out what it meant to be a real college student and a Christian in the 1960s and 1970s.

NOTES

1. P. Andrew Brown, "Apathy on the Way Out?" *Gordon Tartan*, December 10, 1968, 7.
2. Adam Laats, *Fundamentalist U: Keeping the Faith in American Higher Education* (New York: Oxford University Press, 2018); William C. Ringenberg, *The Christian College: A History of Protestant Higher Education in America*, 2nd ed. (Grand Rapids, MI: Eerdmans Publishing Company, 2006); see also George M. Marsden, *The Soul of the American University: From Protestant Establishment to Established Nonbelief* (New York: Oxford University Press, 1994).
3. See Laats, *Fundamentalist U.*
4. Laats, *Fundamentalist U.*
5. Virginia Lieson Brereton, *Protestant Fundamentalist Bible Schools, 1882–1940* (PhD diss., Columbia University, 1981), 304n31.
6. Nathan R. Wood, *A School of Christ* (Boston: Gordon College of Theology and Missions, 1953), 10.
7. Typescript of Culbertson biography, n.d. Culbertson papers, Moody Bible Institute archives.

8. See, for example, George M. Marsden, *Fundamentalism and American Culture: The Shaping of American Evangelicalism*, 2nd ed. (New York: Oxford University Press, 2006); Matthew Avery Sutton, *American Apocalypse: A History of Modern Evangelicalism* (Cambridge: Harvard University Press, 2014); Kathryn Lofton, "Commonly Modern: Rethinking the Modernist-Fundamentalist Controversies," *Church History* 83 (March 2014): 137–44.

9. Marsden, *Fundamentalism and American Culture*, 199–228.

10. Laats, *Fundamentalist U*, chapter 7.

11. Bob Jones Sr., *Bob Jones Magazine* 1 (June 1928): 3.

12. Bob Jones Sr., *The Perils of America, or, Where Are We Headed?* (n.p., n.d. [from a sermon delivered at the Chicago Gospel Tabernacle, March 5, 1934]), 7.

13. See, for example, Helen Lefkowitz Horowitz, *Campus Life: Undergraduate Cultures from the End of the Eighteenth Century to the Present* (New York: Alfred A. Knopf, 1987); Paul K. Conkin, *Gone with the Ivy: A Biography of Vanderbilt University* (Knoxville: University of Tennessee Press, 1985); Beth L. Bailey, *From Front Porch to Back Seat: Courtship in Twentieth-Century America* (Baltimore: Johns Hopkins University Press, 1988); Margaret A. Nash and Jennifer A.R. Silverman, "'An Indelible Mark': Gay Purges in Higher Education in the 1940s," *History of Education Quarterly* 55, no. 4 (November 2015): 441–59.

14. Typescript of questions with student answers; Turner Box, folder: Miss Dorothy R. Seay, Bob Jones University archives, Greenville, South Carolina.

15. Anne Williams Warwick, *Tides: Growing Up on St. Andrews Bay* (Panama City, FL: Boyd Bros Printing, 1984), 123.

16. Warwick, *Tides*, 121.

17. Bob Jones to "Friend," n.d.; Box HC 20/24, folder: Bob Jones College, Crown Point, FL, Letters to New students; Bob Jones University archives.

18. Charles Blankenship to R. K. Johnson, November 3, 1953; Dr. Turner Box, folder: Ted Mercer et al., Bob Jones University archives.

19. Interview with Vincent Leroy Crossett, November 16, 1984. Collection 288, Archives of the Billy Graham Center, Wheaton, Illinois.

20. Anonymous, "Accent on Sin," *American Mercury* 51, no. 201 (September 1940): 18.

21. Roger Dunn to Bob Guernsey, April 21, 1969. Folder: Chimes, The, Student Newspaper Publication Biola, Sutherland papers, Biola University archives, La Mirada, California.

22. Guernsey to Dunn, April 24, 1969. Folder: Chimes, The, Student Newspaper Publication Biola, Sutherland papers.

23. James W. Davis, Memo, June 11, 1932; Box 2, folder 8, Student Records Collection (hereafter SRC), Moody Bible Institute archives, Chicago, Illinois.
24. James W. Davis to Mr. and Mrs. Edward T. Lloyd, February 20, 1932; Box 2, folder 8, SRC.
25. James W. Davis to Ruby A. Jackson, October 28, 1932; Box 2, folder 8, SRC.
26. Ruby A. Jackson, Memo, June 29, 1933; Box 2, folder 8, SRC.
27. Ruby A. Jackson, Memo, May 28, 1930; Box 2, folder 9, SRC.
28. A. F. Broman, Memo, October 21, 1948; Box 2, folder 14, SRC.
29. Interview with Paul Dean Votaw, March 4, 1980, Collection 105, Archives of the Billy Graham Center.
30. Joel A. Carpenter, *Revive Us Again: The Reawakening of American Fundamentalism* (New York: Oxford University Press, 1997).
31. C. David Weyerhauser to William Culbertson, January 1960, cited in George Marsden, *Reforming Fundamentalism: Fuller Seminary and the New Evangelicalism* (Grand Rapids, MI: Eerdmans, 1987), 204.
32. "Announcement," *Gordon Tartan*, February 19, 1969, 2.
33. Bob Cruickshank, "McCarthy for President Delegation Enlists Gordonians for Campaign," *Gordon Tartan*, April 2, 1968, 1; Andrew Brown, Robert Cruikshank, Ed Vaeni, Sue Bingham, "A Choice, Not an Echo," *Gordon Tartan*, February 27, 1968, 2; Brian McLamb, "Letter Blasts Vietnam Editorial," *Gordon Tartan*, March 12, 1968, 2; Dave Sheppard, "Vietnam: An Opinion," *Gordon Tartan*, June 11, 1969, 3; Richard Nixon to Harold Ockenga, November 6, 1969; Richard Nixon to Ockenga, June 29, 1969, President's Office Files, 1966–1969, Box 3, General Correspondence, N-Z, Gordon College archives, Wenham, Massachusetts.
34. Nathan Garnett to James Forrester, November 20, 1967, President's Office Papers, 1966–1969, Folder: G, 1967, Gordon College archives, Wenham, Massachusetts.
35. Angelus Lados to James Forrester, December 7, 1967, President's Office Papers, 1966–1969, Folder: L, 1967, Gordon College archives.
36. William J. Harrison to James Forrester, n.d., President's Office Papers, 1966–1969, Folder: H, 1968, Gordon College archives.
37. James Forrester to Nathan Garnett, December 5, 1967, President's Office Papers, 1966–1969, Folder: G, 1967, Gordon College archives.
38. George Rideout to Harrison, August 6, 1968, President's Office Papers, 1966–1969, Folder: G, 1967, Gordon College archives.
39. James Forrester, "Campus Address," December 21, 1967, President's Office Papers, 1966–1969, Folder: Patton, General (Celebration), Gordon College archives.
40. Harold Ockenga to Norvell Peterson, October 30, 1969, President's Office Papers, 1966–1969, Folder: P, 1969, Gordon College archives.

41. David E. Gillespie to George Rideout, December 31, 1968, President's Office Papers, 1966–1969, Folder: G, 1969, Gordon College archives.

42. George Rideout to David E. Gillespie, January 17, 1969, President's Office Papers, 1966–1969, Folder: G, 1969, Gordon College archives.

43. P. Andrew Brown, "Apathy on the Way Out?" *Gordon Tartan*, December 10, 1968, 7.

44. Letter to the Editor, *Gordon Tartan*, January 30, 1968, 2.

45. "The Dean Speaks Out on Smoking," *Gordon Tartan*, February 13, 1968, 1.

46. Richard Slater, "Reply to 'Smoking,'" *Gordon Tartan*, February 13, 1968, 2.

47. Ed Vaeni, "Englund Discusses Dancing," *Gordon Tartan*, January 30, 1968, 3.

48. Dan Meiners, "Christian Liberty Upsets Campus," *Gordon Tartan*, February 27, 1968, 4.

49. Laats, *Fundamentalist U*, chapter 3.

50. "Trustees Ratify Changes in Behavior Standards," *Gordon Tartan*, May 6, 1970, 1.

51. "Trustees Ratify Changes."

52. John R. Rice, "Editor Visits Bob Jones College," *Sword of the Lord*, June 8, 1945, 5.

53. Resolution passed by BJU Alumni Association, April 2, 1970, Folder: Bob Jones University—Alumni Association, Gordon Stenholm papers, Bob Jones University archives.

54. Michael Jay Sider-Rose, "Between Heaven and Earth: Moody Bible Institute and the Politics of the Moderate Christian Right, 1945–1986" (PhD diss., University of Pittsburgh, 2000), 187.

55. Dave Broucek, "Racial Harmony: Time for Self-Examination," *Moody Student*, February 13, 1970, 2.

56. "Students, Deans to Revise Rules," *Moody Student*, November 20, 1970, 1.

57. "Students, Deans to Revise."

58. Mike Farrell, "Are We Fighting the Wrong Fight?" *Moody Student*, December 16, 1970, 2.

59. "Students Speak Out on Rules," *Moody Student*, December 16, 1970, 5.

60. B. Myron Cedarholm to William Culbertson, January 21, 1971, Culbertson papers, Moody Bible Institute archives.

61. "Our Good Example Is Important," *Moody Memo*, August 1, 1969, 3.

62. Glenn Arnold, "The Christian Collegian After a Decade of Change," *Christianity Today*, November 3, 1978, 22.

CHAPTER 13

Conclusion: New Perspectives on Campus Life and Setting the Agenda for Future Research

Christine A. Ogren and Marc A. VanOverbeke

The chapters in this volume offer a rich, detailed, and complex history of various aspects of campus life in the United States. The collection deepens and expands the boundaries of the historiography of college students in the nineteenth and twentieth centuries. Timothy Cain, for example, describes students breaking strikes as a way to burnish their masculinity, while Margaret Nash, Danielle Mireles, and Amanda Scott-Williams capture those students who donned drag, either for fun or for political purposes, and in doing so challenged gender boundaries and norms. Joy Williamson-Lott highlights black students who challenged entrenched conservative attitudes at some historically black campuses and among

C. A. Ogren (✉)
Educational Policy and Leadership Studies, University of Iowa, Iowa City, IA, USA
e-mail: chris-ogren@uiowa.edu

M. A. VanOverbeke
College of Education, University of Illinois at Chicago, Chicago, IL, USA
e-mail: mvanover@uic.edu

© The Author(s) 2018
C. A. Ogren, M. A. VanOverbeke (eds.),
Rethinking Campus Life, Historical Studies in Education,
https://doi.org/10.1007/978-3-319-75614-1_13

283

black administrators, in a sometimes intergenerational conflict over civil rights strategy. Christopher Tudico uncovers the history of Mexican American students who dedicated much of their campus experiences to expanding access and opportunity to more students from similar backgrounds, and Adam Laats portrays students on evangelical campuses in conflict with themselves and others over what it meant to be a real college student while remaining true to deeply help religious beliefs and practices. Nicholas Syrett and Margaret Freeman detail dating practices among members of fraternities and sororities, and the ways in which these organizations governed much of campus life, even for those students who never rushed a particular fraternity or sorority. Additionally, Christine Ogren and Marc VanOverbeke focus on students at normal schools and state colleges, and Nicholas Strohl discusses students at community colleges, all of whom built full, exciting, and robust student cultures that rivaled those found elsewhere.

While prior research on the history of campus life—including notably Helen Lefkowitz Horowitz's *Campus Life*—has greatly enhanced our understanding of students, this volume builds on and expands that research. Through offering new perspectives on established topics in the field, analysis of overlooked or ignored institutions, deeper work on student groups that scholarship has often marginalized, and innovative research in new areas, the chapters in this volume underscore how rich and vibrant the field of student life has become within the larger historiography of higher education. These chapters offer an extensive view of campus life, and they capture the diversity of students, their organizations, and their behaviors that, as Michael Hevel and Heidi Jaeckle highlight in their historiographical essay, have always been part of student life across many different types of institutions. They add a deeper level of analysis to how students experienced and shaped college-going throughout the nineteenth and twentieth centuries. These essays offer a captivating description of students and the lives they built, shaped, or responded to while on campus and off campus.

In this concluding chapter, we highlight a few of the themes that thread across the chapters and underscore the significant contributions these chapters individually and collectively make to our understanding of campus life. As rich as these chapters are, there is more work to be done in the history of campus life, and these chapters point the way to some interesting, provocative questions that need to be at the heart of future research. We identify some of those questions before offering a few final thoughts on the state of the field.

THEMES AND CONTRIBUTIONS

Together, these chapters underscore key themes that expand our understanding of campus life. While there are many relevant themes, in this section we focus on three: exclusion and exclusivity among students and within campus life; navigation of larger social issues through student life; and fluidity between on- and off-campus life for students. By highlighting exclusion and exclusivity, the first theme also focuses on access and opportunity to attend college and experience campus life, while the second theme emphasizes the ways in which students shaped social issues and were influenced by larger social, political, and economic circumstances. The third theme builds on this connection between campus life and external contexts to consider the fluidity between on-campus and off-campus student life. This latter theme emphasizes that student life does not occur just on campus. Not all chapters emphasize all of these themes but each theme crosses multiple chapters to further our understanding of campus life, and each theme builds on or contributes to the key areas we identified in the Introduction.

Exclusion and Exclusivity/Access and Opportunity

All the chapters to some degree address exclusion and exclusivity, as well as access and opportunity. Indeed, in many ways, college has been—and is—an exclusive institution to which some have access, others do not, and still others fight to expand access to greater numbers of students. Throughout history, even those who were able to gain access to college continued to experience—or enforce—various forms of exclusion and exclusivity through a hierarchy of groups and organizations in which students lobbied to join the most prestigious ones. Gaining access to college alone did not mean that one had broken completely through barriers of exclusivity.

As these chapters underscore, campus life often revolved around identification within a cohesive and similar peer group and the simultaneous exclusion of other types of students. This exclusivity was often overt, as when white fraternities excluded women and male students of other races. Of course, exclusion by race was the choice of the white fraternity members, as Syrett shows, but not the choice of black members on the outside. Also, as Syrett highlights, fraternities were perched at the top of a student life hierarchy and dictated the campus life experiences even of those students who did not wish to become members of a fraternity. Fraternities gained such standing and prestige in large measure because they controlled access to their elite social organizations and excluded many through a rushing and hazing process. Sororities did not have quite the same cachet and standing as their male counterparts, as Freeman argues, but they did enjoy their own exclusivity. And, as both Freeman and Syrett point out, the exclusivity of the Greek organizations affected student dating habits, since the members of more prestigious fraternities were encouraged not to date members of less prestigious sororities, less they risk tarnishing the reputations and thus the exclusivity of their organizations. Nash, Mireles, and Scott-Williams make the point that exclusion revolved not only around dating but also around gender and sexuality more generally. As they detail, some students resorted to drag as impersonation, tomfoolery, or vaudeville to experiment with ideas of gender and sexuality.

The students profiled by Syrett, Freeman, and Nash, Mireles, and Scott-Williams reinforced or challenged exclusion and exclusivity within campus life, especially regarding access to prestigious social activities, groups, and organizations. At the same time, as other chapters in this volume make clear, many students did not have access to higher education in the first place. As Ogren, VanOverbeke, and Strohl underscore, normal schools, state colleges, and community colleges broadened access and made it more likely that greater numbers of young people could experience campus life as college students. In so doing, these institutions challenged the exclusive nature of higher education, and, as Tudico, Williamson-Lott, and VanOverbeke also underscore, many students spent much of their campus lives pushing for, demanding, and campaigning to expand college access to greater numbers of students and, in essence, to make college less exclusive. Williamson-Lott and Tudico, in particular, identify the battles that African American students, often at black colleges in the South, and Mexican American students undertook as part of their campus experiences to chip away at the exclusivity and exclusion that marked higher education and that prevented many of their peers from being collegians. In the process of telling their stories, these authors provide new perspectives on how these students built their campus lives, often in opposition to established authority figures or against great odds.

As part of this push toward expanding access and opportunity and challenging exclusion and exclusivity, many types of students asserted that they were bona fide college students. Laats argues that students at evangelical colleges sometimes protested campus rules out of a desire to be seen as real college students on real college campuses. VanOverbeke similarly argues that students at the new state colleges and the former normal schools that were becoming comprehensive colleges developed campus cultures and student activities that mimicked what they saw on more traditional campuses. This standardization of campus life emerged from students' desire to be seen and to see themselves as legitimate college students earning real degrees. In many ways, as Ogren and Strohl point out, students at normal schools and community colleges ignored their lack of standing in relation to prestigious research universities and instead built vibrant campus cultures that mirrored, or even improved upon, student experiences at more established colleges and universities, even though historians have often assumed that these students did not seek that kind of engaged, meaningful student life. As they pushed toward developing what they saw at other campuses, students at evangelical institutions, community colleges, normal schools, and state colleges asserted their status as real college students and, in doing so, challenged notions of exclusivity that marked many colleges and universities.

Through chapters in this volume, we gain a rich understanding of life on less prestigious, less exclusive campuses, including community colleges, normal schools, state colleges, evangelical colleges, and historically black colleges in the South. We also gain new insights into fraternities and sororities, as well as often ignored students—such as Mexican American and African American students, as well as homosexual students. In the process, these chapters begin to rectify an imbalance in the literature that has too often focused on exclusive institutions and traditional student groups. Indeed, running through all of these chapters is the recognition that over the course of the twentieth century, college was becoming less exclusive and more open. Still, these chapters also raise questions and underscore that there is more to know about those students excluded from aspects of campus life or completely barred from college more generally. We address some of those questions later in this chapter.

Navigating Larger Social Issues

Another theme that crosses multiple chapters is students' use of their experiences and the campus cultures they built to better understand and navigate changing cultural and social issues. Nash, Mireles, and Scott-Williams clearly highlight the role of drag for students who sought to understand gender and sexuality in particular, but they also discuss students who turned to drag to make sense of political issues or to protest political events and, apparently in one case, to mock suffragettes and the larger suffrage movement. Nash, Mireles, and Scott-Williams thus profile students who engaged in campus life as a means of making sense of and even challenging larger social, political, and cultural norms and expectations. At the same time, Ogren explains how activities, social life, athletics, and leadership opportunities at state normal schools allowed women students to cross gender boundaries through participation in campus life. Syrett clarifies that fraternity members were explicitly asserting their sense of masculinity and heteronormativity through their activities and by joining a fraternity in the first place, and Freeman makes a related point that sororities promoted "heterosocializing," through which sorority sisters learned their place in a male-dominated world. In this way, fraternity and sorority members—as well as women students at state normal schools and students who embraced drag—used their campus lives and experiences to better understand themselves, their gender and sexuality, and their identity. Sometimes these students challenged gender boundaries, as was the case at normal schools and with some students in drag, and in other cases, they had no choice but to accept gender norms, as many sorority sisters discovered.

Other chapters highlight how students used their campus experiences to understand their role and place in a changing world in terms of race and social class. In the cases of Mexican American and African American students, Tudico and Williamson-Lott respectively illustrate how students overtly and directly challenged common assumptions and norms about student racial groups. VanOverbeke similarly explores the role of African American and Mexican American students in addressing pressing racial issues and civil rights through their on-campus efforts to push their campuses to be more open and welcoming places. Strohl and Ogren expand this focus to emphasize the low socioeconomic class of students at community colleges and state normal schools. These students, by attending college and becoming campus leaders, challenged norms and expectations based on socioeconomic class and asserted their right to a college education. At normal schools, they also used campus life to acquire the cultural capital and sociability that marked middle-class standing. As all of these students developed campus organizations, engaged in campus protests, or simply participated in campus activities, they sought to find their place in the larger world and to link their campus lives with their lives outside of campus.

Cain makes a direct link between students' lives on campus and the ways in which they sought to use their experiences to make sense of the world around them. As they struggled either to break strikes or to support striking workers—both on campus and off campus—students challenged themselves and their peers to think about the values and ideals they wanted to embrace and promote in the world. While many students remained safely ensconced behind college walls, others struggled alongside the workers or were workers themselves, as Cain alludes to when he discusses the black college students who were also cafeteria workers caught up in the Greensboro strike. Whether they were striking cafeteria workers, students who supported the strikes, or students who aided corporations as strikebreakers, Cain's subjects actively bridged their campus lives and the world outside of college in an effort to navigate the changing world around them.

The students attending evangelical colleges, as Laats argues, engaged in campus life as a way to make sense of their roles and responsibilities as evangelicals in the larger nation. As they protested for or against looser lifestyle rules at their institutions, evangelical students wrestled with what it meant to be religious—and even how to define religious—in a nation in the midst of profound change. As the civil rights movements and the Vietnam War shaped the nation and world, these students debated their roles as evangelicals in converting others, in building their careers and lives, and in tempering the tendencies and habits of a more secular society.

In looking at these social issues and by exploring the ways in which students turned to campus activities to make sense of the world around them, the authors of chapters in this volume have advanced understanding of gender, sexuality, race, social class, and religion among collegians and on college campuses. They have underscored the growing diversity among college students, and highlighted the many activities to which students turned in their efforts to find their way through a changing world. As with the theme of exclusion and exclusivity, these chapters' treatments of students' navigation of social issues also raise a number of questions and suggest areas for further research.

Fluidity Between On and Off Campus

As students sought to navigate larger social issues through their activities, they discovered that the boundaries between on and off campus were fluid and shifting. This fluidity between on campus and off campus is another theme that cuts across the chapters. As Williamson-Lott argues, students did not stop being citizens just because they entered the campus quad, and they did not give up their identity as students when they left campus. She shows that students used their campus experiences to shape larger black freedom movements and they used those movements in turn to shape their campus experiences. Cain explicitly raises this issue of fluidity across campus boundaries in his discussion of strikebreaking and student involvement in labor issues off campus. Students repeatedly ventured back and forth between the campus and the community, as they supported or opposed labor actions. For them, the boundaries between campus and community were never firm. Similarly, as Nash, Mireles, and Scott-Williams describe, students involved in theatricals and vaudeville often traveled off campus to entertain non-students. In this way, these aspiring actors blurred the lines between on- and off-campus student activities, and brought non-students into campus life.

Laats also addresses fluidity of campus boundaries by describing how evangelical colleges sought to govern student behavior in movie theaters and other off-campus venues. He points to the tension that such oversight caused with students and the ways in which students pushed against and sought a relaxation of many of the rules governing student behavior on and off campus. Tudico further explores this theme through a focus on Mexican American students who sought to influence and build stronger communities among students and others. These students leveraged the resources of their campuses and communities to develop organizations that linked the two and connected Mexican American students across multiple campuses. They dedicated many aspects of their campus experiences to making it possible for other young people—who were off campus and not yet of college age—to attend college in the future. In similar ways, students at community colleges constantly had to balance their campus lives with their personal lives, which often included roles as parents and employees of off-campus entities. As Strohl describes, these students had multiple identities as students, parents, and workers, and could never draw firm boundaries between their on-campus and off-campus experiences.

While these authors do not focus explicitly on off-campus activities, they show that the boundaries between on and off campus have been fluid. It is rarely possible to divorce historical developments in campus life from larger, external issues and forces. The boundaries have shifted as students built campus cultures that reflected and challenged, and were shaped by, off-campus cultures and events. Students have not shed their student identities when off campus (often to the dismay of administrators when students protested off campus, as was the case with the 1968 Olympics that VanOverbeke introduces). Students also have not come to campus unaffected by larger events and issues in society.

The fluidity between on and off campus reflected in these chapters raises the question of what qualifies as campus life. Are events or activities student life because they take place on campus, or because students engage in them? These authors imply that student life is defined more by who is involved than by where it takes place. Thus, campus life is campus life because students are involved, and it does not matter whether activities occur on or off campus. These chapters expand the boundaries of student life beyond the campus gates, and in doing so, they raise questions about what actually constitutes campus life. We address some of these specific questions in the next section.

QUESTIONS AND FURTHER RESEARCH

The chapters in this volume add richness and depth to our understanding of exclusion and exclusivity, navigation of larger social issues, and fluidity between on and off campus in student life, while also raising important questions for further research. Some of these questions flow directly from these emerging themes and from the authors' arguments, and some of the questions emerge more indirectly from tantalizing pieces of information that hint at new arguments, or what we might call undercurrents. In addition, even with the depth and complexity of these chapters, gaps in the literature remain. Thus, other questions for additional research flow from the topics that are not part of this volume. Questions for future research fall roughly into three areas: student groups and activities, institutions, and student demographics.

Syrett and Freeman offer crucial insights on student activities through their examination of fraternities and sororities, and in their chapters they begin to explore how these organizations shaped and influenced campus life for students outside of the Greek system. Syrett's argument that fraternities often dominated campus life suggests important new questions. What effect, then, did these organizations have on other groups? Freeman illustrates how the need for attention from and approval by fraternities shaped sororities. What sorts of influences did fraternities and sororities have on the experiences of those students who were not part of the Greek system? Indeed, more broadly, how did competition or even interaction among groups affect how students both inside and outside those groups experienced college? Williamson-Lott talks about black student activists and white allies at universities in the South. What about black students who were not activists? What roles did they play on campus? How did they affect campus life, and what campus cultures did they build?

Connected to this strand of inquiry are questions about how non-students off campus viewed and interpreted college as a result of the actions of student groups. Nash, Mireles, and Scott-Williams, as well as Cain, Williamson-Lott, and Tudico, describe activities in which students interacted very directly with external groups. What these chapters do not address—and is not necessarily their focus—are the ways in which those external groups viewed college students and campus life as a result of those interactions. How did interactions with student life shape how external actors viewed and understood colleges and students? Did the strikebreaking students shape laborers' views of college students, or did the efforts of African American and Mexican American students affect how local citizens interacted with and viewed those students? At the same time, did students in drag shape community perceptions of student activities and life, and, if so, how?

Considering how external groups viewed students and campus life leads to further questions about what constitutes a college campus. If student life is defined by the people (students) taking part rather than the location (campus), then do the settings of off-campus actions and protests by students become part of the campus, if only temporarily? What about students who live off campus, especially those who are raising children? In this case, is parenthood a component of student life, and does being a student influence approaches to raising children? Strohl's chapter on community colleges also suggests further questions about commuter students who live off campus, regardless of the type of institution they attend. What constitutes their campus life? Relatedly, what about students who have off-campus jobs, whether full-time or part-time? Are their work experiences part of student life? Answers to these questions have meaning for how we define student life and how we understand the opportunities, activities, and resources available for students. Should scholarship focus on campus and student life within its boundaries, or would it be more appropriate to focus on the lives of college students across both on- and off-campus dimensions?

In terms of institutions, Ogren and VanOverbeke explore normal schools in the late nineteenth and early twentieth centuries and their state college successors in the mid-twentieth century. What about the history of these institutions between these two time periods? What might we learn by bridging the gap between these two studies? Strohl also identifies a number of areas regarding community colleges where more research is needed. He points to students at community colleges who built active student lives, often in the midst of very busy personal lives. More research is needed to explore the ways in which they built these campus cultures, as well as how campus cultures shaped these and other non-prestigious institutions and the services they provided and continue to provide.

Additionally, the chapters in this volume suggest that specific institutional context has not necessarily been as important as historians have assumed. These chapters detail rich campus life at normal schools, state colleges, community colleges, and historically black colleges and universities, suggesting that institutional type did not determine whether students had access to campus life. Institutional context did shape campus life. For example, Ogren explains that activities at state normal schools did not include fraternities and sororities and actually enhanced students' intellectual and professional growth. But, as Strohl points out, a different context did not necessarily mean big differences in student life. Students at community colleges built active campus lives similar to those on other campuses, contradicting historians' assumptions that community-college students did not focus on campus life. VanOverbeke found similar situations at state colleges in California, where students worked to build robust campus cultures. Context can matter, but it is not destiny when it comes to student life; thus, we need more research to further tease out the influence of institutional type.

Another key area for additional research is student characteristics and demographics. Socioeconomic class, gender, and race are key factors in these chapters as in the history of campus life. While these chapters as well as the historiography described by Hevel and Jaeckle in Chapter 2 pay much attention to class, gender, and race, they are such crucial topics that more research is needed in these and related areas. Regarding social class, Cain points out that strike activities underscored divisions among students, and that some student workers in boarding houses—as well as African American students from historically black colleges and universities who completed their education by working at other campuses—went on strike. We need to know more about these student workers, their experiences, and the relative roles of work, academic studies, and/or extracurricular activities in their campus lives. As Cain states, 60 percent of male students and 25 percent of female students at the University of Michigan in the 1930s worked. Why? How much of their time did they devote to work, and where did they find work? How did their working lives affect their campus experiences and the student lives they built? By looking at student workers, what new and important insights do we gain about socioeconomic class, students, and campus life?

Similarly, what might we learn through more research on gender and sexuality? Women played significant roles in campus life, as Freeman emphasizes, and women were crucial to the work of the Mexican American Movement at the heart of Tudico's chapter. Ogren describes how the distinctive campus culture at state normal schools welcomed women students into public life. What role did these women and their successors on various types of campuses play in struggles for women's and civil rights? While Freeman explains how sororities codified and applied notions of proper femininity, Syrett describes how fraternities enforced changing standards of masculinity. Syrett also suggests that these standards influenced expectations for male students and men in general far beyond the walls of fraternity houses. How, exactly, did sororities' and fraternities'—as well as society's—views of proper gender roles shape campus life for all students? Drag raised questions about gender roles. As Syrett and, especially, Nash, Mireles, and Scott-Williams explain, drag occurred on campus in various settings and for many reasons. These reasons included entertainment and even humiliation (as in fraternity initiation rituals). In other cases, students may have been engaging in drag as a way to push boundaries of gender and sexuality, and this focus especially deserves greater investigation. While both of these chapters advance new research around sexuality and gender—and while other historians have taken up this topic in relation to college and student life, as Hevel and Jaeckle emphasize—far more research is needed to understand how sexuality shaped student experiences, and, simultaneously, how campus life and experiences influenced students' understanding and comfort with their sexual identity and that of other students.

Regarding race, Tudico and Williamson-Lott respectively advance scholarship on Mexican American students, about whom there is a relative dearth of scholarship, and African American students, who have received more attention from historians but who remain underrepresented. Much more research needs to be done not only on African American, Mexican American, and Hispanic students, but on many other student groups defined by race or by other characteristics as well, including Asian and Asian American students, Native American collegians, commuter students, gay and lesbian students, and working students from low socioeconomic backgrounds. These students and their experiences need to be part of future volumes on the history of campus life. Similarly, many student groups that are gaining prominence in the early twenty-first century also need to be the subjects of research going forward: transgender students and undocumented students are two of the most prominent such student groups but not the only ones. Laats stresses religion as a pressing issue for evangelical students, and more research is needed to explore the experiences of Muslim students and others from minority religious and cultural backgrounds. Many of the students in this volume likely were first-generation students, although the chapters do not focus explicitly on first-generation students and their experiences; future historical work could look more directly at this group.

These questions and areas for additional focus are certainly not exhaustive. What of those students who were not protesting labor inequities or breaking strikes, or who were not advocating for greater civil rights and access? What of those students who did not join theatrical societies or vaudeville groups, or parade in drag down city streets? What of those students who steered away from fraternity and sorority parties and instead studied in the library for long hours? What of those students who did not join campus groups? How did they spend their days and college years? We tend to write from the perspective of those who left provocative stories and telling examples, but as colorful as those can be, campus life has also been—as it will continue to be—about those who may have been quiet, studious, or averse to taking the kinds of steps and actions that would get them into the papers or official records that historians would later mine to understand the history of students. Campus life is as much about them, as it is about the more vocal students, the more engaged students, and the students who were active in organizations that created robust archival sources and documents. While it is more difficult to recover the past or piece together the stories of quiet students, we need to remember that they were as much a part of campus life as those who are prominent in archival documents. Whether about these students or others, much more research is needed to understand who went to college, how they experienced college, and how their campus experiences shaped their lives overall.

CONCLUSION

The history of college student life is complex and complicated. Horowitz tried to give it some order through her categorization of students. We have approached this complexity differently by assembling a varied collection of chapters that together offer new perspectives on established topics, consideration of overlooked institutions, deeper work on marginalized student groups, and new work on innovative topics, as well as by identifying common themes in the chapters. Horowitz's approach and our organization here both have merit and value, as, ultimately, student life is rich, complicated, and complex. The essays in this volume underscore that richness and complexity, and showcase historians' grappling with the diversity of campus life in thoughtful, innovative, and productive ways. The historians in this volume—as well as others working in the field and future historians of student life—all will have to continue to wrestle with that complexity. In doing so, they undoubtedly will further our understanding of campus life among diverse groups of students at an array of institutions.

Index[1]

A

Aaron, Marvin, 204, 205
Academic clubs, 96–98, 100, 102, 106, 107, 207
Access and opportunity, 13, 15, 18–20, 31, 92, 154, 191, 194, 197, 206, 214–216, 222–223, 228, 239, 284–287, 293
See also Exclusion and exclusivity
Activism, student, vi, 3, 6, 7, 17, 19, 20, 22, 27, 52, 132, 142, 144–159, 165–185, 213–214, 222–228, 237–254, 261, 263–264, 268–278, 283–284, 287–291
Adams, Ruth, 69, 70
Advisory Committee on Special Sorority Problems (UNC), 129
AFL-CIO, 179, 180, 182, 183
See also American Federation of Labor (AFL)
African American students, see Black students

Afro-American Congress, 250
Agassiz, Elizabeth Cary, 69
Alabama, 97, 101, 103, 105, 124
Alabama, University of, 124
Albany (New York) State Normal School, 93
Alcorn University and A & M College, 242–245, 253
Alemida, Tico, 183
Alexander, Harry A., 72
Alpha Chi Omega, 124
Alpha Delta, 53, 97
Alpha Delta Pi, 121, 133
Alpha Gamma Delta, 129–130
Alpha Kappa Alpha, 25, 116
Altbach, Philip G., 168
Alumni, 5, 12, 14, 15, 17–19, 21, 43, 49, 54, 55, 67, 68, 71, 82, 99, 116, 117, 130–132, 154, 217, 219–222, 263, 269, 270, 273, 274, 277
American Association of Junior Colleges (AAJC), 195, 197, 198

---

[1] Note: Page numbers followed by 'n' refer to notes.

© The Author(s) 2018
C. A. Ogren, M. A. VanOverbeke (eds.),
Rethinking Campus Life, Historical Studies in Education,
https://doi.org/10.1007/978-3-319-75614-1

American Association of University
  Professors (AAUP), 248, 249
American Civil Liberties Union
  (ACLU), 174
American Council on Education
  (ACE), 196, 229n7
American Federation of Labor (AFL),
  167, 168, 179, 180, 182, 183
American Federation of Teachers
  (AFT), 181
American Student Union (ASU),
  173, 176
American Youth Congress (AYC),
  173, 176
American Youth for Democracy, 177
Amherst College, 39, 42, 46, 55, 61,
  66–68, 73, 74, 82
Anderson, James, 18
Animal House, 53
Appleton, Nathan, 75
Arizona, 142, 147, 154, 155
Arizona State College, 153–154
Arkansas, 93, 247, 248
Asian American students, 2, 13, 19,
  20, 47, 56, 295
Asian Movement, 20
Asians, 19, 20, 295
Athletics, v, vi, 2, 4, 7, 12–14, 21, 25,
  29, 38, 39, 43–45, 48, 51, 52,
  57, 72, 94, 102, 104–107, 144,
  145, 152, 153, 201, 205, 207,
  213–228, 288
Athletics and protest, 222–228
Austin, Allan, 19

B
Bacone College, 21
Bailey, Beth, 27–28
Barlow, Andrew, 181
Barnard College, 167
Barnartt, Sharon, 21

Barrow, David C., 120
Baseball, 48, 102
Basketball, 48, 102, 105, 106, 108,
  146, 152, 217, 218
Beach, J.M., 197
Beemyn, Brett, 22
Bérubé, Allan, 62–64
Biola University, 262, 267
Biondi, Martha, 253
Black Awareness Coordinating
  Committee (BACC), 253
Black fraternities, 25
Black freedom struggle, 179–181,
  238–242, 244–246, 249, 250,
  254, 290
Black Panther Party, 253
Black Power, 19, 22, 130, 178, 240,
  249, 250, 253
Black sororities, 25, 116
Black students, v, vi, 1–4, 7, 12, 13,
  17–20, 25–29, 47, 55–56, 93,
  116, 124, 181, 204–205, 215,
  223–228, 237–254, 283,
  286–289, 292–294
Black Students Association, 19
Boardinghouses, 103, 168, 293
Bob Jones College,
  see Bob Jones University
Bob Jones University (BJU),
  262, 265, 266, 273, 274
Bohn, Frank, 169
Boston, 7, 55, 262,
  264, 268
Boston Police Strike (1919), 170
Bowie (Maryland) State Normal
  School, 93
Bowling Green (Kentucky) State
  Normal School, 103
Boyd, John D., 243, 244, 256n17
Boyd, Nan, 62, 63
Brawer, Florence, 202, 209
Bressler, Marvin, 172

Bridgewater (Massachusetts)
State Normal School, 96
Brint, Steven, 196–198, 203, 206
Brockport (New York) State Normal
School, 96, 97, 101
Bronner, Simon J., 64, 68, 71
Brown v. Board of Education, 204, 247
Brown, Isaac Eddy, 102
Brown, Lida, 102
Brown, Steven, 21
Brown University, 39, 41, 169, 170
Bruce, Imon E., 248, 249
Bryan College, 262
Bryn Mawr College, 168
Bucknell University, 14
Buffalo (New York) State Normal
School, 103
Burlesque, 71–75, 77, 78, 82

C
Cain, Timothy, vi, 3, 4, 6, 8, 283,
289, 290, 292, 293
California, 3, 6, 20, 91, 96, 99, 101,
106, 107, 141–145, 147, 148,
153–155, 159, 174, 175, 177,
181, 213–228, 253, 267, 293
California Collegiate Athletic
Association, 219
California State College System,
141, 142, 214–216, 218, 293
California State University, at Los
Angeles, 141, 142
California, University of, at Berkeley,
20, 25, 43, 44, 142, 143, 146,
174, 175, 181, 198, 240
California, University of, at Davis, 218
California, University of, at Irvine, 20
California, University of, at Los
Angeles (UCLA), 141, 142,
149, 156
Campus Crusade for Christ, 26

Carmichael, Katherine, 124
Carmichael, Stokely, 250
Carnegie Council on Policy Studies in
Higher Education, 206
Carson, William Wilson, 45
Castleton (Vermont) State Normal
School, 101
Catholic colleges, 20
Catholic students, 12, 47, 50, 51, 116
Cedar Falls (Iowa) State Normal
School, 94, 97, 107, 110n14
Cedarholm, B. Myron, 276
Ceja, Manuel, 145, 146, 156
Chapman College, 153
Chauncey, George, Jr., 64
Chávez, César, 180
Cheating, 12, 27, 37, 45, 267
Cherokee Female Seminary, 21
Chicago, 7, 19, 167, 168, 173, 244,
262, 264, 267, 275, 276
Chicago, University of, 173
Chicano Movement, 20, 159, 180
Chicano studies programs, 159
Chico (California) State Normal
School, *see* Chico State
Teachers College
Chico State Teachers College,
101, 106
Chi Omega, 126, 138n51
Chi Phi, 44
Chi Psi, 73
Christianity, 14, 20, 26, 72, 102, 143,
239, 261–278
Christiansen, John, 21
City College of New York, 172
Civil Rights Act, 55, 131
Civil Rights Movement, 19, 26, 28,
130, 132, 159, 177, 179–180,
238–254, 263, 268, 284, 288,
289, 294
Clark College, 252
Clark, Robert, 224–227

Clark, Thomas Arkle, 37, 38, 49
Clawson, Jessica, 22
Claxton, Philander P., 199
Clemente, Deirdre, 29
Clergy, 39, 40, 63, 239, 242
Cline, Hazel, 108
Coeducation, 15–17, 43, 47, 50, 65, 76–77, 82, 92–108, 120, 131
Cohen, Arthur, 202, 209
Coleman, James, 243
College enrollment, 11, 26, 48, 52, 118, 142–158, 172, 191, 199–200, 202, 215–216, 262
College men, 2, 12–15, 22, 23, 25, 27, 29, 50, 55, 65, 94, 95, 100, 104, 167, 237, 254
College of William and Mary, 20, 23, 40, 123
College women, 2, 12–19, 22–24, 26–30, 47, 50, 51, 54, 56, 64, 65, 69, 71, 81, 83, 104, 116, 120, 121, 124, 126, 132, 166, 167, 171, 237, 254
Colorado, 104
Columbia University, 19, 22, 147, 170, 173, 182, 183
Commencement, 12, 17, 22, 49, 67, 69, 105, 142, 149, 205, 227
Commonwealth College, 166, 173
Communism, 169, 172, 176, 177, 179, 242, 251
Communist Party, 179
Community colleges, v, vi, 3, 6–8, 141, 145, 146, 149, 153, 191–209, 284, 286–288, 290, 292, 293
Commuter students, 192, 292, 295
Compton Junior College, 141, 146
Congress of Racial Equality (CORE), 180, 246
Connecticut, 94
Cornell University, 19, 22, 29, 46, 47
Corona, Bert, 145, 159

Coronel, Paul, 145, 148, 149, 155–158
Cortland (New York) State Normal School, 98, 102, 106
Council of Federated Organizations (COFO), 244, 249
Covey, Dorothy, 105
Cox, Marcus, 19
Credential, 147, 216, 219, 221, 222, 228, 246, 262
Cross dressing, 65–72, 82
Cruse, Harold, 252
Culbertson, William, 276
Cultural capital, 100, 101, 104, 107, 288
Current, Richard, 23
Curriculum, 14–17, 20, 23, 24, 27, 92, 94, 96, 97, 177, 195, 198, 239–240
Cutting, George Rugg, 66

D
Dartmouth College, 20, 22, 45, 48, 49, 53, 174
Dating, 3, 25, 27–28, 30, 50–51, 54, 119, 122, 124, 125, 202, 278, 284, 286
De la Garza, Jesús, 143
De la Raza, Manuel, see Gutiérrez, Felix
Deaf President Now, 21
Dean of Men, 37, 49
Dean of Women, 121, 124
Debate clubs and debate, 21, 24, 42, 48, 95–102, 105, 107
Delta Chi, 53
Delta Kappa Epsilon, 41, 47
Delta Upsilon, 42, 76
Denton State Normal School, see North Texas State Normal School
Dickeys (D.K.E.), 74

Dilley, Patrick, 22
Dining hall workers, 165
Disabilities, students with, 21
Discrimination, 16, 18, 22, 28, 55,
    148, 157, 182, 184, 205, 214,
    223–226, 228, 250
Divine Nine, 25
Dodge Revolutionary Union
    Movement (DRUM), 180–181
Dorn, Charles, 108–109n5
Dougherty, Kevin, 197
Drag, vi, 3, 5, 8, 61–83, 283,
    286–288, 292, 294, 295
Drinking, 4, 12, 37, 39, 40, 46, 48,
    52, 53, 56, 57, 117–118,
    124–128, 266–270, 272,
    274, 276, 277
Drugs, 272
Du Bois, W.E.B., 252
Duke University, 43, 53, 123, 126,
    131, 132, 181
Duke Women's Liberation, 132

E
Economic Research and Action
    Projects (ERAP), 178
Edwards, Harry, 68, 223, 224, 226
Eisenmann, Linda, 17
El Club Hispano America, 143
Eltinge, Julian, 63
Emory University, 246
Emporia (Kansas) State Normal
    School, 94, 101
Evangelical Christianity, 7, 26,
    262–266, 268, 270, 273, 274,
    277, 278, 289
Evangelical colleges, v, vi, 3, 4, 7–9,
    261–278, 284, 286, 287,
    289, 290
Evangelical students, 261–278, 286,
    289, 290, 295

Evans, Sara, 26
Evans, Stephanie, 18, 19
Exclusion and exclusivity, 46–47,
    285–287, 291
Extracurriculum, v, 1, 12–14, 16,
    23–27, 30, 43–45, 47–48, 51, 52,
    94–108, 166, 207, 293

F
Faculty, 17, 20, 21, 28, 38–42, 47, 73,
    76, 95, 99, 101, 129, 143, 165,
    167, 172, 182, 207, 217, 224,
    226, 227, 237, 247–254, 262,
    266–268, 270, 273
Faculty Committee on Fraternities
    and Sororities (UNC), 129
Faehmel, Babette, 17
Fanon, Frantz, 252
Farnham, Christine, 15, 16
Far Western Conference, 218
Fass, Paula S., 126, 171
Female impersonation, see Drag
Femininity, 25, 63, 120, 134, 294
Feminist Movement, 52, 131–132
Field, Walter Taylor, 44
Finnegan, Dorothy, 26
First-generation students, 194, 202,
    215–216, 244, 295
Fisk University, 239–240
Fitch, Clyde, 61, 66, 73–74
Florence (Alabama) State Normal
    School, 97, 99, 101, 103, 105
Florida, 22, 93, 180, 246, 265
Florida Agricultural & Mechanical
    University, 246
Florida State University, 22, 246
Florida, University of, 22
Football, 7, 44, 45, 68, 92, 102, 108,
    146, 152, 167, 170, 208, 213,
    214, 216–224, 228, 244
Forrester, James, 269, 270

Fort Scott Junior College, 207
Franklin and Marshall College, 14
Fraternities, vi, 2–5, 8, 12, 14, 23–25,
  27, 37–57, 73, 76, 92, 94, 95,
  107, 115–119, 124–130,
  132–134, 136n20, 146, 153,
  192, 207, 208, 223–225, 246,
  284–288, 291, 293–295
Frazier, E. Franklin, 252
Fredonia (New York) State
  Normal School, 102
Freedom Summer (1964),
  240, 244, 249
Freeman, Margaret, 3, 5, 8, 284, 286,
  288, 291, 294
Free Speech Movement, 181, 240
French, George B., 72
Friedan, Betty, 17
Frye, John, 197, 198, 203, 204
Fundamentalism, 7, 262–278
Furness, Horace, 75

G
Galarza, Ernesto, 143, 144
Gallaudet University, 21
Gallogly, Owen, 24
Gasman, Marybeth, 20
Gay students, see Homosexual students
Gender, 3, 13, 15–17, 22, 27, 42, 45,
  50–51, 54–55, 63, 68, 69, 71,
  74, 82, 83, 94, 99, 104–107,
  116, 118–125, 128–134, 184,
  185, 196, 265, 283, 286–289,
  293, 294
Geneseo (New York) State Normal
  School, 96–99, 101, 102,
  105, 107
Georgia, 44, 120, 133, 246, 252
Georgia Institute of Technology, 246
Georgia Students for
  Human Rights, 246

Georgia, University of (UGA),
  44, 120, 133, 246, 252
Gettis, Tyrone, 253
Gibbs, Thomas, 55
GI Bill, 123, 216–217
Giddings, Paula, 25
Glee clubs, 44, 48, 72
Goldin, Claudia, 216
Gompers, Samuel, 168
Goodin, Peggy, 125
Goodman, Andrew, 249
Gordon College, 7, 262, 264,
  268–275, 277, 278
Gordon, Lynn, 15
Graduate student unionization, 183
Graduation, see Commencement
Grambling University, 245
Great Depression, 52, 120, 171–176
Greek letter organizations (GLOs), v,
  3, 25, 43, 45, 48, 52, 95, 115,
  116, 125, 126, 134, 225, 246,
  250, 257n21, 286, 291
  See also Fraternities; Sororities
Greeley (Colorado) State Normal
  School, 104
Green, Jennifer, 14
Greensboro, North Carolina, 181,
  244, 289
Grinds, 47, 95
Gross, Richard, 271
Gutiérrez, Felix, 144, 146–152,
  154, 156
Gutiérrez, Johnny, 149, 150
Guzman, Bartolo, 143

H
Hall, Benjamin, 41
Hamilton, Charles, 250
Hamilton College, 41, 42
Hampton Institute, 21
Harbeson, John, 200, 201

Harbin, Billy J., 73
Haresfoot Club, 76–78
Harlan County, Kentucky, 172
Harper, Charles A., 100
Harsha, Albert K., 72
Harvard Dramatic Club, 74
Harvard University, 14, 20, 22, 65,
    68–71, 74–78, 82, 83, 165,
    168–170, 172, 175, 176, 262
Hasty Pudding Club, 68, 74, 76,
    81, 82
Haugen, Nan, 205
Hazing, 4, 37, 39, 46, 48, 52, 53, 55,
    56, 133, 286
Heagerty, David, 220
Heterosexuality, 4, 22, 27, 28, 39, 50,
    52, 54–57, 63, 64, 119, 121,
    122, 125, 129, 133
Heterosocializing, 5, 115–134, 288
Hevel, Michael, 2–4, 9, 24, 110n14,
    284, 293, 294
Higgins, Judith, 172
High school, 142–144, 146, 148,
    149, 152, 153, 191–193, 195,
    197, 199–206, 216, 225, 227
Hill, Walter, 44
Hispanics, 152
Hispanic students, 254, 294
Historically Black Colleges and
    Universities, 3, 7, 8, 13, 19, 21,
    30, 204–205, 215, 237,
    239–245, 252–254, 283, 286,
    287, 293
Hitchcock, Edward, 39
Hollywood, 63
Homophobia, 11, 22, 55
Homosexual students, 2, 13, 21, 22,
    28, 50, 52, 54–57, 62–65, 71,
    76, 78, 82, 83, 182, 287, 295
Hopkins, C. Howard, 171
Horak, Laura, 65

Horowitz, Helen Lefkowitz, v, vi, 2,
    3, 8, 12–17, 22–24, 27, 30, 31,
    92–95, 100, 104, 107, 108,
    110n12, 166, 192, 214,
    237–238, 246, 254, 284, 296
Howard, Thomas, 24
Howard University, 245
Howe, Stewart, 54
Hubbard, Minnie Allen, 121
Hubbell, John Dana, 75
Hunter, Charlayne, 252
Hussey, George, 65, 66, 71
Hutcheson, Philo, 193, 203, 210n8

I
Ibáñez, Dora, 146, 147, 159
Illinois, 19, 21, 37, 38, 49,
    52, 55, 77–80, 93,
    100–103, 183, 204
Illinois State Normal University,
    100–103
Illinois Union Dramatic Club, 77
Illinois, University of, 19, 21, 37, 38,
    49, 52, 77–80, 176, 258n31
Immigrant students, 47, 93, 141, 144,
    146, 172, 176
Industrial Workers of the World, 169
In loco parentis, 131, 132, 172, 245,
    251, 278
Insull, Samuel, 173
Integration and desegregation, 18, 55,
    123, 124, 131, 204, 244,
    247–250
Intercollegiate Socialist Society (ISS),
    168–170
Iowa, 24, 94, 107, 110n14, 146
Iowa, University of, 110n14, 199
Ithaca College, 165
Ivy League, 21, 262
    See also names of institutions

J

Jabour, Anya, 16
Jackson State University, 181, 254
Jaeckle, Heidi, 2–4, 284, 293, 294
Japanese American Student
    Relocation Council, 19
Jefferson, Thomas, 24, 241, 245
Jewish students, 12, 25, 47, 50, 51,
    93, 116
Johns Hopkins University, 183
Johnson, Lyndon, 180
Jones, Bob, Sr., 265–266
Joseph, Wilhelm, Jr., 252–253
Junior colleges,
    see Community colleges

K

Kalamazoo (Michigan)
    State Normal School, 99
Kansas, 94, 101, 207
Kansas, University of (KU), 28
Kappa Alpha, 39, 40, 46, 53
Kappa Alpha Theta, 116, 119, 122
Kappa Kappa Gamma, 123, 126
Kappa Sigma, 43
Kappa Sigma Epsilon, 42
Karabel, Jerome, 196–198, 203, 206
Katz, Lawrence, 216
Keek, Charles, 78, 80
Kelley, Mary, 16, 24
Kent State University, 181
Kentucky, 24, 103, 172, 178,
    179, 247
Kentucky, University of, 24
Key, V.O., 242
Kick line, 75, 76, 78, 88n63
King, Clennon, 242–243
King, Martin Luther, Jr.,
    181, 251, 253
Kisker, Carrie, 202, 209
Knapp, Martha, 91, 103

Knowles, Tim, 227
Koos, Leonard, 199–202
Kozol, Jonathon, 268

L

Laats, Adam, vi, 3, 4, 7, 8, 284, 286,
    289, 290, 295
Labor, students and, 4, 6, 165, 166,
    170, 171, 173, 176–178, 180,
    182–185, 295
Labor unions, 3, 6, 8, 166, 176, 179
Ladd-Taylor, Molly, 182
Lafayette College, 41
Lambda Chi Alpha, 48
Land grant institutions, 17, 24,
    43, 113n46
Lange, Alexis, 198
Latinos, 2, 13, 20, 56, 143
Latino students, 20
Lawsin, Emily, 19
League for Industrial Democracy
    (LID), 170, 173, 178
League of Revolutionary Black
    Workers, 180
LeGarratte, Carlos, 180
Leggett, Mortimer, 46
Lehigh University, 49
Leibovitz, Liel, 19
Leitch, Alexander, 67
Lesbian students, 13, 28, 295
Leslie, Bruce, 14, 26
Levine, David O., 196, 198, 199,
    203, 206
Levy, Peter B., 177, 178
Lewis, John L., 173
LGBTQ students, 2, 13, 21, 22
Liberal arts, 14, 17, 18, 23, 55, 192,
    196, 203, 208, 209, 240, 262
Liberty University, 262
Lincoln Junior College, 204, 205
Lindsey, Donal, 21

Literary societies, 23–25, 40, 78, 95–98, 100–107, 110n14, 207, 208
Liuzzo, Viola, 249
Long Island University, 165
Los Angeles, 99, 141–143, 145, 146, 152, 153, 157, 262
Los Angeles City College, 141
Los Conquistadores, 153, 154, 159
Louie, Steve, 20
Louisiana, 245, 246
Louisiana State University, 126, 246
Louisville, University of, 246
Lowe, Margaret, 28–29
Ludwig, Erik, 185

M
MacDonald, Victoria-Maria, 20
Maine, 95
Maranatha Baptist College, 276
Marra, Kim, 66, 73
Marsden, George, 265
Martin, Becky, 275
Masculinity, 4, 12, 25, 38, 39, 43, 45, 47–52, 55–57, 63, 64, 72, 83, 116, 125, 167, 283, 288, 294
Massachusetts, 91, 93, 94, 96
Massachusetts Institute of Technology (MIT), 53, 169, 170
McCandless, Amy, 17, 18
McConn, Max, 49
McCosh, James, 45
McDonald, Ellen, 105
McEwan, Ernest, 243
Mexican American Movement (MAM), 6, 141–159, 160n1, 160n15, 294
Mexican Americans, 6, 141–159, 226–227
Mexican American students, v, vi, 3, 6, 8, 141, 143, 148, 150, 153, 158, 159, 222, 223, 225–228, 284, 286–288, 290, 292, 294

Mexican Girl's Conference, 155
Mexican immigrants, 141, 144, 159
Mexican students, 6, 141
Mexican Voice, The, 142, 144–157
Mexican Youth Conference, 144, 145, 148, 149, 155, 160n1
Michel, Gregg, 247
Michigan, 18, 94, 96, 99, 169, 174
Michigan Agricultural College, 175
Michigan, University of, 48, 168, 169, 174, 175, 177, 293
Middlebury College, 41
Mihesuah, Devon, 21
Military, 15, 19, 63, 64, 167, 268, 275
Military schools, 14
Miller, Matthew, 19
Minnesota, University of, 199
Mireles, Danielle, vi, 3, 5, 8, 71, 72, 283, 286–288, 290, 292, 294
Mississippi, 19, 180, 242, 244, 245
Mississippi Freedom Democratic Party (MFDP), 179, 180
Mississippi Freedom Labor Union (MFLU), 179
Mississippi Industrial College, 252
Mississippi Summer Project, 179
Mississippi, University of, 246
Missouri, University of, 28, 204
Model minority, 20
Moody Bible Institute (MBI), 7, 262, 264, 267, 274–278
Moody, Kim, 178
Morality code, 63
Morelock, Kolan, 24
Morgan, J.P., 173
Movimiento Estudiantil Chicano de Aztlán (MEChA), 159
Muñoz, Carlos, J., 20
Muñoz, Rosalio, Jr., 159
Muñoz, Rebecca, 153, 154
Muslim students, 295

N

Nash, Margaret, vi, 3, 5, 8, 16, 21, 283, 286–288, 290, 292, 294
Nasmith, J.S., 95
National Association for the Advancement of Colored People (NAACP), 242
National Organization of Women (NOW), 132
National Panhellenic Conference (NPC), 116, 121, 124
National Student Association (NSA), 180, 205, 246
National Student Forum, 171
National Student League (NSL), 172, 173
National Women's Trade Union League (WTUL), 167, 168
Native American students, 20, 21, 26, 28, 93, 295
Nebraska, 94, 96
Neckwear Makers Union, 170
Nelson, Lawrence, 28
Neuman, Lisa, 21
Nevada, University of, 218, 219
New evangelicals or neo-evangelicals, 261, 263, 268–272, 274
New Left, 177, 178
New Orleans, 246
New Paltz (New York) State Normal School, 98
New York, 62, 63, 93–96, 98, 101–103, 105–107, 167, 172, 179, 184, 192
New York City, 168, 172, 178
New York University, 183
Nguyen, Thai-Huy, 20
Normalites, *see* Normal schools
Normal schools, v–vi, 2, 3, 5, 8, 16, 17, 22, 24, 91–108, 142, 215, 284, 286–288, 292–294
North, 15, 18, 19

North Carolina A&T University, 181, 254
North Carolina, University of, at Chapel Hill, 15, 53, 124, 127–130, 181, 251
North Carolina, University of, at Greensboro, 181
North Texas State Normal School (Denton), 64–65, 98, 101
Norwood, Stephen H., 167

O

Oak Park Junior College, 204
Obama, Barack, 191
Oberlin College, 18
Occidental College, 143
Ockenga, Harold, 270
Oglethorpe University, 246
Ogren, Christine, vi, 3, 5, 8, 16, 24, 284, 286–288, 292–294
Okihiro, Gary, 19
Oklahoma, 21, 95, 108
Old Left, 177, 178
Olympics (1968), 226, 291
Omatsu, Glenn, 20
Ombudsman, 225, 227
Oneonta (New York) State Normal School, 96, 97, 101, 107
Oregon, 94, 192
Oshkosh (Wisconsin) State Normal School, 96–101, 103–105
Oswego (New York) State Normal School, 94
Otis, Jesse R., 242, 243
Outsiders, 2, 12, 14, 22, 23, 27, 30, 93–96, 100, 104, 237, 238, 254, 277

P

Pace, Robert, 14
Panhellenic Council, at Duke, 131

Parades, 66–68, 71, 82, 168
Parietals, *see In loco parentis*
Pasadena Junior College (PJC), 153, 200, 201
Patton, Cornelius Howard, 44
Pedersen, Robert, 206–208
Perkins, Linda, 18
PerLee, Grace, 106
Peru (Nebraska)
    State Normal School, 94, 96
Pfister, Joel, 21
Phi Beta Kappa, 23, 40
Phi Kappa Psi, 55
Phi Lambda Alpha, 143
Phi Mu, 123
Phi Sigma Upsilon, 153
Pi Eta Society, 74
Pincus, Fred, 196
Pine Bluff (Arkansas)
    State Normal School, 93
Platteville (Wisconsin)
    State Normal School, 95
Poblano, Ralph, 227
Pony ballet, 73, 77, 78, 88n63
Poor students, 2, 12, 40, 43, 47, 93, 94, 206, 207
Port Huron Statement, 178
Powell, Adam Clayton, 242
Predominantly white institutions, 3, 7, 237, 238, 247, 250, 251, 258n31
President's Commission on Higher Education, *see* Truman Commission
President's Commission on the Status of Women, 131
Presque Isle (Maine) State Normal School, 95
Princeton University, 14, 39, 45, 67–68, 71–73, 77, 82, 83, 170
Progressive Labor Party (PLP), 179
Prohibition, 97, 126
Protestantism and Protestants, 12, 14, 20, 26, 116, 118, 262, 264

Protests, student, 3, 4, 7, 8, 11, 21, 26, 28, 29, 62, 107, 165, 166, 171, 172, 176, 178, 181–184, 214, 223–228, 239, 240, 245, 247, 249, 251–253, 261–264, 268–274, 276–278, 286, 288, 289, 291, 292, 295
Psi Upsilon, 41, 48
Publications, student, 12, 24, 95, 97–100, 105, 107
Putnam, Robert, 101

Q
Quilty, Harriet, 106

R
Radcliffe College, 69, 75, 81, 82
Radke-Moss, Andrea, 16, 24, 113n46
Reagan, Ronald, 224
Rebels, 2, 12–14, 22, 23, 110n12, 237, 238, 254, 263, 268, 269
Redlands University, 141, 147
Reeb, James, 249
Reserve Officers' Training Corps (ROTC), 19, 172, 173, 249
Residential colleges, 192, 202, 208, 209
Reyes, Stephen, 149
Rhoads, Robert A., 182
Rice, Alexander Hamilton, 41
Rice, John R., 273
Richardson, Elizabeth M., 81
Richardson, Leon B., 49
Richmond (Kentucky)
    State Normal School, 103
Rituals, student, 46, 55, 56, 61, 62, 64, 66, 68, 71, 218, 294
Rivers, Bryan, 77
Rodriguez, José, 145, 146
Roe Cloud, Henry, 21
Romecin, Eduardo de Antequera, 143

Roosevelt, Theodore, 45
Ross, Lawrence, 25
Rudolph, Frederick, 1, 2, 9n2, 11, 24, 193
Ruehl, Adoph, 105

S

Sacramento State College, 213–219, 221–222, 228
San Francisco Junior College, 195
San Francisco State College, 20
San Jose (California) State Normal School, *see* San Jose State College
San José State College, 91, 94, 96–99, 101–104, 106, 107, 108n5, 214–215, 219, 221–228
San Marcos State Normal School, *see* Southwest Texas State Normal School
Santa Barbara State College, 141, 153
Santa Clara University, 20
Sanua, Marianne, 25
Sawyer, Corinne Holt, 68
Schanke, Robert A., 73
Schrecker, Ellen W., 177
Schwerner, Michael, 249
Scott-Williams, Amanda, vi, 3, 5, 8, 283, 286–288, 290, 292, 294
Seashore, Carl, 199
Seay, Dorothy, 266, 267
Secret societies, 39, 40, 45, 115
Segregation, 17, 18, 26, 28, 43, 52, 55, 56, 93, 124, 142, 148, 156–158, 177, 204, 214, 224–226, 228, 242, 246, 247
Setran, David, 26
Seven Sisters, 15, 17, 18
Sex, 12, 18, 28, 50–52, 54–57, 63, 119, 124, 125, 127, 128, 133, 202, 205
Sexual assault, 4, 39, 118, 127

Sexuality, 22, 27–30, 63, 74, 127, 133, 286–289, 294
Shepard, Elizabeth, 96, 105
Sigma Chi, 48, 128, 133
Silverman, Jennifer, 21
Sit-ins, 183, 224, 238, 240, 244, 264, 270, 273, 274, 277
Slosson, Edwin, 142
Smith College, 29, 69, 81, 82, 169, 170, 172
Soccer, 48
Social clubs, 68, 76, 115, 207, 208, 286
Socialism, 168
Socialist Party, 168
Socioeconomic class, 13, 51, 288, 293, 294
Solomon, Barbara Miller, 15
Sororities, 2, 3, 5, 6, 8, 12, 17, 23, 25, 27, 47, 48, 51, 54, 92, 95, 104, 107, 115–134, 138n51, 192, 207, 223–225, 246, 284, 286–288, 291, 293–295
Sorority pledge guidebooks, 123, 126, 119
South, 3, 14–20, 93, 170, 180, 240, 244, 245, 249, 258n31, 286, 287, 292
South Carolina State College, 251, 254
South Carolina, University of, at Columbia, 251
Southern California, University of, 53, 141, 177, 183, 218
Southern Christian Leadership Conference, 239
Southern State College, 247–249
Southern Student Human Relations Project, 246
Southern Student Organizing Committee, 180, 247

Southern University and A&M
    College, 245, 246, 254
Southwestern State Teachers College
    (Weatherford), 95, 108
Southwest Texas State Normal School
    (San Marcos), 93, 96–98,
    101, 104
Spelman College, 29
Sport, see Athletics
Stanford University, 44, 46, 143, 207,
    218, 221
State colleges, vi, 3, 4, 7, 108,
    213–228, 262, 284, 286,
    287, 292, 293
State normal schools,
    see Normal schools
State universities, 24, 206
Stevens Institute, 170
Strikebreaking, 6, 166–170, 175, 184,
    185, 289, 290, 292
Strohl, Nicholas, vi, 3, 6–8, 284,
    286–288, 290, 292, 293
Student government associations,
    7, 13, 23, 27, 44, 52, 106,
    175, 223, 238, 241–246,
    251–253, 257n21
Student Labor Action Coalition
    (SLAC), 183
Student League for Industrial
    Democracy (SLID),
    173, 177, 178
Student Nonviolent Coordinating
    Committee (SNCC), 179, 180,
    238, 239, 244
Students for a Democratic Society
    (SDS), 178–180, 249, 251
Students for Labor Action, 165
Students United for Rights and
    Equality (SURE), 247–249
Student Workers Federation (SWF),
    174, 175

Supreme Council of the Mexican
    American Movement, 158
Supreme Court, 204, 242
Susman, Warren, 121
Sutherland, Samuel, 267
Swarthmore College, 14, 170
Syracuse University, 49
Syrett, Nicholas, vi, 3, 4, 8, 21, 25,
    116, 125, 284–286, 288, 291, 294

T
Tallahassee (Florida)
    State Normal School, 93
Teachers colleges, 13, 92, 106–108,
    215, 218, 221
Teaching and teachers, 16, 17,
    19, 91–96, 98, 99, 105, 107,
    143, 145, 147, 156, 195, 205,
    215, 265
Teaching Assistants Association,
    University of Wisconsin, 181
Tennessee, University of, 172
Tennis, 48, 102, 207
Texas, 101, 146
Texas, University of, 174
Textbook burning, 66, 73, 82
Thelin, John, 109n5, 216
Theta Nu Epsilon, 37, 38
Thomas, Norman, 170
Title VII of the Civil Rights Act, 131
Title IX (1972), 205
Transgender students, 13, 295
Transylvania University, 24
Tri Delta, 122, 123, 127, 128
Truman Commission, 194–196
Tudico, Christopher, vi, 3, 6, 8, 284,
    286, 288, 290, 292, 294
Tufts College, 169
Tulane University, 246, 250
Turk, Diana, 25, 116, 128

Turner, John, 26
Turpin, Andrea, 17
Two-year colleges,
   see Community colleges

U
Ullman, Sharon, 62
Umemoto, Karen, 20
Uncle Tom's Cabin, 242
Undocumented students, 295
Union College, 40
Unions, 143, 165, 166, 169–171,
   173–176, 178–184
United Auto Workers (UAW),
   175, 177, 178
United Farm Workers (UFW), 179
United Packinghouse Workers of
   America (UPWA), 179, 180
University employee unions, 165

V
Valadez, Gualberto, 156
Van Cleave, Kendra, 65
Vanderbilt University, 246
VanOverbeke, Marc, v, vi, 3, 4, 7, 8,
   213, 284, 286–288, 291–293
Vassar College, 29, 69, 70, 81, 82,
   168, 170
Vaudeville, 5, 62–64, 72, 76, 78,
   86n37, 286, 290, 295
Vermont, 101, 174
Veterans, 123, 192, 205, 216,
   217, 242
Veysey, Laurence, 14, 193
Vietnam War, 26, 130, 177, 179, 249,
   251, 263, 275, 278, 289
Virginia, University of, 24, 183,
   241, 246
Voorhees College, 253

W
Waite, Cally, 18
Ward, Phebe, 195
Washington, DC, 245
Washington, University of, 175
Wayland, Francis, 39
Wayne State University, 180, 181
Weatherford (Oklahoma) State
   Normal School, see Southwestern
   State Teachers College
Wellesley College, 168
Whaley, Deborah, 25, 116
Wheaton College (Illinois),
   262, 266, 268
White, James H, 253
White students, 12, 14–18, 21–29,
   31, 100, 115, 119, 124, 180,
   223, 224, 226, 240, 245–247,
   249, 251, 252, 254, 255n2,
   255n11, 275
Whitewater (Wisconsin)
   State Normal School, 97
Whittier College, 153
Whittington, Erica, 246
Wilkie, Laurie, 25
Williams College, 42
Williams, Timothy, 15
Williamson, Joy Ann,
   see Williamson-Lott, Joy
Williamson-Lott, Joy, vi, 3, 4, 7, 8,
   283, 286, 288, 290, 292, 294
Willimantic (Connecticut) State
   Normal School, 94
Wilson, Gordon, 103
Wing, Yung, 42
Winstead, J. Lloyd, 29
Wipf, Donald, 275
Wisconsin, 99, 105
Wisconsin, University of,
   at Madison, 71, 76, 77, 83,
   168, 172, 181, 183

Woman's College of Duke University, 123, 126
Women's colleges, 15, 17, 29, 30, 65, 66, 81, 82, 104, 119, 167
Women's Rights Movement, 22, 130
Woodson, Carter G., 252
Worcester (Massachusetts) State Normal School, 94
Working class students, 169
World War I, 29, 64, 78, 169, 196, 198–200, 206
World War II, 19, 21, 25, 52, 55, 63–65, 83, 123, 126, 156, 158, 176, 194, 196, 198, 200, 201, 203, 204, 206, 215, 216, 242, 262
Wright, Bobby, 20
Wright, Conrad, 14
Wright, William, 21, 76

X
Xavier University, 246

Y
Yale University, 21, 29, 42, 45, 47, 70, 77, 78, 170, 174, 176, 182, 183, 262
Young America for Freedom, 181
Young Communist League, 177
Young Men's Christian Association (YMCA), 14, 26, 102, 143–145, 168–171, 177, 246–247
Young Women's Christian Association (YWCA), 26, 102, 103, 106, 168, 171, 177, 246–247
Ypsilanti (Michigan) State Normal School, 94, 96–97, 99

Z
Zeta Psi, 44, 127, 128
Zeta Tau Alpha (ZTA), 121
Zook, George, 196
Zoot Suit Riots, 156

Made in the USA
Columbia, SC
06 September 2020